THE ROUTLEDGE COMPANION TO PUPPETRY AND MATERIAL PERFORMANCE

The *Routledge Companion to Puppetry and Material Performance* offers a wide-ranging perspective on how scholars and artists are currently re-evaluating the theoretical, historical, and theatrical significance of performance that embraces the agency of inanimate objects. This book proposes a collaborative, responsive model for broader artistic engagement in and with the material world. Its 28 chapters aim to advance the study of the puppet not only as a theatrical object but also as a vibrant artistic and scholarly discipline.

This Companion looks at puppetry and material performance from six perspectives: theoretical approaches to the puppet, perspectives from practitioners, revisiting history, negotiating tradition, material performances in contemporary theatre, and hybrid forms. Its wide range of topics, which span 15 countries over five continents, encompasses:

- visual dramaturgy
- theatrical juxtapositions of robots and humans
- contemporary transformations of Indonesian *wayang kulit*
- Japanese ritual body substitutes
- recent European productions featuring toys, clay, and food

The book features newly commissioned essays by leading scholars such as Matthew Isaac Cohen, Kathy Foley, Jane Marie Law, Eleanor Margolies, Cody Poulton, and Jane Taylor. It also celebrates the vital link between puppetry as a discipline and as a creative practice with chapters by active practitioners, including Handspring Puppet Company's Basil Jones, Redmoon's Jim Lasko, and Bread and Puppet's Peter Schumann. Fully illustrated with more than 60 images, this volume comprises the most expansive English-language collection of international puppetry scholarship to date.

Dassia N. Posner is Assistant Professor of Theatre at Northwestern University. A theatre historian, dramaturg, and puppeteer, she is the author of numerous articles and chapters on Russian theatre, the history of directing, and puppetry and is peer-review editor for *Puppetry International*. Recent dramaturgy includes *Three Sisters* and *Russian Transport* at Steppenwolf.

Claudia Orenstein is Associate Professor of Theatre at Hunter College and the Graduate Center at CUNY. Publications include *The World of Theatre: Tradition and Innovation*, and *Festive Revolutions: The Politics of Popular Theatre and the San Francisco Mime Troupe*. She is a board member of UNIMA-USA and Associate Editor of *Asian Theatre Journal*.

John Bell is Director of the Ballard Institute and Museum of Puppetry and Associate Professor of Dramatic Arts at the University of Connecticut. An active puppeteer with Great Small Works and Bread & Puppet Theater, as well as a theatre historian, his publications include *American Puppet Modernism* (2008) and *Puppets, Masks, and Performing Objects* (2001).

THE ROUTLEDGE COMPANION TO PUPPETRY AND MATERIAL PERFORMANCE

Edited by
Dassia N. Posner, Claudia Orenstein,
and John Bell

Routledge
Taylor & Francis Group
LONDON AND NEW YORK

First published in paperback 2015
First published 2014
by Routledge
2 Park Square, Milton Park, Abingdon, Oxon OX14 4RN

and by Routledge
711 Third Avenue, New York, NY 10017

Routledge is an imprint of the Taylor & Francis Group, an informa business

© 2014, 2015 Dassia N. Posner, Claudia Orenstein, and John Bell

The right of Dassia N. Posner, Claudia Orenstein, and John Bell to be identified as author of this work has been asserted in accordance with sections 77 and 78 of the Copyright, Designs and Patents Act 1988.

All rights reserved. No part of this book may be reprinted or reproduced or utilized in any form or by any electronic, mechanical, or other means, now known or hereafter invented, including photocopying and recording, or in any information storage or retrieval system, without permission in writing from the publishers.

Trademark notice: Product or corporate names may be trademarks or registered trademarks, and are used only for identification and explanation without intent to infringe.

British Library Cataloguing in Publication Data
A catalogue record for this book is available from the British Library

Library of Congress Cataloguing in Publication Data
The Routledge companion to puppetry and material performance / edited by Dassia N. Posner, Claudia Orenstein, and John Bell.
    pages cm
1. Puppet theater. I. Posner, Dassia N. II. Orenstein, Claudia. III. Bell, John, 1951-
IV. Title: Companion to puppetry and material performance. V. Title: Puppetry and material performance.
  PN1972.R68 2014
  791.5--dc23
                                                    2013049987

ISBN: 978-0-415-70540-0 (hbk)
ISBN: 978-1-138-91383-7 (pbk)
ISBN: 978-1-315-85011-5 (ebk)

Typeset in Goudy
by Taylor & Francis Books

To our children:
Sophia and Isaac Posner,
Caleb and Sophie Carman,
and Isaac Bell.

CONTENTS

List of Figures   xi
Notes on Contributors   xvi
Acknowledgments   xxi
Foreword by Kenneth Gross   xxiii

Introduction   1
DASSIA N. POSNER, CLAUDIA ORENSTEIN, AND JOHN BELL

PART I:
Theory and Practice   13
EDITED AND INTRODUCED BY JOHN BELL

Section I: Theoretical Approaches to the Puppet   17

1 The Death of "The Puppet"?   18
  MARGARET WILLIAMS

2 The Co-Presence and Ontological Ambiguity of the Puppet   30
  PAUL PIRIS

3 Playing with the Eternal Uncanny: The Persistent
  Life of Lifeless Objects   43
  JOHN BELL

Section II: Perspectives from Practitioners   53

4 Visual Dramaturgy: Some Thoughts for
  Puppet Theatre-Makers   54
  ERIC BASS

5 Puppetry, Authorship, and the *Ur*-Narrative   61
  BASIL JONES

CONTENTS

6 Petrushka's Voice 69
ALEXANDER GREF AND ELENA SLONIMSKAYA

7 "Clouds Are Made of White!": The Intersection of Live Art and
Puppetry as an Approach to Postdramatic Children's Theatre 76
RIKE REINIGER

8 Movement Is Consciousness 84
KATE BREHM

9 The Eye of Light: The Tension of Image and Object in
Shadow Theatre and Beyond 91
STEPHEN KAPLIN

10 The Third Thing 98
JIM LASKO

11 Post-Decivilization Efforts in the Nonsense
Suburb of Art 105
PETER SCHUMANN

PART II:
New Dialogues with History and Tradition 111
EDITED AND INTRODUCED BY CLAUDIA ORENSTEIN

Section III: Revisiting History 115

12 Making a Troublemaker: Charlotte Charke's Proto-Feminist Punch 116
AMBER WEST

13 Life-Death and Disobedient Obedience:
Russian Modernist Redefinitions of the Puppet 130
DASSIA N. POSNER

14 The Saracen of *Opera dei Pupi*: A Study of Race,
Representation, and Identity 144
LISA MORSE

15 Puppet Think: The Implication of Japanese Ritual
Puppetry for Thinking through Puppetry Performances 154
JANE MARIE LAW

16 Relating to the Cross: A Puppet Perspective on the
Holy Week Ceremonies of the *Regularis Concordia* 164
DEBRA HILBORN

Section IV: Negotiating Tradition — 177

17 Traditional and Post-Traditional *Wayang Kulit* in Java Today — 178
MATTHEW ISAAC COHEN

18 Korean Puppetry and Heritage: Hyundai Puppet Theatre and Creative Group NONI Translating Tradition — 192
KATHY FOLEY

19 Forging New Paths for Kerala's *Tolpavakoothu* Leather Shadow Puppetry Tradition — 205
CLAUDIA ORENSTEIN

20 Integration of Puppetry Tradition into Contemporary Theatre: The Reinvigoration of the *Vertep* Puppet Nativity Play after Communism in Eastern Europe — 218
IDA HLEDÍKOVÁ

PART III:
Contemporary Investigations and Hybridizations — 225
EDITED AND INTRODUCED BY DASSIA N. POSNER

Section V: Material Performances in Contemporary Theatre — 229

21 From Props to Prosopopeia: Making *After Cardenio* — 230
JANE TAYLOR

22 "A Total Spectacle but a Divided One": Redefining Character in Handspring Puppet Company's *Or You Could Kiss Me* — 245
DAWN TRACEY BRANDES

23 Reading a Puppet Show: Understanding the Three-Dimensional Narrative — 255
ROBERT SMYTHE

24 Notes on New Model Theatres — 268
MARK J. SUSSMAN

Section VI: New Directions and Hybrid Forms — 279

25 From Puppet to Robot: Technology and the Human in Japanese Theatre — 280
CODY POULTON

CONTENTS

26 Unholy Alliances and Harmonious Hybrids: New Fusions
in Puppetry and Animation 294
COLETTE SEARLS

27 Programming Play: Puppets, Robots, and Engineering 308
ELIZABETH ANN JOCHUM AND TODD MURPHEY

28 Return to the Mound: Animating Infinite Potential in Clay,
Food, and Compost 322
ELEANOR MARGOLIES

Index 336

LIST OF FIGURES

1.1	Pierrot (1973). Photo courtesy of Philippe Genty Company	19
1.2	*Tragédie de Papier*, created and first performed by Yves Joly (1956). Photo: © Yves Joly and courtesy of Théâtre de la Marionnette à Paris	20
1.3	*Piccoli Suicidi* (1984): Creator and performer Gyula Molnár with sweets and a glass of water. Photo: © Francesca Bettini	21
2.1	*Cuniculus*, Stuffed Puppet Theatre (2008): Neville Tranter and pal. Photo: © Michael Kneffel	32
2.2	*Twin Houses*, Compagnie Mossoux-Bonté (1994): performer Nicole Mossoux. Photo: © Mikha Wajnrych	35
3.1	"Doubt as to whether … a lifeless object may not in fact be animate": Trudi Cohen in Great Small Works' *Terror As Usual: Episode 7: Metro Section* (1993). Photo courtesy of Great Small Works	47
3.2	Freud's "discarded beliefs" in the active power of objects came back not in the form of primitive culture but as avant-garde performance: Maryann Colella in Bread and Puppet Theater's *Things Done in a Seeing Place*, Glover, Vermont (2013). Photo courtesy of the author	51
4.1	*Between Sand and Stars*, a collaboration among Sandglass Theater, Gemini Trapeze, and Rob Mermin (2003) based on images from Antoine de St. Exupéry's *Wind, Sand and Stars*: as the pilot lost in the desert struggles to make his way through endless sands, the marionette's lifelines are visible. Photo: © Richard Termine, richardtermine@nyc.rr.com	57
4.2	*Un Cid*, Compagnie Émilie Valantin (1996). Photo: © Hubert Charbonnier	58
5.1	*Confessions of Zeno* rehearsal, The Dance Factory, Johannesburg (2002): puppets designed by William Kentridge and made by Adrian Kohler and Tau Qwelane. Photo: © Ruphin Coudyzer	62
5.2	The cast of *War Horse* at the New London Theatre (2009): puppets by Handspring Puppet Company. Photo: © Brinkhoff/Mögenburg	65
6.1	Petrushka, Vagrant Booth Theatre. Photo courtesy of the authors	70
7.1	*Mrs. Sun and Mr. Moon Make Weather*, Deutsch-Sorbisches Volkstheater Bautzen (2007): performers Christian Pfütze and Christiane Kampwirth with the model stage. Photo courtesy of the author	79
7.2	Mrs. Sun puppet (2007). Photo courtesy of the author	80
7.3	Performer Susan Weilandt and the rainbow (2007). Photo courtesy of the author	80

LIST OF FIGURES

8.1	Early sketches of the performing scenery (which itself functions as a puppet) and its transformational frame: designed by Kate Brehm. Image courtesy of the author	85
8.2	Later sketches of the performing scenery, including a wall of windows: designed by Kate Brehm. Image courtesy of the author	86
9.1	Photo montage created by and courtesy of the author	92
9.2	Traditional shadow troupe in rehearsal, Northern China (1936), Pauline Benton Collection. Photo courtesy of Chinese Theatre Works	96
10.1	Rice paper and bamboo constructed spectacle objects for Redmoon's *All Hallows' Eve Ritual Celebration* (October 1997) on the streets of Logan Square. Photo © Katja Heinemann	99
10.2	Performers manipulate large-scale puppets, masks, and objects during Redmoon's *Frankenstein* parade (September 1995) at Chicago's Navy Pier, soon after the North Avenue parade. Photo © Tria Smith	101
10.3	Actors in *Dis/Replacement* take their positions on the stages perched atop a twin forklift engineered for Redmoon's Urban Interventions Series, here seen on a street corner in the Wicker Park neighborhood of Chicago (summer 2012). Photo © Christina Noel	104
11.1	Drawing by Peter Schumann (2012)	106
11.2	Drawing by Peter Schumann (2012)	107
11.3	Sleeper puppet, from Bread and Puppet Theater's *Things Done in a Seeing Place*, Glover, Vermont (2013). Photo courtesy of John Bell	108
12.1	Inspired by Charke's tale of stealing her brother's and father's clothes to imitate her father, the engraving reads, "An exact Representation of Mrs. Charke walking in the Ditch at four Years of Age, as described by herself in the first Number of the Narrative of her own Life, lately published" (F. Garden, 1755). © The Trustees of the British Museum	117
13.1	Demon puppet from *The Forces of Love and Magic* (1916): puppet design by Nikolai Kalmakov. Image reprinted from Iuliia Slonimskaia, "Marionetka," *Apollon* (March 1916), PSlav 122.5, Houghton Library, Harvard University	135
13.2	Nina Simonovich-Efimova and Big Petrushka (1930). Photo courtesy of the Museum Archive of the Obraztsov State Central Puppet Theatre, Moscow	140
13.3	Nina Simonovich-Efimova, the witches of *Macbeth* (1931). Photo courtesy of the Museum Archive of the Obraztsov State Central Puppet Theatre, Moscow	141
14.1	Saracen soldier created by Vincenzo Argento. Photo courtesy of the author	147
14.2	Saracen trick puppet designed to split in half, created by Vincenzo Argento. Photo courtesy of the author	149
15.1	A rare example of a body substitute known as an *amagatsu* (heavenly child): these infant-shaped effigies were used widely in the Tōhoku region of Japan to safeguard newborn infants against illness, sudden death, and disease by serving as surrogates (from Morioka, Iwate prefecture, 1988). Photo courtesy of the author	156

LIST OF FIGURES

15.2 Members of the Awaji Puppet Theatre in Fukura, Japan, perform the *Ebisu-mai* (a deity play) at its traditional location of Susaki Island in the Fukura Harbor (August 1991). The use of *kuroko*, though not traditional for this play, shows the dominance of this theatrical medium today. Photo courtesy of the author ... 162

16.1 The Cloisters Cross: English; twelfth century; walrus ivory; 22⅝" × 14¼"; The Metropolitan Museum of Art, The Cloisters Collection, 1963. Image © The Metropolitan Museum of Art. Reproduction of any kind is prohibited without express written permission in advance from The Metropolitan Museum of Art ... 169

17.1 *Kitab Sucineng Manusa*, performed by Purjadi, Bodesari (March 14–15, 2009): Bathara Guru (center) consults with his vizier Narada (left). Photo courtesy of the author ... 184

17.2 Sigit Sukasman (1937–2009) explaining *wayang* visual theory in his studio (April 26, 2009). Photo courtesy of the author ... 186

17.3 Rehearsal for *Berlian Ajaib*, Cemeti Art House, Yogyakarta (March 3, 2009). Photo courtesy of the author ... 188

19.1 A forest scene from the traditional *tolpavakoothu* performance, Kerala, India (July 21, 2013). Photo courtesy of the author ... 208

19.2 Ramachandra Pulavar (center) with his family, holding up both new and traditional *tolpavakoothu* puppets, Kerala, India (July 22, 2013). Photo courtesy of the author ... 212

19.3 Backstage after an off-season ritual *tolpavakoothu* performance: the puppet of Hanuman wears a *dhoti* cloth given as an offering; Kerala, India (July 21, 2013). Photo courtesy of the author ... 214

20.1 *Vertep*, Bryzhan Family Theatre, Chmelnickij, Ukraine (premiered 1995): Director: Sergij Bryzhan; designer: Michail Nikolaev; from left: Olga Bryzhan, Natasha Bryzhan, and Sergij Bryzhan. Photo courtesy of Sergij Bryzhan ... 221

20.2 *A Christmas Mystery*, Rovenski County Puppet Theatre, Rovno, Ukraine (premiered July 1, 2000): Director: Sergij Bryzhan; designer: Michail Nikolaev. Photo courtesy of Sergij Bryzhan ... 222

20.3 *Resonances*, Chmelnickij County Puppet Theatre, Chmelnickij, Ukraine (premiered July 1, 2003): Director: Sergij Bryzhan; designer: Michail Nikolaev. Photo courtesy of Sergij Bryzhan ... 224

21.1 "A Wonder of Wonders ... ," 1651 broadsheet recounting the story of Anne Green © The British Library Board General Reference Collection E.621(11). Image published with permission of ProQuest. Further reproduction is prohibited without permission. Image produced by ProQuest as part of *Early English Books Online*. www.proquest.com ... 233

21.2 *After Cardenio*, University of Cape Town, South Africa (2011): Dylan Esbach as Cardenio; vellum puppet made by Gavin Younge; Marty Kintu as primary puppeteer. Photo: © Ant Strack 2011, www.antstrack.com ... 238

21.3 Puppet by Gavin Younge; Marty Kintu as primary puppeteer. Photo: © Ant Strack 2011, www.antstrack.com ... 238

21.4	Dylan Esbach as Doctor Petty; Marty Kintu as primary puppeteer; puppet by Gavin Younge; and Jemma Kahn as Ann Green. Photo: © Ant Strack 2011, www.antstrack.com	239
22.1	*Or You Could Kiss Me*, National Theatre, London (2010) presented in association with Handspring Puppet Company: written and directed by Neil Bartlett; Basil Jones (left) and Adrian Kohler (right) animate Old B and Old A. Photo: © Simon Annand/Arena PAL	248
22.2	Basil Jones animates Old B. Photo: © Simon Annand/Arena PAL	251
22.3	Basil Jones lifts Young B. Photo: © Simon Annand/Arena PAL	252
23.1	Enno Podehl with Hermann performing his morning gymnastics. Photo: © Sharon Baronofsky	258
23.2	Anne Podehl, Rosa, Hermann, and Enno Podehl. Photo: © Sharon Baronofsky	260
23.3	Enno Podehl and Hermann light a match. Photo: © Franz Kramer	262
24.1	*Mnemopark: A Model Train World*, Rimini Protokoll (2005): Director: Stefan Kaegi. Photo: © Lex Vögtli	271
24.2	*The Great War*, Hotel Modern (2001): created and performed by Herman Helle and Pauline Kalker (pictured) and Arlène Hoornweg. Photo: © Joost van den Broek	273
24.3	Fixing tracks at the Toy Train Society (Berlin, 1931). Photo: © Alfred Eisenstaedt/Time & Life Pictures/Getty Images	275
25.1	The Wakamaru robot, Takeo, converses with his employer, Yúji, in *I, Worker* (2008): written and directed by Hirata Oriza. Photo: © Osaka University & Eager Co. Ltd	282
25.2	Ishiguro Hiroshi and his Geminoid HI-1 (2006): Geminoid HI-1 was developed by Hiroshi Laboratory, Advanced Telecommunications Research Institute International (ATR). Geminoid is a registered trademark of ATR. Photo courtesy of ATR Hiroshi Ishiguro Laboratory	284
25.3	Diagram of Masahiro Mori's "Uncanny Valley." Image courtesy of Karl MacDorman. Originally published in *IEEE Robotics and Automation*, 2012, 19(2): 99	285
25.4	Geminoid F and Bryerly Long in *Sayōnara* (2010): written and directed by Hirata Oriza. Photo: © Tatsuo Nambu/Aichi Triennale 2010	287
27.1	Dancers Stephen Loch and Stephanie Johnson (Brooks & Company Dance) performing choreography that was recorded using motion-capture technology; Georgia Institute for Technology, Atlanta (January 2009). Photo courtesy of the authors	316
27.2	A computer rendering of marionette choreography based on motion-capture data and simulated using the original Trep software program. Image courtesy of the authors	316
27.3	Three robotic controllers operate a wooden marionette suspended from a plastic ceiling that covers a stage at the McCormick School for Engineering at Northwestern University: the robots each control two puppet strings and collaborate with each other to generate marionette	

	motion; Evanston, Illinois (January 2011). Photo courtesy of the authors	318
28.1	Leek nobleman from Nada Théâtre's *Ubu Roi* (1990; photo from 2013 remounting). Photo © Nada Théâtre	326
28.2	The Sugar-Eating Sea Monster. Photo © Sally Todd/Indefinite Articles	329
28.3	Map dated 20 August 2011 showing the location of individual stalls in that year's Feast on the Bridge in London. Image courtesy of Clare Patey	331

NOTES ON CONTRIBUTORS

Editors

John Bell is Director of the Ballard Institute and Museum of Puppetry and an Associate Professor of Dramatic Arts at the University of Connecticut. He is a founding member of the Great Small Works theatre collective; was a member of the Bread and Puppet Theatre company from 1976 to 1986; and received his doctoral degree in theatre history from Columbia University in 1993. He is the author of many books and articles about puppet theatre, including *American Puppet Modernism* (Palgrave Macmillan, 2008) and *Strings, Hands, Shadows: A Modern Puppet History* (Detroit Institute of Arts, 2000). He also edited *Puppets, Masks, and Performing Objects* (MIT Press, 2001) and is an editor of *Puppetry International*, the publication of the US branch of UNIMA.

Claudia Orenstein is Associate Professor of Theatre at Hunter College and the CUNY Graduate Center. Her publications include *The World of Theatre: Tradition and Innovation*, *Festive Revolutions: The Politics of Popular Theatre and the San Francisco Mime Troupe*, and many articles on puppetry, political theatre, and Asian theatre. Her dramaturgy work includes *Wind-Up Bird Chronicle* and other puppetry-related productions. She is executive producer of the documentary on Indian puppetry *Magic in Our Hands* and serves as a board member of UNIMA-USA, peer reviewer for *Puppetry International*, and associate editor of *Asian Theatre Journal*.

Dassia N. Posner is Assistant Professor of Theatre at Northwestern University, where she teaches Russian theatre history, history of directing, dramaturgy, and puppetry. Her articles and reviews have appeared in *Theatre Survey*, *Theatre Topics*, *Slavic and East European Performance*, *Communications from the International Brecht Society*, *Theatre Research International*, and *Puppetry International*. She is currently working on a book, *The Director's Prism: E. T. A. Hoffmann and Russian Theatricalist Directors*, and is peer-review editor for *Puppetry International*. For many years she designed and performed with giant and shadow puppets with the Puppeteers' Cooperative and with Luna Theatre. She is also a dramaturg; recent projects include *Three Sisters* and *Russian Transport* at Steppenwolf Theatre Company, with a variety of additional credits at Connecticut Repertory Theatre.

NOTES ON CONTRIBUTORS

Authors

Eric Bass founded Sandglass Theater in 1982 in Munich, Germany, with his wife, Ines Zeller Bass. Since 1986, he has made his home in Putney, Vermont. In 1991, Mr. Bass was awarded the Figurentheater Prize of Erlangen, Germany, for his contributions to puppet theatre. He currently co-directs an intensive training in puppet theatre at Sandglass during the summer, directs internationally, and tours extensively with Sandglass performances.

Dawn Tracey Brandes is a Ph.D. candidate at Northwestern University and a Teaching Fellow in the Foundation Year Programme at the University of King's College. Her dissertation considers contemporary puppet theatre and the philosophy of consciousness.

Kate Brehm is a movement artist who devises original works with performing objects and physical theatre. Her company, imnotlost, is known for unusual and uncanny puppetry, often utilizing performing scenery or costumes. She is trained in the Margolis Method of physical acting and has toured extensively with renowned puppeteer Basil Twist. She trains adults how to move objects and conceive performing design.

Matthew Isaac Cohen is Professor of International Theatre at Royal Holloway, University of London and performs *wayang kulit* internationally under the company banner Kanda Buwana. His most recent book is *Performing Otherness: Java and Bali on International Stages, 1905–1952* (Palgrave Macmillan, 2010).

Kathy Foley is a Professor of Theatre at the University of California, Santa Cruz. She is author of the Southeast Asia section of *Cambridge Guide to World Theatre* and editor of *Asian Theatre Journal*. She was the first non-Indonesian invited to perform in the prestigious all-Indonesia National Wayang Festival.

Alexander Gref is an artist and director. In 1989, he founded Vagrant Booth, reviving the Russian traditional puppet *vertep* and fairground Petrushka traditions. He is the author of three books and two dozen articles devoted to the history, technology, and therapeutic uses of puppets. Gref is a board member of UNIMA's Russian branch.

Kenneth Gross is the author of *The Dream of the Moving Statue* (1992), *Shakespeare's Noise* (2001), and *Shylock Is Shakespeare* (2006). His most recent book, *Puppet: An Essay on Uncanny Life* (2011), published by the University of Chicago Press, was co-winner of the 2011–2012 George Jean Nathan Award for Dramatic Criticism. He teaches English at the University of Rochester.

Debra Hilborn is a Ph.D. candidate at The City University of New York (CUNY) Graduate Center and a Communication Fellow at the Bernard L. Schwartz Communication Institute, Baruch College, CUNY. Her dissertation explores how performative encounters with medieval material remains produce various ways of understanding "the medieval" in later historical periods and today.

NOTES ON CONTRIBUTORS

Ida Hledíková, Ph.D, is a professor, theatre historian, critic, dramaturg, and author of documentary films. Since 1999 she has taught in the Department of Puppetry and is a researcher at the Academy of Arts in Bratislava (VŠMU), Theatre Faculty. She is the author of the monograph *Strolling Comedians, Actors, Puppeteers*, in addition to one other monograph on contemporary puppetry.

Elizabeth Ann Jochum is a postdoctoral researcher in Human-Centered Robotics and lecturer in Art and Technology at Aalborg University in Denmark. She is also the co-founder of the Robot Culture and Aesthetics research group at the University of Copenhagen. She earned a PhD in theatre from the University of Colorado, Boulder and BA from Wellesley College.

Basil Jones was born in Cape Town, South Africa. He majored in sculpture at the University of Cape Town before co-founding Handspring Puppet Company in 1981 with its artistic director and his husband, Adrian Kohler. Jones's role in the company was as a puppeteer and producer. Since the company's production of *War Horse*, he has focused his energies on the not-for-profit Handspring Trust, introducing puppetry arts in rural areas and townships.

Stephen Kaplin studied puppetry at the University of Connecticut and received an MA at New York University in performance studies. In 2006, his puppet designs for Ping Chong's *Cathay: Three Tales of China* won the American Theatre Wing's Henry Hewes Award for Notable Effects. His book (co-written with Kuang-Yu Fong) *Theatre on a Tabletop: Puppetry for Small Spaces* was published in 2003. He is co-artistic director of Chinese Theatre Works and a founding company member of Great Small Works.

Jim Lasko is an award-winning artist who creates theatrical events that reveal and celebrate overlooked and hidden cultural assets. His work with Chicago's Redmoon Theater has activated a wide range of public spaces ranging from the Museum of Contemporary Art to urban interventions in Chicago's most underserved communities. In 2011 he designed the staging for a talk by His Holiness the Dalai Lama. Lasko is a Harvard University Loeb Fellow.

Jane Marie Law is the H. Stanley Krusen Professor of World Religions, Director of the Religious Studies Program, and Associate Professor of Japanese Religions at Cornell University. In the field of puppetry, she is best known for her 1997 book *Puppets of Nostalgia: The Life, Death and Rebirth of the Awaji Ningyô Jôruri Tradition* (Princeton University Press).

Eleanor Margolies is a writer and theatre-maker based in London. She has been published in *New Theatre Quarterly*, *Visual Communication*, *Performance Research*, and *The Smell Culture Reader*. She founded *Puppet Notebook* magazine and edited it from 2004 to 2012.

Lisa Morse is an Instructor of Theatre at the College of Marin. She holds a B.A. from the University of Rhode Island, an M.F.A. in acting from the University of Alabama, and a Ph.D. from the University of Colorado.

Todd Murphey received a Ph.D. in control and dynamical systems from the California Institute of Technology and is an Associate Professor of Mechanical

Engineering and Physical Therapy and Human Motion Sciences at Northwestern University.

Paul Piris is a French researcher and theatre director based in London. Since 2005, he has been the artistic director of Rouge28 Theatre, a company that produces interdisciplinary performances rooted in puppetry. He recently completed a Ph.D. at Royal Central School of Speech and Drama. His research explores the puppet as a figure of alterity, as well as the interaction between perception and imagination in the fabrication of the presence of the puppet on stage.

Cody Poulton is Professor of Japanese literature and theatre in the Department of Pacific and Asian Studies at the University of Victoria, British Columbia, Canada. Author of numerous books on Japanese theatre, he has also translated *kabuki* and contemporary Japanese drama for such multivolume series as *Kabuki Plays on Stage* and *Half a Century of Japanese Theatre*. He is co-editor with Mitsuya Mori and J. Thomas Rimer of *The Columbia Anthology of Modern Japanese Drama* (2014).

Rike Reiniger worked in a traditional traveling puppet theatre before she studied directing and dramaturgy for Puppet Theatre at the Prague Academy in the Czech Republic and Applied Theatre Studies at Giessen University in Germany. Following her Master's degree she devised and directed performances in Berlin, where she continues to work as a director and playwright.

Peter Schumann founded Bread and Puppet in 1963 in New York City. Since 1970 in Vermont, he bakes sourdough rye bread in outdoor ovens as part of annual, giant outdoor spectacles that address political urgencies and take place on the Bread and Puppet farm. Bread and Puppet also maintains a touring company that performs worldwide.

Colette Searls is Associate Professor of Theatre at the University of Maryland, Baltimore County (UMBC), where she has devised award-winning puppet plays and collaborated on several digital puppetry projects for live audiences. She has received grants from the Jim Henson Foundation and Puppeteers of America for her original found-object puppetry productions and served on the UNIMA-USA Board of Trustees.

Elena Slonimskaya is an actress and musician with Vagrant Booth Puppet Theatre in Moscow. She is the co-author with Alexander Gref of a book devoted to art therapy and works in a children's oncology hospital providing psychological aid to patients through art and music. Slonimskaya is a member of UNIMA's Russian branch.

Robert Smythe was the founder and Artistic Director of Mum Puppettheatre in Philadelphia. He has earned fellowships from the John Simon Guggenheim Foundation, the NEA, and the Pew Charitable Trusts, and he has won six Barrymore Awards for Excellence in Theater and three UNIMA-USA Citations for Excellence in Puppetry. He teaches at Temple University and is the director of the writing program at the International Puppetry Conference at the Eugene O'Neill Theater Center.

Mark J. Sussman is Associate Professor of Theatre and Associate Dean in the Faculty of Fine Arts at Concordia University, where he teaches courses in performance studies and puppetry. A director, designer, and performer, he is a founder and co-artistic director of Great Small Works in New York City. He earned a doctorate in performance studies from New York University in 2000 and lives in Montréal and Brooklyn.

Jane Taylor first worked with puppets in 1996 when she wrote *Ubu and the Truth Commission* with William Kentridge and Handspring Puppet Company. She is currently CEO of Handspring Trust and the Wole Soyinka Chair of Workshop Theatre at the University of Leeds. She has been a Visiting Professor at the University of Chicago and Visiting Fellow at Oxford and Cambridge. Taylor has a Ph.D. from Northwestern and an M.A. from the University of Cape Town.

Amber West is a feminist poet and theatre-maker originally from California. She earned her Ph.D. in English at the University of Connecticut and her MFA in creative writing at New York University. Published in journals such as *Calyx*, *The Feminist Wire*, and *Puppetry International*, she is co-founder of the artist collective Alphabet Arts and director of the annual Puppets & Poets festival in New York City.

Margaret Williams was educated at Melbourne and Monash Universities and lectured in theatre at the University of New South Wales, Sydney, from 1973 to 1998, where she introduced undergraduate and postgraduate subjects in puppetry and material theatre. She is currently exploring the vocabulary of puppetry discourse in her forthcoming book, *An Incomplete Book of Puppetry*.

ACKNOWLEDGMENTS

Bringing this book to light has been a three-year process, during which we have relied on the support of many institutions, as well as dedicated colleagues, collaborators, and friends.

This book would not have been possible without the generosity of the many participants of "Puppetry and Postdramatic Performance: An International Conference on Performing Objects in the 21st Century" at the University of Connecticut, Storrs, in April 2011. This conference was planned by this book's editors with Janie Geiser and Susan Simpson of the Cotsen Center for Puppetry at the California Institute of the Arts; Bart Roccoberton, Director of the University of Connecticut's Puppet Arts Program; School of Fine Arts (SFA) Assistant Dean Ted Yungclas; SFA Fiscal Manager Mary Mell; and Puppet Arts graduate student Nicole Hartigan. Sincere thanks to former SFA Dean David Woods; Vincent Cardinal, Chair of the University of Connecticut's Department of Dramatic Arts; our many student and staff volunteers; the UNIMA Research Commission, UNIMA-USA; the UNIMA North American Commission; and the conference's more than 200 presenters and guests.

We are grateful to our institutions and home departments – the Theatre Department at Hunter College; the Department of Theatre at Northwestern University; and the Department of Dramatic Arts and the Ballard Institute and Museum of Puppetry at the University of Connecticut, Storrs – each of which has supported our work in myriad ways. Thanks to Dr. Bríd Grant, SFA Dean at the University of Connecticut, whose support of the Ballard Institute and Museum of Puppetry made John Bell's contribution to this volume possible. The Northwestern School of Communication gave Dassia Posner valuable time and resources to work on the project, and Harvey Young, Tracy Davis, Liz Son, Mary Poole, Linda Gates, and Brian, Betsy, and John Posner offered support along the way. Our warm gratitude also to Adrienne Macki Braconi, Bonnie and Andrew Periale, Jeungsook Yoo, Nenagh Watson, and Kara Reilly.

We are extremely grateful to Ben Piggott and Harriet Affleck, our editors, and to everyone at Routledge who patiently dealt with our queries at every step in the process. We also sincerely thank our peer reviewers for their invaluable feedback.

Eternal thanks to our editorial assistants, Dawn Tracey Brandes and Tim Cusack, for their extraordinary work, Dawn early in the process and Tim in preparing the manuscript for final submission. The Northwestern Department of Theatre provided funding for Dawn's work, and the George N. Shuster Faculty Fellowship Fund and Hunter College Mid-Career Faculty Seminar Grant funded Tim. Thank you to Robert J. Buckley and Barbara Medina for their help with the awards and to Andrew J. Polsky and the other seminar participants for their advice.

We are proud and humbled by the inspiring work of our amazing authors and for their willingness to endure multiple revisions of their chapters in our joint goal of raising the conversation about puppetry and material performance to a new level. Our deep gratitude to Kenneth Gross for his Foreword, which lends grace, beauty, and insight to our endeavors.

Additional thanks to the many scholars and artists on whose work we have drawn and built. You have made puppetry a rich and rewarding world to explore, and it is on your shoulders that we stand.

Above all, we thank all our family members, who patiently supported us through this process, giving up our time and attention as we completed our work.

FOREWORD

Kenneth Gross

> Marionettes open like umbrellas in late October.
>
> Dennis Silk

The puppet is an unpredictable creature. It always crosses between worlds and ferries *us* between worlds. Decidedly a made, material thing, the puppet has the toughness of ordinary objects – the pebble and the paper clip – yet also the resilience of more hidden and elusive entities, things of mind and spirit. Actors that are moved by others, puppets live double lives, often controlling those who seem to control them, controlling the audience's eyes and ears as well. They tend towards metamorphosis, always shifting their shape and scale, by turns innocent and violent, fiercely alive yet never quite living. You think you know the thing, what it can do, old as the puppet is, and suddenly, as if to mock your certainty, it turns into something else. Just as suddenly, the puppet can make other things in its vicinity its mirrors or doubles – the human walker in the street, the walker's shoe, a struck match.

In their long history, puppets have found their way onto a myriad of stages. You discover them not only in the nursery but in the recesses of a temple, in the opera house, the cemetery, in the city square, at a political rally, on a bare tabletop, as a thing driving the inventions of filmmakers, designers of video games, and robotics engineers – sometimes in forms you might not even recognize that require a new name. Ask people what they remember of puppet shows they have seen, and what they report is likely to be something strange, unsettling. Plain as it can be, the thing keeps its secrets.

The editors of this collection have brought together scholars, theorists, and working artists – often they are the same person – to do the complex job of making sense of this strange entity, the puppet, in its old strengths and its ever-expanding place in the world of theatre and media. What you sense among the chapters gathered here is a richly expanding conversation, open to new possibilities, with lines being thrown continually between traditional and experimental performance, between concrete theatrical practice and speculative theory. The collection invites you to see ancient shadow puppets in the light of film animation and to listen to the shrill traditional sounds of a tiny Petrushka puppet alongside the breathings of the grand animals of *War Horse*. Moving among theatres and artists in North America, Europe, Africa, Asia, and Australia, we see the puppet as a material thing deeply embedded in historical time, leaving complex legacies; it is an object in performance, an ally and challenger of the living body of the actor. We also are made aware of the puppet as *idea*, as a piece of our mental furniture, a tool of thought, a spur to reimagine parts of our ordinary life, our play and work. As much as the force of individual essays, what makes the book feel genuinely companionable is the sense of a shared project, the passionate exploring of the diverse shapes of this theatre, and what those shapes themselves explore. These pieces speak to one another in ways that continue to surprise and offer important resources for future work.

Introduction

Dassia N. Posner, Claudia Orenstein, and John Bell

In 2011, the editors of this book and several collaborators organized an international scholarly puppetry conference, "Puppetry and Postdramatic Performance," at the University of Connecticut.[1] The aims of this conference were "to explore new approaches to critical thinking and theorizing about puppetry and performing objects" and "to enrich, expand, and enliven the field of discourse" in a performance form that is as ancient as the stones and is becoming increasingly visible in contemporary theatre, but still is viewed by many as a form that is intellectually and artistically less substantive than theatre in which text or the live body of the actor is central.[2]

Several things became clear over the course of the conference, which brought together 150 scholars and artists from 14 countries across six continents: that numerous individuals were thinking about puppetry in the same kinds of ways, that there was a hunger for a more comprehensive investigation and articulation of the poetics of the puppet, and that there was profound excitement at the prospect of uniting scholars whose publications had previously often appeared piecemeal, scattered in journals or book volumes, without a clear means for their ideas to participate in direct conversation with one another.

This book, therefore, unites common threads of observation about the puppet that have emerged in disparate nations, time periods, minds, and forms – ideas that have not yet been fully understood in terms of their interconnectedness and with which we seek to hone a vocabulary. This volume's authors investigate and embrace multiple definitions of puppets, performing objects, and related forms with the aim of advancing the study of the puppet not only as a theatrical object but as a vibrant artistic and scholarly discipline.

This book, the most expansive collection of English-language puppetry scholarship to date, examines the philosophical, historical, and theatrical value of puppetry and material performance. Its essays dance between history and the present, drawing from what is useful in past understandings of the puppet, testing the boundaries of its definitions, and empowering readers to look at theatre (and beyond) through the lens of a humble responsiveness to performance in and with the material world. While this book aims to significantly shape puppetry scholarship as a discipline, we aim not to exhaust its study but to nurture its growth. In selecting the book's chapters from over 70 submissions, we have pursued temporal, geographical, critical, and thematic breadth; but there were important forms, time periods, geographies, productions, and artists that we were not able to include and which we leave to future studies.

Similarly to how *bunraku*, often described as a "theatre of threes," allows its audiences to fragment and reassemble character and story, the introduction to this volume frames the necessity and interventions of this book in three different ways, each by one of its editors: Claudia Orenstein muses on our contemporary "puppet moment," during which we interact with "smart" objects in new ways; Dassia N. Posner introduces the term "material performance" to explore the value of a puppet-centered approach to theatre; and John Bell writes about the "omnipresent" yet "invisible" puppet in his reflection on performing object historiography. The final portion of the introduction then synthesizes these perspectives into an explanation of the logic, structure, and aims of the book.

A puppet moment

Although puppets and puppet-like figures go back to the earliest periods of human culture, today they seem to be springing forth in astonishing abundance. Puppets, performing objects, and a wide variety of manipulated creatures appear on Broadway stages (*The Lion King, Avenue Q, War Horse*) and their international equivalents, garnering some of theatre's most coveted awards. They show up likewise in avant-garde venues, clubs, cabarets, and puppet slams, and on both our small and large screens. With such a preponderance of puppets, we find ourselves in what we might call "a puppet moment," a juncture when cultural attention has turned forcefully towards the manipulated theatrical object.

Puppets and related figures that combine anthropomorphic elements with craftsmanship and engineering serve both as important metaphors and tangible expressions of our continually changing understanding of what it means to be human. They emerge as vital artistic elements at times when we question and reconceive long-standing paradigms about human beings and our relationship to the inanimate world, offering concrete means of playing with new embodiments of humanity. To understand our engagement with puppetry is to chart and reveal new expressions of ourselves.

Today's proliferation of expressive objects reflects a current cultural context beyond the stage, concerns that preoccupy *our* times. As we revise our understanding of humanity in regard to both the man-made and natural elements that surround us, these new views simultaneously transform our concept of what a puppet is and how puppets manifest in performance. Describing this new understanding of puppetry and the themes and questions that emerge from it is a central project of this collection.

Objects invade every aspect of our lives. We are inundated with ever newer and more enticing commodities and, thus, are compelled to engage with a growing array of *things* and encouraged continually to assess their value and our interactions with them. Capitalist society, spreading globally, habituates us to see *things* as a means of satisfying our desires, expressing our personalities, and somehow completing us – *things* as an essential extension of ourselves.

INTRODUCTION

The theme of the object as an adjunct of the self extends to many areas of modern, daily life, especially in our relationships with new technologies. The omnipresent smartphones and tablets are expressive tools, as well as repositories of easily accessed information, acting as additional, portable brains. The way we reveal ourselves through such new technologies has increased concerns about personal privacy and how much we share of ourselves with the outside world.

The puppeteer's inquiry into the object, while drawing on our heightened responsiveness to *things*, takes us beyond simple consumer models. As Peter Schumann writes in this volume, "it is the job of the de-artified artist to push the obscure, hypocrisy-injured ordinary into the sun's or the light bulb's brightness."[3] As our authors show, puppetry redeploys objects to express the complexities of contemporary life; creates, questions, or strengthens communities; reforms relationships with technology and nature; balances tradition and modernity; and delves into metaphysical questions of existence.

Today's puppetry highlights the relationship of actor and object, connecting them in new, varied ways. Rather than simply standing in contrast to one another – human actor versus puppet – a paradigm that Edward Gordon Craig articulated in his famous "The Actor and the Über-marionette," human flesh and material constructs now intermingle in an endless array of configurations. As puppeteers play with connecting to the material world and drawing focus to or from their own presence, they physically embody larger cultural practices and preoccupations while engendering new interrogations into the puppet's nature: how does one understand subjectivity, agency, or character in this intermingling of flesh and matter, in the theatrical co-presence of puppet and puppeteer? The age-old question of what defines a puppet also requires reassessment in this context. Might puppetry, as Margaret Williams proposes in "The Death of 'The Puppet'?" rest not on particular kinds of objects or means of manipulation, but rather on a form of spectatorship?

The puppet's ability to oscillate between states of life and death has long engendered philosophical contemplation. Today the demarcations between life and death may not be as simply construed as in the past. Medical advancements connect humans with machines, keeping critically ill patients alive. More and more, we replace pieces of our failing bodies with more durable crafted parts. How do we understand the metaphysical "self," given these new *material* realities? How do we conceptualize the division between animate and inanimate when the inanimate sustains life? To manipulate the puppet is to explore this blurred line between life and death, between the self as a discrete being and one intertwined with inanimate matter.

Many cultures do not articulate distinct dichotomies between animate and inanimate, living and dead, seeing all matter as endowed with spirit or as providing sites for hosting a world of passing beings: divine, demonic, or the spirits of the deceased. As Cody Poulton reminds us, "The Japanese since ancient times accorded a sense of spirit or consciousness (*kokoro*) to all natural phenomena, from insensible stones to plants and animals." The human-shaped figures used to negotiate the spirit world and deal with highly charged emotional situations, like those Jane Marie Law analyzes, pave the way not just for Japan's *bunraku* puppet tradition, but also for contemporary experiments using androids and robots in performance. When cultures with differing beliefs meet around performing objects, new questions emerge: how do objects carry and transmit the beliefs of those who crafted them? Can a culture share its ritual performance but not its gods or its beliefs? Can one manipulate the puppet or embody the mask without embracing its spirit, or at least the spirit in which it was constructed?

Virtual worlds engineered through computer technologies engender further philosophical explorations – and concomitant social anxieties: how does the virtual replicate, replace, reconfigure, or misconstrue the non-virtual? Both real performing objects onstage and virtual ones on screens provide opportunities for grappling, physically and directly, with answers. New technological experiments that intersect directly with puppetry include robot performers, robots manipulating string marionettes, computer-generated imagery (CGI), and motion capture. Puppeteers and scholars wrestle with how traditional ideas of puppetry and new technologies can inform and enrich each other, and find, despite the innovative tools and techniques at work, that these experiments re-invoke puppetry's recurrent philosophical issues: what constitutes a puppet? What is human agency?

The puppet's visual nature also speaks to our current moment. Abundant exposure to film, television, and computers, which inundate us with images, has turned viewers into adept readers of the visual. Puppets, as bearers of precise visual meaning, can, perhaps even more than human actors, serve the needs of such visually trained audiences. They form a bridge between the human actor and digital media onstage. Moreover, divisions between artistic disciplines are now productively blurred, with art forms mixing all manner of technology and expression. Dancers who speak and plays that incorporate digital projections are but two examples. The puppet, as both art object and kinetic character, is thus a valuable medium for contemporary artists who merge dance, theatre, film, literature, and visual arts.

Increasingly in the current performance context, when we say "puppet," we are no longer speaking exclusively of the figurative, crafted characters dangled from strings, gloved on hands, or attached to rods that the word has previously evoked: the Punch, Guignol, Howdy Doody, Lamb Chop, Kukla, and Kermit characters of our childhoods. It is this expanded understanding of "puppet" that the chapters in this volume point to and that Dassia Posner describes below as "material performance." The view this term provides places our attention on the material world around us, its action on us, and our interactions with it.

In a world of material performance, why use the term puppet at all? The iconic idea of the puppet is an anchor within this new model of performance that links the physical world and all its associations with the realm of human concerns and human mediation. Puppetry gives unique focus to objects in performance, often conspicuously in contrast to the live-actor theatre. By examining the history, practice, and artistic vocabularies of puppetry, we can more fully understand and activate the new material nature of the stage. Additionally, because the puppet is a technological object manipulated through technological means, it serves as a bridge between the world of the human actor and a multitude of media. Within this new paradigm of puppetry performance, the puppet, no longer an inferior echo of live-actor theatre, becomes a new central figure through which we can enter into a broader notion of performance in and with the material world.

– *Claudia Orenstein*

INTRODUCTION

Material performance(s)

In using the word "puppet," the authors of this book mean many different things – a leather shadow, a coffee bean, a leek, a toy train, a cross, a handful of clay, an image on a screen, a robot that animates a marionette – and thus expand far beyond notions of the puppet as necessarily figurative or anthropomorphic. One important constant, however, is that the life and agency of the puppet is a recurrent, central point of inquiry. At its broadest and yet its simplest, we define puppetry as the human infusion of independent life into lifeless, but not agentless, objects in performance.

In 1983, Frank Proschan revolutionized the definition of the puppet by articulating this performance form as a subgenre within a much wider category of "performing objects" – that is, "material images of humans, animals, or spirits that are created, displayed, or manipulated in narrative or dramatic performance" (Proschan 1983: 4). Interestingly, given the rise in Europe of *théâtre d'objets* – theatrical performance that animates everyday objects – during the same decade in which Proschan's essay appeared (Margolies 2013), Proschan centered his discussion on objects – masks, puppets, ritual objects – that were designed with performance in mind. Common usage has since conflated the two terms, "performing objects" and "theatre of objects," so that many puppetry scholars and practitioners now consider any object that is given independent life in performance – a match that self-immolates, a flying metronome, a piece of swirling cloth – to be a performing object.

The stubborn resistance of the puppet to a single definition says a great deal about its chameleonic nature. The puppet exists in an inherently ambiguous, fundamentally dual state: it operates, as Margaret Williams notes, "in the collapsed boundaries between the living and the inanimate;" it remains independent even as it is manipulated; and it expresses the will and persona of its animator while imparting meaning of its own. In the words of Peter Schumann, puppetry is "an anarchic art, subversive and untamable by nature … representing, more or less, the demons of … society and definitely not its institutions" (Schumann 1991: 75).

Rather than simply pondering what a puppet *is*, this book is concerned with what the puppet *does*: to paraphrase Jennifer Parker-Starbuck (2013: 385), our authors investigate the puppet not "as object" but "as do-er." And it is in this sense that the book forays into new territory, into "material performance": performance that assumes that inanimate matter contains agency not simply to mimic or mirror, but also to shape and create.

By "material performance," I mean several things. At its simplest, this term assumes that puppets and other material objects in performance bear visual and kinetic meanings that operate independently of whatever meanings we may inscribe upon them in performance. The sheer phenomenological "thereness" of objects (Sofer 2003: 15) can supersede or even erase spoken words because an audience's fascination with them is so intense; examples of this range from real water or animals on the stage to puppets that, in the words of Handspring Puppet Company's Basil Jones, "ignite … a smoldering coal of ancient belief in us that there is life in stones, in rivers, in objects, in wood" (*Lincoln Center Theater Review* 2011: 12).

Performing with food or with everyday household objects also "ghosts" our previous associations with such objects outside the theatre (Carlson 2003: 7).

The physical materials of which objects are comprised – cloth, metal, papier-mâché, leather – also have unique dramaturgies. John Bell observes that puppet theatre is "inextricably linked to long-standing human desires to play with the material world in performances focused on wood, stone, plastic, metal, glass, paper, bone, and other objects that … move around, speak, and otherwise seem to possess life."

In her recent book *Vibrant Matter*, political scientist Jane Bennett argues that all matter, even matter that is not technically alive, contains agency and efficacy, what she terms "vitality." She explains: "By 'vitality' I mean the capacity of things – edibles, commodities, storms, metals – not only to impede or block the will and designs of humans but also to act as quasi agents or forces with trajectories, propensities, or tendencies of their own." Bennett, paraphrasing Bruno Latour, also describes matter as an "actant," that is "a source of action that can be either human or nonhuman; it is that which has efficacy, can do things, has sufficient coherence to make a difference, produce effects, alter the course of events" (Bennett 2010: viii). Bennett describes the agency of the inanimate material world in terms that are similar to how puppeteers have long articulated their interplay with puppets.

Like Proschan's "performing objects," the term "material performance" broadens the sphere of the puppet, but it additionally infuses this breadth with the centrality of vibrant matter. If we begin with the assumption that objects contain life, will, and intent by virtue of their design and inherent nature, rather than taking for granted that humans wield (and thereby dominate) inert matter, such a view allows for a productive rethinking of how we interact with objects on the stage. Puppets have often been viewed as inanimate beings that *mimic* human ideas and content (by being representationally or anthropomorphically tied to the human form or by being controlled by a human operator), while lacking agency to *shape* or *alter* them. Yet one of the most recurrent refrains uttered by nearly anyone who has ever held a puppet is that the puppet is unruly, that it wants to do things that differ from what we would impose upon it, and that we can best bring out its life if we listen to it.

This leads us to ponder how the material (i.e., physical, phenomenological) world performs, not in the sense of how we might manipulate it or dominate it, but of how we might respond to it. This book thus encourages a fundamental perspective shift, one in which actors do not interact in hierarchical superiority over objects on the stage but engage in equal interplay or "collaborative interchange" (Parker-Starbuck 2013: 392) with them. Theatrical performance then shifts to focus not only on the interplay of actors but also on the interplay of actants.

As Kathy Foley has argued, theatre in the West has often approached the puppet as a machine, seeing "the puppet *qua* object obediently carrying out the intention of the puppeteer." Many Asian theatre forms, by contrast, view "the puppet as having a life, law, and logic of its own, which it imposes on the manipulator" (Foley 2000: 14). This allows puppeteers, in Foley's words, "to be moved by their imaginative embrace of the object … in a way that allows us to re-imagine our world. … The manipulator is danced by a reality that is not his/her own by … becoming a person, animal, thing she will never be" (Foley 2000: 15). As Jim Lasko similarly notes, shifting focus from one's self to an object of common collaboration can unleash creative thought. There is thus an important difference between material performance and performance with materials – productions that use puppets or performing objects in an auxiliary way (Francis 2011: 6). The latter complements performance, but the former has the power to generate or inspire it.

Puppetry and what Debra Hilborn calls "a puppet perspective" are thus material (i.e., substantial and necessary) to much broader kinds of theatrical conversations. Indeed, many artists in contemporary theatre are engaged with material performance, even if they may not yet articulate it this way. For instance, Moisés Kaufman (inspired, in turn, by Mary Overlie and Tadeusz Kantor) has advocated for "horizontal theatre" that "topple[s] the vertical hierarchy of the text to build theatre around the equal interplay between all of the theatrical elements" (Brown 2005: 54). The vocabulary and sensibility of material performance also lends valuable contextualizing insight to the sensory immersions of Punchdrunk, Emma Rice's playful interplay with film, Dmitry Krymov's infusions of theatrical design into the fourth dimension of time, William Kentridge's "stone-age animation" (Tomkins 2010: 53), Basil Twist's fantastical plays with fabric, Agus Nur Amal's contemporary object performances, and many, many others.

In viewing the theatre from the wise perspective of the puppet, this book proposes a model for malleable, collaborative, and responsive artistic engagement with the material world. Light can be something with which to collaborate rather than to bend or focus; billowing cloth can speak louder than words; a sword or a book or a glass of water can be a partner rather than a passive, inert object. The idea that we might heed rather than simply manipulate objects is also causing waves in multiple fields at present – political science, philosophy, robotics, media studies, theatre, and beyond – demonstrating the value of puppet and material performance to larger systems of creative thought.

– Dassia N. Posner

Omnipresence and invisibility: Puppets and the textual record

Although puppets might seem to have only recently emerged urgently into our cultural range of vision, they have, in fact, been with us all the time. Likewise, although many might consider the literature and criticism of material performance to be scant if not nonexistent, it can, in fact, be found within a rich network of interwoven discussions among a variety of disciplines. The histories of puppets, objects, and other elements of material performance are not told simply by dramatic texts, histories of theatre practice, artists' accounts, and theories of performance, but also by philosophical, theoretical, and scientific studies that attempt to understand the nature of *things*; by oral histories connected to puppet practices around the world; and by the "texts" of the actual puppets, masks, and performing objects.

The first, and in some ways most powerful, literature of puppetry is the performing object itself, which instructs us clearly about its preferred movements, aesthetics, stories, and social contexts. A puppet's structure and its ability to let the performer know what it "wants" to do constitute an instruction manual and an aesthetics of performance. As Robert Smythe argues in this volume, "the puppet *is* the text." A related, similarly unconventional literature of the puppet is oral history, which is embodied in the transfer of knowledge from master to apprentice in generations of puppet ensembles around the world. This word-of-mouth literature embodies design and performance codes, aesthetics, and community beliefs. The literatures marking the history of technology, such as the accounts of Hero of Alexandria's automata from the first century CE or Ibn al-Jazari's similar mechanisms from the thirteenth century, can also be viewed likewise as a literature of the puppet, as much a tool as it is an artwork or ritual object. The eighteenth and nineteenth centuries' many new mechanical viewing systems, the precursors of film (camera obscura, magic lantern, eidophusikon, peep show, panorama, zoetrope), created new paradigms for mechanical image performance, which still dominate culture today. The puppet's status as tool fosters a unique body of knowledge about its functionality and practices.

Since the nature of things is an essential metaphysical question, the literature of puppetry also necessarily includes philosophy. Plato's references to performed objects in *The Republic*'s "Allegory of the Cave" helped him to explain a foundational idea of Greek philosophy – the nature of the real and the ideal – in terms of a metaphorical shadow theatre, the dynamics of which were apparently familiar to his students. The advent of modernity and its separation of nature and culture led to Immanuel Kant's eighteenth-century idea that objects are never experienced directly in themselves but only through human cognition. During the twentieth century, Martin Heidegger responded that objects exist independently of human cognition in "a reality that cannot be manifested by practical or theoretical action" (Harman 2002: 1). This sense of an autonomous power of objects led Graham Harman and other ecological theorists to develop object-oriented ontology, which considers the material world as an independent force and questions human relationships.

The literature of artists' analyses, theories, and prescriptions offers another important strand of historical literature on the puppet. A fascination with puppets emerged in European Romanticism as eighteenth-century artists and thinkers rejected the political status quo, ideas of industrial progress, and rationalism itself. A return to the idea of powerful objects appeared most prominently in Heinrich von Kleist's 1810 "On the Marionette Theatre" but also in Goethe and Schiller, as well as with E. T. A. Hoffmann's interests in object theatre as part of the popular culture of fairground performance and persistent pagan rituals like carnival. Avant-garde theatre makers associated with late nineteenth-century Symbolism – Maurice Maeterlinck, Alfred Jarry, Edward Gordon Craig, and others – took up Romanticism's concerns with objects and puppets and proposed puppetry and puppet dynamics as viable and revelatory means of making modern theatre. The avant-garde movements to follow rejected stage realism and actor-centered theatre, instead exploring the possibilities of bodies, texts, objects, puppets, masks, and machines. These artists also made a real contribution to the literature of puppets with the development of the artist's manifesto. Jarry, Fernand Léger, and Oskar Schlemmer (to name a few) wrote eloquently about how to reinvent human-object relations on stage. Such mixtures of theory and experiment contributed to the 1960s manifestos of the New York avant-garde by members of Fluxus and the Judson Church artistic community, both influences on Peter Schumann's practice and theory. The writings and artistic works of these artists form a rich mine of thought on the puppet to which scholars and practitioners continue to return.

The social sciences of the nineteenth century – from the development of antiquarianism into folklore and anthropology – created another stream of performing-object literature as they documented and analyzed object-based ritual and performance in Asia, Africa, and the Americas, as well as in Europe. At a time when mainstream European and American cultural ideologies were increasingly certain about puppetry's confinement to children's culture and low-brow entertainment, anthropologists explored the intricacies of international object performance forms, initiating Western efforts to understand puppetry as a worldwide phenomenon that has become deeply intercultural.

Another important contribution to the literary history of the puppet came in the early decades of the twentieth century from scholars of semiotics – the scientific study of language – who expanded its purview from the language of words to the language of objects. Writers of the Prague Linguistic Circle considered both folk performance and avant-garde theatre, analyzing puppet techniques and their relationships with humans.[4] Frank Proschan's 1983 *Semiotica* issue ("Puppets, Masks, and Performing Objects from Semiotic Perspectives") was both a culminating moment for the energy of Prague School studies and a new opening for subsequent examinations of puppetry and material performance, ranging from the history of popular theatre to ritual studies, linguistics, and the nature of communication systems. These semioticians provided puppetry scholars with a theoretical model for and academic validation of their pursuits. Semiotics continues to inform analysis of puppetry today, though it has been expanded upon by an interest in phenomenological models that go beyond thinking of puppetry as exclusively a sign-system to take into account its multifaceted experiential nature.

During the latter half of the twentieth century, puppetry studies was given another scholarly boost with the development of the new discipline of performance studies, which expanded Western theatre analysis to embrace ritual and social performance from a global perspective, necessarily involving puppet, mask, and object performance. Although some other aspects of critical and cultural theory neglected studies of the material world to focus instead on texts (*pace* Jacques Derrida) and the body (*pace* Michel Foucault), in the 1980s the material world became crucial to studies of science history by Bruno Latour and others, initiating analyses of the agency of that world as a critical and ecological need. Such studies have more recently connected with multidisciplinary work focused on objects and material culture: Victoria Nelson's *The Secret Life of Puppets*, Sherry Turkle's *Evocative Objects*, Susan Stewart's *On Longing*, Jane Bennett's *Vibrant Matter*, and the object-oriented ontologists mentioned above.

In Western culture, the literature of theatre history and theory has tended to see puppetry as an occasional and often inconsequential addendum to the history of dramatic texts and actors' theatre, although intriguing exceptions abound.[5] One such exception is Charles Magnin's impressive 1852 *Histoire des Marionnettes en Europe*, which recounted the progress of puppets from Egyptian, Roman, and medieval religious rituals to popular and aristocratic entertainments, taking into account not only familiar hand and string puppets but also masks, automata, giant puppets, and crèche plays. Magnin's work was followed by a small but impressive group of twentieth-century puppet historians focused on specific companies, movements, or regional traditions, including Paul McPharlin and Stefan Brecht for American puppetry; Henryk Jurkowski, George Speaight, John McCormick, René Meurant, Brunella Eruli, Didier Plassard, Harold Segel, Penny Francis, and Antonio Pasqualino for

European forms; and James Brandon, Donald Keene, Jane Marie Law, Stuart Blackburn, Fan Pen Li Chen, and Matthew Cohen for Asian puppetry.

During the past two decades, English-language puppetry scholarship has burgeoned significantly as writers respond to the current puppet moment by placing puppetry at the center of critical inquiry. To name but a few, *Puppets, Masks, and Performing Objects* (Bell 2001) and *Puppetry: A World History* (Blumenthal 2005) embrace a wide geographical and historical scope of forms, performers, and productions. *American Puppet Modernism: Essays on the Material World in Performance* (Bell 2008) examines US puppetry from the past 150 years; *Handspring Puppet Company* (Taylor 2009) provides a revelatory view of a South African company; *Über-Marionettes and Mannequins: Craig, Kantor and Their Contemporary Legacies* (Guidicelli 2013) reimagines the theory and practice of two of puppetry's most dynamic twentieth-century innovators; *Puppet: An Essay on Uncanny Life* (Gross 2011) articulates wide-ranging responses to puppet theory as an inspired form of literary criticism; and *Puppetry: A Reader in Theatre Practice* (Francis 2011) is the first recent practical English-language textbook for the field.

There is no single, straight trajectory through the literature of puppetry and material performance. That history is told in many ways and through many disciplines – a network of literatures whose connections to each other might not always be obvious yet are always compelling. The chapters in this book are informed by this network of disparate approaches – theatre history, oral history, objects as teachers, history of technology, philosophy, performance studies, social sciences, artists' perspectives, and critical and cultural theory – that relate to long-standing, though often under-acknowledged, conversations about puppet and object performance. We necessarily address essential elements such as sculpture, painting, music, choreography, text, acting style, aesthetics, and the social, religious, political, aesthetic, and philosophical contexts of puppet and performing object practices over many centuries and around the world.

– John Bell

The book

Each of this book's three parts muses on two related issues and their intersections: how the puppet is theorized by both scholars and artists; how we might understand material performance by re-examining both history and tradition; and how we analyze the vocabularies of the puppet in both live and mediated performance. With the exception of Basil Jones's "Puppetry, Authorship, and the *Ur*-Narrative," none of these chapters has previously appeared elsewhere.

Part I, "Theory and Practice," edited by John Bell, engages with the nature and function of the puppet as articulated in written theory. Its authors expand beyond the oft-cited Kleist and Craig to propose a productive rethinking of the puppet's poetics through the lens of its scholars, puppeteers, and scholar-puppeteers. Its two subsections, "Theoretical Approaches to the Puppet" and "Perspectives from Practitioners," explore puppets as they have been historically theorized and as puppeteers frame their work by viewing the puppet's meaning not as fixed but as something to be discovered. This fusion of scholarship and artistic insight features a mix of writing styles and perspectives that are united by a common aim: to expand and articulate how objects function in performance.

Part II, "New Dialogues with History and Tradition," edited by Claudia Orenstein, prompts a re-examination of puppetry history and traditions. The first section, "Revisiting History," reclaims lost and undervalued voices in the history of puppetry and advocates for the value of rethinking the meanings of objects in performance from "a puppet perspective." The second, "Negotiating Tradition," focuses on case studies from India, Indonesia, Korea, and Ukraine to explore what Cohen terms the "post-traditional," productively troubling oversimplified notions of traditional forms as codified and unchanging rather than fluid, responsive, and dynamic.

Part III, "Contemporary Conversations and Hybridizations," edited by Dassia N. Posner, investigates how the puppet is defined in live theatre and in hybrid forms, such as motion capture and robotics, with case studies drawn from South Africa, England, Germany, Switzerland, France, the Netherlands, the United States, and Japan. The first section, "Material Performances in Contemporary Theatre," engages in close analyses of contemporary puppetry performances, grappling with how puppetry functions theatrically. The second section, "New Directions and Hybrid Forms," begins with three perspectives on hybridizations of puppetry and technology: string marionettes controlled by robots, robots performing onstage with humans, and live motion capture as a kind of puppet. It concludes with a piece that ponders puppetry, ecology, and the implications of both on a cosmic scale.

Our authors reflect on a wide variety of themes that also transcend section divisions. They ponder why the puppet (or robots, motion capture, etc.) is often read as uncanny (Bell, Poulton, Searls, and Jochum and Murphey), how it fragments and reassembles character (Taylor, Brandes), how it mediates between spatial and perceptual planes (Brehm, Smythe), communities and societies (Lasko, Schumann), understandings of the self (Morse, Piris), life and death (Jones, Law), and history and the present (Cohen, Hilborn, Hledíková, Foley). They advocate for reclaiming the innovations of women who found in this form an arena for artistic autonomy (Orenstein, Posner, West). They also investigate the potential of heeding rather than wielding lifeless matter (Bass), the value of adopting the wise fantasy of the child (Reiniger, Sussman), of engaging creatively with intangible substances, such as light (Kaplin) or the unearthly sound of the swazzle (Gref and Slonimskaya). The book begins with an investigation of the "death" of the figurative puppet (Williams) and ends with its rebirth and infinite potential in new, broader realms (Margolies).

Dancers have long understood that music can be made visible through the poetry of the body. Russian puppeteer Nina Simonovich-Efimova once compared the puppeteer to a pianist and the process of performing with a puppet to trying out its movement "scales" to explore its expressive potential. In this book's essays, we do not claim to play all the pieces in the puppet's repertoire, but we do hope to demonstrate the expansiveness of its range and the tremendous breadth of its resonance.

Notes

1 See the Acknowledgments for details on conference collaborators and participants.
2 Quotations from the Puppetry and Postdramatic Performance conference program. The conference also explored performing-object theatre in relation to Hans-Thies Lehmann's

INTRODUCTION

Postdramatic Theatre (1999, translated into English in 2006), positing that puppetry has always been "postdramatic," that it "has always thrived independently of a dependence on dramatic text."
3 Quotations for which no citation is given are drawn from chapters in this book.
4 Anthologies of Prague School essays include Matejka and Titunik (1986) and Garvin (2007).
5 For an earlier attempt to delineate a historiography of puppetry, see Bell (2001). For an excellent bibliography of puppetry scholarship in English, see Francis (2011).

Works cited

Bell, J. (ed.) (2001) *Puppets, Masks, and Performing Objects*. Cambridge, MA: MIT Press.
—— (2008) *American Puppet Modernism: Essays on the Material World in Performance*, Palgrave Studies in Theatre and Performance History. Hampshire, England: Palgrave Macmillan.
Bennett, J. (2010) *Vibrant Matter: A Political Ecology of Things*. Durham, NC, and London: Duke University Press.
Blumenthal, E. (2005) *Puppetry: A World History*. New York, NY: Henry N. Abrams.
Brown, Rich (2005) "Moisés Kaufman: The Copulation of Form and Content," *Theatre Topics* 15: 51–65.
Carlson, M. (2003) *The Haunted Stage: The Theatre as Memory Machine*. Ann Arbor, MI: University of Michigan Press.
Foley, Kathy (2000) "The Dancer and the Danced: Approaches toward the Puppeteer's Art," *Puppetry International* 8(Fall): 14–16.
Francis, P. (2011) *Puppetry: A Reader in Theatre Practice*. Hampshire, England: Palgrave Macmillan.
Garvin, P. (2007) *A Prague School Reader on Esthetics, Literary Structure, and Style*. Washington, DC: Georgetown University Press.
Gross, K. (2011) *Puppet: An Essay on Uncanny Life*. Chicago, IL: University of Chicago Press.
Guidicelli, C. (ed.) (2013) *Über-Marionettes and Mannequins: Craig, Kantor and Their Contemporary Legacies*. Charleville, France: Institut International de la Marionnette.
Harman, G. (2002) *Tool-Being: Heidegger and the Metaphysics of Objects*. Peru, IL: Open Court.
Kleist, H. (1810) "On the Marionette theatre," trans. R. Paska (1989) in M. Feher with R. Nadaff and N. Tazi (eds) *Fragments for a History of the Human Body Part 1*. New York, NY: Zone.
Lincoln Center Theater Review (2011) "The Magical Life of Objects: An Interview with Adrian Kohler and Basil Jones," 55: 10–14.
Magnin, C. (1852) *Histoire des marionettes en Europe*. Paris: Michel Lévy Frères.
Margolies, E. (2013) "Arthur Rimbaud and the Puppets in Charlestown," *Times Literary Supplement*, 25 September, <http://www.the-tls.co.uk/tls/public/article1318371.ece> (accessed December 7, 2013).
Matejka, L. and Titunik, I. (1986) *Semiotics of Art: Prague School Contributions*. Cambridge, MA: MIT Press.
Parker-Starbuck, J. (2013) "Animal Ontologies and Media Representations: Robotics, Puppets, and the Real of *War Horse*," *Theatre Journal* 65: 373–393.
Proschan, F. (1983) "The Semiotic Study of Puppets, Masks, and Performing Objects," (also ed.) *Semiotica* 47(1–4): 3–44.
Schumann, P. (1991) "The Radicality of the Puppet Theatre," *TDR/The Drama Review* 35(4): 75–83.
Sofer, A. (2003) *The Stage Life of Props*. Ann Arbor, MI: University of Michigan Press.
Taylor, J. (2009) *Handspring Puppet Company*. Cape Town, South Africa: David Krut Publishing.
Tomkins, Calvin (2010) "Lines of Resistance," *The New Yorker*, January 18: 53.

Part I
THEORY AND PRACTICE
Edited and Introduced by John Bell

Puppetry, which allows a performer to create the illusion of life by combining objects with motion and sound, is an art form that raises many fundamental questions. What exactly is life? How is it created? Who creates it? What, in fact, do puppets actually do? How should we think about and respond to our experience of puppetry? Such basic questions about the nature of human and material existence constantly wait beneath the surface of puppetry's benign or seemingly inconsequential existence and inspire performers, audience members, and scholars to engage in theoretical thinking, some of which we present in Part I of this book, "Theory and Practice." The first section, "Theoretical Approaches to the Puppet," presents the work of three scholars concerned with the meaning of different kinds of puppet practices; while the second, "Perspectives from Practitioners," offers writings by nine puppeteers who analyze the form from the viewpoint of their own experience. These two perspectives, from both sides of the puppet stage, complement each other by investigating what it means to make puppet theatre and what it means to experience it.

Puppets and performing objects have been part of global culture since its beginnings, but theoretical writings about the form began to constitute their own field only relatively recently. Puppet theory first existed as observations puppeteers shared with each other, and it seems to have been only in the modern era that theories of puppetry have been written down for more general audiences. Perhaps such thinking emerges with an understanding of the form as art, more than ritual or popular performance. In Japan a brief record of playwright Chikamatsu Monzaemon's thoughts about meter, nonrealism, and the articulation of pathos through words and objects in *jōruri* puppet plays appears in a 1738 memoir, *Naniwa Miyage*, after the playwright had established puppet plays as serious theatre. In Europe, the modern engagement with puppet theory could be said to have begun less than a century later with Heinrich von Kleist's 1810 essay "On the Marionette Theatre." Kleist's unassuming text (a dialogue, really) analyzes the connections between movement and consciousness in dance, everyday life, and with animals and marionettes. However, like much of puppet theory to follow, it expands itself into a contemplation of identity and being which embraces metaphysical issues and conundrums in an epiphanic style befitting Kleist's Romantic bent. Although not all the essays in Sections I and II here strive for epiphany, their subject matter forces the authors to engage in stimulating thinking about the nature of humans, life, and inanimate matter in the context of often-humble performances with various combinations of wood, metal, plastic, leather, and papier-mâché.

The three essays in "Theoretical Approaches to the Puppet" reflect the expansive and heterodox range of contemporary puppet and object theory in the early twenty-first century. Margaret Williams's investigation of the "death" of the puppet marks a particular moment of expansion from traditional notions of puppetry into the "theatre of objects" movement that began in Europe during the 1980s, placing both on a continuum of manipulated materiality. In his chapter, Paul Piris asks basic questions about new forms of puppet and object theatre from a phenomenological perspective, attempting to understand how the simultaneous presence of manipulated puppet and manipulating puppeteer creates ontological ambiguity. Finally, my own chapter argues that puppets are always "uncanny" and that our modern sense of that sensation as a problem connects to the metaphysical complexity of puppetry's consistent resistance to modernity's attempts to separate nature and culture.

Puppeteers always have to think about the nature of their medium in a kind of applied theory. In purely practical terms and for wholly practical reasons, they figure out how to move the puppets; what kinds of objects, settings, sounds, and texts to add to them; and what makes for the most effective means of communicating with and through them. Some puppeteers have been further inspired to address issues of puppet theory on the page as well as the stage. Theorist/practitioners Edward Gordon Craig and Alfred Jarry set the tone for such writings about puppetry, establishing an audacious and willfully shocking attitude befitting the avant-garde desire to redefine modern culture. In the century that followed, puppetry has become a complicated mix of practices encompassing old traditions, new aesthetics, and technological innovations that have intertwined it deeply with other strands of contemporary culture. The various "Perspectives from Practitioners" in Section II express differing combinations of theory and practice as experienced in each author's work and show that the artist's need to articulate puppet theory offers vital insights applicable to a broader understanding of the field.

Considering the increased importance of the body in contemporary performance, Sandglass Theater founder Eric Bass argues for a similar awareness of the puppet's function, pointing out that, although when an actor appears onstage she or he *needs* to make a statement, the appearance onstage of a puppet already *is* a statement – a dynamic principle with profound implications for all types of performance. Basil Jones, co-founder of South Africa's Handspring Puppet Company, pursues similar goals on a different path, describing the independent "*Ur*-narrative" of the puppet as a "dignified hunt for life" that exists almost independently of story, in the "micro-movements" that give puppets life. Moscow puppeteers Alexander Gref and Elena Slonimskaya, who work with the archetypal Russian glove puppet Petrushka, examine the function of the noise instrument known as a swazzle in order to interrogate its function for modern audiences and consider the semiotics of such music-making in international contexts. German puppeteer Rike Reiniger explains the development of a different kind of contemporary puppetry: the invention of object performance for very young audiences by artists inspired by the "live-art" experiments of Bauhaus and other avant-garde traditions and informed by contemporary early-childhood education theories. New York puppeteer Kate Brehm links her own process of creating theatrical structure and dramatic affect to theories of the cinema and the comic book articulated by Gilles Deleuze and Scott McCloud, thus discovering a means by which critical theory can have practical value for object performance. Chinese Theatre Works co-founder Stephen Kaplin looks at the nature of shadow theatre – one of the oldest idioms of puppetry – as a practical technique that, even with the new technological possibilities of image projection and performance that saturate our environment, inexorably leads to mystical phenomenology by means of its essential dependence on the elusive properties of light. In "The Third Thing," puppeteer and director Jim Lasko follows the development of applied theory by Chicago's Redmoon Theater as it creates participatory spectacle in public spaces where puppets and objects become essential mediators between people, creating what Victor Turner termed "communitas." Finally, Bread and Puppet Theater director Peter Schumann – who has long shared the proclivity of avant-garde artists to use the manifesto as a modern literary form that declaims, proclaims, teases, and provokes – provides an enigmatic and evocative analysis of the ordinary life of the capitalist system in which we live, calling for a revolution against "the holy cathedral of our civilization" by means, of course, of puppet theatre.

While the practitioners of Section II have been compelled by personal experience to explain how puppetry manages by its very essence to address larger questions of human existence in the material world, the theorists of Section I have made a conscious decision to examine puppetry as a legitimate field of inquiry that embodies multiple theories of performance and modes of existence. Both perspectives illuminate the work examined in the following sections of this book.

Note

Chapters in Part I by Bell, Gref and Slonimskaya, Jones, and Lasko are edited by Dassia N. Posner.

Section I
Theoretical Approaches to the Puppet

1
The Death of "The Puppet"?
Margaret Williams

In his message via the Internet to puppeteers for World Puppet Day on March 21, 2011, Henryk Jurkowski celebrates the vitality and diversity of international puppetry today. Yet he suggests that "from now on the object will replace the figurative puppet," and ends with the hope that "the tradition of the figurative puppet has not disappeared over the horizon" and "will always remain as a valuable point of reference" (Jurkowski 2011). If it seems a rather wistful conclusion, it echoes a concern shared by some devotees of the puppet theatre. Many people at festivals of "puppetry and related arts" still complain that there weren't any puppets. That might not trouble many of us, but the complainants do have a point – is it puppetry if there are no puppets in it? And just how are the "related arts" related to puppetry?

Three classic short performances in which puppets or objects seem to commit suicide might serve to illustrate the "death" of the figurative puppet, perhaps even of "the puppet" as a concept, in the contemporary Western puppet theatre. The death or suicide of the puppet is a recurring theme in puppetry, since it exposes the problematic nature of the puppet's "life." There is a parallel theme of the death of the puppeteer at the hands of the puppet, but it's the puppet's potential demise we're concerned with here.

In Philippe Genty's famous short untitled piece, a Pierrot marionette becomes aware of the strings connecting it to its manipulator and asserts its independent life by breaking them one by one until it falls "dead" when finally detached from the puppeteer.[1] It's the classic metaphor of puppetry – the godlike puppeteer both gives life to and withdraws it from a creation made in his/her own image. Genty, a black-clad figure manipulating the controls high above the Pierrot, is an impassive superior presence whom the puppet resists, only to invite its own destruction. When the last string breaks, Genty simply picks up the puppet and walks off with it, now just an object. But its reduction to object status is incomplete; even as it is carried offstage, it still retains that "after-life" that lingers around any figure with which an audience has emotionally identified. It remains a human form, able to be empathized with and to be revived and to "die" all over again at the next show. The piece has reduced many audience members to tears, yet it demonstrates, quite literally, that the puppet's "life" exists only as an *effect* of the puppeteer's control.

Figure 1.1 Pierrot (1973). Photo courtesy of Philippe Genty Company

In the French puppeteer Yves Joly's *Tragédie de Papier* (*Tragedy in Paper*), the puppets are animated drawings rather than lifelike figures, two-dimensional cutouts with stylized facial features and arms painted onto them. The physical properties of paper (in fact, light cardstock) are exploited in the portrayal of the two lovers' deaths: the female figure is brutally slashed by a large pair of scissors wielded by a jealous villain, and the male figure is set alight and reduced to ashes. It remains ambiguous whether this apparently spontaneous combustion of grief is to be read as suicide, since, unlike Pierrot, the figures can seem to take only limited action by themselves. Both the slashing of the first figure and the setting alight of the second are performed by the puppeteer's black-gloved hands, visible at times, which must substitute for the puppets' painted ones. If, as Victor Molina (1998: 177) writes, a puppet cannot be called dead until its body has completely disappeared – "as long as we can see the smallest fragment of its destroyed body, there is a potential puppet" – Joly's paper figure consumed by fire can truly be said to have "died," reduced to matter that is impossible to revive or re-create. The audience is denied even the semblance of a human form to empathize with, the figures reduced to a formless materiality that it is impossible to revive and re-personalize. The puppets are shown to be simply matter in a quasi-human form, and a temporary and unstable form at that.

Gyula Molnár's tabletop show *Piccoli Suicidi* (*Small Suicides*) is an early example of the Theatre of Objects in which everyday objects are substituted for humanoid figures.[2] In such performances there is no attempt at visual illusion – the objects are moved about by a visible manipulator and imaginatively transformed into notional characters suggested by their shape and movement, although they can also be used in counterpoint to their inherent form and function, in Jurkowski's words, either in

Figure 1.2 *Tragédie de Papier*, created and first performed by Yves Joly (1956). Photo: © Yves Joly and courtesy of Théâtre de la Marionnette à Paris

accord with or against their "iconicity" (Jurkowski 1992: 103). Some recent performances have bypassed character and narrative altogether and simply explore the various physical properties and imaginative evocations of the objects in what is often described as a form of "adult play." *Piccoli Suicidi* is of the former narrative kind. Molnár sits behind the table on which he moves his objects, and in contrast to Genty's remote impassivity, his hands-on manipulation and exaggerated facial responses to the story's events make him an integral part of the show. In the first little suicide, an Alka-Seltzer tablet and a handful of sweets play out a comical yet touching drama about the rejection of the outsider. The Alka-Seltzer tablet, consistently spurned by the sweets, finally "dives" into a glass of water in which it instantly dissolves. In the second story a despairing match sees the coffee bean it loves tossed with a handful of others into a coffee grinder. The cup containing coffee made from the beans is overturned by the match, who signs his lover's name with the spilt liquid before striking his head in despair and setting himself alight.

In all three performances the most poignant moment for the audience is when the "puppets" revert to being objects or inanimate matter, though in Molnár's case it's tempered with (slightly guilty?) laughter. But their reversions to the status of object are of very different kinds. Genty's marionette seems to "act" of its own volition, but it must detach itself physically from the manipulator to prove it's alive, which only demonstrates that it's not. Yet it remains a complete human figure, able to be reanimated in the same form. Joly's two-dimensional stylized figures have little capacity for simulating independent movement and can "die" only by being defaced or destroyed by the (at times) visible hands of the puppeteers. No revivable puppet figures remain, and new ones must be made for each performance. Molnár has no constructed figures and simply assembles a new set of objects for each show. Any sense of life or independent action in them is a matter of imaginative suggestion, and

Figure 1.3 Piccoli Suicidi (1984): Creator and performer Gyula Molnár with sweets and a glass of water. Photo: © Francesca Bettini

their "death" is expressed as a transition from one form of materiality to another, bypassing the human form altogether. As with Joly's figure destroyed by fire, Molnár's objects "die" by disintegrating into a form of matter that allows no possibility of theatrical resurrection. They are chosen for their inherent instability of form, and, as quasi-puppets, are as disposable and replaceable as the ordinary objects we discard every day.

But Molnár's recycling of puppet "life" into physical matter includes, by implication, the puppeteer – and, by extension, the audience – in the cycle of material disposability. Items of food were often used in place of puppets in the early days of Theatre of Objects.[3] It's an obvious choice for hard-up performers – it's cheap, the universal "found object," and if not too damaged, can be eaten after the show. Yet at the interface between the animate and inanimate that is the territory of puppetry, food exists in an ambivalent state: it might be seen as an inanimate object before it's eaten, but it's always potentially animate. Like the Alka-Seltzer tablet and the coffee bean, its disposability lies in its becoming part of a human body. Objects of food used as substitute puppets become an implicit comment on the contingent status of the puppet's theatrical life in relation to the real biological life of the puppeteer, since the "puppet" is potentially subsumable into the living performer.

"Puppeteer swallows puppet" would seem to epitomize – depending on how you look at it – either the *raison d'être* or the *reductio ad absurdum* of contemporary Western puppetry. It encapsulates the collapsed boundaries between the living and the inanimate that are characteristic of today's puppet stage, where the human performer and inanimate matter are often presented side by side as a composite stage subject or a form of "thing theatre" (Silk 1992: 89).[4] Puppeteer and puppet, creator and character, living human and inanimate matter become aspects of a single reality with all these elements in constant flux. "The puppet" is no longer an autonomous "living" figure but an object, as is the body of the human performer, and the only constant reality, it seems, is their shared materiality.

But this relationship of symbiotic equivalence between animate and inanimate matter on stage, no matter how theoretically seductive, is not quite what it seems. The relative absence of the human form from the recent puppet/object stage effectively puts the focus on what "the puppet" is in reality – a manipulated object. Yet that implies a manipulator. No matter how much impersonal matter becomes the sole medium of performance, by itself it can't do anything that would keep an audience watching the stage. Objects can express a great many things in themselves – they can evoke emotions, convey associations, create states of mind – but not by themselves. Object and human performer might share a physical reality, but while Molnár could drink the coffee, thus making the bean seem an organic part of him, the bean can't consume Molnár. Even if he were swallowed up in coffee, he wouldn't *become* coffee – and in any case there wouldn't be another show!

As part of a studio performance at the University of New South Wales some years ago, a postgraduate student created a complex machine that, once set in motion, operated all by itself. A small ball rolled through a series of different planes and inclinations, bounced off various surfaces, made sudden changes of speed and direction, until it finally dropped and abruptly stopped. In describing it, I've had to resist saying that it seemed to make an elaborate journey – it climbed laboriously upwards and then raced downhill, was tumbled about and righted itself, and finally fell and "died." Certainly there was an audible "ah" of regret when it stopped. Did that mean that the audience had identified something human about it, or were they just sorry that the fun had ended?

It seemed that a certain personal narrative was imposed onto the ball in an otherwise impersonal machine by the audience's perception, or perhaps expectation, of a theatrical event. That expectation of being able to identify with something human in a performance setting can become a demand. At a major exhibition of early twentieth-century avant-garde art, a number of films were screened that showed only moving objects or machines, with no human context or intervention.[5] Many in the audience for the screening at which I was present showed obvious restlessness, even anger, as if a joke were being played on them, and some people stormed out of the cinema, slamming the door in protest. Yet kinetic art and impersonal mechanisms operating in open gallery spaces do not seem to create a similar outraged response.

Context sets up certain expectations, and expectation molds perception. It was certainly possible to anthropomorphize the ball in the machine – indeed, hard not to! – but it could equally be seen simply as going through a series of ingenious mechanical interactions. Might the ball in the machine be perceived differently at a puppet festival and in a gallery setting? Might it become puppetry in one context (a theatre) but perhaps not in another (a gallery) and almost certainly not in a factory workshop? A factory context, in which the machine's purpose would be viewed as simply functional, would seem at the opposite pole from a theatrical event. Yet even with a machine in a purely functional context, an imaginative viewer might find a suggestion of anthropomorphic performance in its impersonal action.[6] Is puppetry then a mode of spectatorship rather than a specific form of performance? For the moment I'll just leave that question hanging!

The four examples I've discussed might seem to suggest an evolution in puppetry from the "living" figurative puppet to the non-anthropomorphic moving, but not necessarily performing, object. (There is no chronological progression implied in the relation between these examples, simply a conceptual one.[7]) If they are seen in terms of a linear progression, one might draw a line between any of them and say that up to this point the event is "puppetry" and then it starts to become something else. Genty's Pierrot is a traditional figurative puppet, and despite their two-dimensionality and limited potential for autonomous action, virtually everyone would class Joly's paper figures as puppets. Most people today would extend puppetry to include Molnár's show, although it has no puppet figures, since its objects stand in for fictional characters enacting a narrative. But for many people the tilt from puppetry into "something else" would still be at the point where obvious character and narrative disappear – between Molnár's objects and the ball in the machine. If the ball can be empathized with as a quasi-character, perhaps it counts as a puppet – just! But that would imply that puppetry is to be defined by its approximation to the human dramatic theatre of character and narrative and that it cannot exist in its own right outside the realm of the dramatic.

Hans-Thies Lehmann's term "postdramatic theatre" embraces the various forms of contemporary performance that are not based in fictional character or dramatic narrative but which combine the energy of human performers' bodies and elements of the physical setting into a nonlinear theatrical event, happening in real time and within a space that includes stage and auditorium, performers and audience. Apart from postulating some of Robert Wilson's slow-moving performers as analogous to puppets in their apparent lack of volition, as if moved by mysterious forces, Lehmann (1999: 78) does not discuss any specific forms of puppetry. But he does consider the possibility of an impersonal theatre of nothing but interacting physical realities (including the performer's body), a post-anthropocentric theatre that might include "the theatre of objects entirely without human actors, theatre of technology and machinery ... and theatre that integrates the human form mostly as an element in landscape-like spatial structures." This fusion of animate and inanimate forms into a single reality he appears to see as still largely potential, "utopically" prefiguring a theatre that would challenge the human dominance of nature (Lehmann 1999 [2006]: 80–81).[8]

Are we now in the age of postdramatic puppetry? Certainly we seem to be in an age of post-puppet puppetry. The progression (or regression, some would say) of puppetry in the four above examples might seem to parallel the change from the dramatic theatre to the postdramatic and even to the post-anthropomorphic – from the puppet as a character within its own narrative to a continuous present of interchangeable physical realities, both animate and inanimate, and even to a theatre of interacting material shapes and images with no human reference at all. If seen only in terms of a dramatic spectrum, the figurative puppet of Pierrot and the ball in the machine might well seem to be at opposite poles or even from two quite different genres.

The Catalan puppeteer and theatre academic Joan Baixas, writing in the puppetry journal *Puck*, makes a distinction between animating a puppet into life and the movement of objects in a theatre of performing materiality. The puppet arises from the world of real living things, of "zoology," he writes, whereas a theatre of material images develops from virtuality and metaphor. The physical control of objects requires manipulation, whereas the animation of a figure into life demands acting on the puppeteer's part (Baixas 1994: 40). Baixas is himself a master of both figurative puppetry and the theatre of dynamic images, but he makes a fundamental distinction between them in their mode of performing.[9] I'm happy to accept that for a performer (I'm not one) they are fundamentally different ways of working, but I'm less sure that from an audience's perspective the difference between acting through a puppet and manipulating an object is always so clear cut. All of the three "suicides" previously discussed suggest a shifting or collapsing boundary between acting and manipulating. Genty is both acting through the puppet of Pierrot and demonstrating that its own "acting" is nothing more than the effect of his manipulation; the hands of Joly's puppeteers both act on behalf of and act upon the cutout puppet figures; and Molnár's objects are openly acted upon to simulate their enactment of their own stories. None of the puppet or object characters in the three examples can even *seem* to end its own life without visible help from human hands. Conversely, the ball in the machine was acted upon only mechanically, yet seemed to acquire a notional "life" of its own.

Rather than seeing the manipulation of objects in contrast to the acting that animates a puppet into life, it is possible to see "the puppet" as existing at their point of intersection. A puppet only seems to act by itself because it is acted both *through* and *upon*. The various forms of manipulation – strings, rods, hands-on control – have always lent themselves to being read metaphorically and have often been the basis of attempts to define "the puppet" itself. Yet the word "manipulation" has ambivalent associations. It is rightly regarded as one of the puppeteer's most highly valued skills, but it also has overtones of the mere showman, of tricks and cheap effects. Ariel Bufano makes a similar distinction to Baixas in seeing a potential "divorce" between actor and puppeteer, with the latter becoming a simple manipulator of beautiful and astonishing effects or "a kind of 'prestidigitator'" – a word that suggests not just manual dexterity but the conjuring tricks of the stage magician, and even outright deception (Bufano 1992: 94).[10]

Historians of puppetry's origins are always happy to include ancient magic and sorcerer's dolls within the provenance of the puppet, and a number of puppeteers such as the English Punch professor John Styles are also magicians, while others, including Genty, have incorporated magic tricks into their shows. Yet today stage magic is rarely if ever found among the "related arts" at puppet festivals, and I wonder why. Maybe it is because to most puppeteers it seems something *even less* than manipulation – mere manual dexterity or even sleight of hand? Yet perhaps the stage magician might give some clue to the nature of the puppet before its relatively late appearance as a dramatic character and its recent disintegration into objects and material images.

One (just one) possible way of seeing "the puppet" is as a point of intersection between dramatic theatre and stage magic, which, like puppetry, is a point of intersection between acting and a manipulation that is not only physical but visual and psychological. Puppeteer and magician manipulate not only objects but also audience perception – they deal in making objects seem to subvert the outward forms and laws of nature. Both set up an interactive relation between performer and objects, and at times even create the sense of a psychic force between them. Like puppets, the magician's objects can seem to be transformed in defiance of everyday logic, and at times to have a capriciousness, even a will, all their own. One such object is the "floating globe," a sphere that seems to glide around the magician and is "called back" when it drifts too far away – an apparent psychic tug-of-war between object and performer that recalls the classic battle of wills known as "separation" between puppet and puppeteer, which echoes Genty's resisting Pierrot.

Puppeteer and stage magician both manipulate objects in order to create surprising theatrical *effects* so that at times the boundary between puppetry and magic can be hard to define. The late Australian puppeteer Norman Hetherington had a show based on *The Magic Tinder Box* in which the marionette of a king was just one puppet character among others – until, to the audience's astonishment, suddenly the arms became owls and flew off, the legs became frogs and hopped off, and the body turned upside down and became a large purple pig that ran off. Did it stop being a puppet when it ceased to be a character and instead became just a trick? In fact, it's one of the oldest tricks in the puppetry book, a variation on the Grand Turk marionette that flips inside out to reveal a cluster of its own small children.

The traditional puppet has a quasi-human body, yet one of puppetry's obvious advantages over the theatre of living performers has always been its ability to subvert the human form. The physical irreducibility of the human body has been a problematic concern of the twentieth-century stage, as seen in the lengths to which directors have gone to disguise it, ever since the Futurists and the Bauhaus artists encased their performers in machine-like and geometrical shapes.[11] No matter how much the stage tries to objectify the human body, it's not an object *just* like any other, since there's a limit to how one can really distort or dismantle it. Yet traditional puppets, such as dissecting skeletons (breakaways) and transforming figures, still keep audiences happy with no narrative context, simply by changing their bodily forms in ways impossible to real human beings.

We've become so used to seeing "the puppet" as a character and to theorizing about it as a character that we've forgotten that it can be something else.

The magician's secrets are closely guarded, whereas the puppeteer is often happy to have the audience come backstage after the show, but both puppetry and magic invite asking about how it's done, perhaps most of all when they pretend to conceal it. The concept of "backstage" is intrinsic to the puppet theatre, just as it is to the magician's stage. Recent puppetry has brought "backstage" onstage with the presence of the formerly invisible puppeteer, but "how it's done" is an implicit part of the show, even when it's behind the scenes. In this puppetry would seem to diverge from Lehmann's concept of postdramatic performance, in which stage and auditorium together create a single shared time-and-space, continuous-present reality for both performers and audience (Lehmann 1999 [2006]: 150–152). I asked my friend Clare Grant, a member of the Sydney Front, one of the pioneering postdramatic groups cited by Lehmann, whether backstage figured greatly in their concept of performance. Apart from briefly slipping behind a small curtain for changes of costume, she said, there was only one moment in all their shows when it became a significant element – when, in her words, they wanted to create "a moment of magic."[12]

Henryk Jurkowski's term for the puppet that seems to have a theatrical life of its own is the "magic" puppet (Jurkowski 1988: 42), and for many people it is still the pure form of puppetry, its point of reference. Yet the "magic" puppet that is often taken as the benchmark of puppetry might also be seen as a close relation of the transposed and transformed objects of the stage magician. "How it's done" is an intrinsic part of both puppet show and magic show, whether through offstage manipulation, hands-on control, or sleight of hand. Far from effacing the question of how it's done, the magic puppet raises it more explicitly than any other form of puppetry. Puppeteers might like to think that the public believes the puppet lives by itself, but the most common everyday metaphor of the puppet refers to the marionette's supposedly invisible strings, not to its "magical" life.

To return to the question I raised earlier: is there perhaps a puppetry and a non-puppetry way of seeing the ball in the machine? In one sense, it was only too easy to perceive the ball as a little person (or perhaps a hyperactive mouse). That might seem enough in itself to make it a puppet, but I would hope that puppetry is something more than the easy anthropomorphizing, even sentimentalizing, of a moving object. Simply to see the ball as a quasi-character would be to ignore the action of the machine. If it was possible to anthropomorphize the ball, it was impossible not to be aware simultaneously of the rest of the machine's operations, to enjoy the maker's craft and wit, his ingenuity and intention, in its impersonal mechanical interactions. The creator's volition was intrinsic to the event, even though he was physically absent from it after setting it in motion.[13] A theatre of nothing but interacting objects might exclude any human element, whether puppet or performer, from the stage, but no matter how far the audience suppresses the awareness of it, there's always someone backstage. The suspension of that awareness in a theatre of abstract material forms is as much a pretense as the fantasy that the magic puppet lives all by itself.

We're not in the age of post-puppet puppetry, and the figurative puppet will always remain, as Jurkowski trusts, the point of reference because it holds acting, acting-on, and acted-upon in near equilibrium: the three-dimensional puppet of Pierrot both acts as a character and acts on its strings in freeing itself while being visibly acted upon by Genty, who is acting through the puppet. Yet all puppetry plays with all three in varying degrees: Joly's two-dimensional cutouts, midway between figurative puppets and objects, seem to take action by themselves though obviously being acted upon by the puppeteers' hands and external objects; Molnár's acting on and through his objects evokes their own imagined actions; and the ball in the machine is mechanically acted upon, yet suggests activity rather than passivity on its part.

Despite his fundamental distinction between acting and manipulation, Joan Baixas (1994: 40) sees figurative puppetry and the theatre of material images as closely related and complementary – "*deux genres voisins et complémentaires.*" In a later major article he sets "puppets and their relations" in the context of a wide range of sacred and secular forms of which puppets are "really just one aspect," including "a huge variety of forms which prioritize plastic, choreographic or technical aspects in turn," from "the theatrical life of geometric shapes" to "the emotion of the living machine, independent of human control" (Baixas 1998: 173–175). Acting and manipulation, living performer and puppet-object, onstage and offstage, are in constant flux in all puppetry and material performance, and in ever-changing inverse ratio, depending on how one chooses to prioritize them. Perhaps an awareness of their interaction is the "way of seeing," a mode of spectatorship rather than any specific theatrical form, that identifies puppetry and links those unspecified related arts to "the puppet."

The traditional puppet as a "living object" figures the ambivalent nature of the body itself, which as an animate being can act and act on objects but as part of the material world is vulnerable to being acted upon. Yet whether the human form is mirrored on the puppet stage or conspicuously absent from an impersonal theatre of objects, the inextricable relationships between acting, acting on (or manipulating), and being acted upon raise the same questions puppetry has always asked about our relation to the materiality that includes our own bodies. Victor Molina (1998: 176) writes that "the puppet reveals … that man's body is not a space that ensures the indisputability of his I, but right where man (and together with him, anthropocentrism) finds himself contested." The distinction between the "living" puppet, with its basis in biology, and a theatre of purely material forms disappears in the transformation of Molnár's coffee bean: from everyday object to puppet-character to amorphous granules to liquid coffee consumable by the performer, it encapsulates both the puppet's "life" that it shares with the puppeteer and the body's potential disintegration into formless matter. "The puppet" and a theatre of impersonal objects are not the extreme ends of a linear dramatic spectrum, but on a continuum in which, from opposite directions, they come full circle to meet each other.

Notes

1 The antithesis of Philippe Genty's suicidal Pierrot is the Punch-like marionette of the Dutch company Triangel, which defiantly breaks its strings, causing the puppeteer's hands to drop as if lifeless, while the puppet hobbles offstage using its marionette control as a crutch.
2 Objects have had a prominent place in both actors' and puppet theatre throughout the twentieth century, but a Theatre of Objects developed as a specific form in Europe in the 1980s. Among the early performers, Christian Carrignon and Katy Deville of Le Théâtre de Cuisine, Jacques Templeraud's company Manarf, and Tania Castaing and Charlot Lemoine's company Vélo Théâtre used household objects, notably kitchen gadgets. For example, Carrignons's vignette of a tabletop village was created entirely with objects, such as corks, bottles, and a coffee grinder. Performers with objects use bric-à-brac, children's toys, and "found objects" from the site of performance, not necessarily as substitute puppets but to explore their uses, shapes, mechanical properties, and emotional and cultural evocations (e.g. the Catalonian duo La Cònica/Lacònica created near-unrecognizable shadows with everyday objects, such as bottles and electrical components). Though some of its performers reject their work being seen as a variant of puppetry, object theatre is now widely accepted at puppet festivals.
3 In two emails to me, Molnár wrote that he had the idea for the show while making coffee and smoking as he prepared breakfast. The audience sees the unfolding tragedy in the daily actions of an ordinary breakfast, while he remains the creator and observer of the story: "I'm just there to assist the tragedy" (Molnár, pers. comm., December 6 and 8, 2012). Jacques Templeraud's version of *Le Petit Chaperon Rouge* included a potato as the Grandmother (which was boiled and mashed to emit steam), a fish head as the Wolf, and a green apple as Little Red Riding Hood, which Templeraud relayed to me that he

simulated biting when the wolf attacked her (Templeraud, pers. comm., February 28, 2012).
4 Dennis Silk's article "The Thing Theatre and Thing Language" (Silk 1992) is an exploration of the shared physicality of actors and objects and of what actors can learn from objects' theatrical "presence."
5 "Surrealism: Revolution by Night" at the Art Gallery of New South Wales, Sydney, July–September 1993.
6 Some devotees of the puppet (including Edward Gordon Craig) have idealized the impersonality of the machine; its unconscious perfection of movement has been seen as analogous to the aesthetic "grace" of the dancing marionette described in Heinrich von Kleist's famous essay "On the Marionette Theatre" (1810).
7 Genty's Pierrot marionette was made in 1973, and the untitled number has often been presented on stage and television. Joly's show was created in 1956; his wedding scene performed entirely with umbrellas is an early example of object theatre. *Piccoli Suicidi*, subtitled *"tre brevi esorcismi d'uso quotidiano"* (three short exorcisms of daily use), was created by Molnár in 1984 and has more recently been performed by Carles Cañellas. The machine was also made in 1984, and its creator, Philip Parr, is now a performer, musician, and director in Britain and other countries.
8 The contemporary example Lehmann gives of a possible post-anthropocentric theatre is the circus.
9 "La marionnette relève de la zoologie, du mondes des êtres vivants. L'image en mouvement se développe au contraire dans la virtualité, dans la métaphore. L'une demande à s'inscrire dans le biologique, l'autre se repaît de langage. ... L'art des images en mouvement demande des manipulateurs, l'art des marionettes exige des acteurs." As solo performer, theatre director, artist, and teacher, Joan Baixas has created an extraordinarily wide range of original and dynamic performances, which embrace puppetry, masks, objects, and abstract images, and include collaborations of his company Teatre de la Claca (1968–1988) with celebrated visual artists, such as Joan Miró. For a survey of his extensive career in puppetry and visual theatre, see the biography on his website: <www.joanbaixas.com/en/past/biografia>.
10 "A commencé ... ce qui pourrait bien être un divorce entre l'acteur et le marionnettiste. Car ce dernier devenait un simple manipulateur d'effets, beaux et étonnants: une sorte de prestidigitateur."
11 Two contemporary examples of objectifying the body onstage are *Vivisector* (2002), a collaboration between Austrian director Klaus Obermaier and choreographer Chris Haring, which projects images onto near-unrecognizable parts of the performers' bodies, and the Babelfish Company from Germany, who encase the performers' bodies in giant inflated balloons. Both pieces were performed at the International Festival of Puppetry Art in Bielsko-Biała, Poland, in 2006, the former winning the prize for the best show.
12 From 1986 to 1993 the Australian group the Sydney Front (Clare Grant, John Baylis, Nigel Kellaway, Chris Ryan, and Andrea Aloise) staged a number of convention-breaking, anarchic, and often transgressive physically based performances involving both performers and audiences. The "magic trick" involved the substitution of a performer for an audience member dressed as a clown.
13 The machine's creator walked onstage to set it in motion and then exited. This raises the question of "real time" (i.e., that the manipulation must take place in the same time frame as the puppet's actions, a view that would exclude stop-motion and Claymation as forms of puppetry).

Works cited

Baixas, J. (1994) "Le souffle de la marionnette," *Puck: La marionnette et les autres arts* 7: 40–43.
——(1998) "Scenes of the imaginary," in Institut del Teatre (ed.) *Escenes de l'Imaginari* [*Scenes of the Imaginary*]. Barcelona, Spain: Centre de Cultura Contemporània de Barcelona.

Bufano, A. (1992) "A côté de l'homme," *Puck: La marionnette et les autres arts* 5: 94.
Jurkowski, H. (1988) "Towards a Theatre of Objects," in P. Francis (ed.) *Aspects of Puppet Theatre*. London: Puppet Centre Trust.
——(1992) "The Acting Puppet as a Figure of Speech," in M. Waszkiel (ed.) *Present Trends in Research of World Puppetry: A Collection of Papers*. Warsaw, Poland: Institute of Art of the Polish Academy of Sciences.
——(2011) "World Puppetry Day: International Message," March 21, Atlanta: UNIMA-USA, <http://www.unima-usa.org/international/world6.html> (accessed September 5, 2013).
Lehmann, H.-T. (1999) *Postdramatic Theatre*, trans. Karen Jürs-Munby (2006). London: Routledge.
Molina, V. (1998) "Artificial Creatures," in Institut del Teatre (ed.) *Escenes de l'Imaginari* [*Scenes of the Imaginary*]. Barcelona, Spain: Centre de Cultura Contemporània de Barcelona.
Silk, D. (1992) "The Thing Theater and Thing Language," in M. Waszkiel (ed.) *Present Trends in Research of World Puppetry: A Collection of Papers*. Warsaw, Poland: Institute of Art of the Polish Academy of Sciences.

2
The Co-Presence and Ontological Ambiguity of the Puppet

Paul Piris

The renewal of puppetry over the past decades is the result of an exploration of the dramaturgical meaning of the animated figure in theatre. Since the 1980s, artists and companies such as Stuffed Puppet Theatre and Duda Paiva in Holland, Ilka Schönbein in Germany, Compagnie Mossoux-Bonté in Belgium, Dondoro Theatre in Japan, Philippe Genty in France, and Blind Summit in Britain have developed an original form of performance where visible manipulators interact with their puppets. As French scholar Didier Plassard (2009) suggests, not only have the puppeteers entered the space of the puppets by stepping out of the puppet booth, but they have also entered their fictional world. In this particular form of performance, a co-presence takes place between the puppeteer and the puppet. This co-presence is particular because it establishes a relation of self to Other between two beings that are ontologically different: one is a subject (in other words, a being endowed with consciousness) and the other one an object (in other words, a thing). Yet, the particularity of the puppet is to present an ontological ambiguity because it is an object that appears in performance as a subject. Co-presence stresses this ontological ambiguity by confronting the puppet with a human protagonist.

This chapter examines the co-presence and the ontological ambiguity of the puppet through phenomenological aspects of thought developed by French philosophers Jean-Paul Sartre and, to some extent, Emmanuel Levinas. The purpose is to understand why the puppet appears as a subject to the spectator's consciousness.

To answer this question, I will first discuss two productions that present two distinct forms of co-presence: *Cuniculus* (2008) by Stuffed Puppet Theatre and *Twin Houses* (1994) by Compagnie Mossoux-Bonté. I will then look at the Sartrean definition of consciousness and the Other in order to understand the fabrication of a co-presence between the puppeteer and the puppet on stage. The inquiry specifically addresses the argument developed by Sartre in *Being and Nothingness*, first published in 1943, that the relation of self to Other is the result of our presence in the world as embodied consciousness. The representation of the Other by a puppet raises a contradiction, because a relation of self to Other can only exist between two subjects. This contradiction is tackled by examining the particular ontology of the puppet in regards to the theory of image developed by Sartre in *The Imaginary*, first published in 1940.

Defining co-presence

To achieve a co-presence with the puppet, performers use skills drawn from puppetry but also from acting. Although acting and puppetry can be considered as related forms of performance because they both aim at creating characters or personae on stage, they entail two different forms of body schema.

In acting, the body schema of the actor is characterized by his own body on stage interacting with other performers or props. In puppetry, as both French and American scholars Annie Gilles (1994) and Steve Tillis (1996) clearly describe, there is a split between the performer and the character. The experience of the world of the character is evoked through the puppet and requires the puppeteer's body to experience the world in another way than the actor's body. The body schema encompasses two bodies: the actual body of the puppeteer and the apparent body of the puppet.

Co-presence inherently supposes that the performer creates a character through the puppet but also appears as another character whose presence next to the puppet has a dramaturgical meaning. For this reason, co-presence is different from the simple visible presence of puppeteers on stage because, in this case, puppeteers do not bear any dramaturgical presence. Co-presence requires the hybridization of the two forms of body schema described above, which is a challenge because it supposes solving a contradiction. In acting, the actors' aim is to focus the audience's attention on their body, whereas the puppeteers' aim is to focus the audience's attention on the puppets. The co-presence of the puppeteer and the puppet requires that a double focus on both the performer and the puppet is achieved.

Cuniculus and *Twin Houses* establish a co-presence between the puppeteer and the puppet through very distinct method of practice. *Cuniculus* was written, designed, and performed by Neville Tranter, while *Twin Houses* has been initiated and performed by Nicole Mossoux and directed by Patrick Bonté. Using Hans-Thies Lehmann's study of postdramatic theatre (Lehmann 1999), I suggest that *Cuniculus* is a form of dramatic theatre, whereas *Twin Houses* belongs to postdramatic theatre. The representation of the puppet as a figure of the Other in *Cuniculus* is contingent on the training and the approach to theatre taken by Tranter, who initially trained in Method acting. Through his approach to text, characterization, and dramaturgy, his work can be categorized under what Lehmann describes as dramatic theatre. Mossoux and Bonté define their work as theatre-dance, which is a hybridization of theatre and dance, not a juxtaposition of one with the other. Dance is used as a tool that articulates their theatrical work. Mossoux initially trained in contemporary dance at Maurice Béjart's Mudra School in Brussels, while Bonté's theatre influences are Grotowski and Kantor. Their work can be labeled as postdramatic.

Cuniculus: A co-presence through speech

Cuniculus is a piece about survivors living in a world ravaged by violence and chaos. It tells the story of a small group of starving rabbits embodied by puppets. They live confined to their warren in order to remain safe from a war happening above them. Amongst these rabbits lives a human character performed by Tranter. This character does not have a name. He wears a pair of red plastic rabbit ears and thinks he is a rabbit. The rabbits hate human beings but behave as if Tranter is one of them.

There are seven rabbits in *Cuniculus*, and Tranter sometimes manipulates two puppets at the same time. The relationship that Tranter's character establishes with the puppets is mainly based on verbal and gaze exchanges. Tranter's puppets are made in the image of the dramatic actor. They express emotions through text and intentions. Tranter defined the characters in *Cuniculus* as archetypes. They represent different examples of human behavior through psychological characteristics. It is important to specify that Tranter is not a ventriloquist. Spectators can see him producing the voices of all the puppets as well as that of his own character.

Tranter's puppets have a strong physical integrity, as they keep the same size and shape during the entire piece and have limited points of connection with Tranter's body. Most of the puppets share the same design principles. They are about 80 centimeters high. They can sit upright on their own without the intervention of Tranter to stabilize them because the trunk and the legs form one solid element. There are no joints for the torso, the legs, or the feet. This feature gives the puppet a low center of gravity. It frees Tranter's hand that is not in charge of moving the head

Figure 2.1 *Cuniculus*, Stuffed Puppet Theatre (2008): Neville Tranter and pal. Photo: © Michael Kneffel

of the puppet to manipulate one of its arms or another puppet. All the limbs of the puppet seem petrified in a dynamic tension. They do not hang freely even when not animated. The only movable parts of the puppet are the head and occasionally the arms. The skin of the puppets is made out of fake fur stuffed with cotton balls. This material gives some flexibility to the upper part of the torso and enables the shoulders to follow the movement of the head. The head makes similar movements to a human head. The puppets' mouths are articulated and twice as large as Tranter's. The puppets also have big long ears that shake whenever they speak or move their head. The result is an amplification of the movements of the head. Their eyes are the size of a golf ball and are protuberant. A glittering material that reflects light is used to indicate the pupil in order to reinforce its resemblance to a real eye. These elements support the impression of a visual agency that is read as a cognitive activity on the part of the puppet. Manipulation is by direct contact. Tranter places one of his hands inside the head of the puppet through the back in order to move the head as well as the mouth. His other hand can directly grip the wrist of the puppet to move the rabbit's arm. These puppets can stand on their own, speak, and look at the world around them but are not designed to grab objects or to move into space. When a puppet needs to go to a different point of the stage, Tranter simply lifts it in the air and places it in its new location.

To establish a co-presence with the puppet, Tranter is physically positioned next to the puppet he manipulates. In that setting, he becomes part of the surroundings of the puppet because the puppet can potentially "see" him. The character who is supposed to speak is the one who moves. Characters engaged in speech display their mouths and eyes to the audience. When Tranter makes the voice of one of the puppets, he positions his own head in such a way that it is less visible from the audience's point of view. His head is either tilted sideways and looking down or placed behind the puppet's body. He keeps the opening of his mouth to a minimum, and he occasionally uses the hand of the puppet to mask his own mouth. Moreover, the direction of the gaze also indicates to the audience which character is talking. When Tranter's character talks, he always looks at the face of the puppet, except when the puppet does not look at him. When a puppet talks, just before delivering the lines, it looks at Tranter's face for a very short moment but then faces the audience to speak. This coordination of the directions of the gazes between Tranter and his puppets contributes significantly to the construction of co-presence.

Tranter's manipulation is focused on moving the head, the mouth, and one arm of the puppet. The rest of the body remains still. At no moment throughout the whole piece does Tranter animate the legs or the torso of a puppet. This contrast between upper and lower parts of the body is found in Tranter's body itself. Only his head and arms actively play a role in the act of manipulation. The rest of his body is used as a support. There is a homogenized use of body, gaze, and speech between Tranter and his puppets, which is done by giving to the puppets human-like behaviors.

Twin Houses: A co-presence through body movements

Twin Houses consists of a series of situations separated by blackouts that invoke a woman surrounded by five puppets that resemble her. Original music by Christian

Genet is constantly played throughout the piece. A general feeling of oppression emerges from the performance. Most of the time, the puppets seem to control Nicole Mossoux. I refer to some of the puppets as the Androgyne, the Lady, the Double, and the Man. Unlike *Cuniculus*, there is no utterance in *Twin Houses*. Co-presence is based on the physical interactions taking place between Mossoux and her puppets.

Mossoux looks like her puppets, wearing makeup and a synthetic wig to enhance her resemblance to them. Her face remains still but not neutral. There is a strange mixture of sensuality, innocence, and surprise about her. Her movements are stylized in order to have a puppet-like quality. The heads of the puppets are made from a mold of Mossoux's face. Their construction varies depending on whether they are fastened to Mossoux's body or detached from it. To schematize their design, they can be described as a head with a neck prolonged by a piece of cloth, except for the Double, who has also been built with two arms and wears a long dress that hides the absence of legs. The Androgyne and the Lady are attached to Mossoux's body like conjoined twins. Their heads are strapped to one of Mossoux's shoulders, which creates an impression of unity and division: unity, because both the puppets and Mossoux share the same body, and division, because the puppets appear very autonomous. The head of the Man can be attached to Mossoux's right shoulder, held from the neck, or placed on top of Mossoux's head. The Double is detached from Mossoux, who controls it by a direct grip of her hand on its neck. The arms hang freely beside its body when not being manipulated. Most of the puppets have a large range of leg and arm movements, as these body parts actually belong to Mossoux, but they collapse on themselves without the support of Mossoux. Because of the realistic features of the face, the eyes are not made especially prominent and so do not reinforce the direction of the gaze.

Some of the puppets in *Twin Houses* do not have fixed shapes. They are fluid entities whose forms change according to the nature of their relationship with the character of Mossoux. This is particularly the case in a scene between Mossoux and the Man. As the scene unfolds, the growing power of the puppet over Mossoux's character is materialized by the fact that it absorbs more and more parts of her body, up to the moment that she completely disappears inside the puppet. Later, Mossoux operates a deconstruction of the Man by playing his life backwards, starting from a male adult and ending as a fetus inside her.

Co-presence between Mossoux and her puppets does not follow a unique schema of embodiment but varies significantly according to the type of puppet she manipulates. In the case of the conjoined twin puppets, the use of a dance technique called body-parts isolation allows Mossoux to create distinct rhythmic and movement qualities within her body, which give the impression that her body is split lengthways into two parts with a head at the top of each half. These two half bodies can move simultaneously but with distinct gestures.

The puppets attached on Mossoux's shoulders cannot look at her because Mossoux cannot turn her shoulders inward enough for the eyes of the puppet to meet her own eyes. Moreover, the shoulder does not allow fine movements. The result of this is the inability of the puppet to precisely focus its gaze on the objects that surround it. To counterbalance this issue, Mossoux has developed a particular strategy.

THE CO-PRESENCE AND ONTOLOGICAL AMBIGUITY OF THE PUPPET

Figure 2.2 Twin Houses, Compagnie Mossoux-Bonté (1994): performer Nicole Mossoux. Photo: © Mikha Wajnrych

Instead of exchanging gazes, Mossoux and her puppets look at the same object, which appears as the center of the action. Moreover, Mossoux displays an unfocused gaze. For instance, in one scene with a conjoined twin puppet, Mossoux writes in a book without looking at what she is doing but instead slightly above the book. This is not normal human behavior when writing; people usually tend to look at what they are writing. The fact that there is no direct eye contact between Mossoux and the puppet but that their mutual gaze is mediated through an object of vision indicates that Mossoux has built a co-presence based on what the protagonists are physically doing together. Mossoux's ability to gaze is similar to that of the puppet because they seem to share the same limitation of movements. This choice allows Mossoux to balance her presence with that of the puppet. It seems that Mossoux loses parts of her human nature in order to share an equal mode of existence with the puppet. Mossoux establishes a co-presence through a "puppetization" of herself.

Two different Others

Although both productions establish a co-presence between puppeteers and puppets, different decisions have been made about what constitutes the puppet as an Other and how the self relates to it. Ultimately, Tranter and Mossoux do not refer to the same Other.

Tranter presents with brio the relationships between human beings by materializing different aspects of human nature, such as cruelty, fear, weakness, empathy, or love, through the different puppets of *Cuniculus*. The rabbits symbolize human society. The fact that they hate humans constitutes the character of Tranter as their ultimate Other. Dramaturgically speaking, Tranter is not a rabbit, and ontologically speaking, he is the only one not to be an object on stage. In Tranter's work, the Other is the one who is different, which one can be tempted to eliminate. In this production, the human being is the one rejected by the society of the rabbits. Tranter's work foregrounds the ethical commitment of the self towards the Other, as described by Levinas in *Totality and Infinity*, first published in 1961. The rabbits have made the choice of abusing the Other and eventually destroying him if necessary in order to survive. Conversely, Tranter's character makes a different choice. He places the Other at a higher level than him. In *Cuniculus*, the puppet is an outer Other whose existence appears to be detached from that of the puppeteer.

In *Twin Houses* the puppets materialize different aspects of the character performed by Mossoux. She interacts with herself in the manner of a schizoid person confronting the different personalities that inhabit her, which explains the variations of shape of the Other. Unlike Tranter's character, who eventually separates from these Others when he leaves the warren, finally having accepted his human nature, Mossoux cannot escape them because they are inside her. When at the end of the piece there are no more puppets on stage, the relation of self to Other is still present but this time inscribed on her very own body, which seems to be split into different independent beings. Although the Other is autonomous, it is a part of the self that emerges from the body of Mossoux or appears next to her as her own double. This is an inner Other that deprives the self of its physical and psychological integrity.

Body and gaze in the relation of self to Other

Despite the distinct forms of co-presence developed by both practitioners, the relation of self to Other, between the puppeteer and the puppet, is achieved by giving the impression that the protagonists exist in apparently close ontological levels: Tranter's puppets are humanized to behave like him, while Mossoux reifies herself to appear like her puppets. These two examples suggest that it is necessary to balance the presence on stage of the puppeteer and the puppet in order to fabricate a co-presence.

Initially, their presence is unbalanced because the puppeteer appears more alive than the puppet on stage. The fabrication of co-presence in *Cuniculus* and *Twin Houses* shows that the puppeteer and the puppet have to appear distinct from one another. This distinction is materialized by the fact that they seem to have separate bodies on stage. When the distinction from the puppeteer is not clearly established, the puppet appears as an extension of the performer and, thus, is mostly present on stage as an object and not as a protagonist. The result is a weakened form of co-presence. To understand why such a distinction is necessary, I suggest looking at Sartre's definition of consciousness and of the Other.

For Sartre, as scholar Kathleen Wider (1997: 112) explains, the body is "the subject of human consciousness." The unity of the body shows the unity of the subject with regard to the world. The body is actually consciousness and not a screen between consciousness and its objects. As scholar Monika Langer (1998: 112) writes, the existence of flesh is "a vehicle of an interworld in Sartre's philosophy." She argues that the existence of consciousness as body "spells an inevitable and eradicable alienation insofar as it engages consciousness in a world which it continually surpasses, and confers on it an eternally elusive 'being-for-others'" (Langer 1998: 105). The distinction of bodies is a key element of the co-presence between the puppeteer and the puppet because it confers on the puppet its belonging to the world as a distinct embodied consciousness. The performer and the puppet seem to be present to one another because of their presence on stage as subjects. The distinction between the apparent body of the puppet and the real body of the manipulator contributes to the epiphany of an apparent consciousness in the puppet.

To operate a distinction between these two bodies, the physical presence of the puppet through its materiality is not enough. It is essential that the body of the puppet moves in such a way that it seems autonomous from the body of the performer and that it seems to deploy an apparent internal logic of movement. The uncanny feeling that spectators may experience when they watch Mossoux and the Man dancing together comes from the impression that two autonomous subjects are present to each other through the interactions of their bodies, despite the awareness that one of the protagonists is actually an object.

The gaze functions as a second key sign of consciousness of the puppet. In *Phenomenology of a Puppet Theatre*, Jan Mrázek suggests that the eyes of the Javanese *wayang kulit* puppet are its "power of vision. ... The eyes give the sensation of the puppet's subjectivity and visual agency, as opposed to being an object of visual gaze" (Mrázek 2005: 35). The puppet is more than a thing that can be seen; it is also an apparent subject that can see. The gaze of the puppet reinforces the separateness from the puppeteer by stressing the dramaturgical presence of the latter. The visible presence of puppeteers on stage does not imply that they have a dramaturgical presence. However, if the puppet looks at its manipulator and the latter responds to this gaze, the human performer appears as part of the actuality of the puppet.

Discussing the question of the Other in *Being and Nothingness*, Sartre suggests two ideas. First, the Other can only be apprehended by the self as a subject. For this reason, it is important that Mossoux and Tranter react to their puppets as if they were in the presence of human beings and not objects. Second, Sartre argues that the Other is the subject who mediates my relation to myself. In other words, the Other allows me to be aware of aspects of myself. Sartre specifically discusses the gaze of the Other in relation to the feeling of shame to highlight the fact that the Other is the subject who mediates my relation to myself. For instance, in one scene between Tranter and the puppet Sissy, Tranter's character feels ashamed of what he has just said because Sissy abruptly stares at him. By her gaze, she makes him suddenly aware of the inappropriate tone of voice he had used when he previously addressed her. Tranter's character is able to grasp a part of himself of which he was not aware – in this instance, his mocking attitude, because of the gaze of Sissy. The gaze allows the puppeteer and the puppet to acknowledge each other but also to distinguish from one another. The Other appears as the one that confirms and denies the selfness to the oneself but also as not being the oneself. Selfness is defined as the individuality, the set of all the properties, unique or not, that characterize an individual.

To summarize, the puppeteer and the puppet appear co-present because spectators have the impression that they are witnessing two distinct subjects. This distinction results from the apparent presence of two bodies and two gazes on stage.

Contradiction of the puppet-as-Other

Nonetheless, the puppet is only an apparent subject with an apparent body and an apparent gaze and, surely, Sartre never intended his theory of the Other to be applied to puppets, as they are not subjects but objects. Moreover, describing the puppet as an Other raises a contradiction.

In *Totality and Infinity* (1961), Levinas exposes clearly why the relation of self to Other is different from the relation of the self with objects. He argues that to be an "I" consists of being identical to myself. Yet this identity is not static, as in the tautology "I am I," but dynamic. As scholar Françoise Dastur explains, "for Levinas the world is not something different from the 'I' but a mode of existence for the 'I'" (Dastur 2006: 37). Knowledge is only a mode of existence of the self that is part of the dynamic process of identification. The self takes possession of the world in order to "consolidate or extend its own identity" (Dastur 2006: 37). The subject does not find anything other than itself in the object. The self gives a meaning to the object, which Levinas refers to as its finality. Levinas argues that the relation of the subject with objects is a relation of knowledge, and for this reason an object cannot be an Other.

Conversely to the relation of the self with objects, Levinas contends that the Other is not another self. For Levinas, the Other escapes the self because, as Simon Critchley writes, "there is something about the other person, a dimension of separateness, interiority, secrecy or what Levinas calls 'alterity' that escapes my comprehension" (Critchley 2008: 26). The self is alone and has no power over the Other. The Other cannot be an object of knowledge because knowledge is an identification process. If this were the case, it would mean that the Other would be part of the identity of the self, which would be problematic for Levinas. In Levinasean phenomenology, there is an opposition between the relation of the subject with objects and the relation of the subject with other subjects.

If we agree with Levinas, how can we explain that the puppet appears as a figure of the Other despite being an object? I suggest that such a contradiction is possible because of the ontological ambiguity of the puppet. To solve this issue, it is necessary to understand what lies behind the apparent presence of the puppet as a subject. The next section examines the spectating experience of puppetry by looking at the role of perception and imagination.

Perception and imagination

The ontological ambiguity of the puppet pertains to the fact that it seems to share the same existence as subject with the puppeteer but nonetheless remains an object.

For instance, when I look at the puppet of Mutti, one of the rabbits in *Cuniculus*, I may see a piece of brown fur attached to a piece of rigid foam controlled by Tranter, but I also encounter an old and tired rabbit who treats Tranter's character as her own son. The objectness of Mutti – in other words, its quality or state of being an object – manifests itself through its materiality as a thing which includes its appearance, its design, its range of movement, and the type of manipulation used in order to animate it. These elements are perceived. The subjectness of the puppet – in other words, its quality or state of being a subject – appears when the puppet seems to escape its own materiality as an object and thus seems to act freely. I suggest that the subjectness of Mutti is not perceived but imagined. To understand the interplay between the perception of the objectness of the puppet and the imagination of its subjectness, I propose to look at it through the theory of image developed by Sartre.

Following the German phenomenologist Edmund Husserl, Sartre posits that perception and imagination are two different ways for consciousness to be related to an identical object. In the case of perception, the object "is 'encountered' by consciousness" (Sartre 1940 [2004]: 7). In other words, the object is present to the viewer. In the case of imagination, the object is absent. Sartre argues that the image is not a thing but a relation. He defines the image as "an act that aims in its corporeality at an absent or non-existent object, through a physical or psychic content that is given not as itself but in the capacity of 'analogical representative' of the object aimed at" (Sartre 1940 [2004]: 20). What is imagined is an object that is not present but that we bring back to our consciousness. Therefore, between perception and imagination there is a difference of nature and not of degree.

Sartre draws attention to the fact that images can be psychic, such as the memory of someone, but also non-psychic, such as a photograph, a caricature, or an imitation. Sartre makes a distinction between non-psychic images that immediately bring to the consciousness of the viewer the absent object, such as portraits and realistic sculptures, for instance, and those that make use of few signs of the absent object, such as impersonator performances.

Discussing non-psychic images, Sartre argues the following:

> These various cases all act to "make present" an object. This object is not there, and we know that it is not there. We therefore find, in the first place, an intention directed at an absent object. But this intention is not empty: it directs itself through a content, which is not just any content, but which, in itself, must present some analogy with the object in question.
> (Sartre 1940 [2004]: 19)

Sartre calls this content an analogon. The analogon allows the absent object to acquire a kind of presence in our consciousness, similar to the way that a present object appears to consciousness through perception although it does not make real what it represents. As Sartre writes, "In the imaging attitude, in fact, we find ourselves in the presence of an object that is given as analogous to that which can appear to us in perception" (Sartre 1940 [2004]: 117). Sartre stresses the importance of a resemblance between the material content and the object that it represents.

Sartre argues that the perception of these particular material contents can lead viewers to imagine absent objects because memory and affectivity are attached to any perception. As Sartre contends, " … all perception is accompanied by an affective reaction. Every feeling is feeling about something, which is to say it aims at its object in a certain manner and projects onto it a certain quality. To like Pierre is to be conscious of Pierre as likeable" (Sartre 1940 [2004]: 28). The concept of a "pure" perception does not exist. As neuroscientist Antonio Damasio writes in *The Feeling of What Happens*, "The records we hold of the objects and events that we have once perceived include the motor adjustments we made to obtain the perception in the first place and also include the emotional reactions we had then" (Damasio 2000: 147).

I suggest that the puppet is an analogon because it allows the audience to imagine its absent subjectness through its present objectness. Mutti is not perceived as an old, tired, and loving character but imagined as such because her presence and reactions remind us of the emotions that we experienced in the past when we encountered similar persons, such as a grandmother, for instance. The subjectness of Mutti is the result of a double triangulation between the puppeteer, the puppet, and the audience. The first triangulation that takes place between these three entities is internal because the audience imagines the existence of the puppet as a subject by focusing on the puppet itself. This triangulation combines the physical appearance of the puppet and the quality of its manipulation by the puppeteer. For instance, Mutti appears old and tired because of her drooping whiskers and ears, her gray eyebrows, her thin body, and her sad eyes, combined with her way of moving. The second triangulation is external because the audience imagines the subjectness of the puppet by focusing on the interactions between Mutti and Tranter's character. These interactions give a certain meaning or quality to the movements of the puppet, and thus they also contribute to the existence of the puppet as a subject. For instance, the interactions between Mutti and Tranter give to the former a maternal quality because of the tenderness present in their relationship. The sum of these elements is perceived as signs that refer not to the materiality of the puppet but to the character it represents.

Puppets appear more or less immediately as Others depending on their design and the quality of their manipulation but also in relation to the affective response of the audience. The visual similarities between puppets and the real subjects they are intended to depict can be slight. For instance, in object theatre the audience first has to recognize the few signs of subjectness before they may imagine a character. Conversely, realistic puppets, such as those used in *Twin Houses*, provoke a more immediate affective response because of their strong resemblance to human beings.

The puppet maintains a distancing effect because imagination never fully takes over perception. Perception confirms the puppet as a real object, while imagination displays the puppet as an apparent subject. This dual mode of existence of the puppet establishes a synthetic reality because the puppet belongs to two different levels of actuality: its objectness is real but its subjectness is not. The contradiction of a relation of self to Other between a human being and a puppet finds its resolution in the fact that spectators do not experience the puppet as an object, although they know that it actually is one, but as an imagined subject.

The two modes of being of the puppet exist simultaneously because the apparent consciousness of the puppet always refers back to its presence as an object. Nonetheless, there is an asymmetry between the real objectness and the imagined subjectness of the puppet. The objectness of the puppet exists through its presence in the world, while its subjectness only exists after the initial perception of the materiality of the puppet. Its objectness is prior to its subjectness. The subjectness of the puppet is bound to its objectness through an opposition. To appear as a subject, the perceived objectness of the puppet is annihilated in order to create a distance from its essence as an object. The distance enables the emergence of the imagined subjectness of the puppet within its materiality. The annihilation of the objectness of the puppet cannot be realized by the puppet but is the result of the joint actions of the puppeteer's manipulation and the spectator's perception and imagination. Spectators and performers annihilate the objectness of the puppet and constitute the imagined subjectness of the puppet.

Conclusion

The singularity of the co-presence established between a puppeteer and a puppet comes from the ontological ambiguity of the latter. By looking at Sartre's theory of the Other, I have suggested that the alterity of the puppet appears when the apparent body of the puppet seems to separate itself from the real body of the puppeteer in order to confront the latter through actions or dialogue. The puppet is apprehended as an Other because it seems to have an embodied consciousness. Gaze and, to a certain extent, speech complete the fabrication of the alterity of the puppet. The ambiguous relationship taking place between these two beings results from their ontological differences. When one watches such a form of co-presence, one often experiences an uncanny impression. Levinas helps us to identify the reason for this uncanny feeling when he contends that an object cannot be an Other. The Other is that particular being who escapes the self, while the object belongs to the identity of the self. There is an apparent contradiction between the impossibility raised by Levinas for an object to be an Other and the fact that the puppet appears as an Other by means of its manipulation. I have proposed to answer this by examining the theory of image developed by Sartre in *The Imaginary*. I have concluded that the puppet is not an Other but the image of an Other. Although this image is initiated by perception, it appears to consciousness as an imagined being because consciousness is directed towards an absence. The ambiguous co-presence taking place between the puppeteer and the puppet is the result of the encounter on stage of two beings who belong to two different modes of existence and actuality.

Works cited

Critchley, S. (2008) "Introduction," in R. Bernasconi and S. Critchley, (eds) *The Cambridge Companion to Levinas*. Cambridge, MA: Cambridge University Press.
Damasio, A. (2000) *The Feeling of What Happens*. London: Vintage.

Dastur, F. (2006) "La question d'autrui dans la philosophie contemporaine," Lecture notes, Saint-Pons, France, August 12–15, <http://www.artefilosofia.com/pdf/autrui.pdf> (accessed September 4, 2013).

Gilles, A. (1994) "Des Acteurs et des 'Manipulacteurs'," *Etudes Théâtrales* 2: 19–33.

Langer, M. (1998) "Sartre and Merleau-Ponty: A Reappraisal," in J. B. Stewart (ed.) *The Debate between Sartre and Merleau-Ponty*. Evanston, IL: Northwestern University Press.

Lehmann, H.-T. (1999) *Postdramatic Theatre*, trans. K. Jürs-Munby (2006). London: Routledge.

Levinas, E. (1961) *Totality and Infinity: An Essay on Exteriority*, trans. A. Lingis (1969), reprint. Dordrecht, The Netherlands: Kluwer Academic Publishers (1991).

Mrázek, J. (2005) *Phenomenology of a Puppet Theatre*. Leiden, The Netherlands: KITLV Press.

Plassard, D. (2009) "Marionnette oblige: éthique et esthétique sur la scène contemporaine," *Théâtre/Public* 193: 22–25.

Sartre, J.-P. (1940) *The Imaginary: A Phenomenological Psychology of the Imagination*, trans. J. Weber (2004). Abingdon, England: Routledge.

——(1943) *Being and Nothingness: An Essay on Phenomenological Ontology*, trans. H. E. Barnes (1956), reprint. Abingdon, England: Routledge (2007).

Tillis, S. (1996) "The Actor Occluded: Puppet Theatre and Acting Theory," *Theatre Topics* 6: 109–119.

Wider, K. (1997) *The Bodily Nature of Consciousness*. Ithaca, NY: Cornell University Press.

3
Playing with the Eternal Uncanny

The Persistent Life of Lifeless Objects

John Bell

The relatively recent development of so many scholarly studies of the uncanny makes it clear that Sigmund Freud's 1919 essay and the 1906 article by Ernst Jentsch that inspired it continue to resonate strong and clear as touchstones for our understanding of modernity. Just as Bertolt Brecht's concept of *Verfremdungseffekt* – distancing, "alienation," or estrangement – has consistently offered itself as a valuable tool for understanding modern theatre and the performative nature of modern culture, the concept of the uncanny – the "dark feeling of uncertainty" (Jentsch 1906 [1995/2008]: 224) as to whether objects are alive or dead – offers itself as a useful marker of the complexities and contradictions of the recent past and our current condition.

For the puppeteer, reading Freud's and Jentsch's essays is a remarkable experience because both are filled with references to the essential nature of puppetry. By this I don't mean that the two writers are focused on puppets *per se* but that the references they make to uncanny experience involve the animation of objects – the essence of puppet theatre. That essence is inextricably linked to long-standing human desires to play with the material world, in performances focused on wood, stone, plastic, metal, glass, paper, bone, and other objects that, as the result of our human intervention, move around, speak, and otherwise seem to possess life. Thinking of the terminology Jentsch and Freud use to explain the uncanny, we could say that the essence of puppet, mask, and object performance is the animation of the dead world by living humans. Before examining their different versions of the uncanny, I would like to consider why the concept itself is a modern problem.

Ubiquity and invisibility of object performance

Performance with objects, puppets, and machines is a ubiquitous global presence today, as it has been since the mid-nineteenth century. Not only do traditional puppet, mask, and object performances coexist with efforts to reinvent those forms, but also contemporary material culture – in particular, machines and digital media – constitutes a network of intense, daily, human–object performance relationships affecting millions of people. For example, on October 8, 2013 I noticed the following in the Arts section of *The New York Times*: a photo of a vintage flatbed truck adorned with a battering-ram style giant head, installed as sculpture in a park in Queens, New York; a shot of giant puppets emerging from the Pacific Ocean as part of Basil Twist's *Seafoam Sleepwalk* performance in Santa Monica, California; a photo of a traditional Indian masked dance to be performed by Rajika Puri in New York City; a picture of an ornate graffiti design on a New York City subway car entitled "Stay High 149"; and an image of the star of a new digital animation television series, *Sabrina: Secrets of a Teenage Witch*. All of these events are examples of a material performance culture that spans geography and chronology, as well as form: puppets, masks, machines, digital animation. They are intricately connected aspects of our modern interplay with performing objects, and yet in the pages of the US "paper of record," there is no critical or analytical sense of how these forms might connect with each other as aspects of material performance. In that sense their presence as a cohesive cultural force can seem invisible.

The disparate modern methods used to analyze puppet performance – anthropology, folklore, semiotics, ontological philosophy, the history of technology, performance studies, and a smidgen of theatre history and theory – do not yet quite allow for a comprehensive understanding of the field. A variety of analytical tools have been forged, in other words, but they have not yet been placed in the same toolbox, and we are not quite sure how to handle them together. However, interesting advances in puppet and object analysis have begun to appear with increasing frequency. The American scholar Jena Osman, for example, recently connected puppetry to Brecht's sense of *Verfremdungseffekt* by stating that "the puppet theatre is the epic theatre" (Osman 2008: 19): in other words, that every instance of puppet performance is marked by the distanced performance methods that Brecht, Erwin Piscator, Vsevolod Meyerhold, and many others developed in their own experiments to make theatre that, in Dassia Posner's words, "celebrated (rather than trying to erase or hide) its conventional nature" (Dassia Posner, pers. comm., July 23, 2013). In a similar way I would propose that every puppet performance is also an instance of what Sigmund Freud and Ernst Jentsch called "the uncanny."

Latour: Modernity as separation and translation

However, modernity – by which I mean developments in secular, humanist, and rationalist culture beginning in Western Europe during the sixteenth century and continuing to this day – has had a fundamental problem with puppet, mask, and object performance. Puppetry's primitive roots, animism, irrationality, and its basic contradictions with realism mark an art form that would not easily adapt into modern culture's interests in civilization (versus nature), realism, rationality, text, and bourgeois art. By the later nineteenth century, when Western ideas about the nature of childhood entered into a kind of crisis mode due to the challenges of the Industrial Revolution, puppetry began to be more clearly defined as the realm of children, fairy tales, and "primitive" cultures from around the world. This situation has led many Western puppeteers over the past 120 years to lament the often successful efforts to limit puppetry's ambit. Bread and Puppet Theater director Peter Schumann (1990: 3) refers to this as "the habitual lament of modern puppeteers about their low and ridiculous status," a standing that, despite the success of Schumann, Julie Taymor, Basil Twist, Robert Lepage, Adrian Kohler, and Basil Jones, as well as others, is still more or less in place.

Modernity (and its postmodern appendage) is often considered from an artistic perspective, but French sociologist Bruno Latour in his influential book of the early 1990s, *We Have Never Been Modern*, sees this moment of history first of all in terms of science and social structure. Modernity, for Latour, represents "a break in the passage of time," when "an archaic and stable past" was superseded by a dynamic and changing new society marked by reason and science. More important, modernity represents "two sets of entirely different practices" for Latour: "translation" and "purification" (Latour 1991: 10). By "purification" he means the "modern critical stance" of separating "Nature" and "Culture" in a strict dichotomy of "two entirely distinct ontological zones: that of human beings on the one hand; that of nonhumans on the other" (Latour 1991: 10–11). However, "translation" in Latour's schema involves "mixtures between entirely new types of beings, hybrids of nature and culture" – relationships which he also terms "networks." The essence of modernity, Latour argues, has been the consideration of translation and purification as entirely separate spheres. However, if we "directed our attention *simultaneously* to the work of purification and the work of hybridization," he writes, we would "immediately stop being wholly modern" (Latour 1991: 11).

These concepts are relevant to the nature of puppet and object performance and the uncanny. First of all, modernity's "separation between humans and nonhumans" has an immediate relation to the performances of humans and the performances of objects that define the difference between puppetry and actors' theatre (although Latour, like Freud and Jentsch, was not thinking about theatre). The separation Latour has in mind is necessary for such modern political activities as the creation of the US Constitution, which analytically laid out a plan for a new society, and the development of empirical experimentation – the scientific method – which analytically laid out plans for our knowledge of the natural world. Both activities, emerging simultaneously in the seventeenth century, depended upon strict separations of humans (culture) and nonhumans (nature) and the dominance of the former over the latter. In this new modern environment, logic, rationality, and the experimental method were prized, and the idea of strict separations could come to include the many differences between "ancient" and "modern" cultures. Colonialism and anthropology, for example, depended upon the concept of modern culture subduing and studying a separate and pre-modern culture. One problem of pre-modern cultures would be their failure to maintain strict separations between culture and nature, between humans and objects. Instead, in such "ancient" cultures, objects and humans were connected, versions of the same existence. Objects in pre-modern (or non-modern) culture could have agency, could perform. But in modern contexts, performing objects inhabit an "entirely distinct ontological zone" (in Latour's terms) separate from humans.

The animism attached to puppets, masks, and performing objects thus becomes a problem of modernity, one which Jentsch and then Freud represented in the early twentieth century with the concept of the uncanny. And the fact that performing objects fall into the category of the uncanny has made it difficult to understand their communicative powers outside the realms of pathology, which both Jentsch and Freud assigned to the concept. Their concept of the uncanny defines the power of objects as a problem, not a window into the nature of the material world and its agency.

Jentsch: Doubt and the uncanny

Freud articulated the uncanny ("*Das Unheimliche*") as a central element of the repressed mysteries of modern life in a 1919 essay that, in particular, examined E. T. A. Hoffmann's disconcerting 1816 story "The Sandman" as an example of how anxieties about castration, sexuality, and the power of the father can return to haunt our psyches. Freud's essay has become one of the most well-known aspects of his analytical approach to psychology, one that has inspired much recent thinking about weird and mysterious situations and events and how we respond to them.[1]

Jentsch's essay a decade earlier, "On the Psychology of the Uncanny," pays more direct attention to the performance of objects. Jentsch also focuses on the writing of Hoffmann[2] in terms of a concept of doubt that resonates strongly with the dynamics of puppetry. Jentsch writes that:

> Among all the psychical uncertainties that can become a cause for the uncanny feeling to arise, there is one in particular that is able to develop a fairly regular, powerful and very general effect: namely, doubt as to whether an apparently living being really is animate and, conversely, doubt as to whether a lifeless object may not in fact be animate – and more precisely, when this doubt only makes itself felt obscurely in one's consciousness. The mood lasts until these doubts are resolved and then usually makes way for another kind of feeling.
>
> (Jentsch 1906 [1995/2008]: 221)

Of course, the play with inanimate objects is exactly what puppetry is, and the fact that Jentsch ascribes the feeling of "doubt" to such play is an important insight for puppetry studies. However, by associating the uncanny with doubt, uncertainty, abnormality, disturbance, and other undesirable effects, Jentsch also problematizes the uncanny, something Freud would press even further. Jentsch's essay features a rich array of performing objects seen from a turn-of-the-century perspective: automata, puppets, life-size machines, masked balls, tree trunks that turn out to be snakes, the "wild man's" first sight of a locomotive or steam boat, scarecrows, wax figures, panopticons, panoramas, dolls, and other anthropomorphized objects. Jentsch makes it clear that human concerns about the mysterious movement possibilities of objects are grounded in the nature of what was then considered "primitive" life. He writes:

Figure 3.1 "Doubt as to whether ... a lifeless object may not in fact be animate": Trudi Cohen in Great Small Works' *Terror As Usual: Episode 7: Metro Section* (1993). Photo courtesy of Great Small Works

> [an] important factor in the origin of the uncanny is the natural tendency of man to infer, in a kind of naïve analogy with his own animate state, that things in the external world are also animate or, perhaps more correctly, are animate in the same way. It is all the more impossible to resist this psychical urge, the more primitive the individual's level of intellectual development is. The child of nature populates his environment with demons; small children speak in all seriousness to a chair, to their spoon, to an old rag and so on, hitting out full of anger at lifeless things in order to punish them. Even in highly cultivated Greece, a dryad still lived in every tree.
>
> (Jentsch 1906 [1995/2008]: 225)

In other words, belief in the uncanny power of performing objects is connected to the infancy of modern children, or the "infancy" of cultures that the West, from its modern perspective, sees as "primitive." In another reflection of that era, Jentsch finds that "women, children, and dreamers" are more susceptible to the influence of the uncanny because of their "weaker ... critical sense," while fully formed adult Western males need not be troubled by the uncanny, since it is not, in the end, rational (Jentsch 1906 [1995/2008]: 219).

Freud: Surmounting primitive modes of thought

Thirteen years after Jentsch, Freud's sense of the uncanny ("something familiar ['homely', 'homey'] that has been repressed and then reappears" [as "unhomely"]) shifts focus away from objects and back towards the human psyche (Freud 1919 [2003]: 152). Like Jentsch, Freud also sees the uncanny as connected to "primitive" or infantile sensibilities. However, while for Jentsch uncanny objects provoke more benign feelings of "uncertainty" and "doubt," Freud's opinion is much more alarmist and dire. The uncanny, he writes, "belongs to the realm of the frightening, of what evokes fear and dread" (Freud 1919 [2003]: 123). And while Jentsch sees uncertainty about the independent agency of objects as a central element of their power, Freud is certain that such powers are illusions to be explained by "the old *animistic* view of the universe" (Freud 1919 [2003]: 147). Although Jentsch focuses on the performative powers of the objects themselves, Freud is more interested in what performing objects mean to the minds of modern men and women. For Freud, "uncanny effects" are "associated with the omnipotence of thoughts, instantaneous wish fulfillment, secret harmful forces and the return of the dead"; moments when our minds play tricks on us, and we believe irrationally that we can control elements of the physical world or that physical objects can take on a life of their own (Freud 1919 [2003]: 154). Freud writes:

> There is no mistaking the conditions under which the sense of the uncanny arises here. We – or our primitive forebears – once regarded such things as real possibilities; we were convinced that they really happened. Today we no longer believe in them, having *surmounted* such modes of thought. Yet we do not feel entirely secure in these new convictions; the old ones live on in us, on the look-out for confirmation. Now, as soon as something *happens* in our lives that seems to confirm these old discarded beliefs, we experience a sense of the uncanny.
>
> (Freud 1919 [2003]: 154)

For Freud, the uncanny is connected to "animistic convictions" that in human culture were "once familiar and then repressed"; a feature of human society that in the modern West is no longer consciously acceptable for "anyone who has wholly and definitively rejected" such convictions (Freud 1919 [2003]: 154). At one point in his essay, Freud confidently says of himself that "[i]t is a long time since he experienced or became acquainted with anything that conveyed the impression of the uncanny" (124), so confident is he in his grasp of the rational world and of his healthy and sophisticated relationship with his unconscious.

Freud sees the experience of the uncanny as an individual pathology; however, it is also part of our collective cultural history. The rejection of animistic convictions, and the particular time when these beliefs were discarded, marks the beginning of the modern world, as Peter Burke (1978) has pointed out in *Popular Culture in Early Modern Europe*. For Burke, there are specific moments when this rejection or surmounting took place – for example, when the Curé of Nanterre "tore the mask from the face of the leading actor" of a street theatre company in mid-seventeenth-century France, or when the Russian Archpriest Avvakum, "zealous in Christ's service" and faced with a travelling *skomorokh* (a Russian minstrel) who had come to his village to perform with dancing bears, "broke the buffoon's mask and the drums" (Burke 1978: 214). In a similar manner, Protestant reformers cleared churches of icons, paintings, and other Catholic ritual objects that troubled the increasingly logical minds of Europeans. The ascendancy of rationalism and the scientific method during the Age of Enlightenment beginning in the late seventeenth century only strengthened modern confidence in discarding ancient beliefs, and in the world of Western performance the increasing dominance of realism as both a scenic and dramaturgical principle of the stage further marginalized popular performing object forms. The colonial forays of European powers into Asia, Africa, and the Americas, and the consequent invention of anthropology and folklore to explain the old beliefs that the "primitive" inhabitants of these places held, brought back the issue of animist performance with objects as a peculiar, irrational belief system that could be examined at a distance, as distinctly "other" than our own sophisticated modern thinking. In other words, as Burke points out, belief in the animism of objects was a marker of one's relative cultural sophistication. Uncivilized and savage peoples believed in such things, while civilized modern men and women categorically rejected these ways of thinking.

And yet, despite the many centuries of development of modern Western thought, the animate nature of objects persists. We attempt to control it with concepts such as "the uncanny," which want to tame the effects of object theatre by assigning them to the irrational and pathological, rather than to consider the disconcerting possibility of the agency of things. But the world of puppets and performing objects is always breaking free of such efforts, imposing its questions on us in a variety of ways.

Beginning in the eighteenth century, a new autonomy of objects emerged with the increasing presence of machines as fundamental aspects of modern life. Industrial society and the rise of mechanical entertainments forced Europeans to consider how machines function and gave rise to anxieties about the possible independence of machines from humans, which Hoffmann articulated in 1816 in the form of the beautiful automaton Olimpia in "The Sandman." A century later this crucial theme reappeared in an even more socially disturbing form when Karel Čapek invented the word "robot" for his 1920 play *R.U.R.* Art historian Tom Gunning (2003) has shown how the appearance and experience of new technologies themselves in the nineteenth century was itself always uncanny, not in terms of theatrical performance *per se* but in the performance of everyday life.

Some avant-garde theatre-makers of the early twentieth century, inspired by machines and by "primitive" icons and fetish objects from Asia, Africa, and the Americas, rejected realism and actors' theatre and jumped right into the uncanny world of puppets and objects. Part of the shock of this avant-garde was its happiness in returning to the culture of "discarded beliefs." Freud's 1919 essay proposed that "we no longer believe in" the real power of objects, but the experience of the twentieth century seems to suggest that, in fact, we may not have "surmounted such modes of thought."

Tugging back on Modernism

The uncanny is a force that tugs back on the civilizing and rationalizing thrust of modern thinking – but perhaps this is a positive development. Modernity presented itself as an entity slowly but inevitably spreading across the world, enlightening it, changing everything in its path, and leaving behind old beliefs and ways of life as they were replaced by modern technologies, modern societies, modern people; but in fact, the old beliefs and non-modern or anti-modern practices have not all been left behind. Puppets are signs of this, which is why they are uncanny.

Let us consider this in terms of modernist performance, by which I mean the network of old and new performance forms that began to coalesce in the late nineteenth century in the European theatre and continue to this day. The drama of realistic actors' theatre (which since the dissemination of Stanislavsky's early teachings to the United States has been the dominant form of theatre taught in the US and the dominant element of what is considered here to *be* theatre) is a sign of the confidence of modern thought. We see humans onstage making things happen or messing things up, but in either case creating action primarily with their bodies and voices. The moment when the young playwright Konstantin Treplev fails to achieve a cosmic symbolist spectacle in Chekhov's 1895 play *The Seagull* – his play-within-the-play is about the possible union of "Spirit and Matter" and includes "will-o'-the-wisps" and the Devil represented by two red lanterns for eyes (Chekhov 1895 [1988]: 82) – not only reflects Treplev's conflict with his mother Irina but also Chekhov's sense of the substantial cultural obstacles a modern drama of symbols and objects faces in front of an audience quite accustomed to the traditions of actors' theatre. And what was disturbing about the actual nonrealistic theatre of the time – the plays of Maurice Maeterlinck; Alfred Jarry's masked characters, puppets, and proto-surrealist scenery in his 1896 play *Ubu Roi*; or, later, Pablo Picasso's puppets for the 1917 ballet *Parade* (which inspired Guillaume Apollinaire to coin the term "surrealism") – was that Freud's "discarded beliefs" in the active power of objects came back, not in the form of primitive culture but as avant-garde performance.

Modern puppet performances can be threatening, doubt-inducing, and anxiety-provoking events because they remind us that we are not necessarily in control of as much as we thought we were. Modernity has traditionally asserted its confidence in human potential, in our rational minds, in our ability to impose logic over untamed and illogical features of our world, including societies we consider un-modern, and even over nature itself – the ultimate force in need of taming.[3] But play with puppets, machines, projected images, and other objects is constantly unsettling because it always leads to doubt about our mastery of the material world. If that piece of wood, that lump of clay, that shadow figure, that machine, seems to be moving of its own accord, then where are we as humans? The essence of puppet, mask, and object performance (as countless puppeteers have said from their own experience) is not mastery of the material world but a constant negotiation back and forth with it. Puppet performance reveals to us that the results of those negotiations are not at all preordained and that human superiority over the material world is not something to count on, especially since *we* all eventually end up as lifeless objects.

Freud saw instances of the uncanny as moments of psychological trouble when certain anxieties of childhood returned despite our efforts to repress them; such uncanny moments were a problem that needed to be and could be addressed by a healthy psyche that had gotten beyond them. But puppets and performing objects, despite our best efforts to insist that we are not "primitive," pull us back towards the

Figure 3.2 Freud's "discarded beliefs" in the active power of objects came back not in the form of primitive culture but as avant-garde performance: Maryann Colella in Bread and Puppet Theater's *Things Done in a Seeing Place*, Glover, Vermont (2013). Photo courtesy of the author

old, discarded animist beliefs and in this way throw doubt upon modern conceptions concerning the powers of reason and science. By not taking them seriously, we think we can hold back the doubt. But since puppet and object theatre is ubiquitous in modern culture (just as it has been ubiquitous in pre-modern cultures), it relentlessly brings the issue back to us.

Bruno Latour developed his thinking about having "never been modern" by focusing on the characteristics of hybrids and networks, which seek connections among cultures, systems, humans, and objects rather than "purifying" those relationships with a strict dichotomy between culture and nature. This approach, it seems to me, is useful not simply because it gets well beyond the modernism/postmodernism debates that have fueled scholarly thinking in Western academia in recent decades, but because a sense of and appreciation for networks and hybrids is necessary for an understanding of the way in which our culture actually works today. Scientific thought and technological development coexist and are informed by the startling power of object performance. The "ancient" beliefs in animism – in Western religions as well as in Asia, Africa, the Middle East, and the Americas – have not been superseded but instead thrive in and benefit from developments in science and technology. Digital puppetry, motion capture, and stop-motion animation coexist with live street performance, ritual object theatre, and Punch and Judy – a global network of object performance. The "uncanny" power of puppets persists, not necessarily as a problem to be surmounted but as a theatrical sentiment to be felt, appreciated, interpreted, and celebrated.

Notes

1 See, for example, La Capra (2009), Collins and Jervis (2008), and Thorburn and Jenkins (2003).
2 Hoffmann, like Heinrich von Kleist and other Romantics, played an important role in the late-nineteenth-century development of performing-object theory because of his intense interest in objects that come alive in such stories as "The Nutcracker and the Mouse King" and "The Sandman," which were adapted, with profound and lasting effect, for the stage.
3 Dassia Posner notes elsewhere in this volume that literature, art, and performance also showed another kind of fascination with puppets: the idea of humans as puppets controlled by outside, larger-than-life, and often invisible forces.

Works cited

Burke, P. (1978) *Popular Culture in Early Modern Europe*. New York, NY: Harper & Row.
La Capra, D. (2009) *History and Its Limits: Human, Animal, Violence*. Ithaca, NY: Cornell University Press.
Chekhov, A. (1895) *The Seagull*, trans. R. Hingley (1988), in *Five Major Plays by Anton Chekhov*. New York, NY: Bantam Books.
Collins, J. and Jervis, J. (eds) (2008) *Uncanny Modernity: Cultural Theories, Modern Anxieties*. London: Palgrave Macmillan.
Freud, S. (1919) *The Uncanny*, trans. D. McLintock (2003). New York, NY: Penguin Books.
Gunning, T. (2003) "Re-newing Old Technologies: Astonishment, Second Nature, and the Uncanny in Technology from the Previous Turn-of-the-Century," in D. Thorburn and H. Jenkins (eds) *Rethinking Media Change: The Aesthetics of Transition*. Cambridge, MA: MIT Press.
Jentsch, E. (1906) "Document: 'On the Psychology of the Uncanny'," trans. R. Sellars (1995) *Angelaki* 2(1): 17–21; reprinted in J. Collins and J. Jervis (eds) (2008) *Uncanny Modernity: Cultural Theories, Modern Anxieties*. London: Palgrave Macmillan.
Latour, B. (1991) *We Have Never Been Modern*, trans. C. Porter (1993). Cambridge, MA: Harvard University Press.
Osman, J. (2008) "The Puppet Theater Is the Epic Theater," in C. Kuoni and I. Schaffner (eds) *The Puppet Show*. Philadelphia, PA: University of Pennsylvania Press.
Schumann, P. (1990) *The Radicality of the Puppet Theater*. Glover, VT: Bread and Puppet Press.
Thorburn, D. and Jenkins, H. (eds) (2003) *Rethinking Media Change: The Aesthetics of Transition*. Cambridge, MA: MIT Press.

Section II
Perspectives from Practitioners

4
Visual Dramaturgy
Some Thoughts for Puppet Theatre-Makers
Eric Bass

Several years ago, at a conference on ensemble theatre, one participant proposed a workshop on physical dramaturgy to complement text-based approaches to creating and critiquing theatre. For many ensembles, "writing" a piece is actually the physical process of embodying the shapes, gestures, movements, and tableaux that suggest the thread or theme of the work being explored. Devising work in this way redefines what we mean by dramaturgy. In a world in which not all theatre is text based, the body's "mind" may direct us. Physical impulse, rather than thought, may be the "writer."

As a puppeteer, I responded to this physical theatre-maker that, if we are going to talk about physical dramaturgy, we need to talk about visual dramaturgy as well. He responded that they were the same thing. I do not believe this. He, by the way, also no longer believes this.

Physical impulses can certainly lead to visual tension. Look for a moment at Anne Bogart's Viewpoints work. One of the first "viewpoints" that Bogart's SITI Company teaches is spatial relationship, the tension between actors created by their stage positions alone (Bogart and Landau 2004: 11). In every spatial relationship, there is an implied story, a relationship: who dominates the picture? What position implies action or stasis? How might the spatial relationship suggest dialogue that is vertical – that talks to God rather than Man? Viewpoints-trained actors discover their characters as a result of physical impulses, rather than by text analysis. They are working within another dramaturgical realm, one that does not try to give the audience information but rather lets the audience discover the drama together with the actor.

This being said, visual dramaturgy is yet again a different approach.

All theatre-making is play. Serious play, many would say, but play nonetheless. The people we now call "actors" were in Shakespeare's time called "players." We make "plays," although this word so often refers to something that is so rigorously set in text that it might be difficult to play with it at all. Physical play-making puts the play back in theatre. Visual play-making does, too, in a different way.

Some years ago we began work on a new piece. We had brought in a director for the show, a man with a very good sense of the texture and shape of materials but whose forte was clearly physical theatre. In our first week of rehearsals, he witnessed the members of our company moving boxes and boards around the stage, making shapes and structures, playing with the materials. He asked when we would actually begin rehearsals. We replied that we had already begun. This was, in fact, rehearsing. We discovered that the materials created many different shapes that suggested rooftops. From this came the discovery of what this scene would be about and how we would "talk" about it. Rooftops suggested rooms, rooms suggested isolation. The visual dramaturgy in this approach opened up both the content of the scene and the dramatic tension in the elements from which the scene was built.

As puppeteers, the material of our theatre-making is material itself. Our shows might have characters in them, but those characters are made of materials that say as much about who they are as the words they speak. We cannot take for granted that they are human; indeed, even when they represent humans, they are of a different reality. When we begin work on a Sandglass show, the first question we ask ourselves is "Why is this character played by a puppet and not an actor?" If we cannot answer this question, it is probably because the character is too much like a human and should remain in that domain. On the other hand, a character who comes out of dream or memory, a character whose being embodies imbalance or fragmentation, a character who sees us as "other" – all of these (and more) beg to be played by puppets. Each suggests a world that could be other than ours.

The arrangement of materials onstage is a dramatic event. One of the exercises that we often use in teaching goes like this: alongside the stage (but outside the playing area) 12 objects are placed. The objects are of varying shapes, sizes, textures, and functions: a ladder, a window, a barrel, a wine glass, an umbrella, a rope, and a candlestick, for example. A team of "players" gets to place these objects onstage in the playing area. Each player can move only one object in his/her turn. When seven objects have been placed onstage, a turn might involve removing or replacing an object or simply changing its position. The task of the "player" is to increase the dramatic tension of the scene. Most important: do not try to tell a story!

This is the moment when the fun really begins. It is quite amazing how invested people become in their sense of drama and the placement of their objects. Any moment might be a cliffhanger, an exasperating moment in which someone's move has completely changed the direction of a "piece." These static pictures, made up only of objects, are exercises in play-making. They are without human characters (either actors or puppets), and yet they contain the elements of dramaturgy. Again, it is important to say that dramaturgy does not necessarily refer to "telling a story." Creating dramatic tension might imply story, and the audience might find one, but that is very different from making storytelling an intent. In this case, it actually gets in the way of discovering dramatic tension.

Kermit Love, the creator of Big Bird and other characters for Sesame Street, as well as a designer for the New York City and Joffrey Ballets, once distinguished between the puppet and the actor in this way: when the actor comes onstage, he needs to make a statement; when the puppet comes onstage, it IS a statement. For the puppet, speech may be redundant. It is already speaking volumes by its materials, by its role as part of a stage picture, by its relationship to objects, even by its physical limitations. In terms of visual dramaturgy, how do we use these properties to *create*? How do we use them to speak in a way that is as powerful as words? How do we use them to create tension with the text?

One of the problems in using puppets to speak text-based theatre is that the puppets are often reduced to vehicles for delivering language that is, in fact, the language of actors. This might be a powerful use of the puppet, in certain contexts, but only when it recognizes the inherent quality of the puppet as different from the actor.

Citing Bogart (2000) once again (who was herself quoting Friedrich Dürrenmatt, I believe), when what we see onstage and what we hear onstage are essentially the same, we have basically cancelled out the tension that we could have created among these dramatic elements. We have created mere illustration. Images have the power to stand alone as dramatic storytellers, but where text is also included, they have the power to act counter to the text to give the piece an added level of tension and complexity.

Let us look at two applications of visual dramaturgy in puppet theatre. In the first instance there is no text. We begin with an image. The image might be a dynamic still life, a stage tableau. The image contains materials, figures made from those materials, and a spatial relationship of those figures. Perhaps there is also a relationship between puppets and humans, an intersection of worlds. We look at the image. Where does it want to go? If it does not "want" to go anywhere, perhaps there is no tension in it to work with. So we move something, create imbalance. Now where is it taking us? What inspired this image? Perhaps it was a dream? Or a painting by Chagall?

An example of this is from a Sandglass Theater production, *Between Sand and Stars*, which we completed in 2005. The production was a puppet-and-aerial piece based on images suggested by Antoine de Saint-Exupéry's 1939 memoir/novel *Wind, Sand and Stars*. Everything takes place in the mind and memory of a 1930s mail pilot who crashes in the North African desert. As he crawls endlessly in search of rescue, he dreams about the risks he has taken and in what way taking risks has given his life a sense of meaning and passion, whether it is the risk of physical adventure or the risk in making art. The puppet representing him is a ten-string marionette operated by five puppeteers, each about 10 feet away from it. This distance gives the puppet the autonomy it needs to seem to be alone in the desert. At the same time, the visible connections between puppet and puppeteers give the puppet its lifelines, which disconnect one by one as the puppet weakens and approaches death. The physical dramaturgy of the scene lies in the puppet's effort to survive. The visual dramaturgy lies in the puppet's dependence on the five manipulators. It does not recognize the puppeteers, but the audience feels the dramatic tension in this relationship.

The metaphor of the puppet dying as its strings are cut is an old one. Artists such as Henk Boerwinkel in the compilation piece *Metamorphoses* (1991), performed with his company Figurentheater Triangel, and Philippe Genty with his Pierrot puppet in the show *Round Like a Cube* (see Margaret Williams's earlier chapter in this book) have used it to great power. In and of itself, it might be thought of now as a cliché. As visual dramaturgy, however, it can become fresh if it leads us beyond being an end in itself. The challenge of *Between Sand and Stars* was to animate empty space. The distance between the pilot puppet onstage and the aerialists in the air (his

VISUAL DRAMATURGY

Figure 4.1 Between Sand and Stars, a collaboration among Sandglass Theater, Gemini Trapeze, and Rob Mermin (2003) based on images from Antoine de St. Exupéry's *Wind, Sand and Stars*: as the pilot lost in the desert struggles to make his way through endless sands, the marionette's lifelines are visible. Photo: © Richard Termine, richardtermine@nyc.rr.com

dreams? ideals? ambitions?) had to be active. In essence, *Between Sand and Stars* was a piece *about* spatial relationship. It was a piece about *air*. Alone in the desert, the pilot is again surrounded by empty space, and yet he clings to something, some hope, some breath of life. That breath came from the five manipulators, shadows beyond the puppet's world yet breathing as one, giving a physical and visual sense of contact through space. In our scene, the puppet does not die or rebel against its manipulators. At the point of near disconnection, breathing through only one string, the pilot is rescued by the man he thought to be his enemy, an Arab camel rider.

Let us look at a second application of visual dramaturgy, this time in a piece with text. Not all text is dialogue. It is true that many puppets "speak," but not all do and not all should. How do we know? It is perhaps too easy to say, but I think we have to listen. Do we hear the voice? If so, is it the voice of the puppet's speech or its thoughts? Where does it come from? Puppets have a way of defying our intentions. They are not always built to do what we intend.

In this instance, what is the role of visual dramaturgy? One approach may be to separate the text from the visual scene we are staging. How can the scene exist in its own right, separate from the words? If the dialogue speaks of flight, can the puppets be made of stone, suggesting weight, so that our investment in the *need* for flight is enhanced?

In the process of visual dramaturgy, it is not always the text that comes first. Each of us has in himself/herself many dialogues, speeches, poems, songs, cries for justice, exclamations of despair. What words are we connected to when we arrange our stage elements in ways that trigger an awakening of these texts? Conversely, if we begin with a text, what images or materials raise the stakes of these words? Sometimes we are inspired with a text as a starting point, but having created a visual expression of this text, the text itself becomes redundant. We have interpreted text not by speaking it but by embodying it in physical and visual elements.

Here, for example, is one of Hamlet's classic monologues from Shakespeare's great tragedy:

> O, that this too too solid flesh would melt
> Thaw and resolve itself into a dew!
> Or that the Everlasting had not fix'd
> His canon 'gainst self-slaughter! O God! God!
> How weary, stale, flat and unprofitable,
> Seem to me all the uses of this world!
>
> (Shakespeare, *Hamlet*, Act 1, Scene 2, lines 131–136)

I am reminded of the work of a French puppet theatre artist, Émilie Valantin, who in her 1996 production of *Un Cid* made her puppets from ice.[1] They were pre-sculpted (and frozen) before each performance. In the course of the one-hour show, the characters melted before our eyes. What about the Hamlet text? Could this material unlock Hamlet's moment through visual dramaturgy? Could he literally thaw? Could we adopt this marvelous physical/visual effect to embody Hamlet's plea?

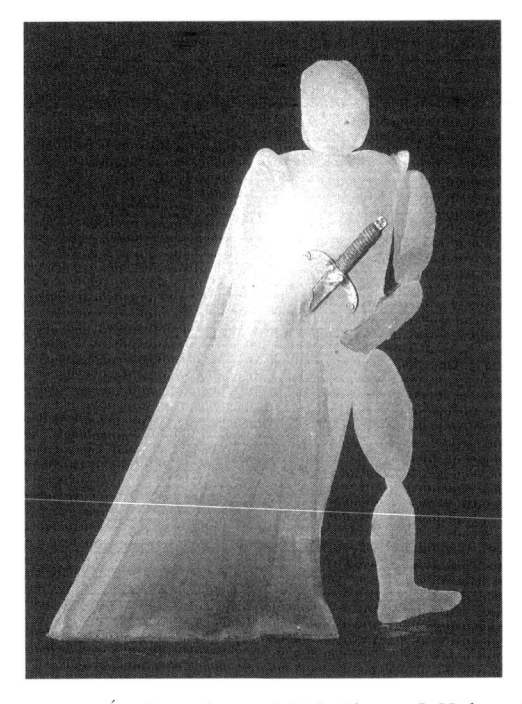

Figure 4.2 Un Cid, Compagnie Émilie Valantin (1996). Photo: © Hubert Charbonnier

As writers of dialogue, we put ourselves in the shoes of our characters to find their voices. As physical dramaturgs, we let our impulses lead us to discover the truth of a moment onstage. As visual dramaturgs, the space, our materials, the imbalance of our images, the actual transformation of our elements, all have the potential to contain dramatic tension (which is the same as comedic tension). Any and all of these can be the tools of our "writing."

Puppeteers are not the only theatre-makers who create visually, but as a puppeteer, this approach is irresistible. In visual dramaturgy, it is the audience who brings psychological content to a scene. They identify with an implied situation, with a need to transform. The visual tension is for them the tension of an imminent life change. The images resonate metaphorically and contain the potential for transformation. What is physical for the performer, whether actor or puppet, triggers emotional and psychological states for the audience. The relation between the physical and the visual is just this: the dramatic visual image, sustaining a special tension, contains the need for an object (or puppet or human) to physically move. Such an image seems to demand that the actors, puppets, or objects fulfill a task in which their identity is at stake. They contain a *need* to transform: the need to achieve balance, for example, or to hold themselves together or to transcend the material of their creation.

In closing, I feel that this potential to move, this dramatic potential of objects, is beautifully captured by the contemporary Polish author Andrzej Stasiuk in his meditation on light, *Dukla*. Describing the dawn, the moment when darkness is poised to become light, he writes:

> Already it's bright enough to see fences, trees, trash, junk-filled yards, broken-down cars sinking into the dirt and disintegrating patiently like minerals; pickets, stakes, slim cold chimneys, shafts of carts, motorbikes with lowered heads, outhouses lurking around corners, telegraph poles festooned with cables that droop in mourning, a spade stuck into the ground and forgotten – all this is there, in its place, but none of these things yet casts a shadow, though the sky to the east resembles a silver looking glass; the brightness is reflected in it but remains invisible. This must have been what the world looked like just before it was set in motion; everything was ready, objects poised on the threshold of their destinies like people paralyzed by fear.
> (Stasiuk 1997 [2011]: 3–4)

Stasiuk's world is about to spring to life, about to become animated. It is tense with drama. Imagine walking into this world. What will happen here? What will happen next? We do not know, but something will begin, launched from the dynamic image into action. All we need is a stage and the artists to help it happen, the artists who are themselves curious where this will lead. Then we have visual dramaturgy.

Note

1 Valantin's piece is an adaptation of Pierre Corneille's 1637 play *Le Cid*. By substituting the indefinite article in her title, Valantin emphasizes that here the audience is witnessing the story of "*a* lord," not "*the* lord."

Works cited

Bogart, A. (2000) Lecture to Saratoga International Theater Institute (SITI) Summer Theater Workshop. Skidmore College, Saratoga Springs, NY, June.
Bogart, A. and Landau, T. (2004) *The Viewpoints Book: A Practical Guide to Viewpoints and Composition*. New York, NY: Theatre Communications Group.
Stasiuk, A. (1997) *Dukla*, trans. B. Johnston (2011). Champaign, IL: Dalkey Archive Press.

5
Puppetry, Authorship, and the *Ur*-Narrative
Basil Jones

The "work" of the puppet

Perhaps it would be useful to begin by asking whether we can define what it is that characterizes the "work" a puppet does onstage and how this form of work is distinguished from the "work" of an actor. The work of the actor is surely to perform the text written by the scriptwriter under the guidance of the director and informed by his or her own research into the character being interpreted.

Ostensibly, the same might surely be said for the work the puppet performs onstage. Both the puppet and the actor are interpreters of the playwright and the director's artistic vision. The traditional chain of meaning and interpretation starts with the playwright, passing through the director and finally to the actor or the puppet.

However, there is another level of activity that actors take for granted, which is central to the meaning and function of the puppet's work. The actor is a living person and therefore automatically possesses life. Both the actor and the audience take for granted this fact. His or her livingness is obvious and certainly doesn't need to be "performed." The actor is in no danger at any stage in the performance of giving away the fact that he is not alive. However, by its very nature, a puppet is an object and therefore, by definition, lifeless. The object which we call a puppet lives and breathes only because the puppeteer takes great care, for however long the performance lasts and at every moment during that performance, to make the puppet appear to be alive.

The designer/maker of the puppet is partially responsible for the life the puppet possesses in performance. The jointing (or lack of it) and the structure of the puppet allow for certain forms of expressiveness and not others. The expert design is acutely sensitive to the movement required by the puppet. So, a large part of the liveliness of the puppet is the responsibility not only of the puppeteer but of the puppet's designer/maker as well.

Thus, the primary work of the puppet is the *performance* of life, while for the actor this fundamental battle is already won. The life – the viability – of the puppet is always provisional. So, a puppet is by its very nature dead, whereas an actor is by her very nature alive. The puppet's work, then – more fundamental than the interpretation of written text or directorial vision – is to strive towards life. This struggle, this "play," is literally in the hands of the puppeteer and need have no connection to the scriptwriter or the director. Every second onstage is a second in which the puppet could die. The life and credibility of the puppet depend entirely on the vigilance of the puppeteer. The audience will take the puppet seriously only so long as they believe in this life. So the puppeteer is literally engaged in a parallel, low-key drama: a life or death struggle, dependent on the puppeteer's strength, stamina, muscle memory, and, of course, artistry or talent.

The ontology of the puppet

The puppet in performance possesses a significantly different ontological status than a human actor. The fact that the puppet is essentially a performing object (the more mechanical puppets could be called performing machines) definitely suggests a different ontology to the human. Also, the puppet's striving to depict and embody life means that it has a different ontological narrative from a human being. I'm not sure how you would describe the human actor's *Ur*-narrative. Perhaps it is the desire to function as the medium for stories and narratives. However, the puppet's *Ur*-narrative is something quite different to, and more fundamental than, storytelling. It is the quest for life itself. It is perhaps worth noting that this "quest" is not an obvious

Figure 5.1 Confessions of Zeno rehearsal, The Dance Factory, Johannesburg (2002): puppets designed by William Kentridge and made by Adrian Kohler and Tau Qwelane. Photo: © Ruphin Coudyzer

part of the puppet's performance. However, it forms the impulse behind every move and every gesture the puppet makes.

Micro-movement

I would suggest that it is this dignified hunt for life, exhibited by all puppets in performance, that fascinates audiences because we ourselves can identify with similar quests in our everyday lives. Thus, apparently minor quotidian functions, like getting out of bed in the morning, or reaching for a cup just beyond one's grasp, or avoiding the clash of spectacles when kissing a friend, can take on epic proportions for many observers when performed by a puppet. Audiences identify with this and feel a resonance with their own interaction with the world. The puppet, therefore, becomes the manifest incarnation of our own struggle to live, to be human, to act.

Once we as puppeteers begin seriously to play and to master these micro-dramas, we see they can trump the macro-action onstage, the action that would normally fall under the heading of choreography. Thus, when the audience becomes engaged with the micro-movement of a puppet's performance, spoken dialogue tends to fade from consciousness, as if it has been bleached out of the performance. Often we hear the comment: "lovely puppets, pity about the text." Most often this remark is made not because the text is poor, but because it is hard to really hear or apprehend the text when one becomes fully engaged with, even mesmerized by, this more profound level of performance. So the puppeteer is performing on two levels, one is the macro-level, which engages with the script and the choreography. The other is the micro-level and is a performance of the *Ur*-narrative: the performance of life.

War Horse

In 2006, Handspring was commissioned to design and make nine life-sized horses for the National Theatre's production of *War Horse* in London. The idea was to make a theatrical interpretation of Michael Morpurgo's novel of the same name. For many reasons, this would be a challenging adaptation. For one thing, in the novel, the central character and narrator is a horse. This horse, Joey, goes to war alongside the British army and it is through his eyes that we experience the horrors of combat. The horse's voice – producing a kind of "equine reportage" – is a powerful narrative device in the novel, though one that we realized would not work onstage. So, the decision was made to keep the horse silent in its theatrical incarnation. This presented the playwright with a problem. How does one "author" a character who plays the leading role in the drama but doesn't speak and is not even a person? Clearly the horse would have to be "articulate" in languages that were not verbal.

From the start, it was clear that the scriptwriter was almost powerless to author scenes where the horse was central. Without an intimate knowledge of the capabilities of the puppet and without weeks of watching the puppet in action, it was impossible to "write" these scenes in any but the sketchiest of ways. And here's where we began to realize how different our role was as puppeteers – different, that is, from the role of the actor. And what I am referring to here is the generative semiotics of our presence onstage.

From a semiotic perspective, the puppet's signing process is made up of two components: the design/making process and the manipulation process. The first is the signing potential that is built into the puppet itself. When designing the horses, for instance, Adrian had to decide which horse-like actions he would be able to include in the puppet's structure and *which not*. A thorough knowledge of the physical skeleton was necessary in order to be able to simplify the jointing and design a *workable* puppet. This was a process that required a deep intuitive understanding of the mechanical capabilities and ergonomics of the human hand and body and how the six hands of three puppeteers could be used to give the horse as much physical articulation as possible.

I would argue that this design process was an act of authorship, because Adrian's design built into the puppet the semiotic grammar of which the horse would be capable. In a sense, then, the puppet design is a meta-script, which the puppeteers must interpret, guided by director, choreographer, and puppet master. Andrew Macklin, of the University of New South Wales, sees this way of generating (authoring) meaning as being *corporeal*, as being *generated by the body* and not reducible to words:

> To create the puppet mechanics is to devise a way of interpreting, hence returning language to its roots in physically actualized discourse from which language is derived. So the puppet-maker who devises ways of articulating concepts of the script (written language) in movement language, is authoring meaning in an embodied language.
>
> (Andrew Macklin, pers. comm., 2008)

The second component of the horse's signing process is the expressive work of the manipulators themselves. Even though Adrian's horses are capable of a wide range of expression, *realizing* that expression through movement requires of the puppeteers the development of a complex set of coordinative skills both personally and as a group. The two main horses each require groups of three operators. A convincing individual horse with a character of its own can be created only by a formidable act of "group mind" – a level of coordination far beyond what a scriptwriter could predict.

Thus, we came to realize that *authoring* a role for the horses functioned at levels that didn't have much to do with the traditional script author. Much of this "authorial" work happened during periods of improvisation. During these periods, the scriptwriter effectively played the role of onlooker. Generally what he did was to observe the various sequences, and those that were approved by the director were sometimes described by the stage managers and incorporated into the working script used to rehearse the play. This was a different script fundamentally from the one published.

So *ex post facto*, the written text incorporates what, in fact, began as a movement text. This is what Juhani Pallasmaa might call the "haptic" text – the text of "active touch" and of the touching body moving through space.[1] The *War Horse* audiences are constantly wanting to know what the horses are thinking and feeling. Only by

Figure 5.2 The cast of *War Horse* at the New London Theatre (2009): puppets by Handspring Puppet Company. Photo: © Brinkhoff/Mögenburg

watching the smallest movements of tail and hoof can they hope to "read" these thoughts.

The authorial audience

Now let us also look at the phenomenon of the performed puppet play from the point of view of the audience. What happens to actors armed with words when they are sharing the stage with a puppet? We were astonished to see what happened in *War Horse* when the horse puppets shared the stage with actors. The audience quickly develops an affinity and fascination with the horses. They clearly want to understand what the horse is feeling and thinking and, as a result, they become avaricious readers of horse semiotics. Whatever the horse puppeteers do (from ear twitching, flank shivering, and eye-line alteration, to whinnying, nickering, and blowing), the audience hungers to interpret.

The audience thus experiences a strong feeling of empowerment. Spectators feel themselves to be in a new interpretive territory concerning the meaning of animals within the context of a theatrical event. There are no rules for such forms of interpretation, and thus the puppeteers give to the audience an *interpretive authority* that is not often imparted in more conventional forms of theatre. Therefore, it could be argued, the audience takes up an auxiliary authorial role as generators of meaning. The intensity of this interpretive focus has an unexpected result: the audience is so intently decoding the visual text that it may experience sections of the performance where the auditory dimension of the play is, as we say, bleached out. In a very real sense, the puppets are stealing the limelight.

The authority of breath

It may be said that there exist levels of authorship that arise neither in word nor in movement, but in stillness. We find that one of the most eloquent ways of communicating onstage is, indeed, not through movement but through such stillness or, more exactly, a *breathed* stillness. Only when the puppet is still and just perceived to be breathing is the audience able to read its thoughts and emotions. So, paradoxically, even in motionlessness there exists a "text" – the text of thought. This is truly an unwritten, an unwriteable text, one that is "authored" by the puppeteers manipulating the puppet and, to some extent, by the puppet designer/maker who engineers such subtleties into the puppet's mechanisms.

But now we are at a curious site of exchange between the performers and the audience as authors. Truly this is the *interplay*: a subtle realm of hermeneutic interchange between viewer and viewed, between actor and those acted upon, where meaning is being created, but we are not sure by whom. Breath and silence on the part of the puppet stimulate, in the minds of the audience, proposals as to the thoughts and emotions in the wooden puppet they are watching. These moments can be some of the most powerful experiences a puppet play produces. The audience, in noticing the tiny in breath and out breath of the puppet, enters into an empathetic relationship with the object that is being brought to life. This breathing is physical, yet it has a profound metaphorical power. This nonexistent substance (air) that is passing through this mechanical being represents the very essence of life: the soul.

Movement as thought[2]

Now we come to a counterintuitive proposal and one that seems to contradict the principle asserted above – namely, that in the puppet's *stillness* the audience can read its thoughts. This is, indeed, true. This is part of what in particle physics might be called "the weak force." However, parallel to this form of thinking (where the audience is really doing the thinking in that spectators "read" the thoughts of the puppet), there exists also a form of thinking which is, one could say, generated more actively by the puppeteer. This may be termed "the strong force" thinking and refers to the totality of movement the puppet makes. This assertion comes out of a phenomenological way of understanding and describing events in the world.

The assertion is that the movement is the thought. Here we are talking about an *embodied* form of thinking, of thinking *incarnate* – well, in the case of the puppet, thinking in and through wood. Here we assert that we refuse to make a separation between mind and body – that is, the mind that thinks and the body that moves. During an improvisation, therefore, we would assert that the puppeteer is using the puppet to *physically evolve ideas that are incommensurate with script and scriptwriting*.

This is thought given expression through gesture, timing, rhythm. Chaplin was the most eloquent and perhaps the clearest example of a performer whose thoughts were utterly embodied. Macklin quotes the philosopher Maxine Sheets-Johnstone, who refers to dance improvisation as an act of thinking: "In such thinking, movement is not a medium by which thoughts emerge but rather, the thoughts themselves" (Harré 1991: 29). Macklin observes:

> What phenomenology is saying is that the body thinks *before* language or concepts, it creates meaning in an immediate act, it is itself a language, both before verbal/written language and in a feedback loop, based on that very language. So when a puppeteer creates meaning with a puppet we have a language beyond language upon which meaning is based.
> (Andrew Macklin, pers. comm., 2008)

I have to admit, then, that we do, indeed, feel a fundamental tension in puppet theatre between the scriptwriter and the puppet manipulator. In a sense, we, the puppeteers, sometimes experience language as a form of repression of our work. Traditionally in the theatre, language asserts its supremacy as thought. However, we the puppeteers instinctively know that we possess a powerful alternate form of thought, and that this form is at least the equal of words.

The work of the puppet, therefore, can be seen implicitly as a rebellion against the word and against conventionalized forms of theatrical discourse. Perhaps this is why so many avant-garde artists have utilized this art form.[3] To grasp the origin of the thinking inherent in any puppet play and to understand how this thinking functions, we have to analyze the work that the puppet performs. We need to understand this process by which the performed play comes into being. Our inquiry has to come to grips with this work of the puppet and its manipulator, where meaning is generated more by process than by content, more by movement than by words. It is this process which reveals the workings of the play's thoughts. As Freud said of the *dreamwork*, so too is the puppet's movement in and through a performance a "disguised form of thought process" where the puppets use the modest gesture and the unassuming walk to embody the deepest meaning. This is where the puppets are doing their thinking and herein lies their authority.

Notes

This chapter is abridged by permission of the author from Jones, B. (2009) "Puppetry and Authorship," in J. Taylor (ed.) *Handspring Puppet Company*. Parkwood, South Africa: David Krut, 253–268.

1 For a discussion advocating touch and "hapicity" in architecture, see Finnish architect Pallismaa (2005).
2 For this section I am indebted to Andrew Macklin, who read an early version of this manuscript and made many insightful comments and recommendations.
3 There are many, as evidenced by *The Puppet Show*, the touring exhibition focusing on the influence of puppetry on contemporary artists, curated by Ingrid Schaffer and Carin Kuoni of the Philadelphia ICA. Willian Kentridge, the artist with whom we collaborated between 1991 and 2002, is one. The list is long and includes Pierre Huyghe, Laurie Simmons, Gavin

Turk, and Deborah Curtis and Nayland Blake. The cohort from an earlier period includes Paul Klee, Picasso, Miró, and Alexander Calder.

Works cited

Harré, R. (1991) *Physical Being: A Theory for Corporeal Psychology*. Oxford, UK, and Cambridge, MA: Blackwell Publishers.

Pallismaa, J. (2005) *The Eyes of the Skin: Architecture and the Senses*. London: John Wiley & Sons.

6
Petrushka's Voice
Alexander Gref and Elena Slonimskaya

Our theatre, Vagrant Booth,[1] has been studying traditional Russian puppet theatre for over 20 years. We focus on exploring traditional culture as it relates to today. We do not seek simply to insert traditional elements into contemporary theatre but rather to determine how traditional theatre can fully exist in the context of today's world. From this perspective, the Petrushka theatre is an ideal model for us. Our more than a decade of experience performing Petrushka shows before a variety of audiences – at universities, before children, in political clubs, before crowds on the streets of Moscow, London, Boston, etc. – has convinced us that the ancient Petrushka theatre is modern, relevant, and vibrant for contemporary audiences.

This chapter describes our role and philosophy in continuing the tradition of using a *pishchik* (swazzle), or voice modifier, in traditional glove-puppet theatre. We examine the role of the voice modifier in creating performance structure, as well as in composing performance rhythm and defining the nature of the central character. Finally, we suggest that the voice modifier is a "proto-instrument" that has been preserved in the theatre since human culture existed in a syncretic state.

The swazzle in Petrushka theatre

The voice of Petrushka is one of the most interesting and ancient tools of this theatre. Petrushka's laughter is absolutely memorable and distinctive enough to be heard above the polyphonic noise of the street. It is produced with a special tool – the voice modifier. Voice modifiers are rarely used in the puppet theatre today. This is probably due not only to the level of skill required to use them but also to an insufficient understanding of their role in performance. In our opinion, there is a sphere in which neglecting to use the traditional technique of modifying a puppet's voice distorts not only the form but also the meaning of the performance. Without using a swazzle, the main character of the traditional puppet theatre loses his connection with his archetype and with the entire history of the puppet theatre and becomes a simple character for children's shows.

There are two basic types of voice modifiers in world puppet theatre: mirlitones and reed aerophones (wind instruments). Mirlitones modify and intensify a sound produced by the artist's voice by means of a vibrating stretched membrane (Likhach 2001: 161). "Comb singing" is a well-known example of a simple mirlitone, as are the

Figure 6.1 Petrushka, Vagrant Booth Theatre. Photo courtesy of the authors

kazoo and the zobo.[2] Such mirlitones are used in the Turkish Karagöz theatre, in African puppet theatre (Darkowska-Nidzgorski and Nidzgorski 1998: 109), in Southeast Asia, and in the Tamil shadow theatre in India (Proschan 1981: 528).

In the Petrushka theatre and in Punch and Judy shows, reed aerophones are more widespread. Reed aerophones produce a sound by making a body of air vibrate as it passes through the reed (Keldysh 1990: 47). *Pischiks* or *govoroks* – the types of swazzles used in the Russian Petrushka theatre – have a reed that is made in the form of a thin membrane (usually cotton twill) stretched in the gap between two curved plates.[3] The principle is similar to that of blowing on a blade of grass stretched between the thumbs. However, the swazzle is placed in the mouth between the soft and hard palate so that it produces a rasping sound; at the same time, it allows the artist to articulate and to speak reasonably clearly while the actual vocal cords don't produce any sound. It also leaves the artist's hands free to manipulate the puppets. A well-trained artist can remove the swazzle and put it back into position with the tongue extremely quickly, alternating between the swazzled sound and the "normal" human voice, thus carrying on a dialogue between the characters at a rapid pace. The main distinctive feature of the swazzle is that sound vibrations are produced by the reed membrane, while the artist's vocal cords are not used; therefore, the vocalized sound becomes distorted and "artificial."

Speech, music, and rhythm

The voice modifier is not an especially suitable contrivance for delivering monologues; furthermore, it is not always possible to articulate all sounds distinctly while using a swazzle.[4] The distinctness of the speech produced with it depends on the construction of the swazzle, on the material from which it is made, on the tension of the membrane, and, of course, on the artist's individual skill. For this reason, questions about how to use this instrument, and, more importantly, why it is useful for the puppet theatre remain of primary importance.

It is common practice for hand-puppet theatres to include in their shows a character, sometimes called a bottler or musician, who serves as an interpreter or narrator and explains and comments on everything that happens on the stage. This narrator, who stands outside the booth both in the Petrushka theatre and in Iranian theatre (Solomonik 1990: 116, 126), but is hidden from view in Chinese hand-puppet theatre (Obraztsov 1957: 254–257), comments on the puppets' actions and explains words that are difficult to understand. The primary way in which the narrator interprets the puppet's speech is by repeating a puppet's phrases in interrogative form.[5] The following example is a dialogue from a puppet play from our theatre:

PETRUSHKA: How much?
MUSICIAN: How much does the horse cost?
GYPSY: One million!
MUSICIAN: One million?!
PETRUSHKA: You're nuts![6]

The role of the narrator in this scene is not only to comment on the puppet's actions and to explain otherwise hard-to-distinguish phrases distorted by the swazzle; the narrator also organizes the performance and provides a link between the puppets and the audience. As O. Darkowska-Nidzgorski writes: "The modification of the voice often makes speech difficult to understand; thus the presence of a narrator is essential" (Darkowska-Nidzgorski and Nidzgorski 1998: 112). She goes on to quote Nigerian puppeteer Moussa Mamane, who observes:

> The function of this kind of artist, who accompanies the entire performance from beginning to end, consists not only in the interpretation of the puppets' words, but in acting as the puppets' partner and messenger. This omnipresent person is always on the move; he is always fussing, sometimes addressing the puppets, sometimes the musician, and sometimes the audience. He interprets, asks, answers and comments; he asks for applause and encourages the audience to be generous. It is he who starts to dance or joins in when the puppets strike up a song.
> (quoted in Darkowska-Nidzgorski and Nidzgorski 1998: 112)

Similar behavior is common in many world traditions (Solomonik 1992: 20–24; Nekrylova 1988: 36).[7] However, the repetition of basic words is not the only way to facilitate a conversation between the puppet and the spectators; there is a range of sound patterns that accentuate the puppet's behavior and that are clear to an audience without verbal dialogue. Laughter, sobbing, sighs, and exclamations – all of these are the instruments of a puppet's speech that are strengthened by the puppet's artificial voice. Petrushka's laughter stands out in this regard. This laughter is a distinct characteristic of the puppet, not comparable to anything and absolutely irreplaceable; it is an inherent feature of the tradition, like Punch's enormous nose. This laughter supports almost every action of the puppet, shapes its character, explains its behavior in many aspects, and, finally, determines the puppet's relationship to other characters and with the audience. When the laughter is not heard, even for a short period, our audiences often look puzzled, as if all the sounds of the performance have been "shut off." A Petrushka performance's vocal range is essentially captured in the alternation between Petrushka's laughter and other sounds.

The swazzle and Petrushka slapstick should be considered an inseparable pair of musical instruments (wind and percussion), a pair that has a long history in the puppet theatre. In this regard, the role of the swazzle in shaping the performance is essential. The duet of swazzle and slapstick is the very music of the performance. This music is so self-sufficient, its rhythm is so clear, so complementary to the performance, and so full of rhythmic movement, that the spoken dialogue often seems unnecessary. "The fact that puppeteers around the globe use voice modifiers," Proschan writes, "suggests to me their profound (albeit unstated) understanding of how they work – that is, their awareness that speech itself is redundant, and that reduction in the sign and restriction of the signal are possible without sacrificing intelligibility" (Proschan 1981: 534). In our experience, this has been confirmed when we have played Petrushka shows before foreign audiences; when the audience laughs, there is no doubt that the stage actions are understood.

The melodic potential of the swazzle as a wind instrument is very diverse: the rhythmic, tonal, and timbral nuances allow for a wide expression of Petrushka's mood range. It is also possible to use swazzles for the mimicking of various sounds – for example, a bird singing or even a fart. We watched a performance of Indian theatre from Rajasthan performed by Puran Bhat, who held a *boli*, an Indian variant of a swazzle, between his teeth to accompany dancing puppets. Puran Bhat manipulated all the puppets, mimicking the energetic singing of the whirling puppet dancers with a voice ideally suited to the puppets, while at the same time, his *boli* was the leading instrument of the accompanying orchestra.[8]

A call from the other world

The question remains as to why the puppet theatre still insists on using this complex contrivance. Proschan has offered two explanations:

> A number of possible motivations are at work, to different degrees in each tradition. ... The distinctive sound of the voice modifier alerts audiences to the arrival of the puppeteers and the beginning of the performance, for example.
> Another ... is ... extremely important: the squeaky voice is inherently funny, especially to the children who often compose the largest part of the audience. ...
> (Proschan 1981: 541)

Half a century earlier, Soviet puppeteer Nina Simonovich-Efimova wrote something similar: "This broken, sharp whistle coming out of curtains that are waving because of its blow ... arouses the interest of the audience and makes the spectators concentrate their attention on the little stage" (Simonovich-Efimova 1980: 116).

We do not deny these conclusions but believe there are additional, more significant reasons to use a swazzle, an instrument particular to the puppet theatre. The modified voice belongs to a particular kind of puppet that has ties with an archaic, ancient theatre, though puppeteers and spectators don't always realize this. Petrushka's strange voice mentioned above – as well as his exaggerated nose, his hump, and his clothes – are all characteristics that separate him from other characters and set Petrushka against "this" world, the human world. By way of example, Darkowska-Nidzgorski's description of Nigerian puppet theatre identifies a connection between a modified voice and *the other world*:

> Listening to puppeteers from Niger and Nigeria, we noticed that all of them spoke in [the] same snuffling voice. ... According to anthropologists, this snuffling voice is connected with death ... so puppeteers' snuffling voices take on special significance. In this specific context, the puppeteer who produces "a voice of the other world" emphasizes the supernatural level of his art and its contrast to the world of living.
> (Darkowska-Nidzgorski and Nidzgorski 1998: 111)

The swazzle is a dual-purpose instrument for modulation of human speech and for musical accompaniment that has maintained its function and construction since the first records of its use in the early seventeenth century.[9] However, this "artificial" voice is also a "proto-instrument" that connects the puppet with the world beyond and with the syncretic period of human culture.

The nature of Petrushka performances changes fundamentally, depending on whether or not the puppeteer uses a swazzle. This is often the case in Russia, where the practice of Petrushka shows was interrupted for at least a half century under the Soviet regime, but also in England, where Punch has been "alive" for centuries. Being educated in the tradition of literary theatre, most contemporary Russian puppeteers pay attention only to the spoken dialogue of the characters published in texts of old puppet plays, forgetting that a folk performance is an evolution not only of text but also of music, sound, and image.[10] Many also neglect the fact that Petrushka's otherworldly voice drives the performance rhythmically and expresses the essence of the performance, creating a dialectic between a strange character "from another world" and the more recognizable characters of the comedy, those who represent human society and speak in "human" voices. Mamane has perhaps expressed this idea best: "I am the one who puts something into my mouth, but it is the thing I hold in my hand that makes me do it" (quoted in Darkowska-Nidzgorski and Nidzgorski 1998: 109). Those who work "inside the booth" have learned that the peculiar voice of the puppet belongs to the puppet and not to the puppeteer, and that this voice is from a world removed in place and ancient in time.

Notes

1 *Brodiachyi Vertep*: literally, "Wandering *Vertep*."
2 The kazoo and zobo are wind instruments that originated in Africa and are commonly used in US jazz bands (Likhach 2001).

3 We believe the ability of flexible material to change a tone's pitch, depending on the intensity of the air supply, to be one of the main reasons that wind instruments with flexible (not "hard") reeds in puppet theatre are so widespread. This construction gives the artist the ability to raise and lower the pitch of the puppet's voice by intensifying or lessening the air supply. Aerophones with "hard" reeds (such as a clarinet) exhibit such characteristics to a lesser degree.
4 I. Komarova and the authors of this essay conducted a number of experiments with Vagrant Booth Theatre studying the "phonetics of the swazzle" before coming to these conclusions.
5 Unfortunately, this method is rarely recorded in many documents of the past. As Nekrylova (2003: 27) observes: "As to precise records of lexical, visual, and playing parts of the performance, they simply don't exist."
6 All performance citations are from our own Vagrant Booth Petrushka production.
7 The narrator is one of oldest characters in the Petrushka theatre. We consider Petrushka to be a representative of the "other" world and the narrator a "link" between "that" world and the world of the living. Consequently, the meaning of the narrator transforms from "an interpreter" to "a ferryman." But the narrator's role, not limited to this, is so varied that it requires a special study that is beyond the scope of this chapter.
8 It should be noted that the performance had a prologue during which the puppets representing gods (who were larger than the other puppets) talked in human voices. Only during the main performance, when "real puppets" appeared, did they begin to sing in "puppet" voices.
9 We believe the swazzle to be a more ancient instrument, despite Proschan's observations that "The use of voice modifiers in folk puppetry is recorded in brief and tantalizing notices scattered throughout the historical and ethnographic treatments of puppetry" (Proschan 1981: 547). By way of evidence, he observes that puppet shows:

> ... in Seville in 1608 used a *cerbatana* ("pea-shooter" or "blow-gun") and Covarrubias ... in 1611 remarks on the use of a *pito* ("whistle") by the puppeteers of Castile, with an interpreter in front of the stage to repeat the lines. Turning to Italy, we learn ... that the seventeenth-century Pulcinella puppeteers used a *pivetta* (diminutive of *pivo*, "whistle") to recite the stories, with one puppeteer providing all the voices, or several, each one with a *pivetta* of a different size, providing the voices of the various characters. ... The earliest evidence from England is ambiguous: in Ben Jonson's *Bartholomew Fair* of 1614, there is a puppet-play-within-the-play, and the puppets are described as "neighing" and "whinnying" with a "treble creaking." But, the puppets' creaking is interpreted to the audience by Leatherhead, who repeats line by line what the puppets are saying. ... By the 1660's Punch had arrived in England, and his use of the swazzle or swotchel (from German *schwassl*, means "conversation, chatter") was firmly established.
>
> (Proschan 1981: 547).

10 Until now there haven't been any serious attempts to analyze records of Petrushka's performances in relation to the phonetic specifics of the swazzle. Several sketches recorded in the form of verbal dialogue could, in fact, simply be attempts of eyewitnesses to describe not only the aural but also the visual impression of the performance. Otherwise, when information is given by professional Petrushka players, they typically don't record details that seem obvious, such as repetition.

Works cited

Darkowska-Nidzgorski, O. and Nidzgorski, D. (1998) *Marionnettes et masques au coeur du théâtre africain* [*Puppets and Masks at the Heart of the African Theatre*]. Saint-Maur-de-Faussé, France: Sépia.

Keldysh, G. V. (ed.) (1990) *Muzykal'nyi entsiklopedicheskii slovar'* [*Musical Encyclopedic Dictionary*]. Moscow: Sovetskaia entsiklopediia.

Likhach, T. V. (trans.) (2001) *Muzykal'nye instrument mira*. Minsk, Belarus: Popurri. English edition: Diagram Group (1997) *Musical Instruments of the World: An Illustrated Encyclopedia*.

Nekrylova, A. F. (1988) *Russkie narodnye gorodskie prazdniki, uveseleniia i zrelishcha: Konets XVIII – nachalo XX veka* [*Russian Urban Folk Festivals, Amusements, and Performances: From the End of the 18th to the Beginning of the 20th Centuries*], 2nd edition. Leningrad, USSR: Iskusstvo.

——(2003) "Teatr Petrushki" ["The Petrushka Theatre"], *Traditsonnaia kul'tura* [*Traditional Culture*] 4(12): 26–47.

Nekrylova, A. F. and Savushkina, N. I. (ed. and intro.) (1988) *Fol'klornyi teatr* [*The Folk Theatre*]. Moscow: Sovremennik.

Obraztsov, S. (1957) *Teatr kitaiskogo naroda* [*Theatre of the Chinese People*]. Moscow: Iskusstvo.

Proschan, F. (1981) "Puppet Voices and Interlocutors: Language in Folk Puppetry," *Journal of American Folklore* 94: 527–555.

Simonovich-Efimova, N. (1980) *Zapiski Petrushechnika i stat'i o teatre kukol* [*Notes of a Petrushka Player and Articles on the Puppet Theatre*]. Leningrad, USSR: Iskusstvo.

Solomonik, I. N. (1990) "Traditsionnye perchatochnye kukly na Vostoke i v Rossii" ["Traditional Glove Puppets of the East and in Russia"], in O. I. Poliakova (ed.) *Chto zhe takoe kukol'nyi teatr?* [*What is Puppet Theatre?*]. Moscow: Souz teatralnykh deiatelei.

——(1992) *Traditsionnyi teatr kukol Vostoka. Osnovnye vidy teatra ob'emnykh form* [*Traditional Puppet Theatre of the East: The Primary Types of the Theatre of Three-dimensional Forms*]. Moscow: Nauka.

7
"Clouds Are Made of White!"
The Intersection of Live Art and Puppetry as an Approach to Postdramatic Children's Theatre

Rike Reiniger

In this chapter I will discuss and analyze my experiences with postdramatic children's theatre derived from live-art and puppetry traditions.

My artistic background as a theatre director and author is based on two rather contrary educational trainings. During the mid-1980s I spent time as an apprentice in a traditional hand-puppet company, the Hohnsteiner Puppentheater, which toured throughout Germany. I also studied directing for puppet theatre from 1987 to 1988 at the oldest puppetry school in Europe, the Academy of Performing Arts in Prague. After this conventional training I completed my drama degree at the University of Giessen, which has a special reputation for its exploratory approach combining innovative forms of theatre and live art.

When I became the director of a puppet theatre with an ensemble of six puppeteers in Bautzen, Saxony, in 2006, I tried to combine these two different traits in some of our performances. This approach was unusual in the field of theatre for very young audiences (ages two and up) but very successful.

Theatre for very young audiences – the development of a new genre

Theatre for an age group younger than four years old has long been thought not only impossible but also unnecessary, since children of that small age are unable to differentiate between an artistic and an everyday experience. Nevertheless, La Baracca, a children's theatre in Bologna, Italy, started to perform for very young children in the late 1980s. Roberto and Valeria Frabetti also organized the first international festival for this form of theatre: *Il Teatro e il nido* (Theatre and the Nursery) in 1989. At about the same time, theatre experiments for the youngest audience target group took place in France. Agnès Desfosses and Laurent Dupont, Phénomène Tsé-Tsé, and Compagnie Skappa! were some of the artistic protagonists there who also collaborated with psychologists and teachers in order to find a new theatrical language for infants. These performances in

Italy and France were the results of individual artistic efforts grounded by personal interests.

In Scandinavia, the Norwegian Ministry of Culture commissioned research into the cultural life of children, which found that small children and toddlers were living in a sort of cultural isolation (dan Droste 2011: 106). A national funding program to support art for small children was therefore set up in 1998: *Klangfugl – kulturformidling med de minste* (Glitterbird – Cultural Education for the Smallest). This national program was followed by the international project Glitterbird – Art for the Very Young in 2003. The aim of this European Union-funded project was to give children under the age of three opportunities to meet and experience art and to promote the idea that art should be a part of small children's lives (Os and Hernes undated).

The Scandinavian, Italian, and French performances began to be seen at international festivals, especially in the field of puppetry, like the Festival Mondial des Théâtres de Marionnettes in France and the FIDENA (Puppet Theatre of the Nations) festival in Germany. Theatre artists in Germany responded to their colleagues' efforts with curiosity but did not at first meet the challenge to work in this area themselves, perhaps because German theatre has been dominated by dramatic literature since the nineteenth century and because children's theatre had been shaped significantly by the socially conscious productions of the 1970s created by groups such as Grips Theater Berlin – which claimed that children's theatre should depict everyday-life conflicts and encourage young spectators to develop their own autonomy.

But in 2006, a *Theater von Anfang an!* (Theatre from the Beginning!) research project was started by the Kinder-und Jugendtheaterzentrum der BRD (German National Center for Children's Theatre) in Frankfurt. For more than two years, two state-supported theatres, two independent theatre groups, and some associated partners, together with theatre researchers and educators, studied theatre for audiences under the age of four. Two conferences, a study trip to Paris, a festival in Dresden, a book publication, and many new theatre productions were the results of this project, as well as an increasing openness to the idea of performing for a very young target group. Now, most of the children's theatres in Germany offer performances for toddlers and small children alongside their usual programming. Across Europe, the Small Size Network for the Diffusion of Performing Arts for Early Childhood has promoted the exchange of ideas on performing arts for very young audiences ever since the organization was initiated by Roberto Frabetti in 2005. The Small Size Network connects theatres in 12 European countries, from Great Britain to Romania, organizing workshops, publishing books and DVDs, cultivating funding resources, and facilitating cooperative projects.

Common practices of theatre for very young audiences

The majority of artists who perform for very young audiences have a children's- or puppet-theatre background; a few come from dance. Some common practices can be observed in most performances.

First there is the practice of exploration. Paralleling small children in their everyday life, the performers onstage explore basic materials, simple objects, and natural principles. These explorations could involve dough, fabric, wood chips, or balls of different sizes and such concepts as the forces of gravity, light, and sound. The materials, objects, or natural principles examined form a kind of frame in which stage action can develop a very simple story.

A second common practice in theatre for very young audiences is reduction. Scenography makes use of only a few distinct colors and basic forms. Elementary music and percussion are produced visibly onstage. Stage figures are limited to positive characters and clear emotional reactions such as surprise, love, sadness, or gaiety.

A third common practice involves the performers inviting the audience to the performance space at the beginning of the show, and even onstage at the end, to play with objects or to explore materials themselves. The boundaries between performer and audience, performance and play, and art and reality dissolve.

Mrs. Sun and Mr. Moon Make Weather

After this general survey, I would like to explain my personal artistic approach to theatre for very young audiences. For my first performance for two-year-olds, *Mrs. Sun and Mr. Moon Make Weather*, I invited interdisciplinary artist Otmar Wagner to work with our puppet company at the Deutsch-Sorbisches Volkstheater Bautzen (German-Sorbian People's Theatre Bautzen) in eastern Saxony. Wagner usually creates live-art performances, which until this point had never overlapped with children's theatre, whereas I had considerable experience with puppet theatre for children. Both of us, though, have a strong artistic connection to such historical avant-garde movements as Bauhaus and Dada, as well as to visual and object theatre. As an experimental performance artist, Wagner was immediately attracted to the idea of working for an audience that does not care for such theatre conventions as story, dialogue, or character and that always feels free to do whatever it likes: an audience of two-year-olds.

We chose the weather as a motif for our performance. Weather, as an everyday reality and an everyday surprise, would be part of the audience's horizon of experience and therefore a good starting point for our theatrical adventure. Wagner invented a performance environment that included designed objects, such as a human-sized flower, waves cut from wood, a wind machine, and a bike that did not move. Next to these objects he arranged a model stage that could be video-projected onto the actual stage, and installed an overhead projector for live rear projection onto three screens to create holographic effects. He also made two-dimensional puppets from photographs of the production's two puppeteers. Through this spatial setting he added the aspects of "big and small" and "material and projection" to the original motif.

The work process began with a two-week phase of exploring and improvising with the material. None of us knew, and none of us wanted to know, what results the exploration would finally have. The puppeteers were, of course, mainly improvising with the performance possibilities of objects and space, not simply animating the

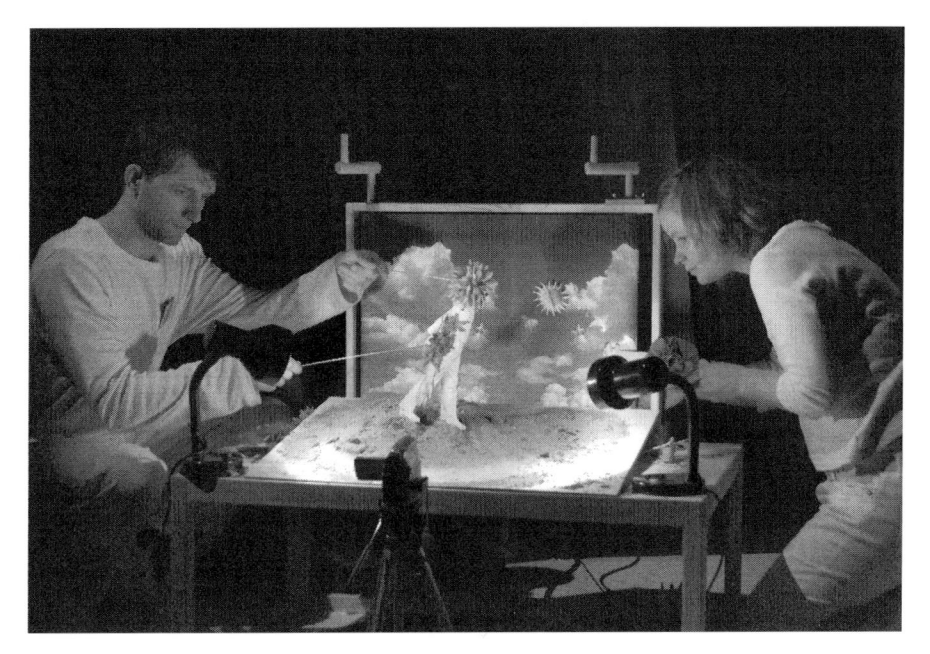

Figure 7.1 Mrs. Sun and Mr. Moon Make Weather, Deutsch-Sorbisches Volkstheater Bautzen (2007): performers Christian Pfütze and Christiane Kampwirth with the model stage. Photo courtesy of the author

rudimentary puppets. We collected these possibilities without initially questioning their sense or non-sense related to the performance.

In the next phase, our directing team (Otmar Wagner and me) considered dramaturgic structure. We decided to define the stage setting as a weather laboratory, with a chief meteorologist, Mrs. Sun, and her assistant, Mr. Moon. And we agreed on a four-section dramaturgic structure to parallel that of the four seasons. The results of our improvisations were assigned to the seasons and linked to the work in the weather laboratory. The opening of the human-sized flower, for example, became part of the spring section; a puppet's dive into the wooden cutout waves belonged to the summer section; the shadow projection of dry leaves and drops of rain became part of the autumn section; and a dance with human-sized snowflakes was part of the winter section.

In terms of language and sound, we were interested in using words not to convey meaning, transmit information, or promote a story, but instead we played with language in the same explorative way as we used material objects. We collected sayings and folk songs about the four seasons. And we asked Jossi, a not-yet four-year-old boy, to explain weather phenomena. Happily, he explained everything we asked him about, coming up with the most poetic texts we could have wished for: "A rainbow feels wet like rain and a rainbow can eat raisins. On the rainbow I easily walk to my grandma who has died," he told us, and "clouds are made of white."

Sayings, folk songs, and Jossi's contemplations were added to the succession of scenic events. We thereby created a dramaturgic structure that did not tell a story

Figure 7.2 Mrs. Sun puppet (2007). Photo courtesy of the author

Figure 7.3 Performer Susan Weilandt and the rainbow (2007). Photo courtesy of the author

(even though we did invent the stage characters of Mrs. Sun and Mr. Moon) but was instead composed of a series of short actions or happenings. I call this a "dramaturgy of incidents."

In the third working phase we conducted regular rehearsals in which the puppeteers developed their characters and rehearsed the course of events and the technicians practiced running the show smoothly. We titled the production *Mrs. Sun and Mr. Moon Make Weather*.

The performance and its audience

Having discussed the working process, I will now focus on the perception of the performance. The target audiences were children aged two or older, but such children, of course, do not attend a theatre performance by themselves; the adults who accompany them have to be taken into account too. Different from shows for older children, the very young audience needs considerably more adult attendants. On average, about two attendants were responsible for each group of not more than ten children attending from nursery schools. Both parents sometimes accompanied one child, especially on weekend performances. Consequently, our audiences consisted of about one-third adults and two-thirds small children: a rather heterogeneous mixture!

Adults think language is an important means of conveying information; but two-year-olds understand an average of 150 words and talk in sentences of not more than three words. Adults restrain themselves, especially in public; but children expect their needs to be met at once and they show their emotions the moment they arise. Adults know how to behave in a theatre, do not move from their seats, and keep silent; children of that small age have never before been to a theatre, have a natural urge to move about, and their expressions of emotion are mostly accompanied by sounds.

Of course, there are many more differences between an audience of adults and of children, but the most important yet to be mentioned is the following: adults are used to having to understand the meaning of a theatre performance. Sometimes that even inhibits them from attending a performance that they might regard as too complicated. They would rather think that they themselves are too ignorant to understand than to question the notion that a performance has to be understood. Children, on the other hand, especially very small children, do not care to understand any meaning. Children care for the sensuous experience of a theatre performance and the emotions that this experience arouses. They *sense* the meaning of art.

We met those differences within the audience by avoiding pretense. Everything was real in our stage setting. All the objects were clearly displayed, all use of technical equipment was openly shown, and the two-dimensional photographic puppets never claimed to be alive. Through the soft use of lights, there was no spatial partition between the seats of the spectators and the stage. We had real people onstage. The two puppeteer/actors never acted as if they were somebody else. Mrs. Sun and Mr. Moon were characters who evolved from the actors' personalities. We performed in real time. There was no difference between the 45-minute duration of the performance and the time onstage. We had a 10-minute break, during which the actors and the children ate fruit together.

These aspects do not seem to describe a typical children's puppet show, but the small children absorbed the whole situation happily. They let themselves be carried away by the beauty of the stage, the rhythm of language and music, their sympathy for Mrs. Sun and Mr. Moon, the excitement of every new incident happening onstage, and the humor and surprise. They simply integrated Mr. Moon's dance with a man-sized flower or a statement like "clouds are made of white" into their life experience. It was interesting that the children's example helped the adults to adjust to a new experience. The children enjoyed themselves. And since there was not just a simple story being acted onstage but instead a whole world of things to discover for the adults as well, they felt free to connect with their own enjoyment too.

Current trends

A small anecdote might illustrate the fact that experimental work in a conventional German children's theatre is not always so easy. In another production Otmar Wagner and I created, *Theo Tinkerer Invents the Hare*, the title character, Theo, builds a bizarre machine that can make popcorn for the entire audience during the performance. However, the artistic director of Dresden's state-funded children's theatre (Theater junge Generation) censored this idea, claiming that we had to teach children how to behave in a theatre, where popcorn eating certainly did not belong!

Nevertheless, *Mrs. Sun and Mr. Moon Make Weather* has been performed approximately 100 times since its premiere in February 2007. It was part of the Theatre from the Beginning! project and is documented in *Theater von Anfang an!: Bildung, Kunst und frühe Kindheit* (*Theatre from the Beginning! Education, Art and Early Childhood*), an anthology edited by Gabi dan Droste (2009). Although parallels between theatre for very young audiences and performance art have often been stated (Taube 2006: 6), *Mrs. Sun and Mr. Moon Make Weather* was, in fact, one of the first collaborations between a performance artist and a children's theatre in Germany and has broadened the understanding of theatre for very young audiences.

Berlin's Theater an der Parkaue, a municipal theatre for children and young people, is currently the greatest proponent for the development of experimental children's theatre and regularly collaborates with performance artists and theatre groups such as Showcase Beat Le Mot, a group of performers (graduates of the University of Giessen's theatre department) who have designed a groundbreaking series of productions for children. The artists of Showcase Beat Le Mot usually start off with well-known children's books or fairy tales, such as "Robber Hotzenplotz" or "The Brementown Musicians," using them freely as material for playful, surprising, and provocative live-art performances that are loved by children and adults alike. Theater an der Parkaue is also devoted to the development of crossover productions of dance and children's theatre.

I would like to conclude with some observations about these new forms of postdramatic children's theatre. The performances certainly are all individually different, but they have a special quality in common: postdramatic children's theatre is perceived in a nonintellectual way. There is no need to decode any meaning, there are no morals to be judged, and there are no conventions to comply with; therefore, adults are not more capable of understanding the performance than small children. There is just the nonhierarchical sensuous theatre experience, a common adventure for all spectators in the otherwise increasingly more fragmented society of today.

Works cited

dan Droste, G. (ed.) (2009) *Theater von Anfang an! Bildung, Kunst und frühe Kindheit*. Bielefeld, Germany: transcript.
——(2011) *Theater von Anfang an! Reflexionen und Positionen für die Praxis*. Frankfurt/Main, Germany: Kinder-und Jugendtheaterzentrum (KJTZ).
Os, E. and Hernes, L. (undated) "Glitterbird – Art for Children under Three: Welcome," <http://www.dansdesign.com/gb/articles/20_07_04.html> (accessed September 14, 2013).
Taube, G. (2006) "First Steps – Erste erträge" in *Zu ästhetischen Eigenarten des Theaters für die Allerkleinsten* [*On the Aesthetic Characteristics of Theatre for the Very Smallest*], <http://www.helios-theater.de/fileadmin/datensammlung/dokumente/Dokumentation_First_Steps_Taube.pdf> (accessed November 26, 2013).

8
Movement Is Consciousness
Kate Brehm

I recently had to make new business cards. And I thought, you know, when I tell people I'm a puppeteer, although they are excited about it, I never feel like they know what I do. Oh *they* think they know what I do, but I ultimately feel misunderstood. So I decided to put something else on my business cards. But what? What do I *really* do? Here is my solution:

Movement is Consciousness.

That's what puppetry is, right? The movement of an inanimate doll breathes life into its soul; the translation of objects through space tells a story; a sudden break in a crescendo of objects swaying together makes meaning. So where did that phrase come from? I derived it from *Cinema 1: The Movement-Image* by Gilles Deleuze (1983 [1986]: 21). But Deleuze isn't talking about puppetry; he is talking about the eye of the camera.

Camera-consciousness/visual storytelling

When a movie camera travels through space while filming, it dictates a viewpoint, a consciousness. The eye of this camera, the camera-consciousness (Deleuze 1983: 77), provides an opportunity for an objective viewpoint outside of the scene. The audience can relate to a character's viewpoint, or they can relate to this outside, godlike viewpoint, which moves through the scene, zooms in on details, or follows the trajectory of a particular character. This is the first law of cinema, the mobile camera. The storytelling possibilities created by this camera-consciousness are fantastic.

As I slowly became obsessed with *Cinema 1*, a realization hit me like a bolt of lightning: film theory has created 100 years of critical writing on visual storytelling, and what is puppetry if not visual storytelling! I was very excited. Diving into film theory, I read and reread *Cinema 1* as a sort of manual of techniques to be applied to live puppetry. And as a puppeteer, I couldn't help but start to conceive a new show. The first thing I did was pick a title: *The Eye Which We Do Not Have*. It was easy; it came straight from the book (Deleuze 1983 [1986]: 83).

Frames

The first concept to catch my attention was framing (something very viable to and already utilized in puppetry). What elements are inside the frame? Outside the frame? Is the frame saturated with elements? Or does it produce a "rarefied image," where the "accent is placed on a single object," like Hitchcock's all-white close-up of a jar of milk? (Deleuze 1983 [1986]: 13). As I got excited about framing, I realized that I had read quite a bit about it in another context: comics.

The discussion about visual storytelling and frames in the world of comics is, most notably, led by Scott McCloud in his book *Understanding Comics: The Invisible Art* (McCloud 1993: 60–117). Here, too, the discussion addresses content inside and outside a frame, but it also addresses the frame itself. What storytelling capabilities do frames have by how they are arranged, their distance from one another, and their size and shape? A long frame can suggest a long time! An excessive amount of space between frames can suggest an excessive amount of time between moments.

I was gripped by inspiration! I started to design a puppet stage for my new show (see Figures 8.1 and 8.2). The stage would itself transform to create constantly

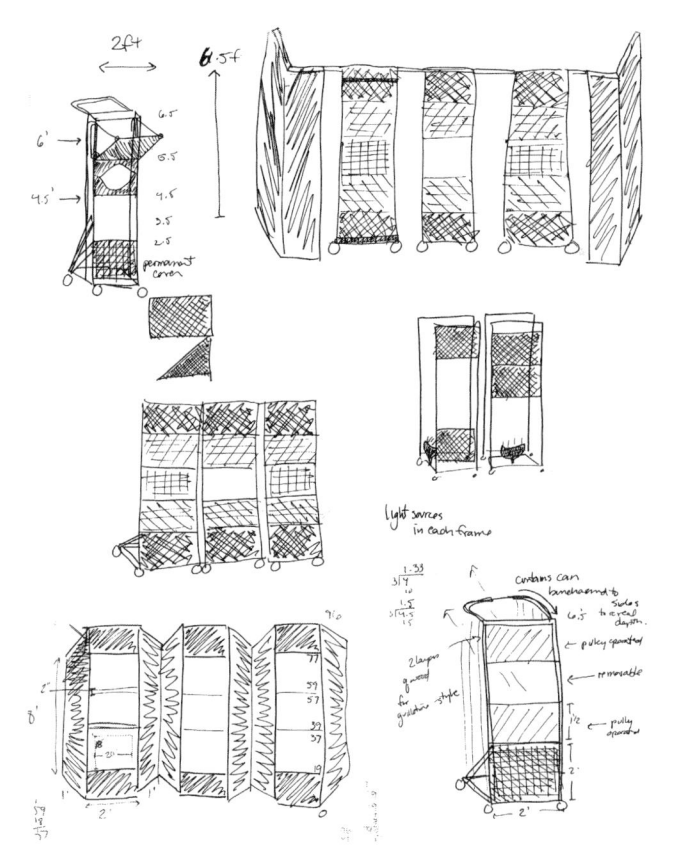

Figure 8.1 Early sketches of the performing scenery (which itself functions as a puppet) and its transformational frame: designed by Kate Brehm. Image courtesy of the author

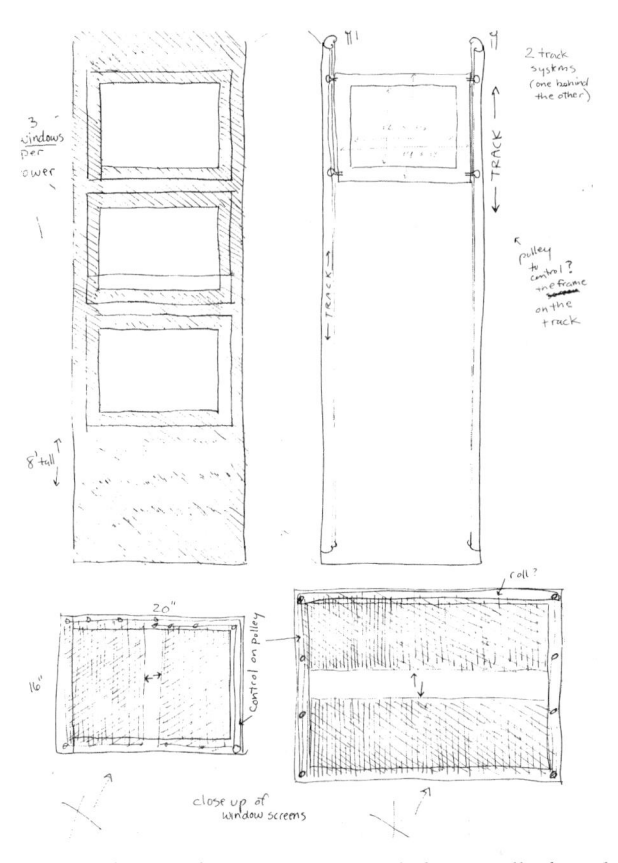

Figure 8.2 Later sketches of the performing scenery, including a wall of windows: designed by Kate Brehm. Image courtesy of the author

different framings. Ultimately, it was designed with six windows, which can each be blacked out individually, so as to create frames of various shapes and sizes. A column of three open windows reads like one long frame. Carefully choreographing the closing and opening windows reads as one frame moving through space. The action behind the windows can move with the frame, as if translating through space, or the frame can reveal different aspects of one large scene, like the roving eye of a camera.[1]

Character

I wanted to use other cinematic techniques discussed by Deleuze too: affection images, action images, and montage. In order to do this, I'd need some objects and people. I really like objects, and cinema theory helped me to realize that I don't need to have characters in my puppet show to drive its action. The consciousness of the camera itself, the viewpoint created by the movement of the camera, can drive the action. But it also convinced me that the connection one can create between an anthropomorphic figure puppet and an audience is nothing to be sniffed at. An audience can relate to a character in deep, meaningful ways. Even though part of me wanted to make an entire puppet show only about furniture, I decided a woman would be the main character of *The Eye Which We Do Not Have*.

The close-up

I'm interested in affect because I want to provoke in my audience an experience of pure sensation, of understanding, of "getting it" and connecting. The affection-image as described by Deleuze "is power or quality considered for themselves, as expresseds. ... These are qualities or powers considered for themselves, without reference to anything else, independently of any question of their actualization" (Deleuze 1983 [1986]: 99–100). In other words, the affection-image is about feeling a particular way – for example, feeling driven or inspired to action. However, the affection-image is not about the action, it is about that feeling of inspiration itself. Pure affect is out of time and place; it belongs to the category of the possible. "It expresses the possible without actualizing it" (Deleuze 1983 [1986]: 101). The affection-image values the power of simple expression. The expression of qualities is itself the point of an affection-image.

The reason I need both objects and people to fully explore affection-images is because they come in two variations. First there is the close-up, which requires a face or a character. It is the definitive way to express affect in cinema. Deleuze spends a lot of time clarifying two different kinds of close-ups: the face can reflect *qualities* or express *powers*. A reflecting face gazes upon something, "thinks about something, is fixed on an object," and *reflects* the qualities of admiration, astonishment, or wonder. "Sometimes, on the contrary, [a face] experiences or feels something" and *expresses* itself through an intensive series of "micro-movements." For example, a face might first express fear, then understanding, and finally acceptance, taking the viewer through an internal experience (Deleuze 1983 [1986]: 89–93).

But with puppets? How is any reflecting or expressing accomplished with the fixed face of a puppet? Well, we've all seen it happen, seen a puppet think and feel. Subtle movements, a change of angle of the face, a slow blink of the eyes: these all allow an audience to project an internal experience into the face of a puppet. Deleuze seems to understand the ability of a fixed face to change, as puppets do. "A very small change of direction of the face varies the relationship of its hard and tender parts, and so modifies the affect. ... It is by turning towards – turning away that the face expresses the affect, its increase and decrease" (Deleuze 1983 [1986]: 108).

The "qualisign"

So what about objects? I am excited about objects! Can they produce affect? Yes. The affection-image is not specific to faces. The close-up of a face successfully creates an affection-image not because it is human but because it is outside of a specific space or time and therefore able to purely express. Even though an expressed affect may be caused by or extracted from a particular space-time (like an empty school in the summer or a quiet hospital at night), the "power" of anger, for example, or the "quality" of victimhood is not actualized in the determined space-time.

This brings me to the second kind of affection image, the "qualisign": a scene or object that expresses pure powers and qualities. To accomplish this expression, the scene or object needs to become disconnected from its determinate space-time. The stereotypical onset of rain when a main character is crushed by emotion is not meant as a description of the science of rain. Rather, reflections in puddles, an endless downpour, or a slow drip express affect. This rain is eternal rain. It is out of space, out of time. It conveys affect, not action (Deleuze 1983 [1986]: 113–114, 123).

An affective object is an exciting way to think about object puppetry. An example of typical object puppetry would be a fork that walks around and looks at things or a pail that loses its shovel. These are thinking and feeling characters that happen to be objects without traditional faces or body parts. Alternatively, I'm excited to explore object puppetry where conveying affect, rather than character, is the intent. In *The Eye* ... , I use a staircase, central to the representation of the main character's psychosis, and disconnect it from reality by presenting it as a large white sheet with only parallel black lines to suggest steps. Rotating it while the main character hovers in front separates it from functionality and a determinate space. And, hopefully, it conveys affect.

How a character handles an object is another way to derive emotional impact. In such instances, the object functions as a symbol. The way it is handled reveals something about the character, the puppeteer, the object, or even the director of the piece. In *The Eye* ... , the central woman cuts out paper dolls.[2] Her handling of the scissors reveals something about her character (she is destructive). It also reveals something about the story (she has and will destroy something). And perhaps it reveals a viewpoint of the director (repression of female sexuality is destructive). The scissors create an emotional link between a "permeating situation and an explosive action" (Deleuze 1983 [1986]: 163). Importantly, though, handling the object is an action, therefore making it not an affection-image. We have arrived at the action-image.

Action-images

At this point I can no longer ignore something I often try to ignore: story. I admit I am, and have been for a long time, averse to story. Narrative is never the first thing I think about when I'm making a new show, never the driving force behind my inspirations. But Deleuze is very analytical about it! He discusses story like an entertaining puzzle or blocks that I can rearrange. No gooey mess. He calls these blocks the "action-image."

Two major elements make up the action-image: first, the *milieu*, or situation that encompasses everyone and everything in a film – powers and qualities plus a state of things that actualizes them; and, second, *modes of behavior* – the way in which people behave naturally within this milieu and embody the powers and qualities associated with it. In a particular story, the milieu and the modes of behavior may function in a correlative way or antagonistically. The behavior of a character can serve the milieu and be at peace with it (a police officer walks into a police station), or the character's behavior may be disjunctive to the milieu (a police officer walks into the station belligerent and drunk).

The action-image also includes *forces* that challenge the characters. The actualized powers and qualities from the affection-images become these forces. For example, in

The Eye ... , the lead character is silent, secretive, troubled, and anxious. These powers and qualities are actualized in her behavior when she is driven to repeatedly sneak up the stairs to a large looming door. She fearfully opens it to find a bed in various states of disarray. This obsessive action is a force that challenges her. She must reckon with her own drive to obsess.

Montage

The last essential cinematic technique I want to discuss is montage. The main thing to realize about montage is that it isn't only the scene set to go-get-'em music where the cheerleader pulls her act together. Montage is every single cut in a film. Early film-makers realized they could create a sense of movement and morph time by placing noncontinuous shots one after the other (much like comics were already doing). The mind of the viewer does the work to connect what is represented in one shot to the next. For example, the viewer discerns that a close-up of a face followed by a long shot represents what that character is seeing. This is very similar to puppetry: the audience fills in the unexpressed *why* when a puppet moves, thereby creating its thoughts and feelings.

But there's more. Montage takes cinema beyond the roving eye of the camera, the camera-consciousness, which was itself revolutionary. All of those images are in relation to one privileged viewpoint: the camera. With montage that singular viewpoint explodes. Montage allows the viewer to connect things and ideas that are otherwise beyond any singular viewpoint. An audience will make associations between the Swedish government and a butterfly, for example, if a film shows images of them in sequence. Montage is a viewpoint "without boundaries or distances." It is "the eye which we do not have" (Deleuze 1983 [1986]: 183).

Finally, time. I take particular interest in how one can convey a sense of time to an audience. This is where film and comics come together. These arts of sequence and framing can create simultaneous time, expanded time, contracted time, and eternal time. The shift from close-up to long shot must happen in sequence, but the viewer understands it as happening simultaneously. One single moment can extend and extend until it takes up an entire two-hour film. A sunset over the desert can represent a man's entire lifetime or the Earth's lifetime or the eternity of everything humans will never know in a lifetime.

This accumulation of shots and cuts creates change in a whole over time. This is montage. It is a film's consciousness. It is what feels different at the end than at the beginning. THIS. This is what I have been after for all of my life in the theatre, a discussion of the technical means for creating affective holistic change through design.[3]

Liveness

In conclusion, I'd like to address one question I never want to be asked: why don't you just make a movie? Answer: I don't want to work with the palette of a screen. I like three dimensions. I like to present an illusion and reveal its device simultaneously. But mainly, it's because I'm interested in *liveness*, that tangible sense of the real, things in space, the present, the now. I don't want to make movies; I just want to steal all of cinema's tricks. Hitchcock said suspense is created when an audience knows something that the character in a movie does not (cited in Gottlieb 1995: 113). There is always suspense in live puppetry, because both the audience and the puppeteers know what the puppets do not.[4]

Notes

1 See <http://tinyurl.com/k29yhyq>, particularly from 1:15–2:00.
2 See <http://tinyurl.com/ljf576j>, particularly from 1:25–3:30.
3 I don't have space in this chapter to discuss the long list of specific montage techniques. However, I recommend reading Eisenstein (1949 [1977]: 72–83) and Deleuze (1983 [1986]: 30–57).
4 *The Eye Which We Do Not Have* premiered in May 2013 in Brooklyn, New York, at Standard Toykraft. Video footage of the completed puppet show is available online at <http://tinyurl.com/mvmkb3r>.

Works cited

Deleuze, G. (1983) *Cinema 1: The Movement-Image*, trans. H. Tomlinson and B. Habberjam (1986), reprint. London: Continuum, 2005.

Eisenstein, S. (1949) *Film Form: Essays in Film Theory*, trans. and ed. J. Leyda, reprint. San Diego, CA: Harcourt Brace & Company, 1977.

Gottlieb, S. (ed.) (1995) *Hitchcock on Hitchcock: Selected Writings and Interviews*. Berkeley, CA: University of California Press.

McCloud, S. (1993) *Understanding Comics: The Invisible Art*, reprint. New York, NY: Harper Perennial, 1994.

9
The Eye of Light
The Tension of Image and Object in Shadow Theatre and Beyond

Stephen Kaplin

The spirit in the flame

This chapter articulates some of the essential aspects of shadow theatre performance and how the root of this ancient performance genre reflects upon the physical and metaphysical properties of light. To do so effectively, it is necessary to blend the languages of the physicist, the Kabbalist, and the artist, since shadow theatre as a performance medium is located at the nexus of scientific, mystical, and aesthetic practices.

Light underpins the very structure of the physical universe. On this both mystics and scientists seem to concur. The biblical account of creation given in Genesis 1:3 cites God's first utterance as "Let there be Light." And there it was. The emergence of this Primal Light is described with painterly precision in the *Zohar* (*The Book of Splendor*, a key text of Jewish Kabbala written by Moses De Leon in the thirteenth century):

> Within the most hidden recess a dark flame issued from the mystery of *Eyn Sof* ["without end"], the Infinite, like a fog forming in the unformed. ... From the innermost center of the flame sprang forth a well out of which colors issued and spread upon everything beneath, hidden in the mysterious hiddenness of *Eyn Sof*. ... It could not be recognized at all until a hidden supernal point shone forth under the impact of the final breaking through.
> (cited in Scholem 1949: 27)

Contemporary astrophysicists have conceived of cosmogenesis in surprisingly similar metaphoric language. They describe the moments after the Big Bang, when a fierce, roiling pinpoint of energy sprang into existence and expanded explosively across 10 or 11 dimensions (depending upon who's counting). In less than a second, the unified forces of space/time/gravity tore apart and unfurled to fill an area the size of the solar system – an unbelievably dense ball of plasma, hotter than the interior of a star. Space itself glowed brilliantly in every direction and from every point so that not a trace of shadow existed from one end of the newborn universe to the

The Eye of Light-- The Tension of Image and Object in Shadow Theatre and Beyond

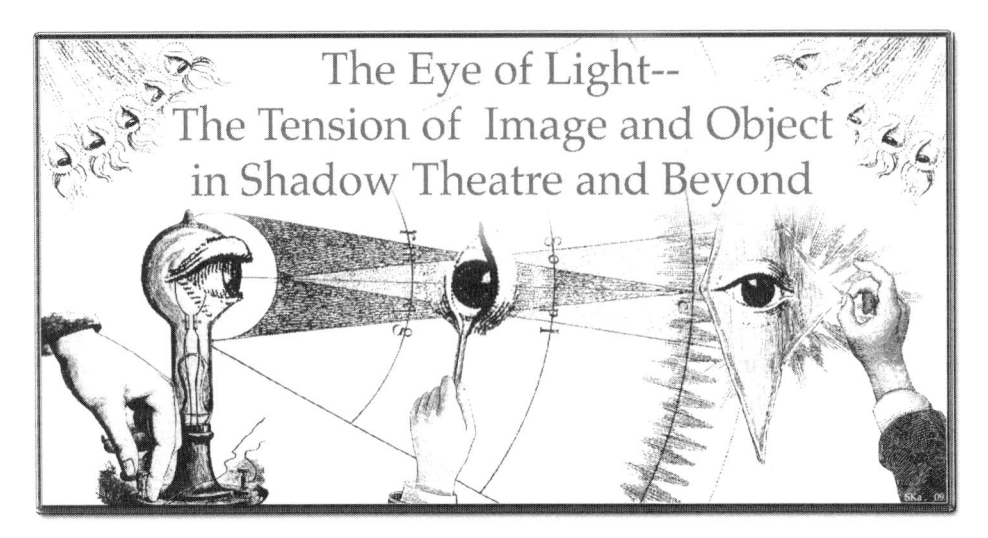

Figure 9.1 Photo montage created by and courtesy of the author

other. Over eons the cosmos cooled and darkened; yet even today, several dozen billion years after the fact, the energy imprint of those first fiery moments of cosmic birth can be detected by our most sensitive radio-telescopic instruments.

Shadow theatre references both of these cosmic narratives. Just as light oscillates between matter and energy states (depending upon how it is observed and measured), the shadow image, spun out of light and its absence, imbued with breath and motion, shifts effortlessly between spiritual realms and the physical plane – an apt model for the human soul/body construct and a perfect performance medium for deep philosophical discourse. How traditional shadow theatre functions as a transmission medium for sacred cultural material is evident in many of the oldest surviving genres of Asian shadow performance – Indian *tholu bommalata*, Thai *nang yai*, and Indonesian *wayang kulit*. The latter is especially demonstrative of how shadow theatre can delineate a schematic cosmic map: the white screen represents the field of physical action, illuminated by the radiance of the Sun; in the middle of the field stands the *kayon*, the Tree of Life; and on either side of the *dalang* (the presiding priest/performer) ranks of shadow figures are arranged according to their relationship to these two polarities of spiritual energy. Likewise, Chinese shadow performance is deeply rooted in both shamanic rituals for communicating with the dead and in Buddhist religious beliefs.

While an affinity for sacred discourse is found across many genres of traditional puppetry, shadow theatre differs fundamentally from other forms of puppet performance because it is not the performing object upon which audience attention is focused but the object's image as it appears projected onto a translucent screen. The physical object and its projected image pull apart as the puppet figure is moved away from the focal plane.

This is critical in understanding the technical aspects of shadow theatre. The image/object gap can be creatively manipulated with various mechanical devices and filters – such as lenses. Since glass, like water, refracts the path of light, a precisely curved arc of smooth, polished glass (such as a plano/convex lens used in theatre lighting instruments) will focus a wide beam of light down to a narrow shaft. A series of lenses can focus a sharp image some distance from its source. These coherent beams can be directed to fall onto photosensitive receptors inside a camera, making the image suitable for transmission over even wider spaces.

Technical mediation increases the distance in space and time that these patterns of light and motion can be transmitted. Modern forms of electronic image broadcasting – film, video, and computer-generated media – require enormous corporate and industrial infrastructures to manufacture and operate the imaging and broadcasting equipment, and to create, perform, edit, produce, and market content for its intended public. In contrast, shadow puppetry maintains hands-on, physical contact between performer and object, as well as real-time, unmediated, line-of-sight connections between object, image, and audience.

The elements of shadow performance

The shadow image is the product of light flowing directly through and around the performing object onto a focal plane. This triad of elements is intimately entwined so that it is hard to refer to one without the others. To gain a clear understanding of the craft, however, it is worth teasing the elements apart and observing their individual characteristics closely.

Light source

The flow of light impeded in some manner gives birth to the shadow image. Therefore, the precise shape of the illuminating source is of particular importance to the definition of the image. The open flame of the *blenchong* lamp used in Javanese *wayang* performance hangs directly above the *dalang*'s head, about an arm's length away from the screen. Its light flickers with every passing breeze, imparting a soulful animation to the shadow images. The effect is similar to that described by the French philosopher Gaston Bachelard:

> Space moves in the flame; time is active. Everything trembles when the light trembles. Is not the becoming of fire the most dramatic and the most alive of all becomings? The world moves rapidly if it is imagined on fire. Hence the Philosopher can dream everything – violence and peace – when he dreams of the world before his candle.
>
> (Bachelard 1961 [1988]: 22)

In contrast to the dynamic shadow produced by a living flame, the steady, brilliant illumination of an artificial light creates a harder umbra that exactly fits the profile of the bulb's filament: a tiny, pinpoint light source (for example, that produced by an LED or a halogen projector bulb) casts a crisp, hard-edged shadow; an elongated light source (e.g., a fluorescent light) creates blurry and diffuse shadows; likewise, multiple light sources will cast overlapping images. Single-point light sources make possible the amplification of the shadow image to many times the scale of the object producing them. A xenon arc lamp, of the type used by Larry Reed's ShadowLight Productions (which makes an incredibly brilliant light from a controlled electrical sparking), can project a massive shadow some 30 feet wide from a relatively small object positioned a foot or so away from the lamp. The size of the light source and its distance from the screen affect the depth of field in which the shadow figure can play, while still remaining relatively in focus. How the light is concentrated or reflected will also affect the quality of shadow cast.

Although in traditional shadow theatres the light source is passive, this is not always the case for many contemporary shadow theatres. Herte Schonewolf's seminal book on modern shadow puppetry technique *Play with Light and Shadow* (Schönewolf 1968) refers explicitly in its title to this change in emphasis. The Italian company Teatro Gioco Vita has developed this idea in performance to the point where the light sources – handheld halogen lamps – are as meticulously animated as the relatively static, cutout shadow figures. The artful choreography of these lights creates images that pan and zoom in and out like a camera.

Shadow figure

In its most elemental form, the shadow figure is defined by the contours of its edges and perforations. Light from the lamp, together with the contoured silhouette of the figure, creates a simple binary composition of black and white. To add intermediate shades of gray or color to the image, one must consider the molecular structure of the material composing the shadow figure. The manner by which materials transmit, bend, absorb, or scatter various frequencies of light gives them their particular qualities of transparency, opacity, refraction, and color. The light-transmission characteristics of different materials are what give the shadow designer a wide-ranging palette with which to paint the image. Most solid materials randomly scatter light passing through them, therefore creating opaque shadows. However, materials with extremely regular crystalline or molecular structures (such as glass or certain plastics) can appear virtually transparent.

One of the oldest materials for the manufacture of shadow figures is animal hide. Opaque in its natural form, it becomes translucent by a laborious process of stretching, scraping, and pounding. The resulting parchment makes a marvelously rich and varied shadow image that is tinted warm ochre or russet depending upon the animal from which it came and the skin's thickness. Its organic irregularity makes it quite different from man-made materials, such as vinyl, acetate, or polycarbonate plastics, products of industrial manufacturing whose utterly uniform molecular structure and surface smoothness results in a sheer, even transparency.

The edges of the shadow figure define the graphic shape of the shadow, so there can be no reliance on the subtlety of three-dimensional modeling of form to assist in revealing the figure's dramatic character. For this reason, the faces of most traditional figures are designed in profile or in a cubistic, three-quarter view. It is interesting to contrast Chinese or Javanese shadow figures with their 3-D puppet or human counterparts in order to appreciate the way their designers are able to compress the particulars of theatrical character types into the two-dimensional image plane.

The shadow figure is generally articulated by rods, since this allows the most direct control without the operator's own shadow interfering with the image. However, a kind of body/shadow figure has become popular for larger-scale shadow theatres in which a shadow mask is mounted on the puppeteer's head. The resulting shadow image melds together the silhouette of the puppeteer with that mask.

Focal plane

The clear, blank surface is the field upon which the shadow image is projected. Traditionally this was a tent wall or a tautly stretched piece of linen or silk. Modern screens include a variety of synthetic rear-projection materials that diffuse the hot spot caused by the light source. The shadow screen defines in formal terms the hierarchy of the theatrical experience, separating the performers from the audience and severing the image from the object and light source creating it. Some traditional Indonesian *wayang* performances allow select audience members to sit behind the screen and watch the *dalang* operate the puppets directly – these guests are considered privileged to be able witness the higher reality of the performance praxis and to watch the *dalang*'s technique.

In most shadow performances the screen tends to be the most passive stage element. However, just as the light source can be brought into play, the screen can also be effectively animated. In the dramatic climax of Julie Taymor's *Lion King*, during the showdown between the pack of hyenas and the pride of lions, a 30-foot-long spandex screen snakes about the stage, alternately opening to reveal the live masked dancers, then closing back up to make a dynamic surface for the images of the relatively static shadow figures.

The architecture of light and shadow

Without the physical stasis of a material body, a shadow projection has no physical limits in terms of scale other than the brightness of its light source. With lasers or brilliant arc-light projectors, shadow images can be thrown onto the sides of buildings and bridges hundreds of feet tall and wide. With improved lamp and projection technology, the sky is truly the limit.

A stunning example of a practical mega-light and shadow spectacle, "Tribute in Light" was on display directly above the site of the World Trade Center in the autumn of 2001 and thereafter on anniversaries of the September 11 tragedy. It consisted of 88 parallel beams of intense light pointing straight up and arranged around the footprints of the fallen buildings. While relatively simple technically, the installation was an emotionally moving experience and a monumental aesthetic construct, visible over 20 miles away. The twin shafts of light did not move or "perform" in any way, but they were in constant interplay with the landscape and with the atmosphere above the city. During the month that they were activated, I often sat near our Brooklyn studio, across the East River about a mile distant from

Ground Zero, and watched their beams dance across the various layers of scudding clouds. On rainy nights they formed a brilliant, glowing mushroom over the skyscrapers of Lower Manhattan; on clear nights they created a silvery shaft that faded as it arced up towards infinity. It was truly a masterful (and totally minimalist) aesthetic gesture.

Curiously, these pillars of light hearken back to one of the earliest references to shadow puppetry in Chinese literature. According to Han dynasty historical accounts, the Emperor Wu (who ruled from the second to the first century BCE) was consumed by grief at the death of his favorite concubine and could no longer rule effectively. His ministers, fearing political chaos, found an old shaman who claimed he could summon back the soul of the emperor's beloved. He set up a silk tent in the palace and had the emperor take a seat in front. Inside the tent a flame was lit and from out of its flickering light, the silhouette of the concubine emerged. The emperor conversed with her and was consoled (Chen 2007: 22). Both the contemporary "Tribute in Light" and the Han Dynasty shaman's illuminated séance illustrate one of the core social functions of the shadow performer: to build a bridge of light and shadow on which the dead and the living, the spirit and human worlds, can communicate effectively with each other.

So what is the utility in our highly secularized, postindustrial culture of an art form that utilizes archaic, analog technology to harness the dynamics of light for building connections between the disembodied realms of spirit and the human world? Can shadow theatre be an effective bridge between ancient and future

Figure 9.2 Traditional shadow troupe in rehearsal, Northern China (1936), Pauline Benton Collection. Photo courtesy of Chinese Theatre Works

performance models? While these questions have no clear answers, I see no reason why contemporary shadow theatre need lose its connection to the primal forces imbuing its prehistoric roots, nor why it should not simultaneously continue to exploit new technologies as practical media for aesthetic expression.

Works cited

Bachelard, G. (1961) *The Flame of a Candle*, trans. J. Caldwell (1988) in J. H. Stroud and R. S. Dupree (eds.) *The Bachelard Translation Series*. Dallas, TX: Dallas Institute Publications.

Chen, F. P. L. (2007) *Chinese Shadow Theatre: History, Popular Religion and Women Warriors*. Montréal, Quebec: McGill-Queen's University Press.

Scholem, G. (ed.) (1949) *Zohar: The Book of Splendor: Basic Readings from the Kabbalah*. New York, NY: Schocken Books.

Schönewolf, H. (1968) *Play with Light and Shadow: The Art and Techniques of Shadow Theater*. New York, NY: Reinhold Publishing Corp.

10
The Third Thing
Jim Lasko

Redmoon was founded as a puppet theatre with an equal focus on creating work in theatres and in streets and parks. Redmoon's current mission is to transform the experience of urban spaces with large-scale theatrical events that promote community, creativity, and an empowered democracy.

An early transformational moment in Redmoon's history was the decision to ban the actor's vocabulary from our process. We replaced the psychological idiom with a materially centered inquiry. The conversation shifted from people to things. What did the material want? What actions aligned with the physical properties of the material? What actions seemed in opposition? How did that fabric, that wood, that bamboo seem to want to behave?

We began to ask the same materially centered questions about our performance objects. What did the puppet want? The mask? A cart, a box, a vehicle? When confronted with a masked performer, we focused our attention on the mask instead of the performer. Rather than occupy ourselves with the problematic hermeneutics of psychologically-centered acting pedagogy and its interest in emotional "truth," we concerned ourselves with the mask. What did the mask "want" or "like"? The mask "came alive" when the performer went low, carrying her weight back a bit, never straightening her knees. The mask "wanted" fast movement, jerky angular movement.

This remarkably simple step had profound impact. We began to work differently. It was as though the puppet assumed the weight of authorship and we were liberated from ourselves. Our attention began to shift.

We began to frame our performance task as service to the puppet. We were not working toward a single artist's vision but allowing a puppet to reveal itself from a materially based conversation among a host of artists, makers, craftsmen, engineers, and amateurs. The vision belonged to everyone and no one. A mask might be formed by the hands of a sculptor but modified by a mold-making process designed by an engineer and then executed by a volunteer. From there it may pass to a painter for surface treatment and then to a craftsperson for hair. In collaboration with a performer, a mechanism for wearing the mask might be devised. Through this entire process, the conversation was focused on the material. We did not speak about preconceived images or intended results but instead talked about the actual physical aspects of the object, about the character that could be seen progressively developing as the mask moved from artist to artist.

A similar process played itself out in rehearsal, where the mask met the actor and its fellow objects. Here, too, it spurred a conversation that continued to shape and transform both the process and product. The mask might reveal itself to work better on the back of a head or appended to an operating stick or manipulated from behind a closed curtain. Each realization led to a new series of exchanges between makers.

This shift in focus from self to object began to alter and reshape our mission. The idea of service moved from artistic methodology to institutional objective. We shifted our project into public spaces where this vocabulary empowered our work in our community; it cleared the way for a surprisingly productive engagement strategy.

What started as a conversation among a group of like-minded artists from similar cultural backgrounds easily accommodated the youth in the neighborhood surrounding our studio. Later, it accommodated the adults in that same community with similar efficiency and then, with similar ease, people from communities all over the city. What started as a conversation about art among artists became a conversation about living, among people from many backgrounds and classes with widely varied interests. Sometimes the results of that conversation were seen in the theatre, but more compelling were those instances when conversations manifested themselves in the public sphere.

In September of 1997, we moved our operations into the highest crime precinct in Chicago. As a predominately white and relatively privileged troupe of artists, we stuck out awkwardly. Our performing objects made the introductions. We

Figure 10.1 Rice paper and bamboo constructed spectacle objects for Redmoon's *All Hallows' Eve Ritual Celebration* (October 1997) on the streets of Logan Square. Photo © Katja Heinemann

rehearsed outside and set up chairs and sometimes on weekends served popcorn. People stopped and asked what we were doing. Relationships were built. A free arts class was introduced. We expanded our artistic conversations to include first our neighbors, then our location, and finally our entire social situation. Our mission began to shift to accommodate that new understanding.

Essential to our process was what I call "radical listening." Radical listening involves an incremental opening of the sphere of influence as mediated through the performing object. Radical listening expands the creative attention in ever widening circles: from the self, to the group, to the site, and finally to the social circumstance in which the theatrical event will be presented. Radical listening means that each voice changes the work itself, takes form, and develops and evokes the next set of iterations, which subsequently must also be heard. This dynamic cycle culminates at the presentation of the work.

At the center of every conversation is the performing object. In her essay "Participation and Spectacle: Where Are We Now?" Claire Bishop asserts the importance of a "third term – an object, image, story, film, even a spectacle – that permits this experience to have purchase on the public imaginary" (Bishop 2012: 45). A vital distinction between artists and participants is mediated through the performing object.

Participatory art is a layered form whose foundation is the manifest process of discovery undertaken by both participants and the artists who have framed the event. Bishop insists that the foundational activity between artists and participants must be arbitrated by a third party, a neutral object able to absorb the input from all collaborators. Bishop refers to a lecture by Jacques Rancierre in Frankfurt, Germany, where he posits a "third thing" through which a participatory process can be elicited (cited in Bishop 2012: 40). This third thing, which he calls "spectacle," sits between artists and those whom they engage. True to our form, "spectacle" is the center point around which all converge and through which the process is made manifest.

The year of *Frankenstein* (1996)

In 1996 we worked in a variety of different communities, each with quite distinct demographic populations. The idea was for each group to engage the myth of Frankenstein in their own distinct way, but for all to work toward the same final, public performance.

At the Association House of Chicago, a social-service organization on the West Side, we led a work study program for "troubled teens." In a borrowed warehouse space across the street, we made puppets and watched movies. We watched innumerable versions of *Frankenstein* – from Andy Warhol's 1973 version to the 1931 Boris Karloff classic, from Roger Corman's futuristic *Frankenstein Unbound* (1990) to *Abbott and Costello Meet Frankenstein* (1948), and all of Frankenstein's offspring and relatives: *Young Frankenstein* (1974), *Son of Frankenstein* (1939), *Bride of Frankenstein* (1935) – we saw them all. We talked about the monster, the part of ourselves that had no place, the part that had been shunned and silenced. And we made large-scale puppets for a parade down a patch of North Avenue that cut through the quickly gentrifying neighborhood where they were raised.

At the same time we were in residency at the School of the Art Institute of Chicago, where we took a more scholarly approach to the same material. We read Mary Shelley's 1818 novel and talked about the Gothic form. We talked about the monster as a metaphor for the creative product. We read neo-Marxist essays on alienation and the role of art as a challenge to the hegemonic forces of capitalism. And we made large-scale puppets for a parade down a patch of North Avenue that cut through the quickly gentrifying neighborhood that was likely to soon become their home.

We also made *Frankenstein* the theme of our ongoing free children's art classes that operated out of our neighborhood-based studio. We ate Frankenberry cereal and read the Classical Comics version of *Frankenstein*. We watched cartoons and looked at Halloween masks and toys based on the monster. And we made a large-scale puppet for a parade down a big street that cut through a neighborhood they had never seen.

The culminating parade was bizarre and wonderful.

We mounted puppets and effigies onto borrowed shopping carts and into the backs of pickup trucks. Additional stick puppets were designed to be carried by teams, while others were to be handed to friends and friendly faces on the route. We deliberated the parade sequence and debated the degree of formality of the choreography, but what happened on the day of the event was a surprise to everyone. Whereas we had put all of our thought into the puppets and their mechanics, into the way the image of the parade would be viewed from afar and from up close, the actuality of the parade revealed a different object of attention altogether. What was on view on the West Side that afternoon was not a parade of objects but a social event. The objects were the intermediating mechanisms that released a spectacle of human interaction.

Figure 10.2 Performers manipulate large-scale puppets, masks, and objects during Redmoon's *Frankenstein* parade (September 1995) at Chicago's Navy Pier, soon after the North Avenue parade. Photo © Tria Smith

When the police showed up, lights flashing, to accompany the parade, the youth with whom we had worked for months to create the parade were certain we were being shut down. It was unfathomable to them that the police were there to facilitate their expression. As that reality sank in, they became increasingly liberated. By the time we crossed through our second intersection against the lights, with police holding traffic for us, things really loosened up. The kids began to interact with the crowd who had spontaneously formed along the sides of the street. Some joined in the dancing and movement. Attention turned from the puppets to the manipulators, and the real content of the parade revealed itself. The event was not the image created by the objects against their urban setting nor was it the kids who carried those objects and their sense of liberty. The theatrical event was the entire social situation. It was the objects, their manipulators, the interactions that they created, and the overall disruption that was left in their wake.

The parade was an ephemeral reconfiguration of North Avenue. The meaning of that place had been altered. Not only for the participants of the parade but also for those who may have considered themselves mere bystanders, North Avenue was no longer a transportation channel or a site of commerce. Convention had been wholly disrupted. The deep and generally unseen social structures that guide and define interpersonal behavior fell away and a new order arose. To use Victor Turner's term, an "anti-structure" had taken hold.

In *Performance Studies: An Introduction*, Richard Schechner reviews Victor Turner's concept of "communitas": "Turner called this liberation from the constraints of ordinary life 'anti-structure' and the experience of ritual camaraderie 'communitas.' … Spontaneous communitas abolishes status. People encounter each other directly" (Schechner and Brady 2012: 70), unencumbered by socially constructed identities.

If only for a moment and in a qualified way, that afternoon on North Avenue some mass of people had an experience of "spontaneous communitas." More than that, others who occupied that same public space, who had no intentional relationship to the event, witnessed the eruption of spontaneous community. They saw social boundaries dissolve and felt the space around them shift and transform. What seemed fixed revealed itself as pliable. While there had been no structural change, the experience of the space, both the physical space and its social context, felt profoundly different.

Place: The meaning of space

In her essay, Bishop refers to Sherri Arnstein's "ladder of citizen participation," which describes varying modes of participation and places them on an ascending ladder, where the lower rungs ("manipulation" and then "therapy") are considered non-participatory and the highest three rungs ("partnership," "delegated power," and "citizen control") involve active engagement (Bishop 2012: 41). Bishop argues that while the ladder provides us with a helpful vocabulary, it does not begin to capture the complex of relationships that develop around a successful work of participatory art. A successful piece of participatory art, she argues, creates relationships that rely on a "continual play of mutual tension, recognition, and dependency" (Bishop 2012: 41).

Perhaps a more apt paradigm for understanding the complex interplay of relationships in a successful participatory art piece is not a ladder but a series of concentric circles that represents the "radical listening" process. In the center sits the artist or artists who initiate the conversation; then moving outward in widening spheres are the groups of interlocutors: artists, collaborators, the formal properties of a given site; and then finally the social situation. The artwork is as successful as the transparency of the conversation. As it was that afternoon on North Avenue for a moment or two, the "third object," the spectacle, holds in lively tension each expanding circle of the conversation, ending with the sphere that includes all those witnessing it and the space around them.

We forget about the pliability of space, as we forget about the pliability of most of our given circumstances. These disruptions remind us that space is structured by the forms that occupy and shape it, but it is interpreted by human beings and is, therefore, inseparable from the personal history of human experience within it. The meaning of a space is an accumulation of a composite of factors, including its shape, its intended use, the policies that govern the activity in it, and, in no small way, the history of human experience within it. This human element, the social experiential history of a space, leaves no immediate physical trace but can have profound impact on the way that a space is understood. To most Americans of my generation, our understanding of Tiananmen Square was dramatically and irrevocably altered by the protests of 1989. At the time of this writing, the meaning attached to the town of Newtown, Connecticut, has recently been radically reshaped by the act of a single man with an automatic weapon. Whether artistically constructed, politically charged, routinely established, or psychotically generated, human experience phenomenologically reconfigures space.

Redmoon performs in public space because public spaces are the symbolic heart of our democracy. In public spaces people encounter one another and their culture on relatively unqualified terms. What happens in public space belongs to everyone and reflects on everyone. From housing density to the patterns of the transportation infrastructure, from social history to formal design, the meanings of our public spaces are both heavily coded and deeply understood. Public spaces are the purest expression of the ways in which we gather, coexist, and resist. They are the texts through which we read our status and our aspiration. This is what makes them exciting to engage as an artist.

For an artwork to reveal the fullness of public space, it must evidence the layered interplay of social and structural forms that constitute public space. The piece itself has to entice and solicit and reveal participation from each of those players. The form can thus expand from the mediating "third object" to embrace the full social situation from which it gains and reflects its power.

Redmoon's *Dis/RePlacement* (2012) was designed to create an invitation. It performs on an adapted forklift featuring two functioning forks, back to back, each holding what appear to be rooms ripped from a typical Chicago apartment. On the front fork teeters a kitchen and the back fork holds a bathroom. On it we perform a silent French farce, with the rooms moving up and down on their masts, creating a constantly shifting dynamic between the rooms and the players who occupy them. The vehicle is a self-contained stage, with its own battery-powered sound-and-light system.

Figure 10.3 Actors in *Dis/Replacement* take their positions on the stages perched atop a twin forklift engineered for Redmoon's Urban Interventions Series, here seen on a street corner in the Wicker Park neighborhood of Chicago (summer 2012). Photo © Christina Noel

It enters a space without warning, attracts an audience with its scale and height and mobility, and keeps them engaged with a broad physical performance style. Most important, it leaves with shocking efficiency. It calls together a broad-based audience, broaches interactions among them, and reveals a previously unimagined range of possibilities. Its departure is carefully choreographed to describe a void and to elicit consideration of how it might be filled.

The object is a mediator. Whether we are working on chicken wire forms around which papier-mâché will be layered, textured, and then painted, or machining joints for a hydraulic hinge that can handle the torque of a teetering tower, the medium is the public itself. Whether steel contraption or giant marionette on a makeshift cart, the puppet is the lever that, properly positioned and addressed with balanced effort, can overcome social resistance and pry open a conversation that demonstrates an unseen potential in civic life. This newly revealed space – which encompasses the people in it – is both the content and the form, both the subject and the object. The puppet is the intermediary, egolessly facilitating the conversation and almost casually posing the open-ended question: "Now what?"

Works cited

Bishop, C. (2012) "Participation and Spectacle: Where Are We Now?," in N. Thompson (ed.) *Living as Form: Socially Engaged Art from 1991–2011.* Cambridge, MA: MIT Press.
Schechner, R. and Brady, S. (2012) *Performance Studies: An Introduction.* London: Routledge.

11
Post-Decivilization Efforts in the Nonsense Suburb of Art

Peter Schumann

Shoe is what you do
Wherever you go it goes with you
Because it has nothing more to do
Than to understand you
In as far as you're a shoe

Shoe is what you wear against dirt and ice. Shoeness is reasonable and allows you to have a down-to-earth relationship with the world. My name is shoe. Shoe is what I am designed to be and to do.

But, instead, I am working against my assignment, and my business is the opposite of shoeness and usefulness because I work in the frivolity business, which caters to the luxury market of society's trifles, providing the decorative nonsense that charms the civilized sense so that the civilized sense can measure the thickness of its seriousness against the flimsiness of nonsense.

Naturally this type of business has its nasty consequences and distorts the frivolity business executive's understanding of the most lavish portion of reality, which is called the ordinary and comes in three categories:

1 The What Ordinary;
2 The Why Ordinary;
3 The Extraordinary Ordinary.

The first category, *The What Ordinary*, is the cluttered house with its straitjacketed tenant inside, the eternal kitchen complete with coffee cup in hands, which are rattled by the daily news.

This in-the-absence-of-heaven ordinary also features the 100-watt light bulb officer in charge of the latest meeting of the We-do-as-good-as-we-can Club, a meeting that starts with the club's anthem: *There must be more to life than this*.

Heaven, the club-members say, is not simply a cloudless sky above whatever confused underneath but is really the product of thought and hand, and just as rain

Figure 11.1 Drawing by Peter Schumann (2012)

pours down from above to fertilize us, so must we pour down and fertilize, even if that fertilization is nothing but Paper-Maché.

The club members, fully aware of their ordinary, absence-of-heaven calamity, admit to be unable to design their life, simply because life refuses to be designable. The *successful* human-animal life, they say, is both horizontal and vertical. The horizontal is known as pillowjoy, lovejoy, and snorejoy. The vertical is the complicated pain-in-the-neck joy of everything else. (By the way, club members are granted privileged access to trickery that allows them to sneak the above-mentioned heaven into the everything else.)

The second category of the ordinary, *The Why Ordinary*, is the holy cathedral of our civilization, the most gigantic architecture ever, the road system with its congregation of ardent believers and forced participants, complete with road-kill slaughterhouse and accidental funeral parlor, officiated by the despised corporate high priests of the beloved auto industry and nourished by the innards of the Earth. No comment.

The third category of the ordinary, *The Extraordinary Ordinary*, consists of all extraordinary minor disturbances and major upheavals surrounded by air, which is stuffed to the brim with music noise, and the indispensable boredom of that noise, as perceived by the hopelessly clogged ear and observed by the one-directional eye, while the kitchen serves its dinner to the eater eating his cow meat thoughtlessly, he who used to be cow or horse himself, wolf or elephant, woodchuck or weasel, heron or hummingbird, goose or woodpecker, cockroach or inchworm.

Allow me to point out that this distance between the eater and his cockroach or elephant self is known as extraordinarily ordinary hypocrisy. What is extraordinarily ordinary hypocrisy and what does it miss to achieve? What ordinary pretense does it represent? What ordinary falsification does it manifest? What truth-proclaiming that

POST-DECIVILIZATION EFFORTS IN THE NONSENSE SUBURB OF ART

Figure 11.2 Drawing by Peter Schumann (2012)

proclaims uncertain truths and nevertheless issues certificates of certainty? These certificates are traditionally cast in stone and proclaim a stonecast Beyond, which also comes in the form of books as printed by ordinary printers and pretended by writers who apparently have never heard of the We-do-as-good-as-we-can Club. It should also be mentioned that the Beyond corresponds to the ordinary dreamer's nonsense-capability and even before dreaming the Beyond, the dreamer brightens his existence with dreaming up nonsense.

And because of these confusing circumstances, all shoes and shoe-related functionaries and committed non-essentialists – who all survive on the flimsy notion which holds that somewhere deep down in the guts of the un-essentials we'll find life's elixir – must nevertheless stop that search and must dirty themselves instead and must de-artify their art, because it is the job of the nevertheless-artist to be ordinary, it is the job of the de-artified artist to push the obscure, hypocrisy-injured ordinary into the sun's or the light bulb's brightness.

It is the job of the hypocrisy-artist to push the straitjacketed tenant of the cluttered house into the stars' vast landscape, even if that landscape is nothing but recycled junk. It is the job of the non-essentialist to service the carefully monitored, government-owned citizen who is only two things: either employed or unemployed and therefore needs the frivolity business to keep his blood from curdling, because what is the ordinary without the trapeze artist's death-defying stunt designed to cheer up the life-defying citizenry?

To sum it up: all the ordinaries – *The What Ordinary*, *The Why Ordinary*, and *The Extraordinary Ordinary* – are all in servitude and are stunted by capitalism's hold on the soul of the population and suffering like the human-animal body suffers from its weakened immune system. The ordinary, its behind firmly glued to the 65-mph seat and flying high in its dream engine that mixes the countries of the world as if they all deserve to be the same, this condemned ordinary must be unraveled. It is the job of the capitalist artist to be unraveled. It is the job of the capitalist unraveled artist to take a pickaxe to the elegant mud with which the dumb ordinary is encrusted and pry it loose and unravel its brilliance.

It is the job of the nonsense artist to access the hidden reality inside the show-off reality of the obvious and to expose the asymmetrical battles that the 400 plutocrats who own this country fight against the occupants of the country or that other asymmetrical battle which the horrorists fight against the terrorists with so much money and religion that all the cops of the world don't dare to arrest their crimes.

It is the job of the aesthete to muscle the aesthetic with revolution. It is the job of the aesthete to revolutionize the revolution with the gut of the aesthetic. It is the job of the aesthete to create an aesthetic that lays bare revolution. It is the job of the revolutionary to discover an aesthetic that creates revolution.

What weapon system is available to the aesthete? What unaccommodated music can be unleashed against the doomed capitalist purposes?

What shoe, what trick, what stick, what tickle-tool, what roaring crocodile from which Punch and Judy show, what cardboard giant, what irresistible light, what irrefutable evidence, what garbage-retrieved model of Paradise, what overwhelming persuasion, what inevitable conclusion, what flight of thought, what idiot-proof argument, what visionary absolute, what final insight, what conclusive fact or heroic

Figure 11.3 Sleeper puppet, from Bread and Puppet Theater's *Things Done in a Seeing Place*, Glover, Vermont (2013). Photo courtesy of John Bell

act or far-out fantasy, what inner certainty or creative doubt, what single-minded stubbornness or communal resolve, what extreme prediction or sober assessment?

And why is the planet so goddamn flat, and why are the trees flying through the air, and why are citizens standing on their modernistic heads, and why is the good-taste-is-timeless furniture rising up against its clients, and why are the cities walking away from their own selves, and what is the meaning of Paper-Maché, and what are the puppeteers doing in the puppetry enterprise?

Part II
NEW DIALOGUES WITH HISTORY AND TRADITION

Edited and Introduced by Claudia Orenstein

Societies of every kind across the globe have given birth to puppetry, endowing crafted objects with life from the earliest periods of human history. Many of these practices have come and gone, while others have bequeathed us iconic figures such as Punch, now inextricably associated with the very idea of "puppet." However, since puppetry is frequently a popular art that de-emphasizes text, written documents that chart its past can be scant and frustratingly incomplete. Sometimes its vestiges remain encased only in objects whose context for use has long vanished. Nonetheless, with the traces of the past carved into their very bodies, puppets and performing objects can attest to anterior practices in concrete, material terms, re-invoking them and drawing them forth from their temporarily inert, sculpted forms.

Contemporary scholars are moving beyond merely documenting puppet histories to reassessing them, applying new theoretical models drawn from multiple academic disciplines to offer fresh approaches and reveal puppetry's connections to myriad academic discourses. Likewise, scholars in contiguous fields, such as literary studies, art history, or material culture, are turning to puppet theory to shed new light on their own areas of research.

Moreover, in many situations puppetry's antecedents have not been erased but persist in performance traditions passed down from one generation to the next. Practitioners refashion these forms over time to accommodate new audiences or their own particular tastes and skills. Such artists must strike a balance between embracing the codes of performance that keep them within their traditional frameworks while meeting the dynamic circumstances that force transformation in their arts. During the last hundred years, rapid technological growth and globalization have put many traditional forms in danger as they lose audiences to television and film. At the same time, many practitioners feel the cultural contexts that previously gave their arts purpose eroding under their feet. Local traditions are changing to respond to global artistic and economic pressures as much as local ones, bringing seismic shifts beyond more familiar incremental transitions.

The lines dividing puppetry's history and contemporary negotiations with tradition are not clearly drawn. Both areas form part of the broader dialogue taking place between puppetry's past and present. This portion of the book, therefore, focuses on contemporary puppetry's engagement with the past. The first section, "Revisiting History," looks at several of the new scholarly models reshaping puppet history, while the second, "Negotiating Tradition," considers the transformation of long-standing puppet traditions.

Chapters in "Revisiting History" bring fresh scholarly perspectives to bear on historical material. Amber West draws on contemporary feminist views to reassess the contributions of eighteenth-century actress and puppeteer Charlotte Charke to the theatre, the culture of her times, and the field of puppetry. West's analysis amplifies our understanding of how women and puppetry have both been undervalued within theatre research. Dassia Posner expands on this theme by bringing to light the mostly forgotten theoretical works of Russian writer and critic Iulia Slonimskaia and visual artist Nina Simonovich-Efimova. During the modernist period, when Russian artists and theorists were enamored of the puppet in metaphorical terms or for what it could contribute to live-actor theatre, these women embraced puppetry itself, theorizing its own artistic potential. Lisa Morse turns to the issue of race in puppetry, analyzing how the problematic image of the Saracen is encoded in many aspects of traditional Sicilian rod puppetry. This racially marked figure, long used by Sicilians as a cultural means of grappling with their own sense of inferiority to other mainland Italian cultures, becomes more problematic today as Arabs and Middle Easterners flood into Sicily as migrant workers. Bringing an anthropologist's view to puppetry, Jane Marie Law details the sustained and ubiquitous Japanese custom of using *ningyō*, or human-shaped figures, as repositories for highly charged emotional experiences, such as the loss of a child. The background she reveals exposes the cultural underpinnings of Japan's exquisite *bunraku* tradition, now widely seen and emulated beyond this original context. Finally, Debra Hilborn draws on theoretical models from puppetry to analyze the worship of the cross in the medieval Catholic Holy Week ceremonies. Hilborn finds that the cross's meaning shifted for participants throughout these rituals as they manipulated and anthropomorphized this object in various ways. Her analysis demonstrates the wider application of puppetry theory to other fields, such as medieval material culture.

The second set of chapters, "Negotiating Tradition," traces the various ways in which practitioners are responding to new forces reshaping their art forms, both in terms of production and reception. Matthew Cohen identifies two important trends within Indonesia's *wayang kulit*, or shadow puppetry tradition, offering the term "post-traditional" to distinguish shows that take the form into radically new territory from those that more practically shift standard performance models to accommodate changing circumstances. "Post-traditional," in Cohen's analysis, delineates practices rooted in tradition but not confined by notions of "traditionalism." It speaks to the attempts of many performers to stake out new artistic territory more responsive to current circumstances and their own creative impulses. Kathy Foley examines the challenges facing traditional Korean puppetry as performers attempt to recast their ribald tradition as an elite art for today's national and international markets. My own chapter outlines the complex web of artistic and personal choices performers of *tolpavakoothu* – or leather shadow puppetry in Kerala, India – face as they struggle to sustain traditional performance within that country's rapidly changing social and economic circumstances.

While the Asian context, with its rich history of puppetry often linked to religious ritual or court activities, offers ample examples of hereditary forms confronting change, Ida Hledíková submits an impressive European case. She describes how, since the fall of Communism, Eastern European directors have revived the previously banned religious *vertep*, or Nativity play, transposing it to reconnect to their lost cultural heritage while simultaneously exercising their new artistic freedoms.

Even as puppetry diversifies today, it is not unbound from its past. Anterior practices and figures continue to link us to a notion of what puppetry is in its paradigmatic forms. To transform puppetry in the present is inherently to be in dialogue with its history.

Section III
Revisiting History

12
Making a Troublemaker
Charlotte Charke's Proto-Feminist Punch

Amber West

"[Y]ou are, without Exception, [one] of the greatest Curiosities that ever were the Incentives to the most profound Astonishment."
    The author to herself, 1755, in A *Narrative of the Life of Mrs. Charlotte Charke*

Charke and the eighteenth-century stage

The eleventh child of one of England's leading theatrical families, Charlotte Charke (1713–1760) was a born performer. Her parents were both well-known actors, particularly her father, Colley Cibber, who was also Poet Laureate, a playwright, and manager of the Theatre Royal at Drury Lane. Charke made her debut there in 1730 and became renowned as a comedic actress deft at breeches roles and impersonations of famous men, most notably her father. Since women were not allowed to perform on the English stage until after the Restoration in 1660, actresses during the eighteenth century were considered novel curiosities and, because they defied gender decorum, frequently presumed to have loose morals.

Charke was an even greater curiosity. Not only an actor but a playwright, she was also an offstage cross-dresser who often passed as a man, one of the first English women ever to manage a theatre company (and later, a puppetry company), and one of the first secular women to publish an autobiography. She gained notoriety, and lost familial class privilege, when her father disowned her for leaving Drury Lane to "become the leading player in an upstart theater troupe run by Henry Fielding ... London's leading avant-garde playwright, and Colley Cibber's bitter enemy" (Shevelow 2005: 5). Their troupe's anti-government satires helped to "inspire" Parliament to pass the 1737 Licensing Act, which restricted dramatic productions to two patent theatres and required all plays to be government-approved prior to performance. Fielding, Charke and other rabble-rousers were effectively banished from the "legitimate" stage. Charke did not let this stop her, taking her subversive parodies to the puppet theatre and traveling the countryside for years as an itinerant performer. Government restrictions on "legitimate" drama in this and the previous century inadvertently helped puppetry to flourish in popularity in England among all classes. Referring to the eighteenth century, George Speaight writes that "never before or since

Figure 12.1 Inspired by Charke's tale of stealing her brother's and father's clothes to imitate her father, the engraving reads, "An exact Representation of Mrs. Charke walking in the Ditch at four Years of Age, as described by herself in the first Number of the Narrative of her own Life, lately published" (F. Garden, 1755). © The Trustees of the British Museum

have puppet theatres so successfully made themselves the talk of the town" (Speaight 1955 [1990]: 92). And though she is rarely given credit for it, the astonishing Mrs. Charke had much to do with puppetry's success and evolution during this time.

Making a troublemaker

Perhaps the only thing more astonishing than Charke's life, more astonishing than the candor and wit of her self-portrayal in her popular autobiography *A Narrative of the Life of Mrs. Charlotte Charke*, published in installments in 1755, has been the glib response of so many scholars to that life. In the first book-length critical study of this enigmatic actress, writer, puppeteer, and theatre manager, editor Philip Baruth writes, "Charke has been treated with notable unfairness for nearly all of the last two centuries, due to a discomfort with her cross-dressing and a concerted attempt on the part of Cibber's biographers to absolve the father through the casual defamation of his children" (Baruth 1998: 11). Reviewing a handful of remarks by scholars makes clear this defamation has been far from casual. Leonard Ashley describes Cibber's "wildly exhibitionistic and uncontrollable offspring" as a "buckeen" whose memoir was merely a desperate attempt for money and "lacking in literary merit" (Ashley 1969: vii, xxiv). Other scholars have described her as a "psychopathic lesbian" with a "perverse predisposition towards vagabondising" (Speaight 1955 [1990]: 108). Likened to "an opium-smoker or a Bedlamite," she was said to have been "disowned by her family as an 'alien'," and rebuked as an unfit mother, a flighty failure at her many business ventures, and a drunken, "bellicose and dissolute woman" (cited in Morgan 1988: 210–211).[1]

From an intersectional feminist standpoint, Charke – an impoverished single mother who lived much of her life as a man, obscured her sexual orientation, and created artistic works primarily categorized as "low" entertainments – has suffered from multiple, overlapping forms of subordination.[2] The same patriarchal systems she actively resisted in her lifetime, in part through her innovative and oft-overlooked puppet shows, have also caused her contributions as an avant-garde, multidisciplinary, entrepreneurial, and proto-feminist artist to go largely unrecognized.

Thankfully, more recent criticism, particularly from queer and feminist theorists, has focused on recovery and correction, illuminating the ways in which sexism, classism, and homophobia led to Charke's discrediting and historical erasure from the late eighteenth to the mid-twentieth centuries (Shevelow 2005: 380).[3] I aim to contribute to the critical conversation by discussing Charke's work as a puppeteer, one of the least examined of her creative endeavors, in part due to the fact that puppetry itself is often disregarded in the West as an artistically valid form of cultural production. Examining her work as a puppeteer, as well as critical misrepresentations of that work, I argue that Charke's puppetry, like her cross-dressing, should indeed be considered an active challenge to, and rejection of, the binary discourses of a patriarchy transitioning from feudalism to capitalism. Charke's puppetry illuminates the ways in which Western hierarchal binaries separating "high arts" like drama from "low entertainments" like puppetry are, in fact, deeply entwined with oppressive, dualistic constructions of gender, race, and sexuality.

Failed puppeteer?

Charke's contributions to puppetry did not begin to be recognized by historians until the mid-twentieth century. Paul McPharlin's seminal 1949 history of American puppetry includes a sizable chapter on eighteenth-century England but acknowledges no particular contribution to the art form by Charke. Describing her experiences in Tunbridge-Wells spa in the summer of 1739, McPharlin characterizes Charke as a failed puppet troupe manager who proved herself incapable of "making money in a watering place" (McPharlin and McPharlin 1949 [1969]: 45). Speaight's 1955 discussion of the same incident stays truer to Charke's own account, though he chides her for not discovering in advance "what a sensible preliminary visit would have told her – that a successful puppet theatre, managed by Lacon, had already been established there for many years" (Speaight 1955 [1990]: 105). Though both puppetry scholars frame it as such, nowhere in her *Narrative* does Charke imply or describe this tour to be a failure. Rather, she tells an upbeat tale of leading her "wooden Troop" into battle against "a General who had taken the Field before [her]." She and her "living Numbers" exhibited professionalism and flexibility by renting Ashley's Great Room and, upon discovering that Lacon had cornered the local puppet show market, performing several comedies with human actors instead of puppets (Charke 1999: 45). Speaight presumes the troupe then "made their way back to London, penniless" (Speaight 1955 [1990]: 105), although based on Charke's own account, this seems unlikely. Her managerial decision to fight "against *Lacon* in *Propia Persona*" (Charke 1999: 45) rather than risking her wooden troupe's defeat at the hands of a veteran army on familiar turf seems, in fact, quite a strategic business choice.

It is also worth noting that this tour was neither Charke's first nor only experience in theatre management. In 1734, she rented the Haymarket, a main London house, for her "Mad Company" of human actors, financing and managing a full summer season in which she also acted in myriad roles, male and female. At only 21, "She may have been, in fact, the first woman on the London stage to assume the sole responsibility of management" (Shevelow 2005: 186). In 1738, shortly after the Licensing Act banished her from the stage, she leased another space in London and created Punch's Theatre, producing and performing at least ten puppet plays in less than three months (Shevelow 2005: 267). Though Speaight spends more time discussing Charke than McPharlin does, his analysis exemplifies the prejudicial tones in most accounts of Charke up until the late twentieth century. Speaight's history was first published in 1955, but the section on Charke in the second edition from 1990 remained unchanged:

> In our portrait gallery of puppeteers Charlotte Charke takes an obvious and important place for her eccentricity. She has, too, provided us with the unique documentation of her autobiography. This fascinating book is neither literature nor history, but the inconsequent and madly egocentric memories of an aging and desperate woman, a glimpse into a twisted and distraught human soul. Modern psycho-analysis would, no doubt, neatly label Mrs. Charke as a psychopathic lesbian, but we need not here peer too far into the deep well of loneliness from which this unhappy woman drew her inspiration. We ... may salute her as a puppet showman of unusual intelligence, taste, and courage.
>
> (Speaight 1955 [1990]: 108)

Speaight's final "salute" is rendered disingenuous by the litany of backhanded compliments and sexist, homophobic remarks pulsing through this and, unfortunately, much Charke scholarship. Speaight remains, however, a primary authority on English puppetry, his research fundamental in an undersized field of study. Though all research on Charke's puppetry, including my own, is necessarily based on Speaight's, more intersectional and interdisciplinary approaches by subsequent critics have shifted the grounds by which we can more accurately acknowledge her contributions.

Correcting the record

In her lively biography, Kathryn Shevelow provides a useful corrective by highlighting the intense physical and mental demands of puppeteering and theatre management in this era (Shevelow 2005: 266). These factors, combined with impoverished single motherhood, more accurately explain the illness that caused Charke to cut short her season at Punch's Theatre and, after the Tunbridge-Wells tour, to lease and later sell at a loss her unique celebrity-faced marionette collection, which I will discuss in more detail below. The short-lived nature of Charke's London puppetry company does not negate the fact that her "grand Puppet-Show over the Tennis Court, in James Street" was highly successful (Charke 1999: 40). Henryk Jurkowski speaks to Charke's abilities as an artist and entrepreneur by acknowledging that she thoroughly refurbished the space she had leased, producing and performing ten different plays in eight weeks at the rate of at least two shows per day (Jurkowski and Francis 1996: 186).[4] Perhaps Charke's puppetry has been overlooked, in part, because her own discussion of herself as a puppeteer focuses almost entirely on those three months in Punch's Theatre. She was, however, a much more devoted practitioner of puppetry than her memoir reveals. Charke worked with two of the most well-established puppeteers of the day, Yeates and Russell (Speaight 1955 [1990]: 102).[5] The former helped her to acquire her marionettes and later leased them from Charke when she fell ill, while the latter hired her to manipulate Punch, his star performer (Speaight 1955 [1990]: 107). Additionally, her sense of fluidity and ease in performing on both human and puppet stages; puppetry's extreme popularity and the resulting abundance of puppet shows by itinerant artists (of which Charke was one for over ten years); and her aesthetic innovations in the genre speak to the significance both of puppetry's place in Charke's repertoire and her contributions to the art form.

Revolutionizing the puppet stage

Charke adapted literary dramas to the puppet stage, which prior to her had been home primarily to folk and biblical tales. Shevelow writes, "Charlotte used her puppets in a way new to the history of English puppet theater ... stag[ing] real plays that might be seen at the same time at Drury Lane or Covent Garden ... compet[ing] with the plays offered by the playhouses, at a cheaper price, and offer[ing] the added attractions of novelty, farce, and parody" (Shevelow 2005: 263). Jurkowski believes Charke had "ambitions to raise puppet theatre to a higher artistic level ... [and] to compete with her previous employers" (Jurkowski and Francis 1996: 185). Speaight, conversely, criticizes this innovation, asserting that "her lack of any previous experience with puppets may have limited her approach." He states that overall her "emphasis was, perhaps, too literary, and not sufficiently in the puppet tradition of folk-drama" (Speaight 1955 [1990]: 104). In light of the modernist puppetry revival initiated at the turn of the twentieth century by Englishman Edward Gordon Craig – which like Charke's work illuminates puppetry's capability for complex artistic expression – Speaight's suggestion that Charke should have stuck with what had been done before seems misguided and denies her contributions as an innovative forerunner in the field. As Shevelow and Jurkowski point out in their more recent analyses, Charke's adaptation of "legitimate" plays to the puppet stage demonstrates her entrepreneurial savvy, undercutting the patent houses while parodying their repertoire with marionettes whose faces she had carved to look like "eminent persons" (Charke 1999: 43) of the day.

Records indicate that Charke obtained a license for Punch's Theatre from the Lord Chamberlain in March of 1738. Scholars wonder why. Since puppetry was not considered "real" theatre because it did not include human actors, such a license was not actually required, a fact that Charke does not mention when she boasts that hers was "the only [puppet theater] in this Kingdom that ... had the good Fortune to obtain so advantageous a Grant" (Charke 1999: 40). Shevelow suggests that Charke obtained the license as a precaution (Shevelow 2005: 260). This seems possible considering that her former colleague, James Lacy, had recently been imprisoned for performing an unlicensed one-man show (Morgan 1988: 63). Charke also used the license as a marketing tool, flaunting a royal connection to distinguish hers from other puppet shows. The license might best be understood, however, as another subversive protest from an artist who displayed an impressive facility for satire. Considering both her scathing critique of sinking artistic standards in increasingly profit-driven patent houses in the first play she penned, *The Art of Management* (1735), and her exit from said houses to become a key player in the rabble-rousing avant-garde theatre that prompted the Licensing Act that left her unemployed, Charke's decision to license her puppet shows seems more significant than the "fear of retribution" or "marketing ploy" arguments suggest. Her description in the *Narrative*, particularly her "*good Fortune* to obtain so *advantageous* a Grant," (my italics) might be better interpreted as tongue-in-cheek wit. The unnecessary license calls attention to corrupt government meddling in the arts, and the inconsistencies and injustice of a system so clearly created to privilege a few well-connected houses, guaranteeing their profits through a virtual monopoly.[6]

In publicizing her uniquely licensed puppet theatre, Charke also regularly "remind[ed] her audience that the plays were to be performed by puppets while announcing them exactly as if they were to be acted by actors: [e.g.,] 'The part of Father Martin [to be] performed by Signior Punch from Italy'" (Morgan 1988: 64). This technique exemplifies Charke's competitive business acumen in presenting "a sturdy classical season" that included many of the day's favorite dramas, such as *Henry VIII* and *Richard III* (Morgan 1988: 64). Scott Cutler Shershow argues that by advertising her marionettes as actors, Charke "burlesques the discourse of [the] commercial stage and pretends to treat puppetry with equal dignity" (Shershow 1995: 158). To suggest Charke merely feigns respect for puppetry overlooks her serious dedication to the art. Treating her puppets as actors seems, in fact, to subvert Western ideologies that figure the puppet as "low" by humanizing her puppets and – in light of her innovative use of portrait puppets – "puppetizing" humans.

Charke writes that she "bought Mezzotinto's of several eminent Persons, and had [her puppets'] Faces carved from them" (Charke 1999: 43). These celebrity-faced marionettes (only one of whose identities is still known: the Italian castrato Farinelli) were "constrained, within the puppet show ... to act side by side with Punch and

Joan" (Shershow 1995: 156). Such a "demotion" might likely have been infuriating to the "legitimate" theatre-makers, including her own father, whom Charke was already notorious for critiquing. Her choice of puppets dissolves the division between high literary drama and low puppet show by outing it as a manipulable construct. Her "curious" (Charke 1999: 43) decision to supplement traditional puppets based on stock *commedia* characters like Punch with portrait puppets might best be understood in relation to her own successful career in male impersonation. She most notoriously played her father in several plays that openly mocked him, written by Fielding, and Shevelow posits that Charke likely had her Punch carved in the likeness of her father (Shevelow 2005: 261).[7] Charke seems to have had a keen, proto-feminist understanding of the ways in which puppetry, perhaps even more so than cross-dressing, can illuminate the human ability to create and re-create ourselves in the likeness of or in opposition to identities socially constructed for us.[8]

Eileen Blumenthal's discussion of portrait puppets further illuminates the effectiveness of Charke's celebrity-faced marionettes. "[P]ortrait puppets have played virtually every head of state. ... [They] spark that peculiar pleasure of recognition that impersonators and impressionists evoke" (Blumenthal 2005: 88). Since puppetry has long been utilized around the world for seditious political satire, Charke was clearly participating in a larger tradition within the art form. Blumenthal cites examples as early as the ninth century in China (Blumenthal 2005: 166). Charke's use of *portrait* puppets for political satire, however, has recently been acknowledged as an original and influential idea that was then "repeated in many theatres of the time." She was "one of the first to introduce personally directed satire in her shows" (Jurkowski and Francis 1996: 186). This aspect of her art must be considered in relation to negative reactions to and portrayals of Charke in her time and since. The specificity of her satire was unapologetically bold. Though Fielding continues to get most of the credit for it, their Haymarket company's critiques were so charged as to inspire legislative censure. At the same time that Britain's first prime minister, Robert Walpole, was driving the Licensing Act through Parliament with support from theatre establishmentarians like Cibber, Charke was starring in *The Historical Register* and *Eurydice Hiss'd*, two satires by Fielding that "specifically and comprehensively" critiqued Walpole and his affiliates (Shevelow 2005: 242–245). She not only spoofed Shakespeare, Dryden, and her father's plays in her puppet theatre, but she also poked fun at religious authorities by performing Fielding's anti-Catholic burlesque *The Old Debauchees* with puppets (Jurkowski and Francis 1996: 187). An acknowledgement of the significance, boldness, and relentless variety of Charke's critiques has been slow to emerge, perhaps because, coming from a poor, outspoken, cross-dressing actress, the criticism was particularly offensive and in need of suppression. Much of what makes Charke so important to the artistic and historical record has nearly erased her from it.

Continued biases against itinerant performers and "lesser" art forms contribute to sluggish acknowledgement of Charke's contributions. Her active opposition to the theatrical powers-that-be and her innovative and bold evasions of a licensing act created in an attempt to suppress dissident artists like her are important both in terms of how Charke ended up becoming a puppeteer and what she did with the art form once she took it up. A closer examination of her 1738 adaptation for the puppet stage of Fielding's burlesque drama *The Covent Garden Tragedy* (first performed six years earlier) reveals Charke's prescient conception of the political and expressive potential of the arts, particularly puppetry. It was precisely in her parodic puppetry that Charke's socially engaged art was most bold.

Punch in petticoats

Shershow examines Charke and Fielding's use of puppetry in his detailed study of the ways in which puppets in Western discourse since antiquity have been appropriated and "enlisted in the construction of a series of interlocking social and aesthetic hierarchies" (Shershow 1999: 8), including man as superior to woman and drama as superior to puppetry. Though Shershow acknowledges Charke's "keen awareness of the puppet's participation in a multiply hierarchical system of literary, class and gender distinction" (Shershow 1999: 144), he ultimately dismisses her puppetry (in the same way so many scholars have pooh-poohed her autobiography) as "little more than a desperate and ultimately unsuccessful effort to exploit her own notoriety for financial gain" (Shershow 1999: 159). He arrives at this conclusion through a somewhat cursory discussion of Charke's casting of Punch as Mother Punchbowl in *The Covent Garden Tragedy*, interpreting her decision through only one side of contemporary feminist debates, represented most extremely by Erin Mackie, who describes Charke's personal and artistic "impersonation of the masculine" as "reinforc[ing], reinstat[ing], and maintain[ing] the value of masculine, patriarchal conventions" (Mackie 1991: 843). Shershow's argument discredits Charke as both a puppeteer and proto-feminist. My perspective on Charke's "Punch in petticoats," and her broader life's work is more aligned with feminist scholars like Kristina Straub, who argues that Charke's "performative, 'unnatural' masculinity ... unsettles newly dominant assumptions about gender as legitimized according to fixed and oppositional categories" (Straub 1992: 138).

Since there is so little information regarding many of her adaptations, and due to her own cross-dressing, Charke's casting of Punch in "'The part of Mother Punchbowl ... being the first time of his appearing in petticoats'" (Charke cited in Morgan 1988: 64) has been of particular interest to scholars. Fielding based the character on Elizabeth Needham, a well-known London brothel keeper who had recently been pilloried to death. Like Speaight, Shershow suggests Charke's casting choice was another easy publicity technique, as it "must inevitably have suggested Charke's own celebrated cross-dressed roles on the stage" (Shershow 1999: 158). Charke likely also could not resist the extra laughs her Punch would get playing this *Punch*bowl madam, whose lines include, "A house like this without a bully left, / Is like a puppet-show without a Punch" (Fielding 1902: 124). The choice may also have been inspired by Fielding's original casting of Mr. Bridgewater in the role, though Fielding's casting was nothing unusual. Male actors had long played female characters because the presence of an actual woman onstage was considered immoral. And though eighteenth-century women performing breeches roles may appear subversive by contemporary standards, "despite their apparent gender-bending, breeches roles played into an entirely conventional sexual system. Appealing to the heterosexual fantasies of men in the audience, breeches emphasized the lower half of the actress's body" (Shevelow 2005: 176). Charke, however, did indeed bend gender, pushing the boundaries even further by developing a notable reputation for performing travesty roles (i.e., playing actual men instead of women disguised as men). This was "considered by many to be a risky and disreputable step" for an actress, but one which helped to solidify Charke's "reputation for eccentricity and masculinity" (Shevelow 2005: 186). Through her acting, writing, puppetry, and in her daily life, Charke actively crossed boundaries of gender, class, and genre.

Although Fielding's original production closed after only one performance in 1732, Peter Lewis believes "[t]he reasons for the thoroughgoing condemnation the play received were moral, not aesthetic" (Lewis 1987: 135), describing it as "one of the few masterpieces of Augustan dramatic burlesque ... [in which Fielding] subjects many features of contemporary tragedy to devastating criticism" (Lewis 1987: 149). Critics at the time ignored Fielding's critique of drama in favor of outrage over the play's brothel setting and prurient characters. There was particular concern for the upper-class ladies in the theatre's boxes, who one outraged critic said Fielding "tells ... without any ceremony, that there's no difference betwixt the best of them, and the bawdy-house trulls they had been seeing on the Stage; and that, pretend what they would, they were all a parcel of downright arrant whores" (cited in Paulson and Lockwood 1969: 58). Both Fielding and Charke show gumption in staging this controversial play, but there are interesting differences in their productions that speak both to Charke's importance as a politically progressive, proto-feminist, avant-garde artist and to her keen understanding of the power of puppetry.

Jurkowski describes *The Covent Garden Tragedy*'s significance as "the first time in dramatic literature that a writer stood up for a prostitute, and presented the nobility of sentiment of a 'fallen woman' – and the practicality of her behavior." He cites Charke's "opposition to the new bourgeois morality" in her decision to adapt this piece to the puppet stage (Jurkowski and Francis 1996: 187). Blumenthal likewise describes the play as a satirical political "farce by Henry Fielding about the brutality of the sex trade" in which, in Charke's adaptation, "Punch (in drag) played a madame, clobbering whores and johns alike" (Blumenthal 2005: 171). Interpretations of the play as a critique of the sex industry, however, are uncommon in scholarship on Fielding's original production. Analyses focus primarily on Fielding's ongoing critiques of the deterioration of "high" theatrical forms, such as tragedy, which in his day "laid itself increasingly open to attack as it became more elevated, heroic, and neoclassical" (Lewis 1987: 3). More politically progressive readings are, indeed, enticing, particularly in light of what were likely the play's most controversial lines. The prostitute Stormandra expresses her humanity and the notion of prostitution as work, separate from matters of the heart, when she tells the man she loves, "But though my person be upon the town, / My heart has still been fixed on only you" (Fielding 1902: 126). In the play's epilogue, Kissinda, the other prostitute, suggests the radical notion that all women enjoy sex but are expected to pretend they do not: "For though some prude her lover long may vex, / Her coyness is put on, she loves your sex" (Fielding 1902: 134). I would argue, however, that Jurkowski and Blumenthal's interpretations are better applied to Charke's adaptation of the play than to the original. Though Fielding may have had some interest in humanizing prostitutes and critiquing the sex industry, more so "his aim is to ridicule ... contemporary tragic drama, especially its language and rhetoric" (Lewis 1987: 135). As is also evident in his more famous 1730 play, *The Author's Farce*, in which he had human actors play puppets, Fielding regularly critiqued "how the purely economic considerations of the actor-managers ... deformed the hierarchy of literary value" (Shershow 1999: 148). Since Fielding ridiculed problematic trends he believed were destroying the theatre (with bad tragedies and puppetry, as I will discuss momentarily, on his list of culprits) by aligning these trends with the "moral reprehensibility" of prostitution, interpreting his version of the play as empathetic to prostitutes is problematic.

Whereas Fielding depicted the lives of sex workers as a metaphor to serve his aesthetic critique of drama, Charke knew personally more than a dozen "Ladies who kept Coffee-Houses in and about the Garden" who were close enough friends that she publicly expresses gratitude to them for their attempt to pool enough money to bail her out of debtor's prison (Charke 1999: 48). These friendships, as well as her own position as an actress and an impoverished woman, arguably gave Charke a different perspective on Needham and her employees. Charke likely had a much more intimate sense of the most controversial sentiment in the play – that all women, regardless of class, are commodities in the patriarchy – as expressed in the epilogue:

> In short, you [men] are the business of our lives,
> To be a mistress kept the strumpet strives,
> And all the modest virgins to be wives.
> For prudes may cant of virtues and of vices,
> But faith, we only differ in our prices.
>
> (Fielding 1902: 134)

With this context in mind, I interpret Charke's casting of the wife-beating Punch in the role of Mother Punchbowl as a scathing critique of a patriarchal system that commodifies all women, which also illuminates the socially engaged possibilities of puppetry.

Punch, the perennial patriarch of the puppet stage, has been described as a working-class hero who rebels against the institutions of marriage, church, and state by beating his wife, the clergyman, and the constable to death. In Charke's hands, Punch in petticoats is "a wolf in sheep's clothing," a symbol of the patriarchy upon which the sex industry should rightly be blamed, rather than the women inevitably contracted to participate in it. Her adaptation draws attention to the oppression of women that is often erased in Punch and Judy. In part because of Punch's position as a working-class man, his abuse of his position of power in relation to his wife is at times overlooked. Charke's proto-feminist Punch in petticoats forces us to take notice.

The differences between Fielding and Charke's versions of *The Covent Garden Tragedy* also illuminate Charke's artistic sensibilities as more radical and ahead of their time than Fielding's, another reason why she is in need of more critical attention. Though he did not completely object to the existence of puppet theatre, Fielding thought it "must be kept in its place ... [He] dislike[d] the puppet's incursion into live theatre, and consider[ed] its proper place to be with simple folk tales and 'Punch and his wife Joan'" (Arnott 1964: 37). Charke had more foresight regarding puppetry's capabilities, radically exploding the divisions between high and low art that Fielding strived to maintain. Time has proven Charke correct. Puppetry continually proves itself at least as capable as human theatre of dealing with complex themes and serious subjects. And although Charke's puppet productions were surely influential in her lifetime, discrimination and oversight by scholars has prevented her contributions from aiding puppetry's recognition as such. As late as 1964, for example, Peter Arnott was still trying to prove that puppetry is "an artistic medium of significant potential" that "could be used for the performance of serious drama" (Arnott 1964: 25) in a study in which he discusses Fielding as contributing to the hindrance of this understanding, but makes no mention of Charke.

As previously discussed, Shershow illuminates the reasons for puppetry's perpetual appropriation as stand-in for all that is "low" or "other." This ideology is no small part of the Western misunderstanding of puppetry's artistic possibilities. Unfortunately, Shershow's focus on the myriad ways in which puppetry has been framed as such causes him to misinterpret Charke's cross-dressed Punch, as well as her own cross-dressing, as "recreat[ing] the theatrical and cultural hierarchies that ... excluded and subordinated her" (Shershow 1999: 159). Rather, Charke's cross-dressing, her manifold *Narrative*, and her petticoated Punch are all, indeed, proto-feminist illuminations of "the discontinuous acts that social custom usually smooths over to produce gender roles" (Wanko 1994: 81), as well as the equally problematic hierarchies of high art versus low entertainment. One final aspect of Charke's puppetry, her use of voice distortion, is key to understanding the ways in which her adaptations of dramas to the puppet stage, like her cross-dressing, reject rather than reinforce patriarchal ideology.

Battling patriarchy with a swazzle

Frank Proschan explains that "[f]olk puppeteers around the world, in diverse and often unrelated traditions ... make use of voice modifying instruments ... to let the puppets speak ... demonstrat[ing] their profound understanding of some of the essential attributes of language and speech" (Proschan 1981: 528). Charke's utilization of voice distortion – she "used the traditional tin or wooden tubes called squeakers to create the puppets' voices" (Shevelow 2005: 263) – demonstrates her sophisticated understanding of puppetry conventions, as well as her innovative spirit in applying long-standing techniques of folk puppetry to literary plays. By doing so, Charke deprioritizes the literary text (and the newly developing authority in this period of the "author-god" who wrote it), while creating space for the audience, puppeteers, and puppets to participate in meaning- and story-making. She does so in adaptations of several plays by Shakespeare no less, the pivotal author-god who, according to Shershow, is second only to Ben Jonson in the theological construction of authorship that emerged in the Renaissance (Shershow 1999: 44). Perhaps Charke's puppetry might be considered a precursor to the socially engaged resistance to authorial and textual dictatorship that appears in the work of modern theorists such as Roland Barthes, who writes:

> [A] text does not consist of ... a single "theological" meaning (the "message" of the Author-God), but is a space of many dimensions ... [R]efusing to

assign to the text (and to the world as text) ... an ultimate meaning, liberates ... for to refuse to arrest meaning is finally to refuse God and his hypostases, reason, science, the law.

(Barthes 1967: 5–6)

Cheryl Walker reframes Barthes's theory from a feminist perspective: "[W]riting is not 'the destruction of every voice' but *the proliferation of possibilities of hearing*" (Walker 1990: 568). Charke's swazzling of literary dramas rejects the sanctity of the author-god and his "sacred" text, as well as longstanding Western patriarchal ideologies that situate man over woman, drama over puppetry. Proschan explains that when puppeteers utilize voice distortion, "the audience's work is increased, their interpretive burden enlarged, as their creative role expands" (Proschan 1981: 551). Proschan's insights lead to an interesting connection between Charke's puppetry, her cross-dressing, and her *Narrative*. Her elusiveness about her sexual orientation and her reasons for offstage cross-dressing, her nonlinear "multifurcated" (Wanko 1994: 87) *Narrative*, and her enthusiastic mixing of seemingly disparate theatrical forms all speak to Charke's bold and subversive refusal of the limits within which the patriarchy sought to fix her.

Power to the puppets

In her *Narrative*, Charke wrote that she was "certain that [learning's] greatest Advantages are to be infinitely improved by launching into the World, and becoming acquainted with the different Places and Objects we go thro' and meet in traveling" (Charke 1999: 17). Her genuine openness to people, ideas, and artistic practices, as well as her stubborn optimism, are still radical necessities in the continuing struggle against systemic inequality. Charke embraced a more difficult life by refusing and resisting the patriarchy in as many ways possible, and despite the inevitable hardships that she suffered because of this (in her own life and in the historical record), she remained convinced "that no Misfortune, of ever so dreadful a Nature, should excite us to despair" (Charke 1999: 51). Christine Cloud argues that Charke's memoir exemplifies the ways in which "autobiographical writing by transvestite figures both constitutes and occupies a third space where identity is hybrid, multiple and disconcerting ... explod[ing] the myths that both underlie and uphold gender-based binary thinking" (Cloud 2009: 858). Similarly, in Charke's Punch in petticoats and swazzled Shakespeare, we see puppetry's potential, perhaps more so than any other art form, to illuminate the socially constructed nature of gender and genre binaries, and thus to help us dissolve categories so often used to divide and control us.

Notes

1 Though Fidelis Morgan usefully summarizes discriminatory scholarship on Charke, she exudes homophobia by arguing that Charke's cross-dressing and long-term relationship with Mrs. Brown do not prove queer identity due to "Charlotte's frequent declarations that her

book was intended to be moral" (Morgan 1988: 203), implying that morality is exclusive to heterosexuals.
2. "[A] theoretical framework of intersectionality ... view[s] race, class, gender, sexuality, ethnicity, and age, among others, as mutually constructing systems of power. Because these systems permeate all social relations, untangling their effects in any given situation or for any given population remains difficult" (Collins 2005: 11).
3. Charke's potential as a feminist or queer hero at times mires critics in discussions of her cross-dressing in relation to her sexual orientation, though the latter is "a question that arguably can never be answered" (Baruth 1998: 50). Related debates regarding whether Charke's cross-dressing and her artistic works (most often the *Narrative* itself) reject or reinforce patriarchal ideology seem more productive. Taking the latter position, Erin Mackie, for example, admits "Charke violates the discretion of the masculine/feminine gender dichotomy," but disagrees with scholars who argue this makes her a feminist because "even Charke's most transgressive gestures – her cross-dressing, her adoption of male roles ... are undertaken not to undermine but to affirm the value of the masculine on which the patriarchy and her own cross-dressing depend" (Mackie 1991: 843). Baruth provides a useful summary of the contemporary feminist and queer debates (Baruth 1998: 52–57).
4. Charke's ten known puppet play adaptations are Shakespeare's *Henry VIII*, *King Henry IV*, and *Richard III*; Fielding's *The Mock Doctor*, *The Covent Garden Tragedy*, and *The Old Debauchees*; Cibber's *Damon and Phillida*; *The Beggar's Wedding* by Charles Coffey; *The Unhappy Favourite* by John Banks; and *The Miller of Mansfield* by Robert Dodsley. John Dryden's *Amphitryon* was announced but never shown (Jurkowski and Francis 1996: 186–188).
5. Yeates's and Russell's first names are unknown.
6. Baruth provides another interesting example of Charke's subversiveness when he frames her short-lived career running an oil and grocery shop once the Licensing Act was passed as antecedent political performance art. "Not only was Charke taking off the London merchant, but part of the point was that her comedic talents were being wasted. By 'div[ing] into the Trade,' Charke could most publicly register a form of absurdist protest ... [keeping] alive ... the memory of the Haymarket Company [and] its place as symbol of the opposition" (Baruth 1998: 31–33).
7. A portrait marionette of her father would be a great attraction due to Cibber's celebrity status, Charke's notoriety for impersonating him, and their tumultuous public relationship, but could likely not replace Punch entirely. We know Charke had at least two Punches (Shevelow 2005: 267) because she advertised that in her adaptation of *Amphitryon* "'[t]he part of the two Sosias [was] to be performed by two Punches'" (Charke cited in Morgan 1988: 64). So perhaps one Punch was indeed Cibber-faced.
8. Considering it in relation to her puppetry would further enrich feminist and queer theorizing on the significance of Charke's cross-dressing.

Works cited

Arnott, P. (1964) *Plays Without People*. Bloomington, IN: Indiana University Press.
Ashley, L. (ed.) (1969) *A Narrative of the Life of Mrs. Charlotte Charke*. Gainesville, FL: Scholars' Facsimiles and Reprints.
Barthes, R. (1967) "The Death of the Author," trans. R. Howard, *Aspen* 5 & 6, <http://www.ubu.com/aspen/aspen5and6/threeEssays.html#barthes> (accessed 22 August 2013).
Baruth, P. (ed.) (1998) *Introducing Charlotte Charke*. Urbana, IL: University of Illinois Press.
Blumenthal, E. (2005) *Puppetry: A World History*. New York, NY: Harry N. Abrams.
Charke, C. (1755 [1999]) *A Narrative of the Life of Charlotte Charke*, R. Rehder (ed.). London: Pickering and Chatto.
Cloud, C. (2009) "The Chameleon, Cross-dressed Autobiography of Charlotte Charke (1713–60)," *Women's Studies* 38: 857–871.

Collins, P. H. (2005) *Black Sexual Politics*. New York, NY: Routledge.
Fielding, H. (1902, reprinted 1967) *The Complete Works of Henry Fielding, Esq: With an Essay on the Life, Genius and Achievement of the Author*, vol. 10, *Plays and Poems Volume 3*, W. E. Henley (ed.). New York, NY: Croscup and Sterling.
Jurkowski, H. and Francis, P. (eds) (1996) *A History of European Puppetry, Vol. 1: From Its Origins to the End of the 19th Century*. Lewiston, NY: The Edwin Mellen Press.
Lewis, P. (1987) *Fielding's Burlesque Drama*. Edinburgh, Scotland: Edinburgh University Press.
Mackie, E. (1991) "Desperate Measures: The Narratives of the Life of Mrs. Charlotte Charke," *ELH: English Literary History* 58: 841–865.
McPharlin, P. and McPharlin, M. B. (1949; 2nd edn 1969) *The Puppet Theatre in America, A History, 1524–1948*. Boston, MA: Plays, Inc.
Morgan, F. (1988) *The Well-Known Troublemaker: A Life of Charlotte Charke*. London: Faber & Faber.
Paulson, R. and Lockwood, T. (eds.) (1969) *Henry Fielding: The Critical Heritage*. London: Routledge and Kegan Paul.
Proschan, F. (1981) "Puppet Voices and Interlocutors: Language in Folk Puppetry," *The Journal of American Folklore* 94: 527–555.
Shershow, S. C. (1995) *Puppets and "Popular" Culture*. Ithaca, NY: Cornell University Press.
Shevelow, K. (2005) *Charlotte*. New York, NY: Henry Holt and Company.
Speaight, G. (1955; 2nd edn 1990) *The History of the English Puppet Theatre*. Carbondale, IL: Southern Illinois University Press.
Straub, K. (1992) *Sexual Suspects: Eighteenth-Century Players and Sexual Ideology*. Princeton, NJ: Princeton University Press.
Walker, C. (1990) "Feminist Literary Criticism and the Author," *Critical Inquiry* 16: 551–571.
Wanko, C. (1994) "The Eighteenth-Century Actress and the Construction of Gender: Lavinia Fenton and Charlotte Charke," *Eighteenth-Century Life* 18(2): 75–90.

13
Life-Death and Disobedient Obedience
Russian Modernist Redefinitions of the Puppet

Dassia N. Posner

One of the striking things about Russian theatre in the first two decades of the twentieth century is that puppets were both everywhere and nowhere. The Russian homage to wooden actors was seemingly ubiquitous; still-famous examples include the trio of dancers who play puppets in Benois/Stravinsky/Fokine's *Petrushka* (1911) and the puppet theatre-within-a-theatre in Blok's *Little Fairground Booth*, directed by Meyerhold in 1906. Although Stanislavsky is often mentally pinned to his naturalistic stagings of Chekhov, his seminal production of *The Blue Bird*, one of Maeterlinck's symbolist plays "for marionettes," is still running at the Moscow Art Theatre over a century after its 1908 opening.

Appearances of actual puppets on Russian modernist stages were, however, few. Tsar Nikolai II's regime had been steadily quashing the Shrovetide fairs, one of the familiar haunts of Petrushka, Punch's Russian cousin. And although many among Russia's artistic intelligentsia – Andrei Bely, Nikolai Evreinov, Sergei Sudeikin, Liubov Iakovleva, to name a few – made attempts to create puppet shows in the new century's early years, most were abortive. Thus, this period of unprecedented theatrical explosion and innovation was marked by a curious paradox: the puppet was one of the major rejuvenating forces in Russian theatre, yet few puppets were to be found.

This changed in 1916 when two women, writer and critic Iulia Slonimskaia and visual artist Nina Simonovich-Efimova,[1] became the first artist-intellectuals to stage professional puppet productions in Russia. Slonimskaia co-created and performed with marionettes in *The Forces of Love and Magic*, originally a French fairground play, at the Saint Petersburg cabaret The Players' Rest. Simonovich-Efimova created a glove-puppet Petrushka for the Moscow Association of Artists and shadow shows for The Bat, a cabaret later known abroad as the Chauve-Souris. Both women also made major contributions to a growing body of theatrical theory about puppets. Their writings, which were deeply informed by their practical puppetry work, challenged widespread interpretations of the puppet that were circulating in Russia's then-raging wars over what the theatre of the future should be.

In looking back at this period, many of the modernist ideas about the puppet that are most famous now – Edward Gordon Craig's that the puppet is obedient, Jentsch's and Freud's that it is uncanny – were primarily developed from outside the puppet theatre looking in. This theory was often more concerned with what Gross calls "the idea of the puppet" than with the puppet itself (Gross 2011: 4). Bensky observes that "the human may be treated in two ways in puppet theatre ... [There is a] constant tendency to humanize the object, endowing it with human characteristics, and alternately to 'depersonalize' it, depriving the puppet of individual features and giving it the function of stereotype or pure theatrical sign" (cited in Jurkowski and Francis 1998: 26).[2] In a modernist context, such "depersonalizations" often focused on the puppet's death or lack of agency.

Simonovich-Efimova and Slonimskaia found such views of the puppet unproductively limiting. They differed significantly from many of their contemporaries in that they aimed to define the specific nature of the actual stage puppet, to clarify its laws and aesthetics, and to establish its artistic legitimacy. Both sought to develop vocabularies for puppetry as a viable theatrical form, to define its laws as unique from the theatre of live actors, and to view theatre, art, and life itself from a puppet perspective.

Two paradoxes regarding the nature of the puppet recur in Slonimskaia's and Simonovich-Efimova's writings, though each articulates them differently with somewhat divergent solutions. Both grapple with what Penny Francis has called the puppet's "life-death,"[3] the idea that an object can be inanimate and yet simultaneously appear to contain life. This belief in the inanimate puppet's innate life led Slonimskaia to write about movement as life and Simonovich-Efimova about the puppeteer as a life-giving force.

The second paradox I will call "disobedient obedience." From the outset, Simonovich-Efimova viewed puppet choreography as a collaborative discovery rather than as an imposition of the puppeteer's will upon her puppet. Slonimskaia, who had no previous experience with marionettes before *The Forces of Love and Magic*, learned quickly that the puppet was a less willingly compliant collaborator than the metaphors about marionettes as obedient beings wielded by omnipotent forces had led her to conclude. Her discovery raised questions about how one might learn not to control but to listen to puppets, material objects with minds of their own.

Slonimskaia and Simonovich-Efimova embraced the artistic autonomy that the puppet theatre provided, a rare sphere in which they could become directors, designers, and performers in their own theatres during an era when the directors in live-actor theatres were almost invariably men. The puppet theatre also gave them a unique opportunity to engage productively and transgressively with forms that had often been held separate: popular and elite culture, theatre for children and theatre for adults, fairground performance and fine art.

Here, however, we encounter another curious paradox. Their intense experimentation led to insights that significantly illuminate the puppet's nature and artistic vocabulary, yet their complete creative freedom lay within a bounded sphere. While the actors' theatre had no difficulty in appropriating puppet metaphors, it was ultimately more concerned with the live rather than the wooden body. The work of both Slonimskaia and Simonovich-Efimova is viewed as foundational among Russian puppeteers and puppetry scholars, but it is still little known beyond this.

This chapter examines their seminal theoretical writings, focusing in particular on their analyses of the puppet's life-death and disobedient obedience. I will first contextualize their work within the Russian marionette craze and in contrast to two contemporaneous symbolist writers, Fedor Sologub and Valery Briusov, before then turning to a more detailed examination of Slonimskaia's and Simonovich-Efimova's writings. My aim is to reclaim a broader, more pragmatic theoretical heritage for the puppet in the modernist period and to illuminate how these two women's insights resonate closely with puppetry theory and practice today.

The Russian modernist marionette

Slonimskaia's and Simonovich-Efimova's work was part of a much larger fascination with the puppet – with the string marionette, in particular – that spanned Europe and the US at the *fin de siècle*, a craze Jurkowski has identified as "an unexpected stroke of fortune" for puppetry in the sense that the form finally "was included in the aesthetics debate, thus establishing its uniquely characteristic features, its essence and its specificity" (Jurkowski and Francis 1998: 1–2).

Several factors contributed to the Russian branch of this marionette madness. One was the concurrent rise in small forms during Russia's Silver Age, roughly the two decades preceding the 1917 Revolution, during which directors and impresarios, inspired by proliferating cabarets in Western Europe, opened "miniature theatres" in defiance of the grandiosity of Imperial and commercial performance venues. Interest in folk and popular traditions also increased markedly in the wake of the decline and eventual erasure of the Russian fairground, as evidenced by many turn-of-the-century books dedicated to folk and fairground traditions.[4]

The pessimism with which Russian artists often linked the marionette is best understood in the context of the failed 1905 Revolution. As Bartlett and Edmondson note:

> The creativity of the Russian modernists was largely inspired by prescience of the demise of their world and way of life; much of their art can be read as a death-wish in terms of its thematics. Yet what came out of that death-wish – music, literature, and art of genius – was ultimately creative, rather than destructive.
>
> (Bartlett and Edmondson 1998: 215)

These artists used the puppet on strings as a metaphor for man at the mercy of fate, as a sign of death, and as an example of a rigidly mechanized being, reflecting the existential issues with which they were then grappling.

Equally significantly, the rise of the theatrical director and the rise of interest in the puppet occurred simultaneously. It is nearly impossible to fathom today how revolutionary it was then for directors to be the primary artistic shapers of theatrical productions. The marionette was a useful symbol for directors attempting to achieve artistic unity in collaboration with actors whose training and methods clashed with this unity. Unsurprisingly, these directors' views of the puppet emerged from their own unique philosophies of the theatre. For instance, while Craig famously viewed the Über-marionette as the ideal actor stripped of messy, unpredictable individuality, Vsevelod Meyerhold lauded wooden actors for their uniquely conventionalized representation of character (Meyerhold 1913 [1969]: 129).

In several early directorial attempts to apply these ideas, actors wore masks, had their bodies replaced with cardboard, used mechanized movements, or even, in Meyerhold's 1908 *Petrushka*, wore false puppet legs in an attempt to explore new physical vocabularies free from the historical and representational constraints of realism (Wachtel 1998: 24). It became common for playwrights and directors to term their plays "marionette shows," meaning that they imitated puppets without using them.

Theatre and the puppet: Sologub and Briusov

These experiments were among a variety of attempts to define theatre in terms of its own inherent *teatral'nost'* (theatricality) and *uslovnost'* (conventionality). In 1902, Russian symbolist poet and playwright Valery Briusov had polemicized against what he called the "unnecessary truth" of the Moscow Art Theatre's early productions (Briusov 1902 [1986]: 30), arguing that it was impossible to mirror life exactly on the stage and futile to attempt to do so. No audience will ever believe that an actual tree is growing onstage or that Hamlet's life is in real danger, he asserted. Theatre should instead embrace its own conventionality in order to engage the "creative urge" of its audiences (Briusov 1902 [1986]: 29).

The question that followed in his essay's controversial wake was *how*. A 1908 collection, *Theatre: A Book about the New Theatre*, proposed several possible solutions. Two of its contributors, Briusov and novelist, poet, and playwright Fedor Sologub, wrote about the new theatre in relation to the marionette. Although both interpreted the puppet in terms that seem remarkably similar to the writings of Edward Gordon Craig, their work was initially better known in Russia than Craig's "The Actor and the Über-marionette" (1908), which was not translated into Russian until 1912.

In "Realism and Convention on the Stage," Briusov probes puppets as a possible solution to the problem of the theatrical actor, whose real body was "out of harmony with a conventionalized production" (Briusov 1908 [1981]: xlviii). Briusov posits that "[t]he only way left for the 'conventionalized' theater to triumph is to replace actors with puppets on strings, with gramophones inside them," adding:

> But the more logical the conventionalized production and the more it tallies with a mechanical theater, the less necessary it will be. By depriving the actor of the possibility of acting and of artistic creation, theatrical conventionality will finally eliminate the stage and art as well.
> (Briusov 1908 [1981]: 177)

For Briusov, a mechanical theatre is no longer theatre "as an individual art form" (Briusov 1908 [1981]: 180). Nor does he believe that forcing actors to behave like puppets is a viable solution:

Once the performers have been retained, one cannot force them to act like machines; a living creature is incapable of it, to any great degree. Once machines have been utilized, one cannot elevate their workings to the level of creativity: We do not have the power to inspire the dead with life ...
(Briusov 1908 [1981]: 180)

Because Briusov views the puppet as a machine, he believes it cannot provide theatre's life-blood: creativity.

A second essay, Sologub's "Theatre of a Single Will," views the puppet as an agentless symbol of death. Sologub advocates for the centrality of the playwright, stipulating that distractions such as the actor's unpredictable personality and the director's interpretive lens be eliminated, as they distort the playwright's vision. Sologub's proposed solution to the "tyranny" of the actor, which threatens to usurp the playwright's centrality, is the monodrama, in which one person reads the entire play, including the title, author's name, cast list, and stage directions (Sologub 1908 [1981]: 138). The actors follow the directions as they are read and speak their lines, prompted by the reader should they forget them. Sologub defends what he called turning actors into marionettes, stating:

> Such is the unalterable law of universal playacting that man is like a wonderfully constructed marionette ...
>
> When the hour ordained for every man comes, each of us, in full, will turn into an inert and unbreathing puppet, no longer capable of playing any kind of role ...
>
> There it lies on sackcloth for the final ablution, a puppet outworn and of no further use to anyone – its arms folded by others – and its legs outstretched by others – and its eyes closed by others – a poor marionette for only one tragic bit of playacting. Yonder, behind the scenes, an indifferent being pulled you by an invisible string.
> (Sologub 1908 [1981]: 140)

Thus, while Briusov saw the puppet as mechanical and lacking in spontaneity, Sologub viewed it as an empty body manipulated from without. Both were more interested in the puppet as a metaphor for mankind rather than in the puppet as a theatrical object. Similar views of the puppet still abound today.

Iulia Slonimskaia: The soul of the marionette

Slonimskaia and Simonovich-Efimova believed that puppetry theory generated from an external perspective – from actors' theatre, psychology, or literature – could generate insights applicable to those fields, but that to write about the puppet without engagement with it was to risk distorting its practical potential. Thus, both women developed their theory simultaneously, along with or in response to their performances.

The Puppet Theatre of Slonimskaia and her husband, Pavel Sazonov, opened its first production, *The Forces of Love and Magic*, in February 1916.[5] Their short-lived

Figure 13.1 Demon puppet from *The Forces of Love and Magic* (1916): puppet design by Nikolai Kalmakov. Image reprinted from Iuliia Slonimskaia, "Marionetka," *Apollon* (March 1916), PSlav 122.5, Houghton Library, Harvard University

theatre was known for lavish sets and marionettes, for designs by World of Art artists Nikolai Kalmakov and Mstislav Dobuzhinsky, and for attracting much of illustrious theatrical Petersburg to its shows.[6] The month after the opening, Slonimskaia published a 42-page essay on the marionette that comprised much of the March issue of the journal *Apollon*.

Slonimskaia's essay was written at the height of the marionette craze and was well known in her day. Because Slonimskaia's work aligned so closely with Meyerhold's views on conventionalized theatre, Meyerhold made her essay required reading in the early 1920s for his State Higher Directors' Workshops students (Zabrodin 2005: 120), among whom were Sergei Eisenstein, Maria Babanova, and Igor Ilinsky. Unfortunately, Slonimskaia's emigration to France shortly after the Bolshevik Revolution curtailed the spread of her influence in early Soviet theatre.

Slonimskaia's essay tied in various strains of thought on the role of the marionette in modern theatre, while offering the historical basis and validation that Konstantin Miklashevsky's research (1914–1917) had generated on the *commedia dell'arte*. She traces the puppet's history from ancient Greece and India to the puppets of her own day, analyzing in detail several specific European forms, including Nativity puppets, the German Faust tradition, *commedia dell'arte*, and Punch and Judy.

Her essay develops several key arguments. First and foremost, she maintains that the marionette has a life of its own and that "the marionette's soul is movement" (Slonimskaia 1916 [1990]: 58).[7] She also defies what she views as a mistaken understanding of the puppet as mechanical: "The theatrical instinct that prompted … the primal songs and dances instilled a desire to animate the marionette with movement – not mechanical movement, but movement that responded freely to the immediate inspiration of its operator" (Slonimskaia 1916 [1990]: 31).

Slonimskaia redirects two familiar formulas that explore the relationship between man and the marionette – the puppet as an imitation of man and man as a puppet of fate:

> Man has created the marionette in his image and likeness. It seems to imitate man, as man seems to imitate nature in his art, but in repeating man, in imitating him, the marionette takes the same path that man takes in the imitation of nature; it contributes something ... and instead of being a copy, it becomes an artistic creation that is full of its own mysterious life. Imitation is transformed into creation.
>
> It is not the marionette that likens itself to man, but, conversely, man who has compared himself to the marionette, which has become a symbol of man in the world.
>
> (Slonimskaia 1916 [1990]: 27)

Slonimskaia aims to demonstrate the puppet's unique contributions to art and philosophy, arguing that it is "a semi-fantastical being," not something dead or free of expression (Slonimskaia 1916 [1990]: 30). The idea that a puppet has a soul runs throughout the essay, particularly in the second chapter, where she writes, "Knowing how it is constructed, [mankind] nevertheless sensed in [the marionette] a hidden magical life that is awakened only by the movement of its strings" (Slonimskaia 1916 [1990]: 30).

Slonimskaia also counters Craig's "The Actor and the Über-marionette," insisting, for instance, that the puppet cannot be a descendent of ancient Greek temple automata, as Craig had suggested, since the movement of these statues was mechanized. Rather, she sees the organic movement of the marionette as having been initiated by women in Dionysian rituals:

> Marionettes did not originate in the temple, but in the folk cult procession. They were not the artificial contrivances of the high priestly caste, but were created from the spontaneous religious thought of the people. ...
>
> This is how the first articulated puppet was born, the strings of which were the conductors of the feelings and thoughts of its creator and poet.
>
> (Slonimskaia 1916 [1990]: 31)

For Slonimskaia the puppet is the inner expression of the artist made tangible.

Slonimskaia's most significant contribution to puppetry theory is her distinction between the marionette and the automaton. If, as she argues, the marionette's spontaneous movement cannot have originated in the automaton's mechanical movement, it therefore also cannot have the very qualities that made it attractive to directors. Her discussion of the problems inherent in this perception of the marionette is worth quoting at length:

> Within the argument of the primacy of the actor or the puppet is concealed a false understanding of the marionette. The marionette is obstinately

identified with the automaton. The tirelessness, submissiveness, and lack of creative individuality that are attributed to it are, in reality, characteristics of the automaton only. In the theatre of the automaton, previously prescribed movements are ... repeated with utter precision at every performance; the automaton's performance is cold and unchangeable, tireless and impersonal.

"Marionettes are obedient, tireless, and always at the ready," says Paul Margueritte. In reality, they don't have a single one of these qualities. The marionette gets tired like an actor because it is moved by human hands. Its voice is human and thus cannot be tireless; it cannot be more tireless or obedient than that of the actor. Its performance cannot always be identical, because it depends on the inspiration of those who move its strings and speak its words.

The marionette is much less submissive than a living person. Its personal qualities are ineradicably strong ... .

The marionette embodies the forces of life – movement – and cannot, as Gordon Craig asserts, be the bearer of death charms. On the contrary, in the marionette is the victory of the forces of life over lifeless matter. A piece of wood moves, lives, and expresses passions as a special kind of creature, created by the magic of art.

The mechanical qualities that have been falsely attributed to the marionette have occluded its real artistic merit. The representation of a marionette as a passionless automaton methodically fulfilling prescribed actions once and forever does not at all resemble the real marionette, which is eternally changeable, ever unexpected, endlessly varied, truly inspired.

(Slonimskaia 1916 [1990]: 56)

Slonimskaia's observation that the marionette represents "the victory of the forces of life over lifeless matter" is particularly significant, as it makes a distinction between dead and lifeless. Dead implies that the life – the unpredictable nature – has been removed, something potentially desirable in dealing with live actors, while lifeless infers that the puppet simply awaits animation. This gives it the ability to bridge life and death, the souled and the soulless.

Nina Simonovich-Efimova: Filling the puppet with life

In 1916, the same year that Slonimskaia's theatre opened in St. Petersburg, Simonovich-Efimova gave her first public shows in Moscow. Her early Petrushka and shadow productions were so well received that she and her husband Ivan founded their own theatre. They initially performed in artistic cafés and cabarets but became itinerant during the lean post-revolutionary Civil War years. They founded what grew into a thriving, established Soviet puppetry tradition. Though Sergei Obraztsov's puppetry style later diverged from that of the Efimovs, they were his first teachers (Simonovich-Efimova 1977: 35).

Looking back in 1940 on their early, itinerant performances, Simonovich-Efimova wrote with satisfaction: "In addition to our direct aim, audience enjoyment, every show was a sermon for what we were doing and, after five years, puppet 'Petrushka theatres' began to appear all over the Soviet Union, first one by one, then by the dozens and hundreds ... ." (Simonovich-Efimova 1940: 3). Simonovich-Efimova's lifelong goal was simple: to advance the art of the puppet. This included expanding the physical vocabulary of puppets, how they were built, for whom they were performed, and by whom they were created.

The earliest formulation of Simonovich-Efimova's theatrical theory was her 1919 "About Petrushka (O *Petrushke*)," but she also published books, pamphlets, and guides for aspiring puppeteers. She is best known for *Notes of a Petrushka Player* (*Zapiski Petrushechnika*, originally published in 1925; adapted into English as *Adventures of a Russian Puppet Theatre*, 1935), through which she became "the first Soviet puppeteer to begin the conversation about the particulars of puppet theatre, a conversation that continues to the present day" (Nekrylova 1980: 20). *Notes* chronicles Simonovich-Efimova's early performances, provides insight into her artistic philosophy, publishes plays and drawings, and provides information on puppet design. It also documents the work of contemporary Petrushka players, about whom we otherwise would know little today.[8]

Everything Simonovich-Efimova discusses in *Notes* emerges from her theatre's mission:

> [T]o show how expressive and subtle Petrushka gestures are, how incredibly many of them there are, how nuanced they are ... and above all – greatness (for puppets that have not been invited to join the ranks of the "great" theatrical arts), above all – a new beauty (for artists singled out as outside the limits of "high" art ...). The concern of our theatre *is not novelty of plot, not novelty of word or of staging, but a new concept of Petrushka gesture* [emphasis in original].
> (Simonovich-Efimova 1980: 43–44)

She worked to define the nature of the puppet, to establish puppetry's validity as a unique discipline within the spectator arts, and to expand glove-puppet movement, design, and repertoire. By "Petrushka," she meant not only the popular entertainment tradition but also glove puppets more generally.

In *Notes*, Simonovich-Efimova validates glove-puppet theatre by comparing and contrasting it with those of live actors and marionettes:

> The theatre of people reaches a certain limit and begins to appeal to the puppet: "Revive me, purify me."
>   Can we talk seriously of parity with the theatre of actors? ...
>   The face is replaced in the Petrushka theatre by the palm of the artist's hand, but this is no worse than a face.
>   The pianist also plays with the hands, and sounds emerge, and images appear ...
>   The artist, who simultaneously has a puppet on each hand, plays with the fingers, and, like a pianist, gives birth to images.
>   The images are not aural, but visual.

There are as infinitely many of them as there are in music, as infinitely great a number of nuances.

(Simonovich-Efimova 1980: 43)

In her understanding, the puppeteer is more versatile than the stage actor because "The actor multiplies his personality with puppets. He does not depend on his partner; he is his own partner" (Simonovich-Efimova 1980: 43).

Simonovich-Efimova "believed that the essential truth lies in the puppet itself, in its limitless expressive capacity," particularly with regard to gesture (Jurkowski and Francis 1998: 105). Simonovich-Efimova outlines in detail gestures at which glove puppets excel:

These little actors do not have facial expressions, but they do have effective gestures: they kiss, fight, bow (what's more, their bow can have all the nuances of a bow), they bless each other ... they die "stupendously," they get frightened; they convey clearly the nature of their good feelings, they tenderly caress, amicably greet one another, warmly or fervently take offense, become angry, trembling with their entire body or head; they applaud, dance.

(Simonovich-Efimova 1919: 7)

When developing shows, she choreographed each gesture, typically in front of a mirror (Nekrylova 1980: 7). She suggested that if a performance is to be unified and the story to fit the character, the artist should be involved in every phase of puppet-theatre creation: even the playwright should wear and interact with puppets during the writing process.

Like Slonimskaia, Simonovich-Efimova responds to contemporaneous conversations about the marionette. She, too, defies the notion of the puppet as an automaton, a lifeless being, or an obedient actor. The assumption of life, she held, provides more fruitful possibilities for movement and repertoire. To her, "a puppet show begins when the audience believes in the puppet as a living being" (Efimov 1990: 80). She celebrated this life through choreography and through a repertoire that explored the life-death of the puppet. Paradoxical though it might seem, she emphasized the puppet's lifelikeness by staging plays in which a puppet dies or triumphs over death.

Interestingly, her response to the widespread marionette metaphor was to reject the marionette. Like George Sand, with whom she felt a particular artistic kinship, she maintained that glove puppets are superior to marionettes, as they are less representational and are in direct contact with the body of the puppeteer:

Marionettes are a mechanism, a system of strings, levers, hooks. They are something forced, melancholic. ... If she offers a bouquet,[9] the scent of its flowers is mixed with the smell of the sweat of the operator who has slaved over the creation of this act of offering. ...

She is a bourgeois among puppets.

But Petrushka is a flame; in him is spontaneously poured the inspiration of the artist.

Because a live human hand is in him! The palm replaces the face ... There is no intermediary in the form of strings and operator.

(Simonovich-Efimova 1980: 49–50)

Figure 13.2 Nina Simonovich-Efimova and Big Petrushka (1930). Photo courtesy of the Museum Archive of the Obraztsov State Central Puppet Theatre, Moscow

For Simonovich-Efimova, the hand (soul) of the puppeteer fills the puppet with life as it literally fills the puppet itself.[10]

The Efimovs experimented insatiably with expressive costuming and with unusual modes of manipulation. They developed shadow theatre as an art form in Soviet Russia and designed puppets worn on the head so that multiple characters could appear simultaneously with one puppeteer manipulating them. During the early Soviet period, when most puppetry was either agitprop or for children, they also created shows for adults, including adaptations of *The Enchanted Pear Tree* (1921) and *Macbeth* (1931) (Nekrylova 1980: 24). For *Macbeth*, they invented a new kind of rod puppet (patented by Simonovich-Efimova in 1926), with rods attached at the elbow to free the movement of the puppet's hands. Macbeth and Lady Macbeth each had two profiles so that when they were pivoted they could change expression (Efimov 1964: 5). The Efimovs also created giant puppet shows, including "Big Petrushka" (1930), in which Simonovich-Efimova danced with a life-sized Petrushka, intentionally blurring the line between agency and manipulation.

Conclusion: Embracing duality

Slonimskaia's and Simonovich-Efimova's writings provide useful models for thinking about how practice can inform theory in the puppet theatre, but also for viewing theatre more generally from the perspective of the puppet. Their assumption of life and agency in the lifeless material world provides expansive opportunities for

Figure 13.3 Nina Simonovich-Efimova, the witches of *Macbeth* (1931). Photo courtesy of the Museum Archive of the Obraztsov State Central Puppet Theatre, Moscow

interacting with the physical environment of the theatre; fabric, light, and sound, from their expanded perspective, might become tangible and intangible characters. Their articulation of the puppet's disobedient obedience invites a humble, responsive means of animating these surroundings, replacing the image of the tireless puppet with that of tireless experimentation by the puppeteer.

These two women's ideas laid a theoretical foundation for the Soviet puppetry of the 1920s and 1930s, including that of Alexandra Exter, Vladimir Sokolov, and Sergei Obraztsov. Exter turned Kamerny Theatre actors "into living sculptures by treating the costumes as fluid plastic entities" (Cunningham 1998: 43) and created cubist marionettes for an unrealized 1926 film. Sokolov, who headed a puppet studio at the Moscow Kamerny Theatre,[11] used puppets as visual representations of ideas or thoughts, much like a painting in motion that was "free from any similarity to the human form" (cited in Jurkowski and Francis 1998: 33). Obraztsov boldly redefined the puppet, using his bare hands to form part or all of its body, challenging notions that a puppet needed to be representational.

The significance of Slonimskaia's and Simonovich-Efimova's ideas extends far beyond the individuals they influenced directly, however. They resonate deeply with many contemporary puppetry experiments, regardless of any traceable genealogy. Basil Twist's abstract shapes and Philippe Genty's dream-like fabrics; Handspring Puppet Company's belief that the life of the puppet springs from direct physical contact with it; Julie Taymor's exposing of the puppet's mechanics to make its life more miraculous; Kneehigh Theatre's innovative interactions with their material environment; and Eric Bass's rehearsal process (described elsewhere in this volume) that "listens" to the puppet's visual dramaturgy are but a few examples.

In challenging common perceptions of the puppet, Slonimskaia and Simonovich-Efimova significantly expanded the puppet's theatrical and philosophical potential.

While Craig, Sologub, Briusov, and others focused on the puppet's deathlike, mechanical, or obedient qualities, Slonimskaia and Simonovich-Efimova explored alternate perspectives and, in so doing, bridged seeming binaries. Both women came to understand that the puppet is simultaneously alive *and* dead, obedient *and* disobedient. As they discovered, the puppet's inherent duality and liminality, its refusal to be defined from a single perspective, may be precisely why we find it so eternally fascinating.

Notes

This chapter builds upon my book chapter "Sculpture in Motion: Nina Simonovich-Efimova and the Petrushka Theatre," in Paul Fryer (ed.) *Women in the Arts in the Belle Epoque: Essays on Influential Artists, Writers and Performers*, McFarland Press, 2012: 118–135. Sincere thanks to Laurence Senelick; Colleen McQuillen and the University of Illinois Chicago Russian Modernism Workshop; and Maria Il'ina and the Obraztsov Theatre and Museum, without whom this work would not have been possible. Thanks, too, to the University of Connecticut School of Fine Arts for awarding me a Dean's Grant to travel to Russian archives, and to the Northwestern University School of Communication for giving me leave time to write. Unless quoted from an English-language source, the translations from Russian are my own.

1 Often referred to simply as Efimova, her married name, in English translations of her work.
2 Jurkowski is summarizing Roger Daniel Bensky's discussion of *Ubu Roi* in *Structures textuelles de la marionette de langue Française* (Paris: Editions A. G. Nizet, 1969).
3 Discussion at Puppetry and Postdramatic Performance: An International Conference on Performing Objects in the 21st Century, University of Connecticut, Storrs, April 3, 2011.
4 See A. V. Leifert, *Balagany* (Petrograd: Izdanie ezhedel'nika Petrogradskikh-gosudarstvennykh akademicheskikh teatrov, 1922); Vladimir Perets, *Kukol'nyi teatr na Rusi*. (Moscow: 1895, reprinted 1991); and Nikolai Vinogradov, *Bielorusskyi vertep* (St. Petersburg: Tipografia Imperatorskoi Akademii Nauk, 1908).
5 Slonimskaia and Sazonov gave private performances before presenting at the Players' Rest.
6 For a list of illustrious attendees, see Sazonov (1990: 24).
7 Slonimskaia's marionette essay has yet to be published in English. All excerpts from it, as well as all other Slonimskaia and Simonovich-Efimova translations from the Russian in this chapter, are my own.
8 These include Ivan Zaitsev, Anna Dmitrievna, Stepan Bulynkin, Pavel Sedov, Vasilii Sizov, and others. See Simonovich-Efimova, *Zapiski Petrushechnika*, 1980: 181–193.
9 Simonovich-Efimova contrasts the gendered pronouns in the original Russian. "Marionette" is feminine and "Petrushka" is masculine.
10 These ideas were likely inspired by a scene in Sand's 1859 novel *The Snow Man* (*L'homme de neige*, 1871: 161–162), in which a puppeteer argues that mechanical, lifelike marionettes are eerily similar to automata and that the puppeteer's hand imbues glove puppets (*burratini*) with life.
11 See Jurkowski and Francis (1998: 32). The Mamonovskii Lane Puppet Studio was transferred to the Kamerny in 1920. At least until Sokolov's emigration to Germany, Kamerny actors were required to train with puppets (Kostrova 1990: 90–91).

Works cited

Bartlett, R. and Edmondson, L.; additional material by Kelly, C. and Smith, S. (1998) "Collapse and Creation: Issues of Identity in the *Fin de Siècle*," in C. Kelly and D. Shepherd (eds.) *Constructing Russian Culture: 1881–1940*. Oxford: Oxford University Press.

Briusov, V. (1902) "Nenuzhnaia pravda. (Po povodu Moskovskogo khudozhestvennogo teatra)," *Mir iskusstva* 4: 67–74; reprinted as "Against Naturalism in the Theatre" in M. Green (trans. and ed.) (1986) *Russian Symbolist Theater: An Anthology of Plays and Critical Texts*. New York, NY: Ardis.

——(1908) "Realism i uslovnost' na stsene," *Teatr: Kniga o novom teatre*. St. Petersburg: Izd. "Shipovnik"; reprinted as "Realism and Convention on the Stage," in L. Senelick (ed. and trans.) (1981) *Russian Dramatic Theory from Pushkin to the Symbolists*. Austin, TX: University of Texas Press.

Craig, E. (1908) "The Actor and the Über-Marionette," *The Mask* 1(2): 3–15.

Cunningham, R. (1998) "Russian Women Artist Designers of the Avant-Garde," *TD&T (Theatre Design & Technology)* 34(2): 38–52.

Efimov, A. (1990) "Dvizhushchaisia skul'ptura," in N. Filina (ed.) *Chto zhe takoe teatr kukol?* Moscow: STD RSFSR.

——(1964) "*Macbeth* at the Puppet Theatre of Nina and Ivan Jefimov," [typescript in English translation], Efimov Collection, Obraztsov State Academic Central Puppet Theatre Museum (GATsTK), Moscow.

Gross, K. (2011) *Puppet: An Essay on Uncanny Life*. Chicago, IL: University of Chicago Press.

Jurkowski, H and Francis, P. (eds) (1998) *A History of European Puppetry, Vol. 2: The Twentieth Century*. Lewiston, NY: Edwin Mellen Press.

Kostrova, N. (1990) "Pervye sovetskie kukol'niki," in N. Filina (ed.) *Chto zhe takoe teatr kukol?* Moscow: STD RSFSR.

Meyerhold, V. (1913) "The Fairground Booth," reprinted in E. Braun (ed. and trans.) (1969) *Meyerhold on Theatre*. New York, NY: Hill & Wang.

Miklashevskii, K. (1914–1917) *La Commedia dell' arte, ili teatr ital'ianskikh komediantov XVI, XVII, i XVIII stoletii*. St. Petersburg: Sirius.

Nekrylova, A. (1980) "Predislovie," in N. Zhizhina, (ed.) *Zapiski petrushechnika i stat'i o teatre kukol*. Leningrad: Iskusstvo.

Sand, G. (1859) *L'homme de neige*; trans. V. Vaughan (1871) *The Snow Man: A Novel*. Boston, MA: Roberts Brothers.

Sazonov, P. (1990) "O teatre Iu. Slonimskaia," in N. Filina (ed.) *Chto zhe takoe teatr kukol?* Moscow: STD RSFSR.

Simonovich-Efimova, N. (1919) "O Petrushke," *Vestnik teatra* 34 (September 23–28): 6–8.

——(1940) "Kukol'nyi teatr khudozhnikov," [typescript], Efimov Collection, Obraztsov State Academic Central Puppet Theatre Museum (GATsTK), Moscow.

——(1977) "Ocherki zhizni i tvorchestva I. S. Efimova," in A. Matveeva and A. Efimov (eds) *Ob iskusstve i khudozhnikakh: Khudozhestvennoe i literaturnoe nasledie*. Moscow: Sovetskii khudozhnik.

——(1980) *Zapiski Petrushechnika, i stat'i o teatre kukol*, revised ed., N. A. Zhizhina (ed.). Leningrad: Iskusstvo.

Slonimskaia, I. (1916) "Marionetka," reprinted in N. Filina (ed.) (1990) *Chto zhe takoe teatr kukol?* Moscow: STD RSFSR.

Sologub, F. (1908) "Teatr odnoi voli," *Teatr: Kniga o novom teatre*. St. Petersburg: Izd. "Shipovnik"; reprinted as "The Theater of a Single Will," in L. Senelick (ed. and trans.) (1981) *Russian Dramatic Theory from Pushkin to the Symbolists*. Austin, TX: University of Texas Press.

Wachtel, A. (ed.) (1998) *Petrushka: Sources and Contexts*. Evanston, IL: Northwestern University Press.

Zabrodin, V. (2005) *Eizenshtein o Meierkhol'de*. Moscow: Novoe iztdatel'stvo.

14
The Saracen of *Opera dei Pupi*
A Study of Race, Representation, and Identity

Lisa Morse

During my first research trip to Sicily, I witnessed an *opera dei pupi* performance featuring stereotyped Saracen warriors, whose racially charged image and fierce treatment made me question why this art form remains popular throughout Sicily. *Opera dei pupi* productions showcasing the Saracen are rooted in the epic adventures of Charlemagne and his "Paladin" warriors, made famous by both medieval French and Italian Renaissance poetry and then popularized in Sicily by Giusto LoDico in his *La storia dei paladini di Francia*. Consistent throughout the branch stories of the Paladins is the ongoing pursuit and destruction of the Saracens in a battle for Christian supremacy over Islam. Following the through-line of the epic narrative, I watched Paladins "kill" Saracens in a grotesque comic battle, which was so artfully performed that the religious and racial markers of Christian/Muslim and Paladin/Saracen fell away. Both "Saracen" and "Paladin" shifted from representational characters to symbolic hero and villain in a mythic battle of good versus evil. At the conclusion of the fight sequence, the figures returned to their original meanings within the medieval narrative, and the once-comic pile of dismembered Saracens suddenly took on a sinister significance echoing the history of human loss in religious and ethnic warfare. At this point I couldn't help wondering, "Should I be laughing at this?" Considering the current state of racial and religious conflict in the Muslim world and the massive influx of immigrants fleeing Northern Africa for asylum in cities such as Palermo, the troubling pro-Christian/anti-Islamic polemic inherent in the chivalric narrative seems wildly out of place on the contemporary puppet stage.

Though *opera dei pupi* has declined in popularity among Sicilian audiences who engage in more modern forms of entertainment, *opera dei pupi* aficionados promote it as a treasured symbol of Sicilian culture. In 2001 UNESCO designated *opera dei pupi* an outstanding example of Oral and Intangible Cultural Heritage. Decades of conservation effort by the Association for the Preservation of Popular Heritage resulted in the creation of the Museo Internazionale delle Marionette Antonio Pasqualino, which boasts an extensive *opera dei pupi* collection along with over 3,000 volumes of material on marionettes and popular traditions. The Museo also sponsors the annual Festival Morgana, which celebrates puppetry from around the world while featuring *opera* performances by resident puppeteers. In addition, agencies within the city of Palermo provide a small subsidy supporting ongoing daily puppet shows during the tourist season. Given the growing status of the *opera* tradition, extensive preservation efforts, and its increasing prestige as a cultural treasure, it is critical to examine and question the significance of these seemingly racist performances and their anti-Muslim content. What can we learn about Sicilian culture, both past and present, by the persistence of the Saracen figure, and how can such controversial performance practices survive in a changing community comprising increased numbers of Muslim immigrants?

Antonio Pasqualino's research offers insight into how Sicilians viewed the Paladin/Saracen stories in the late nineteenth and early twentieth centuries. Pasqualino suggests that, for traditional audiences, the tales of the Paladins and Saracens were not meant as an escape from reality but rather a confrontation with it (Pasqualino 1978: 184) The battles between Paladin and Saracen transcend the epic narrative and parallel a long history of invasion and occupation in Sicily by both internal and external forces continually upsetting the status quo. The Saracen is symbolic of the outsider, and through the ritualized destruction of the Saracen, the Sicilian audience affirms their collective identity. Considering the meteoric rise of *opera dei pupi* from the departure of the Bourbon rulers in 1860 through two subsequent world wars, it is easy to accept Pasqualino's analysis of the *opera*'s function as a politically centralizing force in a chaotic postwar culture. The "chivalric code" within the epic provided a "behavioral code" for Sicilians, which was idealized in the image and actions of the puppets.

Yet what significance does the Saracen figure possess for a twenty-first-century Sicilian audience, as the visceral memories of occupation and invasion slip away? What need is there to collectivize and classify people as Paladin or Saracen? Recent ethnographic studies conducted by Jeffrey Cole (1997) for his book *The New Racism in Europe: A Sicilian Ethnography* provide new research prompting insight into these questions. Cole shows an ongoing sense of marginalization experienced by most Sicilians, which might account for the ongoing need for the Paladin and Saracen heroes as Sicilians attempt to exorcise oppression. Accompanied with this marginalization is a vague understanding of what constitutes race, calling forward the Saracen figure to take his place once again as the generalized historical "other." To gain a better understanding of the Saracen and his progression from page to stage, it is important to examine the literary figure at the center of this controversy.

As a symbolic figure of the "foreign invader," the Saracen of medieval literature embodies significant relevant characteristics that form the basis of the Saracen's representation on the *opera* stage. Interchangeably termed Moor, Pagan, Turk, and Infidel, the Saracen comprises both racial and religious signifiers, which underscore its historically confusing character. According to Norman Daniel in *Heroes and Saracens: An Interpretation of the Chansons de Geste*:

> The word Saracen came into use in late antiquity in both Greek and Latin, and meant simply "Arab." After the rise of Islam and throughout the middle ages, academic and historical writers used *Saracen* to mean "Arab" or "Muslim," or both, according to context.
>
> (Daniel 1984: 8)

Suzanne Conklin Akbari, in *Idols in the East: European Representation of Islam and the Orient 1100–1450*, points out "The *Saracen* identity, like *Jewish* identity, is depicted in medieval texts as being the product simultaneously of religious and ethnic difference, it partakes in both the binarism of religious alterity and the spectrum of bodily diversity" (Akbari 2009: 161).

As will be shown later, it is within the realm of ethnic difference that the Saracen figure intersects most clearly with Sicilian issues of identity. Jaqueline de Weever emphasizes the importance of the Saracen's dual identity as an ethnic and religious figure when she notes:

> While modern constructions of Orientalism center on the idea of the "Arab" or the "Muslim," focusing alternatively on the ethnic and religious identities, medieval constructions conflated categories of ethnicity and religion within a single term that served as a marker of both: "Saracen."
>
> (de Weever 1998: 155)

As described by Lynn Tarte Ramey in *Christian, Saracen and Genre in French Literature*, "At its essence, the term 'Saracen' seems to hold the same place in the medieval imagination that 'foreign,' 'exotic,' or 'outlandish' represent for us." (Tarte Ramey 2001: 8). Additional ethnic identities attributed to the term "Saracen" include invaders from southern Spain, Asia, and much of Northern Africa.

One does not need to look very far into the twelfth-century French poem *The Song of Roland* to find an example of the exoticized Saracen. Within the scene set at the famous Battle of Roncesvalles, the poet describes a formidable and exotic challenger in the Saracen Chernubles, whose native land serves as metaphor for his appearance, behavior, and "overall Saracenness," to use a phrase coined by Conklin Akbari. In the following passage, Chernubles possesses great power and strength and is set off as stark, solitary, and barren:

> Chernubles is there, from the valley black,
> His long hair makes on the earth its track;
> A load, when it lists him, he bears in play,
> Which four mules' burthen would well outweigh.
> Men say, in the land where he was born
> Nor shineth sun, nor springeth corn
> Nor falleth rain, nor dropeth dew;
> The very stones are of sable hue.
> 'Tis the home of demons as some assert.
>
> (O'Hagan 1880: 89)

His estrangement is further amplified by implied damnation on Earth, which renders him a social and religious outcast. The combination of multi-ethnic and religious signifiers, along with a vague characterization of race, form a Saracen stereotype whose facial characteristics, clothing, and behavior are codified on the puppet stage.

Figure 14.1 Saracen soldier created by Vincenzo Argento. Photo courtesy of the author

In an effort to capture the wide-ranging racial characteristics suggested by the medieval literary sources, and to clearly distinguish it from the light-faced Paladin, the Saracen puppet is shown in an assortment of nonwhite skin tones, from tan to shades of black. Additional marks of "difference" identified as "visual signifiers of discredited blackness" by Michael Harris in his text *Colored Pictures: Race and Visual Representation* (Harris 2003: 29) include a wide nose, thick lips, and a heavy brow. The harsh facial expression of the Saracen puppet underscores a lack of refinement, which is set in sharp contrast to the heroic male Paladin depicted as pale with thin lips, narrow nose, and a fine brow. The contrasting facial features distinguishing a villain (grotesque) from a hero (refined) is a common practice in other puppet traditions, such as the *wayang kulit* shadow puppets of Southeast Asia. However, in the case of the Saracen, the soldiers are meant to be lifelike in their proportions rather than stylized, which makes the image noticeably racial. In addition to stereotypical "African" traits, the image of the Saracen puppet also features elements of costuming historically associated with Arab labels. The Saracen wears silk trousers, symbolic of the exotic fabric of the Orient, and bejeweled armor, suggesting what Clara Gallini describes as the "fabled richness" of the Arab (Gallini 1988: 172). The Saracen is depicted wearing a turban as well as armor embossed with crescent moons and stars to signify the eastern Mediterranean and Central Asia. In her article "Arabesque: Images of a Myth," Clara Gallini examines the racist and ethnocentric stereotype of the Arab in post-1945 cinema and print in Italy. She raises questions about the media's ability to make anti-Arab sentiment more apparent and acceptable in the circulation of stereotypes and questions the political power of these images:

> It [racism] exists, but its existence is not recognized. It is so obvious and daily that it is not seen. But this is also because you do not want to see it, since that would mean you would have to denounce it in a world that claimed to be non-racist.
>
> (Gallini 1988: 172)

The consistent repetition and circulation of the Saracen image from one puppet family to the next, as well as throughout the island of Sicily, suggests that the puppet figure with its "African" facial features and "Arab" costuming was a successful rendering of the Saracen in the minds of a nineteenth-, twentieth-, and now twenty-first-century audience. Interestingly, the uniform skin tone and facial features of the Paladins have a strong visual and psychological impact, as they would with any army. However, the various exaggerations given to the Saracen, whether light- or dark-skinned or with varying heights and features, effectively diminish their power.

Medieval texts not only offer a source for the bizarre physical characteristics of the Saracen, but more importantly, provide highly imaginative action describing feats of fantastic strength required to destroy this formidable adversary. The following confrontation between Chernubles and Orlando from *The Song of Roland* is emblematic of many such confrontations that result in the destruction of the Saracen. Similar action is preserved and interpreted on the puppet stage:

> He smote Chernubles' helm upon,
> Where, in the center, carbuncles shone:
> Down through his coif and his fell of hair,
> Betwixt his eyes came the falchion bare,
> Down through his plated harness fine,
> Down through the Saracen's chest and chine,
> Down through the saddle with gold inlaid,
> Till sank in the living horse the blade,
> Severed the spine where no joint was found,
> And horse and rider lay dead on the ground.
>
> (O'Hagan 1880: 105)

In an astonishing display of force, the Paladin Orlando cuts in half not only the Saracen but also his horse. In this verse, superhuman strength and religious superiority are a key part of the literary figure of the Paladin and a significant portion of the puppet performance as well. Francis M. Guercio, as far back as 1939, notes the destruction of the Saracen as wildly popular and appreciated by the Sicilian audience:

> ... struggle against the Moors had become a great national tradition, permeating every form of art and exasperating religious fanaticism. Although now relegated to the sphere of popular tradition, this fanatical aversion to *mori, turchi, infedeli, saraceni, pagani*, as the Moors are indiscriminately named on the marionette stage, still lingers in the Sicilian popular mind.
>
> (Guercio 1939: 249)

Figure 14.2 Saracen trick puppet designed to split in half, created by Vincenzo Argento. Photo courtesy of the author

Coupled with the image of the Saracen is a set of performance conventions regarding his voice and action in performance. Since the Arabic language is not performed, argument is an opportunity to emphasize the "foreignness" of the enemy invader, shown through the inferior pronunciation of his Italian, which further diminishes his status. The Saracen's voice is given an "obscure, throaty, and raucous" timbre and his words are unintelligible (Pasqualino 1983: 238). The following battle sequences from a performance of *Orlando e Rinaldo per amore di Angelica* by Vincenzo Argento e Figli demonstrate the character Orlando and a Saracen King engaging in a brief argument. The *pagano* growls and moves aggressively towards Orlando and the two fight. The *pagano* is knocked repeatedly in the head and eventually (humiliatingly) runs offstage. Orlando chases him into a mysterious wood and, with a mighty blow from his sword, slices the Saracen in half from head to groin. The newly split figure (painted red on the inside for effect) then jumps about screaming in a high-pitched voice (further emasculating the soldier) as the two halves of his body hop farther apart and eventually fall to the ground. Although the action of riving a Saracen in an earnestly fought battle is sincere, the ingenious skill with which it is designed and manipulated undercuts the serious tone of the fight and results in humor.

In a subsequent encounter with another Saracen, the Paladin Rinaldo meets a low-ranking soldier. He is a small-headed, dark-skinned foot soldier who has no shield or armor but carries an oversized spear. In his laborious, slow, and awkward attempts to kill Rinaldo, he misses repeatedly until finally Rinaldo smacks him on the head with the flat of his sword with an outrageously loud "thump," which is emphasized by the puppeteer, who stomps his foot on the floor to underscore the blow. The soldier howls "aiiee yiee yiee" in a high-pitched falsetto voice, leans heavily on the proscenium, and rubs his forehead, confused and delirious. This humorous exchange of blows happens repeatedly until the soldier makes his final attempt and is decapitated. The vandalized body hops about the stage, stops for a moment as if suddenly realizing it has no head, and then drops straight to the floor. In an alternate ending for the same scene, the soldier is decapitated and can be seen running off the stage with his arms held high over his headless body, howling like a wounded animal. Puppeteers indulge the violence to comic effect as characters shriek, howl, and stomp about the stage, simultaneously undermining the Saracen's status as a fierce enemy soldier while delighting an audience of tourists. Humor, irony, and reversals are an important part of an *opera* performance, so amusing confrontations are rife among the various battle sequences leading to a stage filled with butchered bodies. Audiences give meaning to the scenes through laughter and applause as their heroes get the better of the Saracen villain. When the Paladin hero is the butt of a joke, notes Pasqualino, it is intended for a specific purpose. "Derision of Charlemagne is derision of the state; derision of Orlando is a derision of a model of self" (Pasqualino 1987: 22). But what is meant by the derision of the Saracen?

As noted above, customary methods persist in the design and performance of the Saracen, but significant changes in the content of the show strip the Saracen of his complexity. To their credit, puppeteers in recent years diminished the focus on the Crusades at the request of the Catholic Church, though religious difference is still inherent in performance, and instead turned their attention to the romantic pursuits of the Paladin knights. However, the battle scenes are what people want to see, despite the negative connotations in the pro-Christian/anti-Islamic binary. Battles were very popular among traditional audiences, as Guercio notes, yet they were historically less frequent. The serialized stories published by LoDico followed the Paladin and Saracen through a wide range of adventures, romances, and encounters with mythical creatures wherein heroes experienced both failure and success. Over the course of many verses, Saracen warriors were given opportunities to show positive traits along with their stereotypically negative traits, which aligned them more closely with their Paladin counterparts. Sicilian audiences followed their heroes night after night for an entire year, just as a modern-day audience follows a soap *opera*. A traditional audience might see a Paladin lose a battle or fall prey to human failings; they might also hear a Saracen express the same honor code and religious passion as his Christian counterpart. The complex matrix between Paladin and Saracen and their equal balance of positive and negative traits have fallen into obscurity, leaving a modern audience with stark, antagonistic characters and a superficial understanding of the action. In this overly simplistic version of the form, the Sicilian puppet theatre may be encouraging a more negative stereotype of the Saracen than was previously intended in a traditional performance cycle and, thereby, upholding an unfair view of both Arab and African. Pasqualino suggests the Saracens are simply "negative comic characters" functioning as "meaningful comics," for the Saracen is an object to be "laughed at" while the Sicilian audience "strengthens itself and excludes what appears peripheral, inadequate to the central values of the culture" (Pasqualino 1987: 22). Although Pasqualino's theory sees the function of the Saracen figure as a comic foil, his analysis fails to fully appreciate the meaningfulness of the Saracen as a problematized image of Sicilian identity seeking uniformity among an ever-changing demographic.

From 1970 to 1990, as Jeffrey Cole outlines, a lack of immigration control led to a massive influx of foreigners into Sicily from North Africa, sub-Saharan Africa, the Middle East, and Asia seeking residence permits. The impact of this unregulated influx made its immigrant population the third largest in the country: a whopping 7.9 percent by 1990. In his ethnographic study of Sicilian perceptions of race among immigrants living and working in Sicily, Cole characterizes the average Sicilian's opinions on race as "vague" and observes that working Sicilians "tend to lump all immigrants under several Sicilian terms signifying dark skin, such as *marocchini* ('Moroccans'), *nivuri* ('blacks'), and *tuichi* ('Turks')" (Cole 1997: 47). The vague understanding of race noted by Cole echoes earlier comments by Guercio regarding the imprecise identities assigned to the Saracen character. While surveys by Cole show "racist categorizations of immigrants," he suggests the use of these terms is a result of poor education on a variety of levels (Cole 1997: 47). Perhaps the ongoing performance of racial stereotypes in the Saracen of *opera dei pupi* adds to this confusion since the nonwhite, non-Christian is falsely historicized in this beloved cultural tradition. In *Race and Culture: A World View*, Thomas Sowell states that "Race is one of the ways of collectivizing people in our minds. ... How important it is in a given setting can only be determined empirically from an examination of that setting" (Sowell 1994: xiii).

Historically, Sicilians viewed themselves as oppressed by invaders from within and from without, resulting in an overall paranoia of anything remotely foreign. According to Cole, Sicilians today "see themselves as hounded by insecurity and humiliated by marginalization" (Cole 1997: 34). If humiliation and marginalization are significant fears among Sicilians, surely it can be said that the Saracen puppet embodies these same experiences and acts as a metaphorical sacrifice for the cleansing of that fear. In this way, the Saracen functions as a way to destroy their fears of humiliation and marginalization in a satirical manner, making him both Sicilian and Saracen.

What other meanings may be at play in the representation and derision of the Saracen? Cole reveals that Sicilians, as southerners, view themselves as victims of racism by the north of Italy and are often stereotyped as "lazy, rude, and dangerous" (Cole 1997: 20). When migrating to northern Italy for work, Sicilians are labeled as "blacks" and "Africans" by their northern counterparts. In this paradigm, Sicilians are placed in the "ambiguous position of being 'black' in relation to Italy's north, but 'white' in relation to new immigrants" (Cole 1997: 20). Furthermore, Cole's research and surveys indicated, "Just as northern Italians thought themselves superior to southern emigrants, so too do Sicilians consider themselves above Africans and Asians" (Cole 1997: 59–60). In light of Cole's ethnographic discoveries, perhaps the modern-day Sicilian is situated in the uncertainty of a continuum between black and white, and he or she is actively experiencing difference as imagined participants in both the action and characterizations of the Saracen. If so, it may be that Sicilians are using the *opera* to work through issues of identity, and the ongoing performance of these stories provides an opportunity to examine the uniquely tenuous position they occupy between north and south.

Interpretation of the Saracen figure given by Pasqualino, when viewed with recent ethnographic research by Cole, underscores a significant need for *opera dei pupi* preservationists to contextualize the Saracen as a complex figure codifying centuries of ambiguity concerning race and issues of marginalization experienced by Sicilians. As much as the *opera* is problematic with its xenophobic content, it is simultaneously regarded as a symbol of "Oral and Intangible History" and imbued with cultural, political, religious, and social significance, resulting in a highly charged art form. Given the noteworthy change in production format, which was meant to appeal to a "new" audience of tourists, most viewers fail to experience more than one hour of an *opera* show, which pales in comparison to the yearlong season of shows witnessed by a traditional Sicilian audience actively experiencing conflicting identities in the victories and failings of their puppet corollaries, both Saracen and Paladin. The continued performance of *opera dei pupi* is certainly in jeopardy, as remaining puppeteers advance in their years and offer fewer and fewer productions. As performances shrink, so may any understanding of the underlying tensions that separate this distinctly homegrown art form from other cultures. With a greater focus and sensitivity about issues of race at play in the *opera dei pupi* performance, Sicilians have an opportunity to recognize both past and present anxieties regarding marginalization and identity, while discovering ways to address these issues going forward. Preservationists, performers, and historians must work together to educate audiences about the social record contained in the noble figure of the Saracen and his role in the Sicilian's quest for identity, rather than risking misinterpretation of the Saracen figure as an essentialist view on race or culture.

Works cited

Akbari, S. C. (2009) *Idols in the East: European Representations of Islam and the Orient, 1100–1450*. Ithaca, NY: Cornell University Press.

Cole, J. (1997) *The New Racism in Europe: A Sicilian Ethnography*. Cambridge, MA: Cambridge University Press.

Daniel, N. (1984) *Heroes and Saracens: An Interpretation of the Chansons de Geste*. Edinburgh, Scotland: Edinburgh University Press.

de Weever, J. (1998) *Sheba's Daughters: Whitening and Demonizing the Saracen Woman in Medieval French Epic*, Garland Reference Library of the Humanities, vol. 2077. New York, NY: Garland.

Gallini, C. (1988) "Arabesque: Images of a Myth," trans. I. Chambers, *Cultural Studies* 2: 168–180.

Guercio, F. M. (1939) *Sicily, The Garden of the Mediterranean: The Country and Its People*. London: Faber & Faber.

Harris, M. D. (2003) *Colored Pictures: Race and Visual Representation*. Chapel-Hill, NC: University of North Carolina Press.

O'Hagan, John, (ed. and trans.) (1880) *The Song of Roland*. London: C. Kegan Paul & Co.

Pasqualino, A. (1978) "Transformations of Chivalrous Literature in the Subject Matter of the Sicilian Marionette Theatre," in A. Dundes (ed.) *Varia Folklorica*. The Hague, The Netherlands: Mouton Publishers.

——(1983) "Marionettes and Glove Puppets: Two Theatrical Systems of Southern Italy," *Semiotica* 47: 219–280.

——(1987) "Humor and Puppets: An Italian Perspective," in D. Sherzer and J. Sherzer (eds.) *Humor and Comedy in Puppetry: Celebration in Popular Culture.* Bowling Green, KY: Bowling Green State University Popular Press.
Sowell, T. (1994) *Race and Culture: A World View.* New York, NY: Basic Publishing.
Tarte Ramey, L. (2001) *Christian, Saracen and Genre in Medieval French Literature.* New York and London: Routledge.

15
Puppet Think
The Implication of Japanese Ritual Puppetry for Thinking through Puppetry Performances

Jane Marie Law

During the 1980s when I was conducting research on the history, demise, and revival of Awaji puppetry, one of my main contacts on the island of Awaji was an elderly woman who, after her husband was killed during World War II, worked part time as a puppeteer to make a little extra money. We spent a great deal of time together, and because my studies were focused on the issue of revival and on the loss of a context for a tradition that had once been very important in her life, we spent many hours talking about her experiences during the war. She was a follower of a new Japanese religion, Reiyūkai, and one of her core practices was reciting the title of the Mahayana Buddhist scripture, the *Lotus Sūtra*, on a daily basis after reading the names of people who had died on that particular date during the war. (Mahayana refers to the stage of Buddhism that spread to Japan from India via China.) One day, while I was staying at her house, we read a very long list of names of people killed when a passenger boat had been bombed (presumably by American bombers) and sunk. She was very moved remembering how she had heard of the event over the radio as a young woman during the war. We read the names and then she chanted the title of the *Lotus Sūtra*.

Reciting names of war dead and memorializing people one has never met is not a practice particularly unique to Japan. In Japan, though, it can have many layers of political meaning and can form a spectacle in its own right, as the war dead are manipulated for various political purposes. For my friend, it seems, she was always using this ritual to process a deep sense of loss that permeated her life. Over the years, as we met from time to time, she still maintained this Reiyūkai practice.

One day many years after my initial research was completed, I was back on Awaji, visiting. Everyone I knew was lamenting the fate of my elderly friend. Senility had crept in; she seemed to be in a perpetually muddled state, with no awareness of where she was or what year it was. Still very physically fit, she spent all of her time sewing – jackets, bags, trinkets – and in the end, as her ability to complete complex tasks failed her, she stitched at pieces of fabric, often creating seemingly nothing at all. All of her creations followed her around in a large duffle she carried with her.

On a particular (and for her a particularly lucid) day during my visit, she walked over to me, took hold of my hands, and made me form a cup with them. Into them, she poured literally dozens and dozens of tiny fabric pouches, each no larger than a thimble, and all carefully stitched to resemble a swaddled infant in its cradle. As they kept cascading out of the box she was pouring into my hands and fell onto the floor at my feet, I looked a bit surprised. She said to me, "All those names. Remember? All those names." Together we remembered the day we had read all those names.

This experience touched me deeply. It is relevant here, not because there is anything terribly Japanese about it, but rather because it reveals precisely a certain ritual logic that will be the focus of this chapter: that to process loss, we often resort to the use of a ritual substitute to fill that void created by the very absence of what we need ritually present. We use these concrete objects to locate our overwhelming and possibly unimaginable emotional response to the loss itself. It is a fairly obvious point and is seen all over the world in ritual settings: the surrogate, the changeling, the effigy, the body substitute. What I'd like to suggest here is that, while this is not unique to Japan, the extent to which this kind of ritual logic had permeated Japanese social practices is remarkable. In this brief discussion, I'd like to reference several cases in which a ritual object is used to stand for a larger world of meaning that is lost or the loss of which is threatened. The list could be longer than the few cases I cite here, but my hope is that, for scholars and performers working with and thinking through the use of inanimate objects to create ritual or theatre, these cases will serve as reminders of one of the deepest uses of those things, which the Japanese language connotes as "in the shape of the human." I suggest that behind the use of puppets in Japanese theatre, an elaborate and inconvenient theatre choice that fascinates us with its realism and complexity, we can glimpse a more profound, albeit obvious, ritual logic of the use of a human substitute.

Ningyō

In Japanese, the general word for puppet (*ningyō*) is also the word for doll, and the two words, so distinct in English, are used interchangeably. Written with the two-character compound "in the shape of the human" or "person shape," the word suggests that dolls and puppets fill a substitutive space in ritual. When this character compound is read another way, it is pronounced *hitogata*, and ritual objects by this name were used in ancient Japan as surrogates for people as they underwent rites of purification at particular times of the year. Heian period texts make passing reference to these *hitogata*, and even today, the practice of placing sticks on a fire at local shrines at the end of the year to symbolize the negative events of the previous year resonates with the practice of sending sticks vaguely in human shape down streams as a purification rite. All the cases I present here would be recognizable as a form of "*ningyō*" in Japan. While the concept of "doll" may be overly located in childhood in the West, our examples below suggest that the life cycle of people – from the dangers of pregnancy and childbirth to the travails of unwanted pregnancies (whether due to famine or simply bad timing in a woman's life) to removing the emotional charge of negative events that happen to people – is ritually worked out through mimetic action, and a *ningyō* in some form (from the crude to the very refined) serves this locative function.[1] The Japanese scholar Yamaguchi Masao (1991) has argued that Japanese people often negotiate the human–divine interrelationship through representational substitution (*migawari* in Japanese). In this way, he notes, rituals using effigies enable a transformative experience.

Amagatsu

One human experience to which most people who have ever had a child can relate is the intense anxiety surrounding one's concern for the well-being of one's infant, especially during its most vulnerable neonatal days. New parents often confess, almost as if they are sure they are the only people in the history of the human race to have done so, that they have stood over the cribs of their sleeping infants listening for the reassuring sounds of the baby breathing.

In the Tōhoku region of Japan, there was a widespread practice during the 1800s of creating a surrogate baby out of fabric and stuffing and placing the object in a crib or bed where one would expect to find the infant. The *amagatsu* (heavenly child), as these figures were called, served as a stand-in for the actual baby. Should the age-old reapers of young infants – illness, sudden death, disaster – happen their way, those forces would be confused, distracted, and perhaps even fooled.

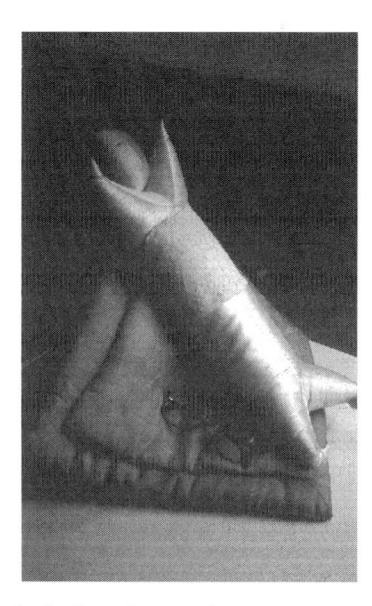

Figure 15.1 A rare example of a body substitute known as an *amagatsu* (heavenly child): these infant-shaped effigies were used widely in the Tōhoku region of Japan to safeguard newborn infants against illness, sudden death, and disease by serving as surrogates (from Morioka, Iwate prefecture, 1988). Photo courtesy of the author

It is always tempting when one looks at the magical rites of other people to assume, "How quaint that they actually believed all that stuff!" – that a parent in rural Japan, in a region beset with famines, poverty, and disease in the nineteenth century, would believe they could save their baby from an unfortunate fate by using a naïve surrogate object to ward off evil! The very idea seems primitive, prescientific, an example of "the savage mind." But if we shift our gaze in this case just a few degrees to the side and choose to look at it not in the harsh light of literalism (i.e., "I do this and therefore must take it at face value") but rather in the realm of the poetry of ritual action, we discern another insight here: the *amagatsu* does not so much protect the baby from evil forces but rather locates the parents' overwhelming anxiety in a secure place so that life can go on and, in the end, perhaps the baby can get more of the attention that would otherwise be squandered on futile worry. In a region where infant death from natural and even unnatural causes sat comfortably between the extremes of the exception and the rule, it is not hard to imagine the anxiety of a parent over the well-being of a tiny infant. But it *is* hard to imagine a worse fate than uncontrollable anxiety when it comes to such a profound human experience. The *amagatsu*, then, is best understood as a ritual place where unimaginable worry can be contained.

I was shown an *amagatsu* by an elderly woman who was the maid in an inn where I once stayed in the city of Morioka, the capital of Iwate Prefecture, during the late 1980s. I had told her I was studying *ningyō*, and from our conversation, it was clear I was talking about the manipulated kind (puppets). But from this term *ningyō* she felt the need to tell me about the *amagatsu* she owned. It was rare, she noted, because few of them still existed. In fact, the lack of physical evidence of this practice is confusing. On the one hand, we might ask, if this practice was so prevalent, why did so few of these objects survive? One obvious answer is that they were fragile, cheap objects. But perhaps another way of seeing this would be to suggest that once a ritual object has done its job (the baby either lived or died, grew up or didn't, and the parents either coped or did not), the object has served its purpose and is no longer important. Having it around is a stark reminder of a more anxious time.[2]

Perhaps this is the task of ritual: to allow in a mimetic space the resolution of deeply tangled emotions, often contradictory and too difficult to process in the normal spaces of human life. This is what ritual affords: a certain suspension of the laws of the human condition and an extraordinary space where the impossible (absolution, resignation, acceptance) can happen.

An *amagatsu*, then, is an example of a ritual body substitute designed to process the overwhelming anxiety of threatened loss. Now we turn to another example of a ritual object, also connected with childbirth but in a starkly opposite way.

Kokeshi

Also from the Tōhoku region, we have the example of cylindrical objects made of wood, often painted to look like young maidens or simple, almost amorphous beings. These objects have been called *kokeshi*, with the word written in phonetic script, leaving us to conjecture as to the original meaning of the name. The most probable answer is that the name is made up of two words, *ko*, meaning "child," and *kesu*, meaning "erase." In an area where droughts and famines were almost normative, the practice of infanticide was a common form of family-size regulation during the Tokugawa period, when this area was under continued but direct feudal control, and peasants and farmers were often the most vulnerable population, unable to accommodate growing families. The hard choice of either "erasing" a child at birth or watching that young child slowly starve to death at a later age was not an uncommon dilemma. The human question this kind of ongoing poverty raises in our minds is this: how do people ritually cope with that kind of Hobson's choice?

A survey of *kokeshi* in museums and older collections (and the occasional flea market, if one is lucky) reveals minimalist, crudely painted objects constructed out of cheap materials – often no more than two eyes on a simple wooden body with little or no neck. While it is likely these objects served different roles for different families and women, here again we see the ritual necessity of attendance by the most absent being, accomplished through a body substitute. In other words, a simple, easily made item became a substitute for a child who never really grew up to see the hardship of peasant life.

Today, if one travels in Tohoku, noted regional folk artists sell elaborately painted *kokeshi* to collectors and tourists – Japanese and foreign alike. The decorative painting of *kokeshi* is a recent phenomenon, dating largely from the postwar era. Before these objects were discovered as souvenir kitsch, we can think of them as functioning as a folk version of the more stylized form seen in the *mizuko Jizō*, discussed next. Clearly, the use of *kokeshi* as ritual substitutes was not as processed and commercialized as the later *mizuko Jizō*, but their current popularity and even iconic status as a "Japanese doll" belies their origins in a much more somber emotional landscape.

Mizuko Jizō

Another significant and oft-seen practice using physical objects "in the shape of the human" to locate grief and process loss is the *mizuko Jizō*, literally "water child" statues of the *bodhisattva* Jizō (Skt: Ksitigarbha). A *bodhisattva* is a figure in Mahayana Buddhism who, having started as a human being and achieved enlightenment in some lifetime in the past, vows to continue to incarnate in the world of sentient beings until all beings have achieved liberation from suffering. Mahayana Buddhism has a retinue of *bodhisattvas* who, through coursing through so many lifetimes, have achieved spiritual superpowers. Among these well-known *bodhisattvas* is the figure Jizō. Jizō is best known in Japanese popular Buddhist practice as the *bodhisattva* who shows his enlightened activity by tending to those who have fallen into hell.[3] According to a most disturbing (but only marginally adhered to) Buddhist idea, all children who die before the age of seven years old go to hell because of the suffering they cause their parents. The widespread application of this idea is that Jizō is always present in hell, helping those poor souls who, through no power of their own, have ended up there. Depictions of Jizō in ritual-specific sculptural form show him as gender-ambiguous, prepubescent, and amorphous, in spite of the highly developed Buddhist iconographic system of which Buddhist sculpture is a major part. What is the ritual use, then, of these small statues of Jizō?

In the postwar era and up through the present day, birth-control services and effective sex education have not been widely available in Japan (though since the 1970s this situation has improved immensely). As a result, abortion, rather than being a last resort, was for many women (married and unmarried alike) a first-line form of birth control. The ritual processing of the difficult emotions involved in aborting a fetus are widely developed (and, some would argue, heavily exploited for financial gain) by some Buddhist temples in Japan. The ritual process is somewhat straightforward: a woman (sometimes accompanied by a male partner) comes to a temple offering *mizuko kuyō* (appeasement) services – rituals for the appeasement and consolation of the aborted or miscarried fetus or stillborn child. She pays a fee (ranging in price, but usually beginning at around 50,000 yen, or about US$500, but often more) and purchases a small (or not so small) statue of the *bodhisattva* Jizō. A service is conducted (often in a group format) for the child who, represented by the small statue, is understood to have been "sent back." In some venues, the woman has the option of writing a wooden placard (*ema*) with a message to the fetus or child. These placards are hung at a public place in the shrine, understood to be messages sent to the other side. The ritual object, the Jizō statue, is often dressed in a child's clothes, given a bib (a common marker of Jizō) and small toys, and placed in the temple grounds amidst thousands and thousands of identical, though individually clad, statues of varying sizes.[4]

There are numerous sites in Japan offering such services, and until recently, many were simply open to the public and one could stroll through the grounds. An astounding feature of the most prominent *mizuko Jizō* site in Japan, Hasedera Kannon in Kamakura, is the sheer volume of the small Jizō statues one encounters in the hills of the site. The vast majority of them show the signs of being forgotten markers of a past agony: the tiny bibs, perhaps once lovingly placed on the tiny Jizō figures, or the toys placed at the feet of the offering, are faded and dilapidated. The state of affairs seems to suggest that, while these objects were once emotionally charged, they have done their work and are now taking up space on the ritual landscape, a testament to a past grief long since overcome or forgotten. Life moves on. The little stone statues don't.

Imon ningyō/migawari ningyō

The final example we briefly consider constitutes one of our most fragile cases, precisely because so few of these objects survived their ritual location – the small homemade dolls made by women or schoolgirls for Japanese soldiers during World War II. Referred to as *imon ningyō*, companion or safeguarding dolls, or *migawari ningyō*, substitute dolls, the dolls were meant to represent the portability of the feminine, the loving, the domestic, and the home – all those things left behind but ultimately longed for – onto the battlefield or into the air in a kamikaze plane.

We have the excellent work of the American anthropologist and *ningyō* scholar Ellen Schattschneider to thank for bringing the existence of these dolls to light.[5] Through her careful reading of popular literature, poetry, diaries, letters, and magazines from the World War II era and her search for extant objects that survived the war, she has re-created for us a vivid picture of the role (real or hoped for) these dolls played in connecting the soldiers on the battlefield with the domestic location back home from which they were separated. Her work raises the awful enigma of objects so tender and feminine and very Japanese being on the battlefield in the presence of horrific atrocities committed by some of those very soldiers carrying these dolls. What did their presence on the battlefields in China, Burma, and elsewhere, as well as in the cockpits of kamikaze pilots' planes, signify? Our concern here is with the use of ritual effigies to stand in for loss – anticipated, actual, or imagined. Schattschneider's work suggests that these *imon ningyō* allowed a surrogate replacement for the kinship that was being lost when a young man went to war. She asks:

> ... what roles did they play in helping to constitute fictive kinship relations among imperial soldiers, Japanese civilians, and colonial subjects and in legitimating the often-violent severing of those putative bonds? And how, ultimately, did those dolls come to play such significant roles in the memorialization of dead soldiers and in managing social and spiritual relations with those destined for death?
>
> (Schattschneider 2005: 330)

The objects were often very simple, made of fabric and frequently dressed in tiny kimonos or other clothing. Family members made them for husbands, fathers, or siblings serving in the war and also for anonymous recipients. The making of these dolls for soldiers was a common task for girls to "support their troops" during the war, and the gifting of these dolls to soldiers, sometimes with the giver's name included and sometimes not, formed a link not only with the Japanese practices of employing dolls in a mimetic fashion, as we have noted above in other cases, but also between the giver and the solider.

Schattschneider surmises that the total number of these dolls made may have been in the hundreds of thousands, perhaps even millions. Her discussion indicates that in many of the popular depictions of the dolls in magazines on the home front during the war, they are often shown as being gifted to Chinese children or young girls. She suggests that part of the role of the narrative of these dolls was to rewrite the history of what was actually happening to local populations under Japanese occupation or attack. They also served as a kind of *o-mamori*, or protective amulet.

Almost always depicting the female form, Schattschneider points out that these *imon ningyō*:

> ... were especially appropriate gifts for male soldiers, who had been separated from the domestic realm and from civilian mainstream society ... and placed into a violent, nearly exclusively male world. The dolls carried multiple messages, marking the male recipient's separation from normal sociality, while also asserting an enduring link, however tenuous, between the "home" world of women and the distant male soldiers on the empire's peripheries.
>
> (Schattschneider 2005: 334)

In spite of their complex multivalence in the history of the war, the very existence of these *imon ningyō* in comfort bags routinely given to soldiers suggests a very Japanese obsession with concretizing a complex sense of loss in a simple object. These simple dolls had a huge job to do – restoring the domestic, humanizing the giver and receiver, intruding into (and therefore transforming) a dominantly masculine and martial landscape with the tender presence of the feminine, and, in the end, through their depiction in the media, helping to anesthetize the population back home to the horrors being conducted by the military abroad.

Conclusion

In the examples above, selected as representations of a much larger cultural dynamic of substitutive representation of many aspects of human existence, I have tried to show how the use of dolls, effigies, and ritual *migawari* in Japan form a strong cultural undercurrent that informs Japanese puppetry. I suggest that it is possible to regard the prevalence of puppets in Japanese theatre as a logical extension of this decidedly ritual and religious sensibility.

As a scholar of Japanese ritual puppetry, I am often asked to comment on the profound influence that the three-person manipulation method we now know as *bunraku* has had on global theatre. As Japan's most ubiquitous puppetry image, it, of course, merits attention. However, the enormous popularity and deep appeal in puppetry circles of this manipulation method – lifelike dolls, manipulated seemingly effortlessly (and very realistically) by up to three puppeteers, who are often clad in *kuroko* (black robes and hoods) – is so pervasive that it has eclipsed anything else we might want to ask about Japanese ritual and theatrical sensibilities. I often feel a bit stifled by this fascination with Japan's most obvious theatrical medium. Use a black hood for a puppeteer or employ more than one puppeteer to manipulate a puppet, and one is immediately referencing a Japanese theatrical trope. And I am not suggesting it is without great effect. Peter Schumann has used *kuroko*-clad figures in his puppetry performances, and Basil Twist has redesigned the method of manipulating a doll with multiple puppeteers in a new and innovative way, also using other dimensions of Japanese puppetry in his work. Nothing about these artists could be called derivative.

But I would argue that, in some cases, the obvious fascination with the *bunraku* methods and styles often not only conceals what is perhaps most fascinating and fruitful about Japanese ritual materials, it can, if not fully appropriated by the artist stealing it (for as we have been reminded – and I paraphrase – bad artists borrow, good artists steal), border on being an orientalist icon for appropriating Japanese theatrical forms without fully engaging the ritual sensibilities that undergird these very forms.

Nevertheless, I would hope that in the case of Japanese puppetry, we can agree to something of a declaration of independence from this normal coupling of the words "Japanese puppet" and "*kuroko*." There is a deeper tradition behind these stylized dolls, one that embraces what puppetry does best – allows a space set apart from the real to explore that which is most disturbing, or overwhelmingly sublime, in human experience.

Figure 15.2 Members of the Awaji Puppet Theatre in Fukura, Japan, perform the *Ebisu-mai* (a deity play) at its traditional location of Susaki Island in the Fukura Harbor (August 1991). The use of *kuroko*, though not traditional for this play, shows the dominance of this theatrical medium today. Photo courtesy of the author

If, in the end, ritual substitutes and locations for complex emotional pain and loss in the form of puppets serve their purpose and then are discarded or lost, it behooves us when we see other such objects on the stage, perhaps in the form of a lovely *bunraku* doll, real and lifelike – and lovingly brought to life by three people – to remember the siblings to these theatrical forms, those very ritual objects used at times in the past to confront our deepest anxieties and suffering. It is often noted that the puppet stage was where the most gory and often violent and disturbing plays of the early modern period in Japanese theatre found their place.[6] On the one hand, it is tempting to accuse puppetry of being a sensational, even debauched medium. But perhaps there is another insight here: perhaps the emergent classical puppet theatre in Japan, drawing as it did on the ritual use of the effigies we have discussed here, recognized the ability of puppets to carry this ritual and cathartic load. And if, for a minute, we open that door, a new level of vulnerability in our experience of the possibilities for puppetry may be attainable. From there, anything could happen.

Notes

1 I discuss these cases in more detail in my book *Puppets of Nostalgia: The Life, Death and Rebirth of the Japanese Awaji Ningyō Tradition* (1997). Readers of Japanese will find a more detailed description of *hitogata* in the work of Nagata Kōkichi (1978).

2 A more detailed study of *amagatsu* is not possible. Not only are the extant objects rare, but due to the perceived "superstitious" nature of their use, in the Taishô and early Shôwa periods (i.e., the early twentieth century), when folklorists in Japan combed the countryside for examples of practices from everyday life, many of those practices that smacked of anti-modernism were intentionally neglected. *Amagatsu* dolls join a long list of many objects and practices in Japan that were thus neglected and, hence, appear to us in evidence only as fragmented examples, as the one *amagatsu* I was shown certainly was.
3 Fortunately for English readers, Yoshiko Kurata Dykstra (1978) has translated some of the miracle tales connected with Jizô into English.
4 Two excellent works by historians of religions offer differing and detailed ethnographic understandings of this ritual practice: William R. Lafleur's book *Liquid Life: Abortion and Buddhism in Japan* (1994) presents the history of infanticide in Japan and places the practice of *mizuko kuyô* within this history, while Helen Hardacre's *Marketing the Menacing Fetus in Japan* (1998) explores the ways in which this ritual practice is implicated in attempts to control women's access to control of their own reproduction through manipulation of feelings of guilt and fear of retaliation from aborted fetuses. The practice *mizuko kuyô* is well described in ethnographic literature and in Japanese anthropology and religious studies.
5 See her detailed article "The Bloodstained Doll: Violence and the Gift in Wartime Japan" (Schattschneider 2005). She also writes about another use of effigy in her article "'Buy Me a Bride': Death and Exchange in Northern Japanese Bride Doll Marriage" (Schattschneider 2001).
6 In this vein, see the recent (2012) translation by R. Keller Kimbrough of Japanese puppet plays based on Buddhist tales. Kimbrough's introduction notes how many of the plays deal with the extremes of human behavior, from torture, human trafficking, and stylized child sexuality to idealized examples of devotion, compassion, and filial piety.

Works cited

Dykstra, Y. K. (1978) "Jizô the Most Merciful: Tales from the Jizô Bosatsu Reigenki," *Monumenta Nipponica* 33: 179–200.
Hardacre, H. (1998) *Marketing the Menacing Fetus in Japan*. Princeton, NJ: Princeton University Press.
Kimbrough, R. K. (2012) *Wondrous, Brutal Fictions: Eight Buddhist Tales from the Early Japanese Puppet Theater*. New York, NY: Columbia University Press.
Kôkichi, N. (1978) *Nihon no Ningyô Shibai*. Tokyo: Kinseisha.
Lafleur, W. R. (1994) *Liquid Life: Abortion and Buddhism in Japan*. Princeton, NJ: Princeton University Press.
Law, J. M. (1997) *Puppets of Nostalgia: The Life, Death and Rebirth of the Japanese Awaji Ningyô Tradition*. Princeton: NJ: Princeton University Press.
Nagata, K. (1978) *Nihon no Ningyô Shibai*. Tokyo: Kinseisha.
Schattschneider, E. (2001) "'Buy Me a Bride': Death and Exchange in Northern Japanese Bride Doll Marriage," *American Ethnologist* 28: 854–880.
——(2005) "The Bloodstained Doll: Violence and the Gift in Wartime Japan," *Journal of Japanese Studies* 31: 329–356.
Yamaguchi, M. (1991) "The Poetics of Exhibition in Japanese Culture," in I. Karp and S. D. Levine (eds.) *Exhibiting Cultures: The Poetics and Politics of Museum Display*. Washington, DC: The Smithsonian Institution Press.

16
Relating to the Cross
A Puppet Perspective on the Holy Week Ceremonies of the *Regularis Concordia*

Debra Hilborn

In the Holy Week ceremonies described in the tenth-century guide to monastic living called the *Regularis Concordia*, the medieval congregant would encounter a cross that sings, is wrapped in cloth and buried in a tomb, and finally disappears over the course of the week's observances. The medieval cross, as an object of study, has been interpreted from countless perspectives in a variety of disciplines. Perhaps the most powerful sign in medieval Europe, probably only surpassed by the Eucharistic host in the later Middle Ages, the cross was also a material object.

Andrew Sofer, in *The Stage Life of Props*, suggests a heavily phenomenological method of studying props that concentrates on the object's reception as a physical entity, in addition to considering its signification to the audience. Sofer proposes what he calls a material methodology, which explores "not only the three-dimensionality of objects as material participants in the stage action, but the spatial dimension (how props move in concrete stage space) and the temporal dimension (how props move through linear stage time)" (Sofer 2003: 2). He attempts to lift the theatrical prop from the page and as far as possible explore its physical life in performance. This approach can certainly be applied to the cross as it is used in the *Adoratio*, *Depositio*, and *Elevatio Crucis* (the Adoration, Deposition, and Elevation of the Cross) – rituals that provide a through-line to the Holy Week observances, in which the object is adored on Maundy Thursday, deposited into the altar on Good Friday, and removed and placed in its usual position before dawn on Easter. Here the cross is by no means a flat or static figure, but a three-dimensional one that is moved within the spatial configuration of the church and undergoes a transformational journey in linear time.

However, Sofer acknowledges that such concentration on a featured object from a text carries the danger of creating an obstructed or distorted view of the whole. And by looking closely at the Holy Week ceremonies of the *Regularis Concordia* it becomes apparent that it is *the conversation between the cross and the celebrants* that is fundamental to the meaning of these observances. Thus, while I incorporate Sofer's emphasis on the material and spatial qualities of the object's journey, I wish to study this particular early medieval cross as an object that can primarily be defined by its relationship with its manipulators. In other words, I analyze the cross as a "performing object" or a "puppet." I use both of these terms interchangeably. As I detail below, in matters of definition I hew most closely to Stephen Kaplin's "puppet tree" (1999), a model of classifying puppets and performing objects that focuses not on the differences in their physical properties but rather charts a spectrum of relationships between object(s) and manipulator(s).

This "puppet perspective" enables me to think about the *Regularis Concordia*'s Holy Week observances as a locus where humans and cross perform in tandem to create meaning and to provide an emotional and spiritual experience for the early medieval congregation. It will demonstrate how even during the early medieval period, when anxiety surrounded the use of three-dimensional figures, a sacred experience could be created for orthodox monastic communities through the manipulation of a material thing. And it will highlight the ways in which, within a document carefully and systematically dictating the behavior and practices of tenth-century monks, a performing object might uncover space for an individualized experience of Christ's crucifixion.

Some medieval attitudes towards performing objects

At the outset I acknowledge that my use of the terms "performing object" and "puppet" to describe the *Regularis Concordia* cross is anachronistic. The expression "performing object" can be traced to classifications in the influential twentieth-century semiotic studies of puppetry – particularly Frank Proschan's much-quoted "The Semiotic Study of Puppets, Masks, and Performing Objects," in which he defines performing objects as "material images of humans, animals, or spirits that are created, displayed, or manipulated in narrative or dramatic performance" (Proschan 1983: 4). And in looking at the historic evidence for puppetry in England, Ian Lancashire argues that the first English puppet play on record took place in 1431, centuries after the period under examination here (Lancashire 1979: 127).

Furthermore, both the creation of puppets and their performance are exceedingly problematic to early medieval teaching about idolatry. Although writing that approved and even exalted artistic creation did exist, there was a definite tension involved in the act of medieval image-making, particularly in the early Middle Ages. Fear of idolatrous behavior prevented the widespread creation of three-dimensional figures until the twelfth century (Camille 1989: 36). Michael Camille cites as influential Hugh of St. Victor's conception of a "hierarchy of creativity," in which the works of man rank the lowest, below the works of nature and the works of God, because "any maker appropriates God's creation in making any image" (Camille 1989: 39). Thus, all human works are simply recombinations of God's raw materials, or, in the case of representational imagery, merely a reflection of the divinely created world.

In the case of puppet *performance*, the tension extends further to what Victoria Nelson describes as "the perceived sacrilege in animating the inanimate" (Nelson 2001: 50). Here the maker not only recombines or reflects what has already been created by God but is heretically attempting to "play God" by giving it life. As many puppet scholars have explored, our historical fascination with puppetry is in large part due to the existential dissonance it engenders, particularly through the seeming ability of the puppet operator to bring life and movement to the inanimate form. As Steve Tillis describes it, "the puppet pleasurably challenges the audience's understanding of object and life" (Tillis 1996: 115). Life-giving powers in medieval Europe, however, were strictly within the purview of the divine. Camille explains that the creators of Gothic-era automatons, for example, were seen as "overstepping the proper paths of human knowledge" and exhibiting an illicit desire to play God (Camille 1989: 250). As Nelson summarizes: "Over the long span of the Christian Middle Ages, a sharp distinction had been drawn between the contrived mechanical wonders wrought by humans and the authentic wonder of *mirabilia*, God's true miracles" (Nelson 2001: 49). Thus, the idea of the cross acting as a puppet, relying on human voices and hands to give it life, would, it seems, have been quite contradictory to the worldview cultivated by early medieval theologians.

Late medieval objects, although operating in a significantly different context, can point us to continuing tensions amassed around image-making and image performance and also provide dramatic illustration of performing crosses within the church walls. The "Rood of Grace," for example, was a crucifix at the Abbey of Boxley in Kent, England, whose corpus was made to bleed and to move in various ways by concealed mechanical means – a subterfuge that supposedly fooled the congregation at Boxley until its discovery, display, and destruction by eager Protestant reformers (who decried the worship of images that were by this point firmly embedded in the Catholic Church) in 1538 (Butterworth 2005: 123–126). Whether the congregation was actually fooled, or if this was an embellishment to the accounts added by the reformers, is not clear. For many of the same reasons that the Protestants smashed the "Rood of Grace," other early reformers of the Catholic Church wrote scathing diatribes against the *Adoratio*, *Depositio*, and *Elevatio Crucis* ceremonies I discuss here. Much of their focus is simply on what they consider the idolatrous nature of the *Adoratio Crucis*, as in Barnaby Googe's translation of Thomas Kirchmayer's *Regnum papisticum*: "Then flat upon the ground they fall and kiss both hand and feet, And worship so this wooden God, with honour far unmeet ... " (cited in Tydeman 2001: 79–80). However, their writings also register great outrage over the fact that in the ceremonies the cross or crucifix cannot move or "live" without human intervention, as in William Barrow of Walden's remarks on the *Depositio* and *Elevatio Crucis* before his execution: "Thys I wotte welle, that on Goode Fryday ye make many goddys to be putte in the sepukyr, but at Ester day they can not a ryse them selfe, but that ye moste lyfte them uppe and bere them forthe, or ellys they wylle ly stylle yn hyr gravys" (cited in Thomson 1965: 134). Here Barrow hits the reformers' anxiety over this liturgical performance on the head: it necessitates the hands of men to resurrect these dead objects, creating the illusion of godly power but lacking a true miracle. Strikingly, William Barrow of Walden's final words come the closest of any medieval source to describing the cross of the *Regularis Concordia* as a puppet.

The cross as puppet

Of course, the use of the cross in the *Regularis Concordia* fits quite easily into a contemporary understanding of "performing objects" and "puppets." Frank

Proschan's definition of performing objects, cited in part above, goes on to describe them as:

> ... images [that] are "created, displayed, or manipulated" in performance; that is, they may be mobile or stationary, permanent or ephemeral. They may, but need not, have movable parts or members. If manipulated, they may be moved directly (as are most masks) or by some mediating device or mechanism (as are many puppets). If displayed, they must then be incorporated into a performance by the indexical words or gestures of the performer calling attention to the image or certain of its part or properties.
>
> (Proschan 1983: 5)

The breadth of Proschan's definition alerts us to the fact that a "performing object" does not necessarily have to look like what one might imagine is the typical Western idea of puppet: a somewhat realistic human or animal figure, manipulated, perhaps via strings, by an operator who remains out of view. And, in fact, attributes of the cross in the *Regularis Concordia* are immediately recognizable in Proschan's definition: the cross is both displayed and manipulated directly; it is incorporated into the ritual by "indexical words" and gestures; and the celebrants call repeated attention to the cross and its properties, all of which I will detail more fully below. Proschan's work is useful for placing the cross firmly within the world of performing objects, but I look to an even more recent and expansive definition of puppetry to further elucidate how the cross was made to live and to mean in performance.

Stephen Kaplin's characterization of puppetry draws on both Proschan's definition and that of Henryk Jurkowski, for whom a puppet is characterized as a "speaking and performing object [that] makes temporal use of physical sources for its driving powers, which are present beyond the object" (cited in Kaplin 1999: 29). Kaplin argues for an inclusive definition of puppet that classifies an object according to its relationship to its manipulator. For him, it is "the complexities of this relationship and its 'constant pulsation' [that] define puppet performance" (Kaplin 1999: 29). By highlighting the interaction between the object and the manipulator, this understanding of puppetry opens up new ways of considering how meaning is generated by puppet performance. Kaplin's definition allows us to go beyond merely analyzing particular qualities of the object to considering what is created and expressed by the relationship between object and manipulator.

Thus, while acknowledging that puppetry was a foreign concept to the tenth-century Anglo-Saxon monastic community (although not necessarily absent from the medieval church), I contend that it is the complexity and the "constant pulsation" of the relationship between the celebrants and the cross that enabled the monastic congregation to see Christ crucified, to witness his body entombed in the sepulcher, and to fully experience the evidence of his resurrection on Easter Day. This does not mean that all the celebrants were manipulators, or puppeteers, in the sense that they physically moved the object or gave it a voice. Although there was a kind of communal activation of the object in these ceremonies and the transformation of the object into the body of Christ was ultimately completed within the imagination of the congregants, it seems that specific individuals were designated to aid in the process. These particular celebrants acted almost as guides whose role was to outline the structure of the internal drama to take place within each participant. It was their direct physical manipulation of the object, their proximity to it, their standing in as the site of signification that gave life to the cross at particular points in the ceremony. As the identities of the cross and the celebrants evolved, it was these celebrants' physical relationship to the cross that guided how the object was to be understood by those participating.

Visualizing the object in context

The cross was an all-pervasive feature of monastic life. Barbara Raw notes that for the monastic community, its image was "visible everywhere they went: in the refectory and chapter-house; on shrines, bookcovers and portable altars; in the shape of pectoral and processional crosses" (Raw 1990: 40). The cross was also the site of individual devotions: many of the prayers that monks recited during the public worship of the cross were also utilized privately, and some specifically indicate that they are to be delivered in front of a crucifix (Raw 1990: 58). It is out of this veritable landscape of crosses that the cross of the Holy Week ceremonies emerges and gains its exceptional status.

It is difficult to reconstruct the physical details of the object that would have been used in the tenth-century ceremonies because none of the extant documents are explicit. We can conclude that the object was a cross and not a crucifix, as is indicated by the use of the word *crux* rather than *crucifixus*. This distinction is extremely important and separates the observances as found in the *Regularis Concordia* (which used a cross) from later versions of the ceremonies that utilized a crucifix with a corpus (a figure of Christ's body attached to the cross). Elizabeth Parker (2001), looking for evidence in continental Europe that might shed light on the nature of the ceremonial cross in England, finds that the practices in the fourteenth-century *Liber ordinarius* from Essen, Germany, can be traced back to the continental observances that shaped the *Regularis Concordia*. Also extant from Essen, and dating from between 972 and 982 and thus contemporary with the *Regularis Concordia*, is a jeweled processional cross with a preserved corpus attached. Although, as already stated, a cross, not a crucifix, was used in the ceremony as recorded in the *Regularis Concordia*, it is tempting to surmise that a jeweled cross, or a *crux gemmata*, was used in English monastic practice. This is even more conceivable if one considers Ian Wood's (2006) theory that eighth-century Anglo-Saxons imagined the true cross (the actual physical object on which Jesus was believed to have been hung) to be jeweled. Wood argues that this conflation of jeweled cross with true cross reflects the descriptions of pilgrims to Jerusalem who perceived the precious reliquary that held the supposed remains not as a container but as the cross itself. If so, the use of a jeweled cross would have heightened the experience of an encounter with the true cross that plays so significantly into the Holy Week observances.

Parker also surmises that a processional cross would have been used in the ceremonies of the *Regularis Concordia*. A processional cross of the tenth to twelfth centuries might have been the size of the "Cloisters Cross," now in the collection of the

Figure 16.1 The Cloisters Cross: English; twelfth century; walrus ivory; 22⅝" × 14¼"; The Metropolitan Museum of Art, The Cloisters Collection, 1963. Image © The Metropolitan Museum of Art. Reproduction of any kind is prohibited without express written permission in advance from The Metropolitan Museum of Art

Metropolitan Museum of Art. At approximately 23 inches by 14 inches, the celebrants would have been able to carry it easily, it would have fit into the sepulcher constructed on or near the high altar, and it could have been removed and returned to its normal position during the *Elevatio Crucis* (Parker and Little 1994: 13). The small scale suggests an intimacy that reflects the private, communal nature of the ceremonies and the close bond between the celebrants and the object.

The cross speaks

At the beginning of the *Adoratio Crucis*, two deacons carry the processional cross – as we might picture it, a jeweled cross, 23 inches by 14 inches, covered with a veil at this point in the service – before the altar of the Cross, leaving some space between it and the altar and holding it aloft, one on each side. They begin to sing the *Improperia*, or the Reproaches (the *Regularis Concordia* does not record the entire observance, indicating the singing of the Reproaches by the first words of the verse, "*Popule meus*," or "Oh my people," but an analogous version can be found in its entirety in the *Sarum Missal*, which was used widely in England later in the Middle Ages).[1] The Reproaches begin: "Oh my people, what have I done unto thee, or wherein have I afflicted thee? Reply to me. Because I brought thee up out of the land of Egypt, thou has prepared a cross for thy Savior" (cited in Tydeman 2001: 70), and the celebrants speak for Christ while at the same time holding up the cross. Thus, the ceremony opens with the celebrants providing a voice for the object and indicating, by their proximity to the object and its placement between their bodies and voices, that the sound is coming from the cross. This reception is reinforced by the *Regularis Concordia*'s instructions that two sub-deacons standing before the cross are to respond to the words; it is almost as if the object has sung to them.

The activation of the object by the celebrants (the singing of the words of Christ) begins the process by which the congregation is able to experience the Crucifixion. The operators are in clear view, but the focus during the Reproaches is clearly directed towards the object, both in its central position in front of the altar, its being held aloft, and its framing by the voices and bodies of the deacons. Here the deacons give voice to the cross very much like a puppeteer would give voice to a puppet or an object. The cross is made to sing Christ's words, and the congregation is able to hear him from the cross, beginning the conflation of Christ with the cross that will play out even more forcefully in the *Depositio Crucis*.

The cross as the body of Christ

After the *Adoratio Crucis*,[2] the cross is again taken up by the deacons who bore it aloft during the Reproaches, and it is again transformed. The deacons wrap the cross in a "napkin" – a piece of cloth meant to signify a shroud – and the object is carried from the altar of the Cross to the high altar, where "there shall be a representation as it were of a sepulchre, hung about with a curtain, in which the holy Cross, when it has been venerated, shall be placed" (Symons 1953: 44). These actions – carrying, wrapping, and placing in the sepulcher – definitively inscribe the object as the body of Christ.

This double vision of cross and body that the rite engenders is reinforced, in part, by aural components of the ceremony so that the congregation is employing multiple senses within these rituals. In particular, certain verses in the *Pange lingua*, the sixth-century hymn by Venantius Fortunatus sung during the *Adoratio Crucis* (as rendered in John Mason Neale's 1851 translation), suggest an anthropomorphizing of the cross:

> Bend, O lofty Tree, thy branches,
> Thy too rigid sinews bend;
> And awhile the stubborn hardness,
> Which thy birth bestow'd, suspend;

And the Limbs of Heaven's high Monarch
Gently on thine arms extend.

(Mitchell 1965: 125)

However, the conflation of the cross with Christ's body was not unique to the Holy Week ceremonies. In Hrabanus Maurus's ninth-century collection of figure poetry, *In honorem sanctae crucis*, the cross represents an underlying cosmic pattern that is reflected in all of the other images of the work so that the shape of the cross seems to undergird all that is spiritual. As Celia Chazelle explains, "*In honorem* insists that the crucified Christ blessed not merely the cross, but its form, a blessing proclaimed in the Bible. ... Apparently, therefore, a visible repetition of the form of the cross may be considered sacred" (Chazelle 2001: 115). Particularly striking is Poem I, in which Christ's body is represented, arms outstretched, but without a cross behind him; the effect is an explicit melding of the body of Christ with the shape of the cross. But while in Poem I of *In honorem* it is the shape of the cross that seems to appear behind the body of Christ, in the *Depositio Crucis* the opposite effect occurs: it is the body of Christ that appears from the shape of the cross.

Perhaps the most prominent melding of the cross with Christ's body occurs in the "The Dream of the Rood," the Anglo-Saxon poem in which a narrator tells of a dream he or she has had of a speaking cross that recounted its experience of Christ's crucifixion. Within the poem (translated by Kevin Crossley-Howard), the cross speaks directly, describing the nails piercing its wood and the blood of Christ flowing over it:

They drove dark nails into me; dire wounds are there to see,
The gaping gashes of malice; I did not dare retaliate.
They insulted both of us together; I was drenched in the blood
That streamed from the side of the Man, when He had set His spirit free.

(Mitchell 1965: 129)

Thomas Hill goes as far as to speculate that the anonymous author of "The Dream of the Rood"

had witnessed or participated in a ceremony similar to the one described in the *Regularis Concordia*, that he was struck by the symbolic association implicit in the ritual, and that a source of the symbolic pattern at the center of the poem was thus some version of this quasi-dramatic ritual.

(Hill 1993: 300)

The "temporal contract"

A consideration of the cross from a puppet perspective begins to suggest the complexity of the reception that would have been involved in the ceremonies. Andrew Sofer's idea of a "temporal contract" that is created between the object and the audience within the space of the performance is useful to employ here. Sofer explains his construct as follows: "Like a character, a theatrical sign is not a semantic given but a temporal contract between actors and audience, in which identity is superimposed on a material object. Such a contract is tenuously constituted in time and thus subject to moment-by-moment renegotiation for the duration of performance" (Sofer 2003: 56–57). Within the temporal confines of the ceremony, the cross as an object and as a "thing-in-itself" becomes the body of Christ for the congregation. The performance of the cross enables the monks to have a unique and affective experience of the Crucifixion in that it allows them to hear Christ's voice and see Christ's body. This effect fits well the purpose of the representational liturgy of the *Regularis Concordia* established by Nils Holger Petersen. Petersen makes a connection between the *Regularis Concordia* and a prayer written by the Benedictine monk Anselm of Canterbury in which Anselm mourns not having been present at Christ's crucifixion to suffer the intense spiritual emotion of the event. Petersen's conclusion is that certain portions of the document allow the congregation to experience what Anselm had missed: they enable the monks "to be witnesses, to be present at the events, although this would have been thought to take place in a spiritual way, outside historical time" (Petersen 2003: 113).

The *Elevatio Crucis*, the removal of the cross from the sepulcher on Easter morning "before the bells are rung for Matins" (Symons 1953: 49), marks the completion of the contract. When the cross is put back, it regains its identity as "cross." As the *Regularis Concordia* states, "The sacrists shall take the Cross and set it in *its proper place*" (Symons 1953: 49) (my italics). While still having considerable resonance as an object, the cross becomes again one of the many other crosses in the landscape of the monastic community. After being put back, it remains a sign of Christ (a sign which would have varying emphases throughout the Middle Ages) but not necessarily a representation of his body.

In some ways the temporal contract relieves the tension involved in the veneration of an object within this ceremony. What – or whom – the monks are led to perceive, through the manipulation of the celebrants, is Christ himself, the body and the sacrifice it would be proper for early medieval Christians to worship – not the "thing-in-itself," a brilliant jeweled object that would not be considered worthy of veneration (Camille 1989: 207). Camille cites Thomas Aquinas's distinction between idolatry and *latria* (the worship due to holy images) as summing up a long-standing theological approach. Aquinas describes the two paths the mind can take towards an image: "one indeed towards an image as a certain thing; another, towards the image in so far as it is the image of something else" (cited in Camille 1989: 207). It is the second movement which is necessary for proper worship of the cross: "we must say that no reverence is shown to Christ's image, as a thing – for instance, carved or painted wood: because reverence is not due save to a rational creature. It follows that reverence should be shown to it, in so far only as it is an image" (cited in Camille 1989: 207). It is precisely the puppet-like manipulation of the material object that achieves this orthodox result: it presents to the congregation an experience of the meaning (the body) behind the image.

The necessity of establishing this "temporal contract" with the monastic audience becomes even more apparent on Easter Day. The final reference to the cross is a revelation of its absence. During the *Visitatio Sepulchri*, three monks representing the three Marys go to the sepulcher and are told by a fourth monk, representing the angel at the tomb, that Christ is risen. The fourth monk then lifts the veil of the sepulcher to reveal that the cross inside has vanished and all that remains is the linen it had been wrapped in. When the empty sepulcher is displayed, the congregation is meant to recall the body of Christ that had been placed there two days earlier. Indeed, if the cross hadn't become the body in the previous ceremonies for the congregation, if it had simply remained a "cross," one would not be able to register its absence. In fact, the cross is clearly present in the community, returned to its "proper place" as the *Elevatio Crucis* dictates, *but it has lost its association with the body*. Another way to look at it: with the temporal contract broken, the body is, indeed, missing. It is this breaking of the contract that allows the monks to witness the event of the resurrection, the pinnacle of their sacred history.

This interpretation of the Holy Week ceremonies leaves open the possibility of heterogeneous responses to the object, varying according to the internal life of each congregant. Performances with objects always result in some amount of space between the stylized movement or crafted expression of the puppet and natural movement and expression – a space, as with the example of the cross, which can be extremely vast. At the same time, it is a space that invites the participation of the audience: the spectator has the active role of filling in the movements, of making connections, of smoothing out rough edges or jerky motions. Spectators are called to be active, placing themselves in the "cracks" in the creation. The gulf between actually seeing Christ on the cross and the experience that is suggested by the manipulation of the cross in the *Regularis Concordia*, an object without a realistic figure of Christ attached to it, gives agency to the spectators and allows them to exercise their imaginative powers. The celebrants manipulating the cross provide an outline, but the transformation of the object into the body of Christ ultimately must be completed within the spectator. Robin Bernstein has referred to particular material objects as "scriptive things" – objects that "broadly structure a performance while simultaneously allowing for resistance and unleashing original, live variations that may not be individually predictable" (Bernstein 2009: 69). Although the *Regularis Concordia* was a document meant to codify and control the life of monastic communities, the performance with the cross produces fissures, albeit small, into which individual interpretation might flow.

A "puppet perspective"

As I've begun to explore through this discussion of the *Regularis Concordia* cross, a puppet perspective can bring a holistic approach to the study of ritual objects, emphasizing the importance of the object's spatial and temporal journey, how it is moved and manipulated, who does the manipulating, where the manipulators are located, and their kinesthetic relationship to the object. It is a methodology that allows the historian to think about how the appearance of life and agency in a material object was both *created* and *perceived*. A puppet perspective can align itself with the move in art history towards thinking about the material and performative qualities of objects and, at the same time, consider these objects as part of a combined human and nonhuman matrix of materiality and meaning.

There are myriad objects from the Middle Ages that might be considered from a puppet perspective: crosses, reliquaries, *palmesels* (wooden figures of Christ riding a donkey that were pulled through towns on Palm Sunday), and "Thrones of Wisdom" (wooden statues of the Christ child on his mother Mary's lap), just to name a few. In addition to the performances of objects, there are also devotional performances from the Middle Ages in which the performer was activated (or stilled) in part by an object. Elizabeth of Spalbeek, for example, was a thirteenth-century Flemish laywoman who enacted the Passion of Christ every day at each hour of the liturgical office. From the *vita* recording her movements, it appears that Elizabeth's performance was inspired in large part by her meditation on a diptych (a two-sided, possibly folding image) of the crucifixion. Elizabeth herself behaved much like a puppet, residing in states of absolute stillness and collapse when not performing, needing literally to be carried to her bed by her mother and sisters. While she performed, her movements appeared so astounding to her audience that it was almost as if something, or someone, were moving her.

It is clear from recent scholarship on medieval objects that a truly interdisciplinary dialogue is in progress. "Objects," "things," and the material world, in general, are garnering greater attention from medievalists of numerous disciplines who have been increasingly drawn to ideas from the fields of speculative realism, object-oriented ontology, and thing theory.[3] Ways of thinking and methodologies from the field of puppetry could be productively added to the conversation. Humans, material objects, and experiences of the divine are inextricably intertwined in the European Middle Ages. A puppet perspective helps us to look back and explore more fully how these elements interact and resonate at the heart of medieval worship. Conversely, the anxiety and debate around proliferating material objects in the Middle Ages can point us forward; studying medieval performing objects might help us to clarify and contrast the ways in which contemporary puppetry both opens space for working through our relationship with the material other and, at the same time, provides audiences with miraculous experiences of wonder and delight.

Notes

1 By featuring Christ lamenting to his people who have crucified him, the *Improperia* lays blame on the Jewish people for the Crucifixion, a sadly common theological stance in the Middle Ages and beyond. Although this chapter focuses on the possibilities for individualized response through performance, it is necessary to remember that these kinds of rituals were meant to instill doctrine and thus would have been instrumental in constructing social attitudes and beliefs, including anti-Semitism.
2 Pamela Sheingorn explains that the Adoration of the Cross was based on the liturgy of Jerusalem where "the impact of the *Adoratio* arose from physical contact with the actual wood used in the Crucifixion at the same season of the year and in the very place in which the Crucifixion was believed to have occurred" (Sheingorn 1987: 13).
3 Two recent symposia entitled "Speculative Medievalisms," held at King's College London (January 2011) and The Graduate Center, City University of New York (September 2011) and organized by The Petropunk Collective, are among the evidence of the increasing popularity in medieval scholarly circles of speculative realism, object-oriented ontology (OOO), and related philosophies and scholarly approaches. Although my inquiry here is concerned with the subjective experience of material objects in performance, OOO and other related theories are provocative (and both resonate and interestingly clash with theories of puppetry and performing objects) in their insistence on the autonomous "life" of a

material thing beyond human perception and control. They also begin to suggest a fascination with a sense of unknowable otherness or thing-ness that a material object might represent in both content and form.

Works cited

Bernstein, R. (2009) "Dances with Things: Material Culture and the Performance of Race," *Social Text* 27: 67–94.

Butterworth, P. (2005) *Magic on the Early English Stage*. Cambridge, UK: Cambridge University Press.

Camille, M. (1989) *The Gothic Idol: Ideology and Image-Making in Medieval Art*. Cambridge, UK: Cambridge University Press.

Chazelle, C. (2001) *The Crucified God in the Carolingian Era*. Cambridge, UK: Cambridge University Press.

Hill, T. D. (1993) "The Cross as Symbolic Body: An Anglo-Latin Liturgical Analogue to *The Dream of the Rood*," *Neophilologus* 77: 297–301.

Kaplin, S. (1999) "A Puppet Tree: A Model for the Field of Puppet Theatre," *TDR/The Drama Review* 43(3): 28–35.

Lancashire, I. (1979) "'Ioly Walte and Malkyng': A Grimsby Puppet Play in 1431," *Records of Early English Drama Newsletter* 2: 6–8.

Mitchell, B. (ed.) (1965) *The Battle of Maldon and Other Old English Poems*. New York, NY: Macmillan.

Nelson, V. (2001) *The Secret Life of Puppets*. Cambridge, MA: Harvard University Press.

Parker, E. C. (2001) "Architecture as Liturgical Setting," in T. J. Heffernan and E. A. Matter (eds.) *The Liturgy of the Medieval Church*, Kalamazoo. MI: Medieval Institute Publications.

Parker, E. C. and Little, C. T. (1994) *The Cloisters Cross: Its Art and Meaning*. New York, NY: The Metropolitan Museum of Art.

Petersen, N. H. (2003) "The Representational Liturgy of the *Regularis Concordia*," in N. Hiscock (ed.) *The White Mantle of Churches: Architecture, Liturgy, and Art around the Millennium*. Turnhout, Belgium: Brepols.

Proschan, F. (1983) "The Semiotic Study of Puppets, Masks, and Performing Objects," *Semiotica* 47: 1–44.

Raw, B. (1990) *Anglo-Saxon Crucifixion Iconography*. Cambridge, UK: Cambridge University Press.

Sheingorn, P. (1987) *The Easter Sepulchre in England*. Kalamazoo, MI: Medieval Institute Publications.

Sofer, A. (2003) *The Stage Life of Props*. Ann Arbor, MI: University of Michigan Press.

Symons, T. (ed. and trans.) (1953) *Regularis Concordia, Anglicae Nationis Monachorum Sanctimonialiumque (The Monastic Agreement of the Monks and Nuns of the English Nation)*. London: Thomas Nelson and Sons.

Thomson, J. A. F. (1965) *The Later Lollards, 1414–1520*. Oxford, UK: Oxford University Press.

Tillis, S. (1996) "The Actor Occluded: Puppet Theatre and Acting Theory," *Theatre Topics* 6: 109–119.

Tydeman, W. (ed.) (2001) *The Medieval European Stage, 500–1550*. Cambridge, UK: Cambridge University Press.

Wood, I. (2006) "Constantinian Crosses in Northumbria," in C. E. Karkov, S. L. Keefer, and K. L. Jolly (eds.) *The Place of the Cross in Anglo-Saxon England*. Woodbridge, UK: The Boydell Press.

Section IV
Negotiating Tradition

17
Traditional and Post-Traditional *Wayang Kulit* in Java Today

Matthew Isaac Cohen

Claims of authenticity and antiquity are attached to puppet theatres worldwide, particularly by advocates seeking patronage from heritage bodies, income from the tourist trade, or a sense of legitimacy and purpose in response to dwindling audiences. However, all we know about puppet theatre indicates that traditions are never, in fact, static but require constant revamping for contemporary audiences and changing performance contexts. Even forms that appear on the surface to be stagnant or inert, such as fusty American holiday marionette shows, the state-subsidized Bunraku company of Japan, or the ritual-bound shadow puppet theatres of India such as *tōgalugōmbeaṭṭa* (Singh 1999), are, in fact, constantly being renewed and altered in sometimes subtle, sometimes dramatic ways. Innovation is not tradition's opposite; change is required to keep tradition vital and meaningful as sociologist Edward Shils (1981) long ago emphasized.

The last century, however, has seen the development of new articulations of puppet traditions – not innovations within traditions but rather strategic departures from them. Puppet artists from Alfred Jarry onward have drawn deeply on tradition's social forms, dramaturgical structures, techniques, and technologies without heeding its rules and taboos. Drawing on the work of British sociologist Anthony Giddens (1994), I refer to such puppet theatre as post-traditional. Productions usually operate outside traditionally mandated time and space, tend to be highly reflexive, and are often politically aware, even subversive. Post-traditional practitioners are sometimes critiqued by conservative traditionalists for "destroying" tradition, but many are, in fact, deeply invested in its transmission while hostile to repressive ideologies of "traditionalism" (Pelikan 1984).

Some post-traditional puppetry has been catalyzed by collaborations with agents coming from outside of traditions – as in *Tall Horse*, a collaboration between South Africa's Handspring Puppet Company and Mali's Sogolon Puppet Troupe (Hutchison 2010). Other post-traditional puppetry has been the result of nonhereditary practitioners entering an established field of practice and remaking it according to nontraditional values, as in Cambodia's Sovanna Phum Theatre, which combines shadow puppetry with circus. There are also examples of transformed tradition resulting from what Shils calls "endogenous factors," the exploration by tradition bearers of new possibilities within the form, the radical rejection of selected precepts, and the bringing of other cultural forms and values into the mix (Shils 1981: 213–239).

Endogenous factors have been the primary causes of change within the traditional puppet theatres, or *wayang*, of Indonesia and the development of post-traditional *wayang* as well. Shadow puppet theatre (*wayang kulit*) on the Indonesian island of Java, my primary focus in this chapter, is in some ways hugely conservative, serving to reproduce ancient Javanese myths and embed Java's versions of the Ramayana and Mahabharata in ritual contexts. *Wayang* "plays" (*lakon*) traditionally are orally improvised in performance and thus always contingent upon context, but one nonetheless observes a high degree of "substantive traditionality," defined by Shils as "the appreciation of the accomplishments and wisdom of the past and of the institutions especially impregnated with tradition, as well as the desirability of regarding patterns inherited from the past as valid guides" (Shils 1981: 21). Shadow puppets carved from rawhide collected more than 200 years ago by T. S. Raffles and now housed in the British Museum could easily be incorporated within Javanese performances today. Puppets are valued as magically potent heirlooms (*pusaka*); performance collections are generally built up over generations rather than being the work of a single maker.

Advances in communication and transportation and the publication of *wayang* texts starting in the middle of the nineteenth century contributed to a blurring of regional *wayang* styles and reduction of local cultural specificities. Dutch scholars privileged literary renderings of *wayang* by the elites of Surakarta, a royal court (*kraton*) city of central Java, and supported *wayang* training courses and associated textbooks (Sears 1996). Texts originating from the royal courts of Surakarta were accepted as authoritative by *wayang* artists around the island. The dominance of Surakarta's courtly *wayang kulit* was further promulgated in the twentieth century by recordings and radio (and later television and digital media). The neo-governmental *wayang* organizations Pepadi and Senawangi, founded in Jakarta during the New Order dictatorship (1966–1998) and patronized by cronies of President Soeharto, promoted Surakarta *wayang* as the *sine qua non* of Javanese tradition in their festivals, publications, and other public representations. *Wayang* was "a carriage-trade item" (Geertz 1990: 52) around East Java by the 1980s, and local puppeteers needed to adopt aspects of Surakarta style to compete (Day 1996). Puppeteers around central and eastern Java purchased colorful and lightweight Surakarta-style puppets tailored to the flashy puppet movement style popularized in the 1980s by Surakarta-style puppeteer Ki Manteb Soedharsono and sold off their old puppets (many of which had long served as *bibit*, or models, for crafting puppets) to antique dealers. Certain regional styles and minority puppet forms, such as *wayang krucil* and *wayang gedhog*, became endangered art forms.

The construction of a monumental, *kraton*-centric "Java" during the New Order dictatorship, critiqued by American anthropologist John Pemberton (1994), has been challenged by dynamic movements in Javanese culture since the 1998 fall of Soeharto. In the carnivalesque demonstrations leading up to Soeharto's ousting, as well as in follow-up celebratory protests against Islamist *sharia*-style regulations of propriety, artists and activists drew upon local forms of cultural performance to combat hegemonic authority. Artists today strive to establish communities of interest (*komunitas*) with local audiences and patrons, reviving and reinterpreting archaic and residual cultural forms of *wayang* and other arts. Endangered *wayang* forms, such as the scroll theatre *wayang beber*, suddenly seem to possess more than antiquarian interest. They are potentially vital cultural resources for "resistance against immanent power" (Nancy 1986). Recent trips I took to Java in 2009 and 2011 confirmed that while *wayang* remains a repository of traditional values, it is a dynamic art, responding to flows of popular culture, political and religious change, and current issues.[1] Far from being "merely" an historical relic, *wayang* is being reinvented on numerous fronts and engaging new audiences through the use of topical humor, social and political commentary, new modes of technology, and philosophical reflection.

Here, I will discuss two broad types or streams of Javanese *wayang* performance. The first I refer to as "traditional." These are Javanese-language performances of standard play-episodes accompanied by gamelan, typically lasting all night, embedded in ritual contexts, and open to the general public free of charge. The second sort of *wayang* is post-traditional, sometimes referred to in Indonesia as *wayang kontemporer*, literally "contemporary *wayang*" (Cohen 2007; Mulyono 1982: 281–289), which is performed outside of ritual contexts in theatre buildings, festivals, or art galleries. Post-traditional *wayang* articulates new relations between performers and their communities of interest and new modes of engagement within and across contemporary art worlds.

It is worth emphasizing that these two streams of *wayang* are not bounded categories. Post-traditional *wayang* artists are often very skilled in traditional practice as well and quite capable of performing traditional *wayang* upon request. Jan Mrázek (2005) in his monograph *Phenomenology of a Puppet Theatre* likens *wayang* to a house that is constructed through performance to be inhabited by performers and spectators for a time. Slamet Gundono, perhaps Java's best known post-traditional puppeteer until his untimely death in 2014, told me there was no fundamental difference between the all-night, gamelan-accompanied traditional *wayang kulit* performances he occasionally gave and his *kontemporer*, intermedial collaborations. Both contemporary and traditional *wayang* offered Ki Slamet houses in which he could live or, as he put it, in which he could *enjoy* (English in the original) himself. Art curator Nicolas Bourriaud's comments on what he calls "postproduction" art are apropos. "The prefix 'post' does not signal any negation or surpassing; it refers to a zone of activity. The processes in question here do not consist of … lamenting the fact that everything has 'already been done,' but inventing protocols of use for all existing modes of representation and all formal structures. It is a matter of seizing all the codes of the culture, all the forms of everyday life, the works of the global patrimony, and making them function. To learn how to use forms … is above all to know how to make them one's own, to inhabit them" (Bourriaud 2001: 17–18). Shils expands further on this metaphor in his discussion of endogenous factors in changing traditions: "The acquisition from the past furnishes their home but it is very seldom a home in which they are entirely at ease. They try to bend it to their own desires; they sometimes discard or replace some of the inherited furniture" (Shils 1981: 213).

Tradition in context: Ritual drama and *komunitas*

Communally sponsored *wayang* performances, though uncommon in much of Central and East Java, remain the norm in Cirebon, Indramayu, and adjacent regencies of western Java. I attended a fair number of these community events in 2009 and performed *Greeting Sri* (*Mapag Sri*) in a number of villages. This is a story episode about the origin of rice cultivation that is enacted as a daytime drama in village halls to coincide with the agricultural year's first planting. Villages that sponsor ritual dramas of this sort, with offerings and incantations to placate spirits, are generally characterized by much substantive traditionality. But Indonesia is a majority Muslim country, and fundamentalist Muslims can be hostile to such customs, which they deem to be polytheistic (*syirik*) remnants of earlier belief systems. I saw the tensions between fundamentalism and substantive traditionality being worked out in 2009 in a small graveside celebration (*unjungan*) in rural Indramayu. The village where this event took place had recently elected a fundamentalist Muslim as village headman – probably due to money politics rather than genuine popularity. At this celebration, a *topeng* troupe performed mask dances with comedy interludes during the day, while a *wayang kulit* troupe performed shadow puppetry at night. The headman had pulled funding for village-wide agrarian celebrations due to his modern religious convictions, to the discontent of many. Despite this, villagers maintained the customary event, sponsored at the neighborhood level and independent of the village bureaucracy, by undertaking door-to-door collections under the sway of beliefs in the power of ancestral spirits to bring blessings and prosperity to descendants. The spirit propitiated was said to be of royal descent, with a proclivity for traditional arts; omitting the customary performance offerings was simply not possible.

Even in this most traditional performance context there were signs of change – including a subsidy from the local government of Indramayu. During the Soeharto era, performances were a cash cow for the local governments. A much-disliked regional regulation (*peraturan daerah*) in Indramayu compelled sponsors of *wayang* and other live performing arts to pay a luxury tax, and in Cirebon, Indramayu, and other parts of Java, cultural inspectors (*penilik kebudayaan*) employed by the Department of Education and Culture showed up regularly at performances to extort money from performers. After the fall of Soeharto, Indramayu's local regulations were dropped, and there were clampdowns on cultural inspectors' corruption. What is more, puppeteers and other performers became aware that villages sponsoring annual ritual dramas were eligible to apply for government subsidies for these events and now work together with patrons to write grant applications. Such funds apparently existed during the Soeharto era but were completely closed to performing artists or their communities of support. We can observe that, even while the dramatic forms and ritual meanings of ritual dramas have remained relatively constant, the context of these events is shifting.

I spent a long weekend in 2009 visiting the field site of folklorist Wisma Nugraha Christianto and discussed at length his research on East Javanese *wayang kulit*, which focuses on the arts management of Ki Surwedi, one of the province's most admired puppeteers. Christianto's research shows that Surwedi maintains his popularity with local sponsors by managerial flexibility and easy familiarity with patrons. Ki Surwedi maintains strong *komunitas* by developing a network of followers and supporters, who hire him to perform more than 100 times a year at the reasonable price of about 5 million rupiah. One of the ways in which Surwedi accomplishes this is through cultivating social ties with his fan base. He encourages the development of credit unions (*arisan*) among devotees so that they can hire his company on a rotating basis. He arrives hours before performances in order to meet with fans in gardens or yards (*perkebunan*) before shows, while receiving a therapeutic massage, rather than arriving just in time to perform or hobnobbing only with elites in hosts' houses. He drinks socially with fans and friends and opens his house and studio to all to play gamelan. In translating Surwedi's client–patron relations to the language of arts management, Christianto is playing an important role in brokering tradition.

In contemporary reconfigurations of tradition, one sees that performance context is no longer bounded at the local level but is increasingly national and even international. Performers and their communities of interest are aware of different models of performance management and are able to hybridize these to suit the circumstances of events.

Tradition in performance: Political critique

The New Order military regime mandated an attitude of political quiescence in *wayang*. Few puppeteers under Soeharto had sufficient power to articulate a political vision or speak up against injustices. Instead, puppeteers were employed as *juru bicara*, spokespeople who parroted official government policy on recommended rice strains, methods of birth control, and the state ideology of Pancasila. In the early years of *Reformasi* (the post-Soeharto period of governmental reform), most puppeteers remained silent, afraid of reprisals even with the promise of freedom of speech.

I saw signs in 2009 that such political attitudes among traditional puppeteers were shifting and that political and religious critiques unthinkable under the dictatorship were being integrated into performances. Educated puppeteers attuned to discourse on human rights and interfaith dialogue were busy restoring *wayang* as a privileged dialogical space. I observed Yogyakarta puppeteer Ki Seno Nugroho interpret the canonical play *Anoman Immolated* (*Anoman Obong*) in May 2009 as a portrait of the authoritarian personality at a performance at the Sasono Hinggil hall of the Yogyakarta royal court and reinterpret *Semar Builds the Heavens* (*Semar Mbangun Kahyangan*) as a critique of government oppression and economic inequality at a performance sponsored by Yogyakarta's high court in February 2009. Mas Seno had recently joined the social networking website Facebook, and we often chatted through this medium about his shows and other activities.

I also reconnected in 2009 with my former assistant and principal informant for my doctoral fieldwork, Purjadi. When I first worked with him during 1994 to 1995, Purjadi was a recent graduate of the State Institute of Islamic Studies, strongly under the influence of a preacher associated with the modernist Islamic movement of Muhammadiyah. Purjadi did not come from a puppeteer family, and as a result his puppet and animation skills were still rudimentary, though he possessed an outstanding singing voice (trained through singing in the local *bujanggaan* club) and an innate talent for vocal impressions. Purjadi performed ritual-drama ceremonies, such as Ruwatan, without offerings to disprove the existence of spirits and repurposed the branch story of *Semar Goes on the Hajj* (*Semar Munggah Haji*) – arguably created as a critique of scripturalist Islam by the radical left-wing puppeteer Abyor – as a piece of Islamic proselytizing (*dakwah*) to inform audiences about the rules of the pilgrimage and the requirements for a pilgrimage to be considered valid (*mabrur*).[2]

I observed in 2009 that years of association with the community of *wayang* performers and supporters had opened Purjadi to values of religious tolerance. For example, he now gave patrons the option of sponsoring the sacred Ruwatan ritual drama with the customary offerings. Purjadi was also involved in local politics, and many of the plays he created, such as *Cungkring Runs for Office* (*Cungkring Nyaleg*), had political themes, with heated debates between representatives of different ideologies.

One of the most interesting plays in Purjadi's repertoire in 2009 was *Human Scripture* (*Kitab Sucieng Manusa*), again based on an Abyor original, which I attended in a performance on March 14–15, 2009 in the village of Bodesari, outside Cirebon. The play concerned a knight returned from the dead in search of an answer to the question that hounded him in life: what is the *kitab sucieng manusa*, the universal "Human Scripture," or sacred text, valid for all humanity? The knight vows to kill anyone who cannot answer his question.

In his quest, the knight makes an assault on Suralaya Kedewatan, the heavens of Bathara Guru, head of the Javanese Hindu pantheon. The assembled forces of the gods cannot turn him back. Then Cungkring, Guru's nephew, the trusted retainer of the Pendhawa brothers (one of the two warring clans in the Mahabharata), arrives in Suralaya, in search of a cure for his ailing master, Darma Kusuma. Guru promises to aid Cungkring if he can defeat the attacking knight. Cungkring confronts the knight, who asks him about the "true" (*sejati*) Human Scripture. Cungkring responds that this question is not clear. We have to know what religious faith a human belongs to first. For Islam, it would be the Qur'an. For Christians, the Gospels (*Injil*). For Hindus, the Vedas. For Jews, the Torah (*Taurat*). The knight protests. Scriptures associated with religion cannot be understood unless you understand the language they are written in. For example, for the Qur'an to have meaning, you have to be able to read Arabic. But the knight insists there is a Human Scripture that can be understood regardless of the language of the reader and can be accepted by all religions, as well as by those without religion. Cungkring, unable to respond, is struck and flies off.

The knight then confronts Bathara Guru, who asks him what his religious faith is. The knight admits that he does not possess a faith. Then follows a theological dialogue, which goes something like this in my own rough, on-the-spot transcription and translation:

GURU: So that is why you don't comprehend the concept of a holy book (*kitab suci*). You need to possess a religion first. Then you will understand.
KNIGHT: What sort of religion would suit me?
GURU: Religion does not work according to suit; it depends on belief and individual faith. Would you consider following my faith?
KNIGHT: All that matters is that I understand Scripture.

Figure 17.1 Kitab Sucineng Manusa, performed by Purjadi, Bodesari (March 14–15, 2009): Bathara Guru (center) consults with his vizier Narada (left). Photo courtesy of the author

GURU: You must first understand the Divine. To do that you must comprehend your inner self first.

Guru then launches into a long explanation about the different dimensions (*alam*) and the relation between the inner and outer world, grounded in the science of Javanese mysticism (*kebathinan*) and reiterating classical monistic theology (see Zoetmulder 1995) in modern, everyday language:

KNIGHT: I have no idea what you're talking about. Tell it to me straight, tell me how things are.
GURU: The Divine cannot be comprehended with logic for God is Most Mysterious (*Maha Gaib*). The taste of sugar or salt cannot be explained to someone who has never tasted these before. Similarly, to know the Lord you need to use *rasa* (feeling), not your brain.
KNIGHT: I want to see God directly.
GURU: The Lord is me, or rather, what is in the heart of a being who believes.

Post-traditional *wayang kulit*

Purjadi and Seno's performances, though contemporary in their religious and political ethos and worldviews, conform to long-established dramaturgical models. Yet, as I have indicated, *wayang* is also taking on new forms and being framed in very new ways. It is being reinvented and reaching new audiences, generating new communities of interest in the process. These efforts are increasingly interconnected, and post-traditional *wayang* practitioners around Java, in Bali, and on other Indonesian islands, as well as in neighboring Malaysia, are operating in mutual awareness of innovations, shared through well publicized public performances, formal and informal gatherings, Facebook, YouTube, and other media.

The beginnings of this movement in *wayang* might be located perhaps in the 1960s, when non-Indonesian practitioners and scholars first began to study practical puppetry in Java and Bali; Indonesian puppeteers taught, studied, and performed abroad; and Indonesian puppet artists came into direct contact with Southeast Asians practicing related puppet forms through festivals and cultural exchange projects following the 1967 founding of the Association of Southeast Asian Nations (Cohen 2007). Intercultural communication and exchange yielded opportunities and tools for theatrical reinterpretations of *wayang*. Indonesian puppeteers personalized the tradition (Susilo 2002: 185) and developed new *wayang* variants with novel puppets, techniques, and scripts. Sociological studies of European art history reveal that the onymous artist emerged over centuries out of artisan guilds and monastic scriptoria (Martindale 1972). The Indonesian puppeteer's transformation from what Ward Keeler calls a "dissembled authority" (Keeler 1987: 268) to charismatic artist, in contrast, has taken less than two generations.

One of the seminal figures in post-traditional *wayang* was the late Yogyakarta artist Sigit Sukasman, who took an experimental approach to making *wayang* following his exposure to modern art in New York and The Netherlands in 1964 to 1965 (Susilo 2002). Sukasman worked with translucent hides and whimsical and idiosyncratic iconographies. His experimental productions of "measured" *wayang* (*wayang ukur*) employed puppeteers in front and behind the shadow screen in collaboration with dancers in variants of *wayang wong* costume – a combination without local precedent. Sukasman's studio in Yogyakarta, up until his death in 2009, was a regular meeting place for Indonesians and foreigners interested in critically exploring the philosophy and aesthetics of *wayang*. He supported himself through the sale of his figures to collectors and complained of how other Javanese puppet makers unscrupulously copied his designs without attribution. Sukasman's experimental attitude provided a model for a stable of Yogyakarta artists who played with *wayang*'s conventions in different ways. Many similar avant-garde creations (*kreasi*) emerged in Yogyakarta and its environs during the 1970s and 1980s.

Many of the experiments under the name of *wayang kontemporer* are ephemeral – "momentarily popular but lacking longevity" in the words of one *wayang* critic (Mulyono 1982: 283). Characteristic of this is a set of figures from a 1975 production created by contemporary gamelan composer Sapto Rahardjo that are on permanent display in Yogyakarta's Kekayon Wayang Museum. These figures, cut from cardboard and painted with fluorescent paint (illuminated in performance by ultraviolet light), depict the city's lively youth culture. A figure dressed in a sleeveless T-shirt and batik sarong listens to music on a portable audio player's headphones. A second is dressed in a tight-fitting, tie-dyed sleeveless T-shirt and miniskirt. A third sports a pink-and-green Mohawk. A fourth wears an outfit crossing combat fatigues with batik and flaunts think eyeliner and lipstick. A *kayon*[3]-like figure notes the cast, referred to with joking nicknames (e.g., "Saptlik Raharjoslaq" instead of Sapto Rahardjo) and English and Indonesian slogans of the time ("Flowers of the War"). The name for this production is *Wayang Kreasul*, said to be jokingly

Figure 17.2 Sigit Sukasman (1937–2009) explaining *wayang* visual theory in his studio (April 26, 2009). Photo courtesy of the author

abbreviated from the phrase *kreasi tanpa melupakan asal-usul* (experiment without forgetting origin).

Some of the ideas initiated in *Legendary Wayang* (*Wayang Legenda*), a 1988 production in Yogyakarta by painter and installation artist Heri Dono, were developed in Dono's subsequent installations and community-based performances in Australia, Canada, New Zealand, and the United Kingdom (Behrend 1999). *Wayang* imagery and ideas continue to inform Dono's work in complex ways. But although Dono is arguably Indonesia's most famous contemporary artist, his *wayang* performance work is little known in his country of origin.

While dialogue is extemporized and no two performances are identical, traditional *wayang* is characterized by its immaculate aesthetic quality, with a clearly defined process of creation. In its ideal form, *wayang* accords to Theodor Adorno's ideal of the monad, "an imminent, crystallized process at a standstill" (Adorno 1970 [2004]: 237). The Surakarta court manual for puppeteers, *Serat Sastramiruda*, prescribes, in an oft-cited list of nine aesthetic qualities, that "a puppeteer should not allude to themes outside the frame of the story, and should especially avoid smutty comedy" (Kusumadilaga 1981: 188). In contrast, post-traditional *wayang* that I have observed tends to be quickly rehearsed, porous to the world, and highly contingent on the circumstances of performance. Such *wayang* is less monadic than what Bourriaud describes as "a temporary and nomadic gathering of precarious materials and products of various provenances" (Bourriaud 2001: 28) – like an outdoor market. A post-traditional *wayang* production staged in Yogyakarta in 2009 offers a sense of post-traditional *wayang*'s processual fluidity.

Porous *wayang*

The first performance of what curator-producer Alia Swastika has called *wayang bocor*, "leaky" or "porous" *wayang*, was offered free of charge at the opening of a solo exhibition by Yogyakarta-based artist Eko Nugroho at the Cemeti Art House in Yogyakarta in 2009. The episodic play, entitled *Berlian Ajaib* in Indonesian (which can be translated as *The Magical Diamond* or *The Wonder of Diamond* in English), was based loosely on stories and figures from the artist's underground comix anthologies *Wart* (*Daging Tumbuh*). This was the second outing for what is described on Nugrohu's website as the artist's "shadow puppet project" (Swastika 2009). The first outing, which used the same set of puppets based on Nugrohu's black-and-white cartoons, was a more conventional scripted drama, *A Wrapped Heart Inside the Refrigerator* (*Bungkusan Hati di Dalam Kulkas*), written and directed by Joned Suryatmoko of Yogyakarta's Teater Gardanella collective and performed at Jakarta's Teater Salihara in 2008. The puppeteer for this earlier performance, the constantly innovative Catur "Benyek" Kuncoro, was unhappy with the script's literalism and the director's lack of sensitivity to *wayang*'s idiom. Swastika thus allowed Benyek, with whom she had worked from 2006 to 2008 on a community arts project with earthquake victims in Bantul, to take over the creative reins. Benyek is an experienced collaborator, descended from a puppeteer family and a graduate of the puppetry department of Yogyakarta's arts high school, Sekolah Mengenah Karawitan Indonesia. He has performed music internationally with the arts company of Padepokan Seni Bagong Kussudiardjo starting in 2004 and with the Acappella Mataraman vocal group. He has also worked with a number of Yogyakarta's other premiere music groups, including Kua Etnika, and puppeteers visiting Yogyakarta, including Damiet van Dalsum. His *wayang kreasi* include *Wayang Kartun* (2005), *Wayang Kontemporer Dual Core* (2006), *Wayang Pixel* (2007), and *Wayang Hiphop* (2010), and he also writes Indonesian-language scripts for Enthus Susmono, currently Indonesia's most highly paid puppeteer. Swastika offered Benyek back issues of *Wart* as stimuli, out of which he drafted a skeletal script, a series of short scenes depicting a carnivalesque night market (*pasar malam*), an alien invasion, and a dysfunctional family.

Nugroho's gallery opening was two weeks distant when I stopped by the Cemeti Art House to see if I might observe rehearsals for this contemporary *wayang*. Benyek, Swastika, and Nugroho, along with a number of other artists (including puppeteer Toro Widyanto, composer Yenu Ariendra, and scenographer Andy Seno Aji), spent the first two days of a six-day rehearsal process lounging around Cemeti, mostly engaging in small talk. I was casually offered the chance to puppeteer alongside Benyek and Toro, and I enthusiastically accepted this role of participant-observer, though no formal parts had yet been decided. Finally, Alia Swastika, anxious about the opening, pressed us to rehearse. Initially we tried to perform sitting down in back of the two *wayang* screens constructed for the exhibition – one painted like the sky in blue and white. This proved awkward with three seated puppeteers, and I suggested loosening the central control rods of the puppets so that they could be held at a distance while standing. This sort of jointing is unconventional in *wayang* (though not unknown for trick figures), but Benyek and Toro agreed, as it allowed for greater freedom and play. It was not long before we were twirling figures around at the screen and tossing them back and forth with abandon across the gap separating the two screens. Toro, who had crafted the figures we were animating, treated the figures with great roughness, in the knowledge that he could always make more if they broke, somewhat to the consternation of Alia, who was hoping to sell the puppets as singular art objects after displaying them at the exhibition.

Alia was more pleased, however, when we propped up figures not in use against the wall behind the screens, perhaps as this allowed a more strategic view of the puppets. She seized upon this casual anti-illusionism as the production's defining characteristic, coining the generic term *wayang bocor*. With the visibility of puppets and puppeteers in mind, we quickly devised a framing prologue in which an itinerant merchant (played by Benyek) and his associate (Toro) hawked magical ointments and potions reputedly fashioned from a magical diamond (*berlian ajaib*). This frame story, which used human actors as well as puppets, although not based on a Nugrohu cartoon, allowed us to use another of the exhibition's set items, a modified food cart that had been prepared and painted by Toro. The conceit was consciously modeled after a then-current news story about a young medicine man (*dukun*) named Ponari who was said to fashion healing potions from a brown "magical stone" (*batu ajaib*). In our telling, the hucksters succeeded in selling one of their potions, before the police showed up, to a licentious but gullible Westerner wishing to sleep with Javanese women (played by the author). The performers ran helter-skelter, which allowed us to take up position behind the screen for the first scene.

As we put together the performance and rehearsed, Ariendra arranged a musical score from sampled sounds and assembled musical pieces, some of his own composition, others taken off the internet, while Seno Aji busied himself with arranging

Figure 17.3 Rehearsal for *Berlian Ajaib*, Cemeti Art House, Yogyakarta (March 3, 2009). Photo courtesy of the author

other parts of the exhibition into an environment for the performance. The last creative player to make an appearance was Ignatius "Clink" Sugiarto, a lighting designer best known for his work with Teater Garasi. Typically for lighting designers unaccustomed to *wayang*, Sugiarto mostly focused his labor on lighting the pre-set and prologue, hanging the crucial lights for lighting the shadow puppets at the end. I protested that standard theatrical lanterns did not yield sufficiently defined shadows, but there was no time to rig special lights nor was there a budget for renting dedicated equipment. Benyek, Swastika, and other members of the creative team deferred to Sugiarto's reputation, even while recognizing that the puppets were not ideally lit.

The audience who attended our performance was young, warm, and enthusiastic and absolutely packed the art gallery. Spectators roared with laughter at even the smallest of jokes – and were particularly appreciative of Toro's broad humor as mime and puppeteer, including a comic bit with an oversexed dog. Ariendra commented that aesthetically the production was "ugly" (*jelek*) – many aspects were very rough indeed, related to the fact that many of the costumes and scenic elements were added at the last minute. However, he added that this roughness was redeemed by the humor and warm atmosphere (including free snacks and an after-show party with a DJ and alcohol). Swastika, cannily realizing in rehearsal that our motley crew would never pull off a polished performance in the time allotted, pushed for the performance to be an "event" after the model of auteur director-playwright Rendra's rough *sampakan* theatre, rather than a finished aesthetic product. The reputation of the venue and of Eko Nugroho, as well as Swastika's connections with the press, meant that this hastily assembled production received attention from the national media, including a preview in *The Jakarta Post* and a review in *Tempo*, as well as coverage on Metro TV's English and Indonesian language news shows. Apparently this mode of working was successful enough to encourage future productions – in Java as well as at the Lyon Biennale 2009.[4]

Reflections on post-traditional *wayang*

Post-traditional *wayang* subverts the structures and forms of Javanese tradition. Unlike the acerbic historical avant-garde of early twentieth-century Europe, though, there is no "desire to wipe out whatever came earlier in the hope of reaching at last a point that could be called a true present, a point of origin that marks a new departure" (De Man 1970: 388–389). As is the case for what theatre historian Harry J. Elam calls "post-blackness," post-traditional *wayang* is a performance turn "simultaneously free from, and yet connected to and perhaps even haunted by, the legacies of the past in the present" (Elam 2005: 382). Post-traditional *wayang* cannot be folded into tradition, though certain innovations (such as the new puppet types invented by Sukasman) might be recycled by traditional practitioners.

Traditional *wayang*, like all traditions, is a "consensus between living generations and generations of the dead" (Shils 1981: 168). Post-traditional *wayang*, in contrast, like much contemporary art, "tends to abolish the ownership of forms, or in any case to shake up the old jurisprudence" (Bourriaud 2001: 35). While the traditionalists helming the national *wayang* associations Pepadi and Senawangi attempt to inscribe regional *wayang* styles within the strictures of a national *wayang Indonesia* complex, a defensive posture to shore up Indonesian cultural territorial integrity against perceived incursions by neighboring Malaysia, post-traditional *wayang* boldly opens the tradition to global cultural flows. Post-traditional *wayang* is thus epochalist rather than essentialist in Geertz's (1973) formulation; it is often more attentive to international media than local spirit beliefs. As such, it offers an ideal footing for collaborations between Indonesian and foreign artists, manifest in such noteworthy international projects as *The MahabharANTa* by Mabou Mines in collaboration with puppeteer I Wayan Wija (1992), *Visible Religion* with puppeteers Sri Djoko Rahardjo and I Made Sidia (1994), *The Theft of Sita* with puppeteers Peter Wilson and I Made Sidia under Nigel Jamieson's direction (1999), *ShadowBang* with composer Evan Ziporyn and I Wayan Wija (2001), *Mahabharata Jazz and Wayang* with the jazz ensemble Luluk Purwanto and the Helsdingen Trio in collaboration with puppeteer Nanang HP (2003), *Semar's Journey* with puppeteer Seno Nugroho (2007), and *Cebolang Minggat* with puppeteer Slamet Gundono (2009). Previous generations of European theatre makers appropriated *wayang* for exotic color. An international collaboration with Indonesian artists today "entails that we [foreigners] understand reflexively that our 'concepts' are only another set of (by Western accident) privileged schemata" (Lash 1994: 156).

Notes

1 I have been studying *wayang* since 1988, when I made my first trip to Indonesia as a Fulbright scholar hosted by the Department of Puppetry at Indonesia's most prestigious conservatoire for the traditional performing arts, now known as Institut Seni Indonesia Surakarta. My studies have been ethnographic and historical, as well as practical: I actually learned how to perform as a puppeteer, something that has been possible for foreigners, even actively encouraged, since the 1960s. Much of the material in this chapter was collected during two recent trips to Indonesia: five months as a visiting scholar hosted by Sanata Dharma University in Yogyakarta in 2009 and a two-week visit to Java in January 2011.
2 For a detailed discussion of Purjadi's interpretation of these plays, see Cohen (1997: 263–332).
3 The *kayon*, or *gunungan*, is the tree-of-life puppet that is used to mark the beginning and end of scenes and serves as an all-purpose prop.
4 For more on Eko Nugroho's "*wayang* project," see the artist's website <http://ekonugroho.or.id/> and YouTube channel <http://www.youtube.com/user/TheEkonugroho> (accessed August 15, 2013).

Works cited

Adorno, T. (1970) *Aesthetic Theory*, eds G. Adorno and R. Tiedeman, trans. R. Hullot-Kentor (2004). London: Continuum.
Behrend, T. (1999) "The Millennial Esc(h)atology of Heri Dono: 'Semar Farts' First in Auckland, New Zealand," *Indonesia and the Malay World* 27: 208–224.
Bourriaud, N. (2001) *Postproduction: Culture as Screenplay: How Art Reprograms the World*, trans. J. Herman (2002). New York, NY: Lukas and Sternberg.
Cohen, M. I. (1997) *An Inheritance from the Friends of God: The Southern Shadow Puppet Theater of West Java, Indonesia*. Unpublished Ph.D. thesis, Yale University.

—— (2007) "Contemporary *Wayang* in Global Contexts," *Asian Theatre Journal* 24: 338–369.

Day, T. (1996) "Performances of East Javanese *Wayang* and the Possibility of 'Internal Otherness' in Contemporary Java," in T. Day and P. Dowsey-Magog (eds) *Performances East/West*. Sydney, Australia: Centre for Performance Studies, University of Sydney.

De Man, P. (1970) "Literary History and Literary Modernity," *Daedalus* 99: 384–404.

Elam, H. J. (2005) "Change Clothes and Go: A Postscript to Postblackness," in H. J. Elam, Jr. and K. Jackson (eds) *Black Cultural Traffic: Crossroads in Global Performance and Popular Culture*. Ann Arbor, MI: The University of Michigan Press.

Geertz, C. (1973) "After the Revolution: The Fate of Nationalism in the New States," in *The Interpretation of Cultures: Selected Essays*. New York, NY: Basic Books.

—— (1990) "'Popular Art' and the Javanese Tradition," *Indonesia* 50: 77–94.

Giddens, A. (1994) "Living in a Post-Traditional Society," in U. Beck, A. Giddens, and S. Lash (eds) *Reflexive Modernization: Politics, Tradition and Aesthetics in the Modern Social Order*. Stanford, CA: Stanford University Press.

Hutchison, Y. (2010) "The 'Dark Continent' Goes North: An Exploration of Intercultural Theatre Practice through Handspring and Sogolon Puppet Companies' Production of *Tall Horse*," *Theatre Journal* 62: 57–73.

Keeler, W. (1987) *Javanese Shadow Plays, Javanese Selves*. Princeton, NJ: Princeton University Press.

Kusumadilaga, K. P. A. (1981) *Serat Sastramiruda*, eds and trans. Kamajaya and S. Z. Hadisutjipto. Jakarta, Indonesia: Departemen Pendidikan dan Kebudayaan.

Lash, S. (1994) "Reflexivity and Its Doubles: Structure, Aesthetics, Community," in U. Beck, A. Giddens, and S. Lash (eds) *Reflexive Modernization: Politics, Tradition and Aesthetics in the Modern Social Order*. Stanford, CA: Stanford University Press.

Martindale, A. (1972) *The Rise of the Artist in the Middle Ages and Early Renaissance*. New York, NY: McGraw Hill.

Mrázek, J. (2005) *Phenomenology of a Puppet Theatre: Contemplations on the Art of Javanese Wayang Kulit*. Leiden, The Netherlands: KITLV Press.

Mulyono, S. (1982) *Wayang: Asal-Usul, Filsafat dan Masa Depannya*. Jakarta, Indonesia: Gunung Agung.

Nancy, J.-L. (1986) *La Communauté désoeuvrée*, ed. P. Conner, trans. P. Connor, L. Garbus, M. Holland, and S. Sawhney (1991) *The Inoperative Community*, W. Godzich and J. Schulte-Sasse (eds) *Theory and History of Literature*, vol. 76. Minneapolis, MN: University of Minnesota Press.

Pelikan, J. (1984) *The Vindication of Tradition: The 1983 Jefferson Lecture in the Humanities*. New Haven, CT: Yale University Press.

Pemberton, J. (1994) *On the Subject of "Java."* Ithaca, NY: Cornell University Press.

Sears, L. J. (1996) *Shadows of Empire: Colonial Discourse and Javanese Tales*. Durham, NC: Duke University Press.

Shils, E. (1981) *Tradition*. Chicago, IL: University of Chicago Press.

Singh, S. (1999) "If Gandhi Could Fly … Dilemmas and Directions in Shadow Puppetry of India," *TDR/The Drama Review* 43(3): 154–168.

Susilo, H. (2002) "The Personalization of Tradition: The Case of Sukasman's Wayang Ukur," in J. Mrázek (ed.) *Puppet Theater in Contemporary Indonesia: New Approaches to Performance Events*, Michigan Papers on South and Southeast Asia, vol. 50. Ann Arbor, MI: The Center for South East Asian Studies.

Swastika, A. (2009) "The Wonder of Diamond," <http://www.ekonugroho.or.id/index.php?page=artwork&cat=Shadow%20Puppet%20Project> (accessed August 16, 2013).

Zoetmulder, P. J. (1995) *Pantheism and Monism in Javanese Suluk Literature: Islamic and Indian Mysticism in an Indonesian Setting*, ed. and trans. M. C. Ricklefs. Leiden, The Netherlands: KITLV Press.

18
Korean Puppetry and Heritage
Hyundai Puppet Theatre and Creative Group NONI Translating Tradition

Kathy Foley

Korean traditional rod puppetry (*kkokdu gaksi noreum*),[1] which was almost defunct at the time of the Korean War (1950–1953), experienced a revival starting in the 1960s. This renewed interest in the art came with the rise of nationalism by way of post-colonial academic work in folklore, which hoped to reconstruct indigenous "roots." Contemporary artists have, since the 1980s, sought strategies to fit *kkokdu gaksi* into modern performance. But the bawdy folk genre called *namsadang nori*, a type of performance that amalgamates farmer's band (*nongak*) music, circus feats, acrobatics, mask performance, and the traditional puppet play of *kkokdu gaksi*, may remain an uneasy match for what the market currently desires in traditional forms: to be able to export a national "high" art in cultural exchanges, to activate child-specific entertainment of modern mediated puppetry, or to energize the urban middle class with a sense of roots in a period of economic growth and democratic freedom. These Korean folk genres, which were low class and critical of the hierarchy in their comic energy, have great potential in times of political urgency and were used evocatively by student protesters in the 1980s to oppose the military dictatorship of President Park Chung-hee and to attack the American military presence (Park 2013). However, they do not approximate elite "art" aesthetics of court or contemporary urban elites. This means that the modern puppeteer must make choices, when purely following the tradition will be seen as too messy, bawdy, or boring. One strategy is to wed selected portions of traditional forms to other arts with which it has no historical link; another is to mold tradition into an avant-garde display where visual aspects may be expanded and recast, becoming more impressive than the original, which was a joke-driven form. Only one government-supported heritage troupe of *namsadang nori* is currently performing the traditional show on a limited basis. But here, after some discussion of the history, we can see how the work of two groups in particular, Hyundai Puppet Theatre and Creative Group NONI, has reworked aspects of Korean traditional puppetry.

"Courtly consort" and the "big bang" in Asian performing arts

For clarifying the situation of Korean puppetry, it is useful first to discuss the two poles of traditional Asian puppetry, which I call the "courtly consort" and the "big bang." Elite arts are or were forms where the artists may live in or by the palace/temple/theatre they serve. They tell epic stories that are generally supportive of the religious or state ideology that assures their daily rice. These forms are relatively high in status and grow as elaborate as the patronage may allow: large sets of figures/impressively large puppets, elaborate musical instruments, and polished presentations are the norm. Some genres from Southeast Asia, such as the court shadow puppetry of the Thai (*nang yai*) and Khmer (*nang sbek thom*), the *wayang* of Java, and court marionettes of Myanmar (*yokthe pwe*), enjoyed court support. The Japanese forms of mask performance (*nō*) or puppet theatre (*bunraku*) could arguably be included as "courtly consorts": while they moved out of the palace and temple, respectively, to play for urban audiences, these Japanese forms were, in the past, genres with elite support.

By contrast, there also exist Asian forms presented by itinerants, who do short skits or episodes that can be quickly grasped by the passerby. In these, the "scene," rather than the ongoing narrative, is a self-standing unit. Big sound, slapstick action, shocking language (sex, political rabble-rousing) can attract attention and garner applause. The puppet figures are rough, small enough for itinerants to carry, and easy to manipulate. Musical instruments are limited and emphasize loudness (drum, gong, oboe/loud stringed instrument). In these forms the musician usually sits outside the simple cloth-draped booth and interacts verbally with both audience and puppets, which are moved by one or a few manipulators. Everything seems a bit fly-by-night, and since the performers are often *persona non grata* (their humor often criticizes the constraints of the upper-class-dominated order), quick exits before official sweeps are sometimes needed. Rajasthani marionettes (*kathputli*), Iranian string puppets (*keimeh shab bazi*), and Korean *kkokdu gaksi* rod figures are all "big bang" forms.

While the court arts may have at one point derived from these faster and more brash materials and may keep traces of this old material somewhere in their structures, the court arts of the powerful have acquired the pomp that is the mark of an elite: palaces generally slow performances down, multiply the number of performers, expand the orchestra, demand extended space, and tell narratively big stories. Court arts are displays of power, resources, and importance. These genres, in an era of the modern nation-state, often garner significant government or elite support, are frequently sent to represent the country in international arts exchanges, and have moved quickly into "Intangible Cultural Heritage" status that UNESCO has created since the turn of the millennium.

Meanwhile, village arts deal with basics. How does one gather a crowd – humans, ancestor spirits, and/or demons? The instruments need to be heard – for example, the brass handheld gong, drums, and the piercing sound of a shawm in the Korean farmer's band. The iconography of figures may be broad and bright, to "read" outdoors and over distance. Narratively, performers turn to basic themes – sex, pecking order, and death – and laughter trumps tears. Since the players depend more on popularity with the masses than approval of a permanent patron, the show's point of view will often reflect the "little guy" and skewer authority. These puppeteers come from the bottom of society, and their clowns playfully expose the viewpoint of the macho-yet-put-upon, lower-class male. In transitioning from traditional societies, these arts may have a more difficult time gaining significant support from national governments or the attention of modern educated urban audiences, and artists may puzzle over how to use them. Traditional puppetry in Korea falls into this "big bang" category, since it was a significant tool in questioning the strict social order, and yet in the last decades, for political and social reasons, there has been an inclination to see how *kkokdu gaksi* and *namsadang nori* might migrate into something a bit more like the "courtly consort."

Translating tradition in post-colonial frames

The migration of Korean folk forms from "big bang" to "courtly consort" during the latter half of the twentieth century posed difficulties. First, there was the traditional class status of the performers and their historical association with male prostitution – modern performers needed to dissociate from this class stigma. Second, there was the spiritual outlook toward shamanism and Buddhism embedded in the performances, scorned by the elite in the Joseon (1392–1910) period and seen in the Japanese period (1910–1945) as primitive or corrupt. This religious root needed to be reframed. Third, there was the narrative – episodic, comic, and antiestablishment. Post-colonial perspectives, nationalist revival, and serendipitous experiments with modernizing the genre led to the reformulations we see in groups such as Hyundai and NONI.

Namsadang nori (literally, "male performers' play") of the Joseon Dynasty were sometimes called *hwarang*, or "flower boys" – a term that some link to early Silla era (57 BCE–935 CE) practices (see Rutt 1961; Kim 1981; and Kim and Hahn 2006: 61; the latter state that other terms used for these male homosexual performers were *kkokdu gaksi*, *midonggaji*, and *namsadang*). They were lower-class males who wandered the countryside performing puppetry and other entertainments and who were generally available as homosexual prostitutes. Working under a single troupe leader for a group of perhaps 40, senior performers for the multifaceted performance were dominant males called *sutdongmo* and "females" who were known as *yeodongmo* (Sim cited in Kim 1981: 10). The apprentices – orphans, children from impoverished and shaman families, and kidnapped boys – fell into this "female" group (Kim 1981: 10). The art during the current era, which frowned upon these homosexual practices, needed to be decoupled from such associations to elevate its status.

Shamanism, though the early Korean religion, was also devalued during the Joseon period, when Confucian ideology prevailed, so this music/performance with shamanic roots, by association, was held in low regard. Exorcisms were probably the first impulse behind farmer's band drums and gongs – agitated rhythms that link to ecstatic shaman performances of the peninsula. *Namsadang* performers, like shamans, were outcasts, and often performers were relatives of the mostly female shamans. Male shamans were a minority, but their cross-dressing and feminine behaviors had parallels to the homosexual culture of *namsadang nori* troupes. Buddhism was a second spiritual root and similarly attacked in the Joseon Dynasty. *Namsadang nori* itself is often linked to an institution of the Silla Dynasty – which reached its zenith by the sixth century CE – a kind of Buddhist Boy Scouts called *hwarang* (Rutt 1961: 3). Farmer's band music, associated with the troupes that did puppet shows, acrobatics, and masks, supposedly derives from marching band performances of these Buddhist youths' military/spiritual training, as they went out to honor the rivers and mountains with their shamanic-Buddhist playing and dancing. These lovely, feminine boys used cosmetics, dressed beautifully, and had homosexual liaisons. *Namsadang nori* of the late Joseon period is argued by some to be a distant, corrupted manifestation of this old Buddhist-shamanist Silla practice, though direct links are impossible to prove (Rutt 1961). In post-colonial Korea, shamanism and Buddhism would be reintegrated and no longer devalued as they had been in the Confucian Joseon perspective.

The narrative of the traditional play did not fit either an elite model during Korea's dynastic period or the various modernized theatre models that emerged in the twentieth century: it shows short episodes of monks, the upper class, or political leaders acting badly. In these plays governors are corrupt and men are self-serving. This brought disapproval first from Confucian officials; while during the colonial period (1910–1945), Japanese authorities saw these low-class performers as politically suspect nuisances who were apt to attack Japanese rule. This genre was, therefore, always important for its critical nature, which questioned class structure and religious orthodoxy, but for that very reason rarely won undivided support from those in power. *Namsadang nori* was largely defunct in the early twentieth century, although some Japanese folklore researchers did begin to write on such forms, laying the groundwork for later studies by Korean folklorists (Ch'oe 2003; Janelli 1986). The form's emblematic characters – Bak Cheomji (Old Man Park), who introduced scenes and was voiced with a swazzle/reed; his well-endowed nephew, Hong Dongji, who saves his uncle from a dragon; the lovely concubine; and the abandoned wife, Kkokdu Gaksi, who squabbles and is sometimes killed to provide the corpse for a funeral – all seemed phantoms of the past.

During the late 1950s, revivalists, government cultural officials, and academic researchers reconstructed the art during a post-colonial search for national roots. Emphasizing Korean folk culture was a way of rejecting Joseon's Confucian court culture, which was held responsible for allowing the Japanese to prevail (Saeji, pers. comm., January 14, 2013). The emphasis on lower-class culture, shamanism, and Buddhism was a way to move beyond both the period of Japanese influence and the Confucian period, where Chinese influence was seen to have dominated, and back to some pristine Korean-ness that might strengthen the nation. The *namsadang nori* genre was declared part of the nation's cultural heritage, and funding from the government was allocated for teaching the genre as it was practiced in the early twentieth century. This reinvented *namsadang nori* was arguably most alive from the late 1970s through the 1980s when the ideas of drumming to gather a crowd and short skits to get political points across were important to university students who wanted to protest the military dictatorship. But with democracy achieved by the 1990s, this brash, youthful energy subsided.

In these more settled times, groups such as Hyundai and NONI restructured elements of *namsadang nori* to see how "big bang" puppetry could morph toward "courtly consort" art to fit better into categories of "national heritage" and contemporary "art" production. Directors think of educating the next generation in their Korean distinctiveness (through a show like Deong deong kung ta kung) or impressing foreign audiences on tour (e.g., Kkok-du in India or Germany) using selected aspects of traditional namsadang and puppet/mask arts to show Korea to all as the serious economic, political, and cultural player that it is.

Hyundai Puppet Theatre

Seoul's Hyundai Puppet Theatre creates an intergenerational music and dance variety show that maintains some of the imagery and sound of the traditional namsadang nori. At the same time, the group melds these commoners' arts with elements from either elevated court arts or modern pop culture to create a fusion performance for local urban audiences and international tours.

A sample of this work is their 2009 show Deong deong kung ta kung[2] – the name comes from the drum syllables used in Korean percussion. This specific work was created in collaboration with Gyeonggi Korean Traditional Music Center and was directed by Lee Mi-yong (Yi Mi-yeong) for both live performance and television in order to introduce children and general audiences to traditional music. The piece includes variations on works introduced years earlier by company founder Cho Yong-su (Jo Yong-su, 1932–1992) – a journalist and graduate from Konkuk University who was hired by KBS-TV (Korean Broadcasting System) in 1962 to oversee children's offerings. Seeing television models from the United States in that era using puppetry as a highlight of children's programming, Cho founded Hyundai in which his brother and current director Cho Yong-suk (Jo Yong-seok, b. 1947) developed his craft. The company mostly began with rod puppets, working from Japanese doll puppet traditions and Western puppet techniques rather than the indigenous model of namsadang nori that performed in Korean commercial centers and the countryside as popular entertainment. Over the years, Hyundai has used a wide variety of puppet forms (black light, marionettes, rod figures) combined with local content. The group began to tour internationally as the Korean economy lifted in the 1980s, and it was useful to have pieces that reflected Korean heritage, both for educational purposes at home and to represent Korea internationally. Thus, Heungbu and Nolbu, a popular Korean tale about the noble Heungbu and his greedy brother, Nolbu, drawn from Korean story singing (pansori), was the company choice for a tour to Japan in 1982. During the same era, Cho Yong-su saw the useful links between puppetry and traditional music for informing youth about indigenous heritage and created pieces for children based on the farmer's band percussion orchestra of namsadang performers, now generally called samul nori, literally "playing four instruments" (the large gong, small gong, hourglass drum, and barrel drum). Cho also did versions of traditional fan and flower crown dances (hwagwanmu) that borrowed from the entertainments performed by courtesans of the pre-colonial Korean court.

The company does not faithfully reproduce kkokdu gaksi, avoiding the play's episodes of marital infidelity, the exploits of the nude, red-bodied Hong Dongji with his large penis, killings, etc. – aspects which the group probably considers inappropriate for their contemporary target audience of school children, middle-class families, or foreigners who can be educated about Korea when the company is on international tour. Though the company borrows from the tradition, it takes selectively. The program for *Deong deong kung ta kung* includes some pieces from *namsadang*-like sources (the farmer's band music, drum dance, and a mask dance number), and these are mixed with examples of court music and dance. Including court genres moves the program away from *namsadang nori*'s characteristic comedy and gives it a kind of cachet that *namsadang nori* lacks on its own. For example, the program begins with a macho masked traditional seller whose big head and deep voice reminds one of the butcher in the mask dance of Hahoe village. But rather than hawking bull testicles as an aphrodisiac to flabby and aging aristocrats (as in the Hahoe original), the character is "selling" the appreciation of traditional music to assembled school children. Tradition is referenced and reworked. It assumes that children, through clips of annual folklore festivals that appear on television, will recognize the character, but the physical image rather than the raucous jokes are appropriated. This is a cleaned-up heritage display and not a messy folk form that has the potential to shake up the social structure.

After a demonstration of some of the softer traditional instruments used in art music, the puppet farmer's band of *namsadang nori* takes center stage. Puppets perhaps 80 centimeters long are attached to the manipulators' feet. A central string comes down from the head of the dancer/manipulator and is attached to the puppet head, while rods manipulated from above activate the puppets' arms. In the stage lighting, the black-clad performers "disappear" as we watch the lively music quartet; the figures dance and play instruments with the sound provided by a recording. Lyrics accompanying the drumming note that music "goes throughout the urban and rural land / ... The *Janggu* [hourglass drum] rhythm / gets exciting / just like a welcome rain." The complex percussion music takes the traditional farmer's band sound and extends it toward the jazz-like improvisations of contemporary *samul nori* music. It also adds lyrics that remind urban children of their roots, providing a positive updating for the genre. Another piece includes an hourglass drum dance by five female drummer puppets. This episode has upbeat energy and uses complex choreographic patterns with the same manipulation style as the farmers' band sequence just described: this is a new music composition by composer Park Byung-oh (Bak Byeong-o) based on tradition, and while the number is not a traditional *namsadang nori* piece, it has some of the same earthy energy.

The puppets dancing in the finale wear costumes and masks that emulate the *talchum*, or mask dance of Bongsan (Pongsan) – a genre formerly of North Korea (preserved in Seoul) and the most virtuosic of the Korean mask dances, related in characters and episodes to *namsadang nori* (see Saeji 2012). But rather than enacting scenes from the traditional mask/puppet play, the figures are just "in the style" of the folk genre. The movement is generic rather than the distinctive mime of the characters presented in a traditional play. The sequence borrows a white-faced Somu (female shaman) mask, a twisted-nose mask that might in a traditional context signal a young and foolish aristocrat (*yangban*), and a dark mask, which might represent an older monk character who tries to seduce a beautiful shaman. But here we have instead generic "Korean mask dance," as the three puppets move in unison rather than doing dance gestures that might indicate their differing characters. The masks provide color contrast rather than specific characters or actions that we would find in a traditional performance. Moreover, they enter to synthesized music (perhaps to aurally signal they are in synch with modernity) – a fast, electric rhythm sounds under their funny, robotic walk. Then they dance to a recording of traditional instrumentation.

This is tradition nouveau, cut loose from expected characterization, wisecracks, and stories. The images are signs of Korean-ness, as is the norm with Korean masks used in TV commercials or displayed on tourist brochures. The *namsadang nori* arts that are included in this performance (farmer's band and mask dance) are comic and energetic parts of the child-friendly program, used to balance out the dances inspired by court-dance tradition. In another item, a court fan dance, puppets are again manipulated by a combination of strings and rods, but the rods are here sometimes held by a second manipulator as the dancing figures flip their fans open and then close them while they gracefully glide and twirl. A fairy dance is another new creation in the program: the white costumed dolls are mounted on a central rod atop the heads of black-clothed manipulators, who see through the sheer skirts. The fabric floats as the dancer-manipulators swirl, moving the figures' arms with rods. The white costumes and flowing movement evoke aspects of *salpuri*, a now classicized female Korean dance genre that is an artistic extension of traditional shaman performance. These floating female dolls of both the fan and fairy dance recalibrate the overall program in a way that *namsadang nori*'s more rough art would not. Perhaps these refined female dances are thought to provide "soft" characters for little girls, as the impression they give is of "princess-like," "ethereal" beings. The intent of the program is to encourage children of both genders to engage with traditional and neo-traditional Korean music and dance, rather than abandoning themselves to Western forms.

This program borrows selectively from *namsadang nori* and *kkokdu gaksi*, taking their music and movement but dispensing with narrative scenes, known characters, and satiric perspectives, probably since these materials are not considered "child appropriate" in current society. By adding courtly dances to the *namsadang nori*-lite program, this becomes a free-floating representation of heritage – bowdlerized and balanced. The pieces can easily be exported and appreciated internationally.

Creative Group NONI

The show *Kkok-Du* by Creative Group NONI, formed in 2006 by a group of graduates of the Korea National University of Arts, takes a different tack. The company keeps aspects of the ribald *kkokdu gaksi* drama, which sometimes earns negative comments from international viewers, but the group also elevates the form and emphasizes the spiritual roots of the heritage, reflecting trends in academic research on this art since Korean independence. Their reframing is done via stylizing the visual design and incorporating sequences not found in *namsadang nori*'s *kkokdu gaksi* to show the shamanic roots of the puppetry/mask dance practices as they have been theorized by Korean folklorists.

The play, using a cast of six and directed by Kim Kyung-hee, is an adaptation of the traditional *kkokdu gaksi* play by Kyoung Min-sun. The musicians (a vocalist and drummer) are on the side of the stage, performing and interacting with the puppets/mask dancers – this corresponds to the practice in traditional *namsadang*. But instead of the simple rod puppet show of *kkokdu gaksi*, which was traditionally staged in an enclosed booth with the puppeteers always hidden, the performance shifts between small rod figures, oversized body puppets of the same characters in front of the booth, shadow sequences, and a dragon character that is painted on the screen during the performance. While the group references the traditional narrative – a love triangle, a monster, and a death – the presentation impresses with a stunning visual display, reorienting viewers toward sacred roots rather than adhering solely to the raucous reality of the traditional show.

The play begins with two unmasked dancers in the white garments of shamans bowing at a table for the spirits. In a ritual opening they dance with the traditional white pompoms used by shamans. The shadow of a bridge appears on the screen – evoking the idea of bridges between life and death. Then we see in the curtained booth the main figure of the traditional play, Bak Cheomji, an old aristocrat, presented as a traditional-looking rod puppet. Bak Choemji then re-emerges as an oversized body puppet, outside the booth, where he interacts with his wife (Gaksi) and concubine (Deolmi), who at first remain small rod puppets. The love triangle and bickering between the three are true to original *namsadang nori*. Soon the serpent-dragon (Isimi), who traditionally eats people, appears. But rather than the small traditional rod figure for the dragon, Isimi magically manifests via quick, calligraphic brushstrokes drawn by designer Won Yeojung all across the back of the extended shadow screen. The small rod puppets pass through the booth as rod puppets and then become shadows as they dance along the extended screen. Their shadow images disappear into the gaping jaws of the large painted dragon. The piece ends, as is customary in *kkokdu gaksi*, with a funeral, as the assembled rod figures carry a decorated bier. Yet, as with the shamanic opening, this scene is given spiritual weight by the music and mood of solemnity. It is not being played for laughs as in a traditional *kkokdu gaksi* show.

Won's design for the puppets draws from traditional characters but presents them with stylization: the concubine has the look of a Modigliani beauty, and the old wife's deeply etched facial lines remind us of a visage that might have been created by expressionists such as Ernst Barlach or Edvard Munch. The body-puppet version of Bak Cheomji is no longer the rough figure we see in *namsadang nori* but has moved toward the figural abstraction reminiscent of Mummenshanz or the polished lines of Cirque du Soleil representations. We recognize the body puppets as Bak Cheomji or his old wife from their grotesque characteristics, but the stylization gives the figures an added coolness that the rough folk puppetry does not have. This is sculptural performance art rather than costumed folk figures. The comedy is here, but it is a *namsadang nori* that has been passed through an abstracting aesthetic in the same way *commedia* in the hands of Lecoq-trained artists is transformed into something new. The overall actions, from the opening appearance of performer/manipulator/dancers in shaman white to the closing funeral, are presented within a theatrical frame: we are inside a shaman ceremony (*gut*). The company's press material states: "There is both recognition and confusion – an acknowledgement of the strange and foreign and of the known and native; of traditional practice and its contemporary meaning; of particular stories and universal truths" (*The Hindu*, August 5, 2011).

Serious visual art characterizes the group. Their other work, including *Playing Wind* (*Param Nori*, 2010), which uses mask images and music from the traditional mask dance, also shows their emphasis on design. In *Playing Wind* the masks, lighted from inside, create ethereal faces as the performers parade through the dark in white traditional clothing and pure white masks (unusual for the tradition): white references both the traditional hemp clothing mandatory in the Joseon period and the color of purity and shamanic power. The company's *Monkey Ddance* (sic) (2012) and *Ignis fatuus Rin* (2010) use aspects of traditional performance (monkey masks and movements, acrobatic spinning, and flags), mixing them with digital projections and shadow puppetry.[3] All NONI presentations bring together striking visual design, elements of Korean performance tradition (distanced from their source), and an emphasis on natural materials sculpturally conceived. The NONI website gives their principles: "Natural Material, Analogue Object, AlterNative View, TraditIonal Play" (Creative Group NONI undated)

International reactions to *Kkok-du* have ranged from highly laudatory to dazed and confused. Indian viewers, as attested by their letters to *The Hindu* on the performance, were often critical, bewildered by the skits when they wanted a narrative plot and shocked by the ribald English subtitles, which emulate the original *kokkdu gaksi*. C. Venugopal noted:

> *Kkok-Du* opens as most Korean theatre productions do – strikingly stark, with exquisite lighting, and cleverly crafted paper lanterns adding to the mood. Characteristic Korean percussion is heard along with clanging cymbals. The backlight shows dancing musicians in scintillating silhouette. One waits for the promised storyline ... but all one gets are shockers – gutter humour which the brochure calls "earthy." One prepares to get up and leave. Again the magic ... The screen comes alive with a python writhing across the screen ... stagecraft that any theatre person would kill for ... again the crass humour laced with crass action ... Finally, one can take it no more and leaves the show with a lot of mixed feelings. Awe for the craft but tinged with anguish for the trash that is shown as art.
>
> (*The Hindu*, August 14, 2011)

Hariharan agreed:

> Twenty minutes of the 80-minute production was devoted to an elegiac epilogue to an old debauch who supposedly drowns to death in a cup of water. Such criticism could be overcome if contextualised and studied within the framework of traditional Korean music and puppetry. But the predicament here was locating the art of ribaldry which was its driving principle.
>
> (*The Hindu*, August 14, 2011)

However, Taroon Kamar praised the show:

> We were all blown away by what is undoubtedly one of the most creative collage[s] I have seen in theater: brilliant set design, great costumes and choreography, amazing puppetry, exhilarating live rhythms – woven together in a funny yet poignant story. Subtitles are provided and they work very well. Superb!
>
> (*The Hindu*, August 14, 2011)

A German reviewer of *Kkok-du* focused on the stylization and was not concerned with words or narrative:

> All in all this exciting performance showed an interesting way to deal with traditional art forms. At no time [did] it seemed outdated. The free combination of different artistic elements produced interesting effects of recognition and confusion. It was not a problem that at times the projected subtitles (the piece was performed in Korean) were difficult to follow. The images, the sounds of drums and voices behind the curtain – and, of course, the wonderfully manufactured puppets – stood for themselves.
>
> (Creutzenberg 2007)

The publicity material for a second piece the group has staged in Germany discussed NONI's use of related techniques:

> The Korean Ensemble Creative Group NONI of Seoul presents a summary of their shadow play Ignis fatuus Rin. The play takes the audience into a fantastic world of ancient Korean rites and legends, … throw[ing] light and shadow … The Shamanism and Buddhism entertainment arts of the rural population of Korea meets … Commedia dell Arte, Sound art, Jazz, Tango and Physical Theatre.
>
> (Huguet 2011)

It was probably easier for the European viewership, accustomed perhaps to greater sex or profanity in modern performance as compared to their South Indian middle-class counterparts, to appreciate the work and not be put off by *Kkok-du*'s borrowing from *namsadang nori*'s ribaldry.

NONI's work clearly moves away from the political-critical-comic potential that was a central aspect of traditional performances and toward the shamanic-visual-ethereal. There are clowns and attention to the source material, but these are the clowns one encounters in the avant-garde – archetypes, not belly-laugh beings. The production goes toward "roots," indigenous Korean shamanism that the post-colonial research community has emphasized as the motivating spirit behind *namsadang nori* and linked to Korean national beginnings. NONI's performance puts the viewer in touch with Korean shamanic distinctiveness by way of a modern, visually stylized spectacle. The result is a performance that is more easily exportable to international festivals and more appealing to local viewers than the original puppet show, which is presented in Seoul more as pure heritage than "art."

The title communicates NONI's intention: *kkok-du* are small figures carved on the sides of traditional funeral biers who "accompany" the deceased to the next world. This, of course, reminds one of the Northeast Asian use of figures/dolls placed in tombs to "serve the dead," of which the terracotta warriors of Xian (third century BCE) are merely the grandest example. While *kkokdu gaksi* may have first stemmed from related archaic practices, this was not the play's function during its documented history in the Joseon Dynasty, when sexual innuendo and satire of class and power prevailed. NONI's way of raising the performance's status is by aesthetically cleaning up the visual lines, making the depictions more abstract and modernist, and pushing the content toward cosmic questions of life and death. The use of shadow theatre, which was very rare in Korea in the past, helps the company's transition to "other" worlds. The shadow's ephemeral nature and the play of light and dark make it a genre conducive to tropes of the spiritual and mystical. That the *kkokdu gaksi* itself was played out of doors with three-dimensional figures and was secular and satiric in content does not matter. The group's intention is to move back to what members, along with contemporary Korean researchers, believe to be the root of the theatre. They link their Intangible Cultural Heritage genre to what they see as spiritual needs in modern society, to "question how traditional techniques can continue to have relevance for contemporary audiences and explore how their creative processes can be eco-friendly to mirror the strong bonds between Man and Nature" (*The Hindu*, August 5, 2011) in a primordial and timeless Korean space.

Though Hyundai and NONI are only two examples of contemporary redeployments of the traditional puppet arts, each is engaged in figuring out how the past as represented by *namsadang nori* can fit present audience expectations. They are dealing with the reality of how a low-class and previously frowned-upon folk genre can be retooled for a modern educated audience. These companies show how the material can be alternatively transformed into art that communicates selective parts of the tradition to a contemporary child audience or how young artists may approach aspects of tradition as "roots" for an adult viewership. In each case they are addressing some of the same issues that Punch and Judy performers may encounter in Anglophone countries in an era when presenting violence or sex if children are watching is frowned upon or when political correctness may censor some traditional scenes. Heritage is a powerful lever and yet it cannot always immediately address what may be the central issue – "big bang" arts by their nature fit uncomfortably inside a "courtly consort" frame that heritage efforts sometimes tend to favor. Instead, they are always exploding out.

Notes

I acknowledge Lee Young-oak, CedarBough Saeji, Chan Park, and an anonymous reviewer for translation and corrections. All opinions and errors are my own. Support came from the UCSC Committee on Research and Arts Research Institute and the Yale Institute of Sacred Music.

1 "Old wife's play," also known as Bak Cheomji's play, *deolmi* (concubine's [play]) or Hong Dongji's play. All the names are of significant characters in the show. For background see Cho (1979, 1988), Jeon (2005, 2008), Lee (1981), and Sim (1970, 1997). The puppet play was made a Korean Intangible Cultural Property in 1964 and inscribed in 2009 as part of *namsadang* as a UNESCO Intangible Cultural Heritage of Humanity genre. The UNESCO webpage features a short video of *namsadang nori*, which includes the puppetry; pictures of the Anseong-based, government-supported heritage troupe; and documentation submitted at the time of inscription. See <http://www.unesco.org/culture/ich/RL/00184>. This Anseong group is the only group currently presenting the traditional puppet show. Called Baudeogi Pungmulden Anseong (Anseong Municipal Namsadang Baudeogi), it is named after the first female leader of a *namsadang* troupe. This group's mission is to preserve not innovate. This chapter instead focuses on groups that attempt to rethink the art. See Anseong Municipal Namsadang Baudeogi Pungmuldan at <http://www.namsadangnori.org/e3.htm>.

2 See "Hyundai puppet theatre presents 'Deong deong kung ta kung'," (July 22, 2011) at <http://www.youtube.com/watch?v=sh4JqbCblh4>. This discussion is based on the YouTube version. Many of the pieces are also included in the more musically eclectic *Puppet City*. See "The Puppet City – Hyundai Puppet Theatre," (March 28, 2011) at <http://www.youtube.com/watch?v=KzAXk8MYUyI>. *Puppet City* has toured internationally since the 1990s and has other musical numbers, including an "Elvis" impersonation.

3 Clips of Creative Group NONI's work can be seen on YouTube. *Kkok-du* (December 24, 2010) can be viewed at <http://www.youtube.com/watch?v=yaSJuQr3Iv0>. For *Playing Wind* (December 26, 2010), go to <http://www.youtube.com/watch?v=TyDG9mdGHAg>. For *Monkey Ddance* (September 10, 2012), go to <http://www.youtube.com/watch?v=7AJnsXeVuZk>. For *Ignis fatuus_Rin* (December 26, 2010), go to <http://www.youtube.com/watch?v=N9Sw7bnqvRM>.

Works cited

Cho, O. K. (1979) *Korean Puppet Theatre: Kkoktu Kaksi*, East Asia series, vol. 6. East Lansing, MI: Asian Studies Center, Michigan State University.

——(1988) trans. and intro. *Traditional Korean Theatre*, Studies in Korean Religions and Culture, no. 2. Berkeley, CA: Asian Humanities Press.

Ch'oe, K. (2003) "War and Ethnology/Folklore in Colonial Korea: The Case of Akiba Takashi," A. Shimizu and J. van Bremen (eds). Osaka: National Museum of Ethnology, <http://ir.minpaku.ac.jp/dspace/bitstream/10502/1036/1/SES65_008.pdf> (accessed September 4, 2013).

Creative Group NONI (undated) Homepage, <http://www.cgnoni.com/we.php> (accessed August 17, 2013).

Creutzenberg, J. (2007) "Korean Puppet Theatre in Berlin: *Kokdu Gagsi Norum* by the Creative Group NONI from Seoul," *OhmyNews International (OMNI)*, June 27, <http://english.ohmynews.com/articleview/article_view.asp?menu=c10400&no=368967&rel_no=1> (accessed August 17, 2013).

The Hindu (August 5, 2011) "Kkok-du," <http://www.thehindu.com/arts/theatre/article2235502.ece> (accessed August 17, 2013).

——(August 14, 2011) "Be a Citizen Reviewer," <http://www.thehindu.com/life-and-style/metroplus/be-a-citizen-reviewer/article2356505.ece> (accessed August 17, 2013).

Huguet, R. (2011) "Collaboration with Creative Group NONI from Korea," January, <http://www.rosabelhuguet.com/collaboration-with-creative-group-noni-from-korea/> (accessed August 17, 2013).

Janelli, R. (1986) "The Origins of Korean Folklore Scholarship," *Journal of American Folklore* 99: 24–49.

Jeon, K.-W. (2005) *Korean Mask Dance Dramas: Their History and Structural Principles*, trans. E. Do-seon. Seoul, Republic of Korea: Youlhwadang Publishers.

——(2008) *Traditional Performing Arts of Korea*, trans. M. Eun-young. Seoul, Republic of Korea: Korea Foundation.

Kim, Y.-G. and Hahn, S.-J. (2006) "Homosexuality in Ancient and Modern Korea," *Culture, Health & Sexuality* 8: 59–65.

Kim, Y.-J. (1981) "The Korean 'Namsadang'," *TDR/The Drama Review* 25: 9–16.

Lee, D.-H. (1981) *Masks of Korea*. Seoul, Republic of Korea: Korean Overseas Information Service, Ministry of Culture and Information.

Park, J. (2013) "Yeonwoo Mudae and the Korean Theatre Movement in the 1980s," *Asian Theatre Journal* 30(1): 67–89.

Rutt, R. (1961) "The Flower Boys of Silla (*hwarang*)," *Transactions of the Royal Asiatic Society Korea Branch* 38(October): 1–68.

Saeji, C. (2012) "The Bawdy, Brawling, Boisterous World of Korean Mask Dance Dramas: An Essay to Accompany Photographs," *Cross-Currents: East Asian History and Culture Review* 1: 439–468.

Sim, U.-S. (Woo-Song) (1970) *Introduction to Korean Folk Drama*. Seoul, Republic of Korea: Korean Folk Theatre Troupe "Namsadang."

——(1997) "*Namsadang*: Wandering Folk Troupes" *Koreana: Korean Art and Culture* 11(2): 44–49.

19
Forging New Paths for Kerala's *Tolpavakoothu* Leather Shadow Puppetry Tradition

Claudia Orenstein

In his 1999 essay "If Gandhi Could Fly ... Dilemmas and Directions in Shadow Puppetry in India," Salil Singh analyzed attempts of performers at the National Shadow Puppetry Festival in Dharmasthala, Karnataka, to revitalize their endangered art forms. While many troupes at the festival offered traditional shows based on India's Hindu epics, government agencies commissioned companies from five states to take episodes from the life of Gandhi as a new subject, hoping to reach out to contemporary audiences. For Singh the experiment proved unsuccessful:

> Puppeteers in whose hands shadows of mythical heroes had danced and cavorted, accompanied by passionate songs and cascading music, suddenly found themselves struggling awkwardly with bland images of a national hero, uninspired and uninspiring.
>
> (Singh 1999: 154)

Singh felt the festival revealed a few distinct paths for shadow puppetry, "either to abandon precedent expediently, without recourse to an equally powerful aesthetic which could propel the art into the future; or to repeat tradition without adapting it to today's cultural realities." Puppeteers could also follow the middle path taken by a troupe from the Bellary region of Karnataka and "successfully create an updated folklore outside of the ancient epics, yet not as contemporary as the Gandhi episodes" (Singh 1999: 166).

Among the troupes that in 1999 stuck to their traditional form was *tolpavakoothu* (also *tholpavakoothu*) or leather shadow company, from the Palakkad district of Kerala, under the direction of master puppeteer Krishnankutty Pulavar.[1] Today, with his son Ramachandra (also Ramachandran) at the helm, the company continues to struggle with the complex issues of preservation that faced them then but which have become more pressing in the last decade during India's rapid economic growth and accelerated transformation of traditional lifestyles. As India dedicates itself to becoming a major economic power, important questions persist: what role does traditional performance play in Indian life, more than embodying and preserving a reminder of the past? How can traditions continue to be living arts, relevant to the lives of spectators and practitioners alike as India moves towards further urbanization, globalization, and mastery of new technologies? For puppetry to entice new generations of performers, increasingly lured away to more attractive careers in computers and engineering, it must not only promise to sustain them economically but offer engagement in a purposeful, culturally relevant, and appreciated activity.

Ramachandra's company exemplifies the challenges facing traditional Indian puppeteers. While the Indian government and other organizations like the Sangeet Natak Akademi (India's National Academy of Music, Dance and Drama) have programs to help traditional artists, in the end it falls to individuals – the practitioners and caretakers of these forms who often must dedicate their entire lives to the work – to make choices about their commitments and whether to preserve, transform, pass on, or abandon their heritage.

While in 1999 Singh outlined various distinct, possible options for shadow puppetry, with puppeteers choosing between an adherence to new or old models, today the Pulavars take an eclectic approach to sustaining their art, following all the different paths Singh suggested and more. They attempt, in a more hybrid style, to keep their ritual form of puppetry intact, continuing those annual performances associated with temples, while exploiting their skills in carving, performing, and storytelling in various new ways outside the temple grounds. In its new incarnations *tolpavakoothu* is as much a business proposition as an artistic one. Trying out new stories for performance is only one of many ways the company is confronting today's cultural realities.

Ramachandra, in response to present circumstances, embodies a new and perhaps increasingly prevalent model of the artist-entrepreneur. He combines artistic skills and practices passed down over generations with a modern aptitude for seizing new opportunities to bring visibility to his art and promote it to a wider audience, hoping to make it economically viable. He shares his knowledge and skills liberally so *tolpavakoothu* can be widely recognized. In 2008, when he resigned from his post office job, he became the first *tolpavakoothu* performer to devote himself full time to puppetry, no longer solely as a ritual form but also as a wider secular occupation, reaching beyond local interests to connect with a national and international artistic world. He has committed to refashioning an art and way of life handed down over 12 generations into one that can engage fruitfully with the contemporary world, hoping his children will carry on the family tradition.

The tradition

Kerala's shadow puppetry derives its depth and beauty from formal practices developed over the tradition's long history, reportedly going back 1200 years (R. Pulavar, pers. comm., July 22, 2013).[2] The puppets enact events from the Hindu Ramayana epic, as recounted in the Tamil language version composed by the poet Kambar (also known as Kamban), the *Kamba Ramayana*[3] (Venu 2006: 8). Today's performers continue to use a mix of Tamil, Sanskrit, and Malayalam, the local language of Kerala. The main text, verses from the *Kamba Ramayana*, are in Tamil, but the puppeteers also engage in deep narration beyond the written text, explaining the background and other aspects of well-known events.[4] They participate in question-and-answer repartee in which the head puppeteer, known as the *pulavar* (a term which means "scholar"), answers questions, posed by the other puppeteers, that emerge from the telling and which can lead him into philosophical territory, as well as tangential stories. His astuteness at providing the answers for these traditional questions earns him his honored title. Each puppet company explores its own interests via its additions and explanations. Ramachandra's group, for example, enjoys cosmological questions. Malayalam creeps in during these explanatory passages to help communicate the text to the local audience. Younger performers, who don't know Tamil, now use more and more Malayalam in these sections (R. Pulavar, pers. comm., July 22, 2013).

The primary intended spectator for this sacred show is the goddess Bhagavati, also known as Bhadrakali. According to myth, the goddess was busy fighting the demon Darika when one of the major events of the Ramayana took place: Rama's killing of Ravana, the demon King of Lanka.[5] Since Bhadrakali was unable to witness Ravana's defeat, the shadow performance re-enacts it for her. Today, the once-abundant human spectators for the show are largely absent. Television, film, other entertainments, and the demands of changing work schedules have usurped the previously captivated audiences in rural areas. Ramachandra remembers full crowds of 500 or more for the shows of his childhood (R. Pulavar, pers. comm., July 22, 2013). Performers continue to adhere to their sacred performance task, often playing only for the goddess. Because of the benefits performance brings as a ritual offering, an ample number of organizations and individuals remain interested in sponsoring temple shows during the four-month performance season, but the grounds in front of the puppet theatres remain largely empty.

Performances take place in long, thin, permanent structures called *koothoo-madam*, or drama- (or play)-houses, dedicated exclusively to shadow puppetry and built on temple grounds. Around 70 of these unusual buildings exist throughout Kerala (Venu 2006: 15). The shadow screen covers the long open front end of the building, usually set directly across from the goddess's temple, so Bhadrakali can enjoy the play of shadows from her sacred abode. Elaborate rituals before the show, including a procession accompanied by music bringing fire from the puppet house to the temple, further connect the puppets with the presence of the goddess.

Up to 150 puppets may be used over the course of performances that can last for 7, 14, 21, 41, or 71 days. These figures were once carved from deer hide, but as this practice is now illegal, today's puppeteers use buffalo skins (*Borrowed Fire* 2000). The hides are cleaned and puppets carefully cut out based on pre-existing patterns, then painted. Puppeteers traditionally fashion the paints from local plants for a predominantly earthy palette of browns, reds, and yellows, enhanced by green, black, and blue. Variously shaped chisels punched into the leather create elaborate ornamental designs on the figures. These project rich patterns of light on the screen during performance. Important characters like Rama appear in three forms: a seated version that has one independently moving jointed arm (this form includes the character's throne and a frame surrounding the image; such puppets are more like pictures with moving parts than independent figures, comparable to some Thai and Cambodian shadow figures); a standing/walking figure with one movable, jointed arm; and a fighting version with two movable, jointed arms.

Figure 19.1 A forest scene from the traditional *tolpavakoothu* performance, Kerala, India (July 21, 2013). Photo courtesy of the author

The tradition is also remarkable for the many animal puppets that fill the scenes of Rama's famous exile in the forest: birds with flapping wings, slithering snakes, deer that gambol and spin, and voracious tigers and lions. The stylization of the figures echoes the aesthetic of Kerala's mural paintings, which apparently go back to ancient times, as well as regional temple carvings and the images from local snake rituals that are shaped on the ground from colorful spice powders (Venu 2006: 30).

A dying art?

These long cultural roots and practices belie the form's seemingly precarious existence over at least the last 100 years. The form was already thought lost by Western scholars before 1935 when an American journalist and a German scholar reported seeing shows (Blackburn 1996: 2). Even then, *tolpavakoothu* remained an obscure form from a global perspective, "known to the outside world only by a handful of essays until 1986, when Dr. F. Seltman published his excellent monograph" (Blackburn 1996: 2). When scholar Stuart Blackburn saw his first full-length *tolpavakoothu* in January 1984, the audience of living spectators had already abandoned the form. Puppeteers had also dwindled in number and commitment:

> Forty puppeteers were reported to be active in 1982, of whom only twenty-five still performed in 1989, and many of them were too feeble to chant through the night. Over the five-year span of my research, three puppeteers died and one retired from illness, but not a single new man entered the drama-house.
>
> (Blackburn 1996: 238)

The tradition's survival remains in question in Anurag Wadehra, Salil Singh, and Marc Stone's documentary *Borrowed Fire* (2000), which focuses on Krishnankutty's company, with Krishnankutty introduced as "the last surviving master of a thousand-year-old form of shadow puppetry." The film honors his commitment to keeping the tradition alive, with all its adherent protocols, and to passing it on to his sons through rigorous daily instruction and recitation, but also leaves viewers concerned for its future. On camera, Krishnankutty's sons acknowledge the debt they owe their father, while asserting that they don't feel the forced model of learning they endured throughout their childhood – to memorize the 1,200 to 2,000 verses needed to chant the play's text – can continue into the next generation.[6]

When I asked Ramachandra if there was ever a time he thought he might abandon puppetry, he confirmed that as a young man he got himself a driver's license as part of a plan to become a taxi driver. Long nights of sitting in chilly puppet houses several hours' drive from home with little recompense – sometimes only a few rupees per night – left him hungry and with only one shirt to his name. These circumstances made him question the significance of the form and the dedication it required. His father would allow him to choose his path but still insisted family members know the Ramayana in depth for its religious benefits and because of the family's reputation as *pulavars* (R. Pulavar, pers. comm., July 22, 2013).

In the modern era, loss of royal patronage contributed to worsening conditions for puppeteers throughout India. The final blow came in 1971 when the Twenty-Sixth Amendment to the Indian constitution ended royal status and the financial privilege of the privy purses distributed to royal houses. The Pulavar's company was the *kavalapura*, or palace or king's group, and historically had enjoyed royal patronage expressed through lavish multicourse meals that fed the troupe during their performing months. Their work was honored in concrete terms that showed appreciation and kept performers fed and happy. When this patronage dissolved, other sponsorship did not match the former models. Puppeteers have had to make a conceptual shift from being cared for within a patronage system to having to fend for themselves by creating their own entrepreneurial models.

Borrowed Fire suggests that Krishnankutty's ardent commitment to the tradition grew from losing his father at 17, driving him to seek guidance in the art on his own (*Borrowed Fire* 2000). This kind of personal initiative is not always present with practitioners of inherited traditions today, although it may be important for ensuring these forms' survival. Watching *Borrowed Fire*, one can imagine that once Krishnankutty, already elderly and frail on camera, passes away, his sons might let the tradition go. However, since his father's death in January 2000, Ramachandra has embraced his leadership role and put the company on a relatively thriving path, maintaining the traditional art while also taking it into new artistic territory, following a path Krishnankutty first opened up.

Eclectic strategies for renewal

In 1969, already seeing the thinning crowds and his children's ambivalence about continuing the tradition, Krishnankutty took a significant and unprecedented step in creating the first version of the troupe's Ramayana performance to take outside the temple grounds.[7] The initial show was done for the Kerala government in Trivandrum (R. Pulavar, pers. comm., July 22, 2013). The artists reduced the marathon epic to one hour, focusing on the main tale and its dramatic highlights. The presentation was appreciated by the audience and covered by several newspapers, allowing the company to offer this shorter presentation again on other occasions. In 1979 the troupe made its first international appearance at a UNIMA[8] puppetry festival in the USSR at the behest of Meher Contractor, an important figure in Indian puppetry.[9] Ramachandra attributes his own renewed commitment to the family art to this international tour and the experience of seeing puppetry appreciated within a wider global and artistic context (R. Pulavar, pers. comm., July 22, 2013).

Of the five existing *tolpavakoothu* troupes today, Krishnankutty's is the only one to have moved outside the temples. Some members of other companies and locals have been critical of this move, feeling it debases the art, but Ramachandra points out what Blackburn's study already suggested: that other companies on the whole no longer have disciples (either their own children or other young people in the community) continuing the tradition. Absent Ramachandra's troupe of about ten, including his own children, Rajeev, Rajitha, and Rahul, the traditional art would soon die out. It seems that the company's new work outside the temples, both the shortened version of the Ramayana and other projects that I will describe later on, as well as the visibility and interest it generates in puppetry, is sustaining the traditional practices and the tradition's future as a whole.

Krishnankutty brought one more significant change to the tradition. The family shows off with pride their now-aged palm leaf manuscripts of the *Kamba Ramayana*, the text the puppeteers memorize and recite. But in performance they have always veered away from Kamban's text or added to it. Blackburn's intricately documented study of the practice shows "that the puppeteers do not 'tell' Kampan's Rāma story as much as they explain it" (Blackburn 1996: 178). Krishnankutty notably wrote down the first full record of the text of the play as it actually takes place in the long ritual performances. This record is invaluable for preserving and recording the form. But in a largely unprecedented change, Ramachandra's children and other disciples can, if need be, rely on the written text during traditional performances, not just for reference but also to read from. Reading parts of the text changes the performers' relationship to it and truncates the deeper understanding and elaborations of it that have always been the *pulavar*'s charge.

In the past puppeteers would have been embarrassed in front of their colleagues if they didn't know the text by heart, but Ramachandra's children were not subjected to the same rigorous early-morning memorization sessions as their father. With the many other commitments of today's young puppeteers, including formal education and full-time jobs, and the dwindling interest of performers willing to dedicate themselves to the form, the tradition must accept accommodations if it is to continue.

Ramachandra notes that, concomitantly, some of the show's songs are sung more quickly now than in the past and sound different. During my interview in July 2013, an impromptu visit by Sreedharan Nair, an 85-year-old man who had performed 65 years earlier but hadn't continued, corroborated this view. He sang the verses at the speed and in the musical style he remembered while Ramachandra made notes on his rendition. Sreedharan Nair also relied on the written text to jog his memory before launching into his chanting. The text is the same, but the songs have become more rapid over time.

Outside the four-month season of temple performances, *tolpavakoothu* performers have always sustained themselves with other work, usually farming. Today the Pulavars have left commercial farming, now growing crops only to meet their own needs. While Ramachandra's older children have regular jobs, he has dropped his other employment to cultivate puppetry as a full-time endeavor. He works instead to promote his art and translate his traditional skills into new creative and commercial arenas.

Whereas in the 1980s Blackburn lamented that "when the puppets become damaged, new ones are no longer manufactured because the skin (of deer and buffalo) has become too expensive and the skill of puppet making too rare" (Blackburn 1996: 178), today Ramachandra's family has discovered commercial value in puppet-making. They all know how to craft puppets and regularly create new ones for performance and for sale to tourists and puppet enthusiasts.[10] With their leather-crafting skills they produce other merchandise, too, such as lampshades and key chains. Moreover, whereas previously women played no role in the *tolpavakoothu* tradition, Ramachandra has enlisted his wife and other female family members in the production of leather goods, distributing among more hands the meticulous labor required, increasing the family income, and giving women the opportunity to master puppet-crafting skills.

The family also teaches puppet-making to others. In January 2011 they offered a one-day workshop to students on the Hunter College Education Abroad program in India, just after hosting a small troupe of French performers who spent several weeks with them learning to build and perform. These workshops are not just attractive to foreign artists. In July 2013 students from Shristi Arts and Design College in Bangalore worked with the Pulavars, while sharing their own skills in technology and lighting with the puppeteers. The Pulavars may draw on this new technology in future shows of their own. Ramachandra's blog (another new practice for puppeteers, along with using Facebook and creating websites to promote their work), dated March 11, 2013, lists the following additional teaching experiences [sic]:

- Trained 10 persons on behalf of Delhi handicrafts in 1995 in leather puppet craft.
- Trained 40 school-teachers in CCRT New Delhi for about 10 years regularly.
- Conduct demonstration in many schools in Kerala.
- Participated every year *pragathi* maiden national handicraft museum, New Delhi from 1980 to 1995.

(Pulavar 2013)

By running workshops that help support them financially, the Pulavars spread the knowledge of their traditional carving skills as they master new pedagogical skills of their own.

The ability to carve new puppets and perform outside the temples has allowed the Pulavars to create and expand their repertoire with shows on novel themes beyond the Ramayana. Their first foray in this direction was in 2000, with a production based on the Indian animal fables of the *Panchatantra*.[11] This show capitalized on the company's traditional animal figures. More ambitious was a commission in 2007, when the troupe finally did take up the theme of Gandhi's life. This project brought them out of the world of fable and mythology to deal with historical material. New puppets for the show included motorcars, guns, airplanes, and contemporary figures in modern dress. The Pulavar's *Gandhi* might not allay Singh's concerns about addressing new themes with traditional puppetry, but it challenged them to expand their techniques as they adapted a modern story for presentation. It also opened up to them additional performance opportunities in schools and elsewhere.

In 2012, the family created another new play, this one about Jesus Christ. Kerala boasts a strong Christian population, with accounts, true or apocryphal, of conversions going back to a first-century visit to Kerala from the apostle Thomas himself, and there are churches in the region that continue to sing hymns in Aramaic. Ramachandra's Hindu troupe created the show in consultation with local Catholic priests and, as of July 2013, had presented it at 25 Kerala churches (R. Pulavar, pers. comm., July 22, 2013). Dealing with Christian themes in the context of Christian churches truly takes them outside their ritual work for the Hindu goddess but also connects them with different local communities.

In 2012, Ramachandra's son Rajeev created his own new production about the Demon King Mahābali, elaborating on an episode that is itself folded into the puppeteer's traditional telling of the Ramayana (Blackburn 1996: 140–143). This project reflects the third path Singh outlines, expanding the repertoire but staying within the world of myth. An audience of several hundred attentively watched the show at a local fair near Shornur in January 2011, very close to the puppeteers' home.[12] This kind of audience presence, unheard of at the temple shows, renews the puppeteers' and the community's engagement with the work. It is especially invigorating for young puppeteers like Rajeev. He plans another new work, based on a Shakespeare

Figure 19.2 Ramachandra Pulavar (center) with his family, holding up both new and traditional *tolpavakoothu* puppets, Kerala, India (July 22, 2013). Photo courtesy of the author

play, and he told me he is eager to expand his puppetry techniques by studying abroad (R. Pulavar, pers. comm., July 22, 2013).

To date, in designing new productions, the puppeteers have retained the basic elements of their tradition: the wide shadow screen, intricately carved and painted leather puppets, chanted storytelling, and explanations between the puppeteers during performances. But the novel themes allow them to reach out to different audiences in previously unexploited venues, such as schools, churches, and local fairs. It promotes the art of shadow puppetry – traditional and contemporary – while offering new fare to spectators and to performers, who now have a chance to develop their own creativity.

The puppeteers went even farther afield in January 2011 when they performed with the contemporary acting company Lokadharmi in *Lanka Lakshmi*, a 1974 play by C. N. Sreekantan Nair, directed by Chandradasan. The story is based on events in the Ramayana involving Sita's rescue. Here human actors played the central characters, performing in a heightened realistic style. The puppeteers, behind an upstage screen, presented the battle scenes using all their traditional skills. Although the puppeteers' work itself diverged little from their usual practice, this novel venture, initiated by the director, occurred within a very different genre and context and reached contemporary theatre-going audiences at a local Cochin venue designed for modern theatre. Ramachandra says he would consider doing another similar project, should the opportunity arise, showing his continued interest in staking out new ground for his art (R. Pulavar, pers. comm., July 22, 2013).

The truncated one-hour Ramayana continues to be popular and profitable for the company during the off-season from regular temple performances. The upper floor of the family home serves as a performance space for anyone wishing to commission a show, as my students and I have done on several occasions. In July 2013, however, I witnessed the space host the familiar performance for a more specific ritual purpose. A troubled family from Trivandrum, over 160 miles away, was advised by an astrologer to offer a *tolpavakoothu* presentation as a *puja*, or form of ritual worship, to alleviate their situation. (The astrologer did not know the Pulavars and had never seen a shadow play himself.) The performance on this occasion, though not at the temple, included special prayers, fires, and offerings of food and cloth wraps for the puppet figures.

New opportunities for women

When Krishnankutty moved shadow puppetry out of the temples, he opened another important door for the transformation of his art. The sacred temple venue had always prohibited women from acting as puppeteers. As Dr. F. Seltmann states:

> Only the male members of the family are connected with the profession of shadow play. Women have nothing to do with it; they should not come in touch with the figures, and they are not allowed to enter the special area where the performances will go on.[13]
>
> (Seltmann 1982: 11)

Figure 19.3 Backstage after an off-season ritual *tolpavakoothu* performance: the puppet of Hanuman wears a *dhoti* cloth given as an offering; Kerala, India (July 21, 2013). Photo courtesy of the author

One explanation for this, offered to me by Ramachandra's daughter, Rajitha, is that the goddess herself wishes to be the main female presence at the show (R. Pulavar, pers. comm., July 22, 2013). But there are many regulations and prescriptions concerning women in Hinduism, especially keeping them from sacred areas and practices when they are menstruating, so this prohibition is not surprising. Ramachandra, however, has extended the role of women in the form beyond also involving them in puppet building. Today Rajitha performs alongside her brothers in shows done outside the temple grounds. She is also, like her mother and aunt, an excellent puppet-maker and in 2013 was awarded a two-year grant from the Sangeet Natak Akademi to create a new show of her own, using her traditional skills. Her show, she says, might focus on women's issues (R. Pulavar, pers. comm., July 22, 2013).

Ramachandra is generous about letting women from abroad who are interested in puppetry accompany him to the drama-house. However, he relates a story to me about one such visitor, the only spectator at the time to watch with rapt attention for the full seven days of a performance, who was the cause for a particular temple to discontinue inviting his troupe for future shows (R. Pulavar, pers. comm., July 22, 2013). Nonetheless, Ramachandra persists in sharing his art in a multitude of ways rather than sequestering it, promulgating opportunities for future life.

Ramachandra's acceptance of women in the tradition may derive partly from necessity (i.e., the need to enlist all family members in the work and its economic pursuits). But it is also timely, reflecting larger changes taking place for Indian women. According to a global poll of experts, "Infanticide, child marriage and slavery make India the worst" country to be a woman among the world's leading economies

(Baldwin 2012: 1). Nonetheless, more and more women in India's changing economy are entering the workforce, often in technically skilled jobs, and moving to urban environments, away from family strictures and traditional lifestyles. In so doing, they are embracing new ways of living and new professions, transforming their own and India's future.

While *tolpavakoothu* temple performances remain off-limits to women performers, Rajitha suggests that it may be only a matter of time before she and other women are accepted in temple shows (R. Pulavar, pers. comm., July 22, 2013). As master performers die off, leaving no disciples behind, Rajitha and her brothers will end up among the few, if not the only, living inheritors of the temple form. Those who want to receive blessings from sponsoring these shows may have little choice but to accept a female performer.

Conclusion

The Pulavars of Kerala, like many traditional artists and craftspeople in India, by virtue of inheriting a long-standing tradition, are also inevitably its caretakers. It is ultimately left to them, even with strong government or other support, to endeavor to sustain their art or not. Whereas in the past the pursuit of the profession of puppetry for *tolpavakoothu* family members went unquestioned, now each new generation needs motivation to continue in work whose original cultural purpose and footing have eroded, even though temple performances currently persist. Many older puppeteers throughout India see, and sometimes encourage, their children to abandon puppetry for more lucrative and contemporarily relevant careers. Ramachandra, by contrast, in line with his father, has thrown his lot in with puppetry, exploiting his skills and knowledge in new directions, hoping to make the family inheritance more enticing to his children. To do this he has become an experimental artist and savvy entrepreneur, seeking out new opportunities and developing new skills in the process. He is mastering new media – webpages, blogs, Facebook – to advertise his work and has even become an author, with an upcoming Malayalam-language book on *tolpavakoothu*.

It may not be easy for a traditionally trained, rural performer like Ramachandra, tasked from an early age with memorizing thousands of verses and carefully crafting designs in leather, to also become a computer-savvy, enterprising businessman. It may also not even be desirable for artists to become entrepreneurs. But today's cultural realities, in India as elsewhere, may demand this of them if they hope to sustain their art. Ramachandra is trying to do it all. He models his practice for others and invites fellow artists, some who have not developed these skills on their own, into programs he organizes, sharing performance and networking opportunities with them.

The Pulavars may have an advantage in balancing their traditional art with new performance forms and opportunities. The sacred context for *tolpavakoothu* is so circumscribed by its seasonal time, temple location, and repertoire that new experiments can be fairly clearly demarcated from the tradition. Still, temple performances necessarily change in these circumstances. True mastery of the form and the difficult texts and explanations required for it fall away when artists attend to other demands.

Will performers continue to know, and audience members to appreciate, the deep philosophical knowledge and interpretive skills that have been the true accomplishment of the *pulavar*?

Tolpavakoothu performers are not alone in being caught between making compromises to sustain their tradition and trying to adhere to the rigorous demands and precedents of their art. Traditional artists have been performing this balancing act for quite some time. Today the Pulavars choose to venture down many paths at once in their work, hoping this multifaceted approach will both sustain and enrich the tradition for the next generation. In the end, *tolpavakoothu*, if it survives, falls into their hands.

Notes

1 The company's website <http://puppetry.org.in/index.html> offers information on performance schedule, the puppetry form, and how to contact the performers, who are grateful for any opportunities for commissioned performances, workshops, and other ventures.
2 My interview with Ramachandra Pulavar on July 22, 2013 provides a good deal of important information for this chapter. Additional material is also based on my many encounters with him and his family and the viewing of his performances, both traditional temple presentations and other works, during six separate month-long trips to India since January 2008. I am grateful to Hunter College President Jennifer Raab's Presidential Travel Awards that have helped to support my research.
3 The text dates from the twelfth century (Blackburn 1996: 1).
4 Stuart Blackburn's book *Inside the Drama-House: Rama Stories and Shadow Puppets in South India* (1996) offers, among other important contributions, an excellent, in-depth study of how Kamban's text is and is not followed within the puppetry tradition.
5 Rama represents the ideal man and king in Hindu culture, and his exploits, as he is exiled from his palace home to the forest and then ultimately gains his rightful position as King of Ayodhya, is the subject of the Ramayana. Ravana's abduction of Sita and the battle to save her, which brings the monkey god Hanuman and his armies into the tale as Rama's allies, is at the center of the Ramayana, and innumerable traditions through South and Southeast Asia draw on these episodes as material for performance.
6 Ramachandra says that in order to learn these verses, his father woke them up every day at 4:30 a.m. He put 400 stones in a bowl and removed one stone each time a verse was recited. After 400 repetitions, the verse was memorized.
7 He did this with the help of Gopal Venu, who has been instrumental in the preservation and development of many Kerala performance traditions, notably *kutiyattam*.
8 UNIMA is the Union Internationale de la Marionnette, the international organization for puppetry, founded in 1929, which is the oldest international arts organization in the world, with chapters in more than 40 countries.
9 For further information on Contractor, see my chapter in *Gender, Space and Resistance: Women and Theatre in India*, (Orenstein 2013: 245–272).
10 Traditional puppeteers around the world make puppets for tourists as a way of enhancing their income. In some cases performance itself flounders, as puppet sales become the main support for puppeteers. This was true for many years in Burma, before a recent revival, and for some puppeteer families in China.
11 The *Panchatantra* is a collection of ancient animal fables, originally compiled in Sanskrit, probably around the third to fifth centuries BCE, that teaches moral values.
12 I personally observed this performance.
13 Both the men and women in my group were invited into the puppet house to try out the puppets.

Works cited

Baldwin, K. (2012) "Canada Best G20 Country To Be a Woman, India Worst," *Reuters*, June 13, <http://in.reuters.com/article/2012/06/13/g20-women-idINDEE85C00420120613> (accessed August 26, 2013).

Blackburn, S. (1996) *Inside the Drama-House: Rama Stories and Shadow Puppets in South India*. Berkeley, CA: University of California Press.

Blumenthal, E. (2005) *Puppetry: A World History*. New York, NY: Harry N. Abrams.

Borrowed Fire: The Shadow Puppets of Kerala (2000) Motion picture, Kathajali Productions, Austin, TX.

Orenstein, C. (2013) "Women in Indian Puppetry: Artists, Educators, Activists," in A. Singh and T. T. Mukherjee (eds) *Gender, Space and Resistance: Women and Theatre in India*. New Delhi: DK Printworld.

Pani, J. (1986) *Living Dolls: Story of Indian Puppets*. New Delhi: Indian Ministry of Information and Broadcasting.

Pulavar, R. (2013) "Biography," March 11, <http://ramachandrapulavar.blogspot.com/> (accessed August 26, 2013).

Seltmann, F. (1982) "Shadow Play in Kerala," in *Our Cultural Fabric: Puppet Theatre in India*. New Delhi: Indian Ministry of Education and Culture.

Singh, S. (1999) "If Gandhi Could Fly … Dilemmas and Directions in Shadow Puppetry of India," *TDR/The Drama Review* 43(3): 154–168.

Venu, G. (2006) *Tolpava Koothu: Shadow Puppets of Kerala*. New Delhi: Sangeet Natak Akademi.

20
Integration of Puppetry Tradition into Contemporary Theatre
The Reinvigoration of the *Vertep* Puppet Nativity Play after Communism in Eastern Europe

Ida Hledíková

A tradition of "crèche" performances, representations of the Christian Nativity, existed in many countries of Central and Eastern Europe (e.g., Austria, Bohemia, Poland, Slovakia, Ukraine, and Russia) during the eighteenth and nineteenth centuries. This tradition primarily came from folk plays presented at Christmastime, but the oldest traditions were derived from pastorals with a Christmas theme, which appeared in the European Baroque theatre around 1555 when the first modern-era plays performed in Latin, called *pastorales sacrae*, were staged in Italy (Slivka 1992: 90). Alongside this tradition, which was developed by Jesuits, came popular presentations of the Nativity story performed in the language of the local populace, the "folk." These Nativity scenes, presented as folk plays, existed in both puppet and human form or as a combination of the two.

By the beginning of the twentieth century, the socialist revolution in Russia and later political changes in Central European countries, such as Czechoslovakia, Hungary, and East Germany, following World War II, brought a definitive end to the traditional puppet theatre. Such performances were considered private commercial activities, which were forbidden under Communist governments because they were incompatible with the principle of public ownership. At the same time the presentation of crèche folk plays with their religious themes was illegal. The strictest ban on religious performances was established in the republics that made up the Soviet Union after the revolution of 1917. Traditional Christmas plays (called *vertep* in Ukraine and *batlejka* in Belarus) have strong roots in the countries of the former Soviet Union, but their presentation disappeared for 70 years. The ban had an ideological rationale: it was a ban on any manifestation of religion.

However, during the 1990s a revival of old traditions was launched spontaneously in the USSR after Mikhail Gorbachev instituted *perestroika* – a process of liberation immediately preceding the collapse of the Communist regimes in Central and Eastern Europe. It was a new chance for free expression and independent theatre. Many professional puppet theatres of the former Soviet Union resumed the practice of presenting Nativity scenes and other traditional productions. At the same time the popular Russian street glove-puppet show with its "hero" Petrushka was once again seen. Nowadays these post-traditional shows are played mainly by professional soloists and professional puppet companies. The actors, directors, and scenic and puppet designers of these plays are educated in theatre schools or schools of fine arts. The majority do not copy the old models completely but take inspiration from them to create new performances derived from traditional content, such as the Nativity scene.

Interesting examples of this type of theatre come from Ukraine. We can see the process of alteration of the Ukrainian *vertep* through three stagings of the Nativity scene, all directed by Sergij Bryzhan and designed by Michail Nikolaev. Both are eminent puppetry artists who work in the County Puppet Theatre in the town of Chmelnickij. These productions show the crèche tradition being used in new, contemporary forms, while maintaining some principles of the original tradition. The Nativity play has become a scenic artifact.

The presentation of three different stagings of the *vertep* Nativity play in Ukraine created by the same director and scenic artist is an excellent example of experimentation with one theme in the puppet theatre. While the first two productions by Bryzhan maintain the status of classical storytelling with regards to the nativity of baby Jesus, his third staging for the most part offers conceptual changes, in the spirit of a modern approach, to become a decomposition of the well-known biblical story. By breaking up the story, the creators make room for a loose interpretation of the narrative and for their presentation of puppetry and visual ideas. At first glance, this version of the story has little in common with the traditional account. Disrupting the story to allow a free flow of associations is one of the characteristic features of postdramatic theatre, which is related to post-traditional puppet theatre.

Post-traditional puppet theatre, in general, is a form of puppet theatre that has attributes of the theatre of objects, usually involving figurative puppets, and that deliberately engages with the elements of traditional puppet theatre dramaturgy, including inspiration, puppetry technique, and specific staging procedures, but which are stylized to create an original new form.

In its formal aspects, this modern presentation of the Nativity play is far removed from folk traditions. Only the story, characters, and structure of the play remain. A postdramatic staging, such as in the third Nativity play by Bryzhan entitled *Resonances*, is devoid of story. The creators do not copy old forms but are, rather, inspired by the story's theme in creating original work.

The crèche story is always simple and short: in the first scene characters, such as shepherds, peasants, and the Three Kings, go to see the baby Jesus with their offerings. The second scene is with King Herod. A sage announces to Herod that a new Jewish king has been born. Herod expresses his fear that he will lose his crown. Then Death comes and beheads Herod. The Devil, who accompanies Death, rejoices and takes Herod away to hell. The play has other versions in different regions, but they all include the same basic events. In Slovakia, for example, a Roma ("Gypsy") character is presented instead of a Jewish man. The story is usually staged in something resembling a small house, of one to three floors, according to regional tradition. The puppets are small, usually between 15 and 25 centimeters, fixed on a stick, and animated from below.

Out of Bryzhan's three new stagings of the crèche, the first, and the one most influenced by tradition, was done in 1995. The last one is a new performance that was conceived – to use terminology from Hans Thies Lehmann in his book on postdramatic theatre – as a framed "state": "The state is an aesthetic figuration of the theatre, showing a formation rather than a story, even though living actors play in it" (Lehmann 1999 [2006]: 68). On the one hand, Lehmann's idea can be perceived as the form tackling the theme while abandoning classical storytelling through characters, relationships, and dramatic conflicts. On the other, however, Bryzhan composes the staging of the scenes with great creativity. He addresses the audience through visual metaphor. He focuses on the abstract scenic form, which allows the audience to make their own associations. The director achieves this provocative abstraction by applying textual and visual fragments, which more or less correspond to the basic structure. It is a free treatment of the theme through theatrical visualization with puppets. This is the principle of the postdramatic treatment of subject at work in his production of *Resonances*.

The first Nativity performance created by Bryzhan and Nikolaev, called *Vertep* after its genre, was done in "family-theatre" style. The family theatre is a type of theatre built on the idea of joint performances by family members (the director cast himself, his wife, and daughter in the play; however, they are not amateurs – both Bryzhan and his wife are members of the Chmelnickij County Puppet Theatre). The stage has an intimate character, consisting of a classical booth with three stories arranged in a hierarchical order: at the top there is the Heavens – where angels usually fly; life on Earth, represented by the Christ child; Mary and Joseph (i.e., the Holy Family); the Three Kings; a typically Ukrainian character "Don Cossack"; and a donkey, is situated on the middle level; and in the lowest space, the scene with Herod, the Devil, and Death takes place.

This staging of the Nativity play is devoid of unique interpretative shifts. The content and message remain true to the spirit of the story and celebrations of the birth of baby Jesus. The content corresponds to the tradition, while the form differs. The puppet technique is identical with that tradition. Simple puppets on a stick are moved up and down and back, as well as from left to right and back, by the actor. The visual arrangement of the scenery and use of puppets fulfill traditional aesthetic requirements. In traditional theatre, the concern is artistic naïveté, although here the staging is performed by professionally trained puppeteers, not folk actors. Contemporary theatre-makers, by contrast, seek inspiration from both self-exploration and ethnological research, since this tradition was interrupted for more than 60 years.

Bryzhan directed his second Nativity staging, *A Christmas Mystery*, in the Rovenski Puppet Theatre in Rovno, Ukraine. The concept, image, and philosophy of this staging are based on an East European religious-art tradition (mainly Ukrainian,

Figure 20.1 V*ertep*, Bryzhan Family Theatre, Chmelnickij, Ukraine (premiered 1995): Director: Sergij Bryzhan; designer: Michail Nikolaev; from left: Olga Bryzhan, Natasha Bryzhan, and Sergij Bryzhan. Photo courtesy of Sergij Bryzhan

Ruthenian, or Russian) called "writing," but which is, in fact, painting icons. "Writing icons" in actuality involves painting biblical stories from the life of Jesus Christ and the saints on wood as a specific manifestation of faith. Therefore, icons are not "painted" but "written." Icons appeared in Russia as early as the fifth and sixth centuries. As with Nativity plays, the tradition of writing icons was also interrupted by the Communist regime, but a change occurred after the fall of the government.

The scenic design of *A Christmas Mystery* reminds one of an iconostasis – a large wall of icons. The iconostasis is placed in front of the altar in churches that adhere to the Greek Orthodox and Eastern Orthodox liturgical rites. It consists of several icons arranged as a wall and includes other larger and smaller paintings with Christian motifs. This markedly stylized scene design and the actors' costumes were created mainly in blue and white. In iconic symbology blue means eternal wisdom and godliness. It is also a symbol of the tunic of the Mother of God, who unifies the lives of Earth and Heaven. White is a symbol of holiness and godly light. The paintings are combined with puppets.

The scenery consists of images that can be rotated, thereby producing windows. This stylized screen evokes an iconostasis. The creators chose this form to depict the Nativity play because it directly corresponds to the biblical stories portrayed on the icons, which capture the life, death, and resurrection of Jesus Christ. The design also recalls the iconic style in its lack of perspective, since the oldest icon painters did not use perspective.

The puppets and the faces of the actors are visible in empty windows. The actors play with small puppets on a stick and sing beautiful Eastern liturgical chorales. To

Figure 20.2 A *Christmas Mystery*, Rovenski County Puppet Theatre, Rovno, Ukraine (premiered July 1, 2000): Director: Sergij Bryzhan; designer: Michail Nikolaev. Photo courtesy of Sergij Bryzhan

be present at this performance is a wonderful cultural experience. It blends stylized artistic conception, contemporary aesthetic taste, iconic tradition, and church singing.

The creators' objective in these numerous productions is to explore different variations on a theme that is one of the pillars of Christian culture. A return to the old forms is no longer possible. The puppet theatre and its creative potential, however, can offer new possibilities.

The biblical model offers the possibility of different interpretations, but most stagings present the classic biblical story. The audience's interest springs from a thirst for a theme whose prohibition symbolized the loss of freedom and religion, which is why it is still captivating, even after more than 20 years of freedom. New festivals of Nativity plays, especially those held in Ukraine and Poland, are proof that there is a growing interest in this genre.

Resonances, Bryzhan and Nikolaev's third *vertep* staging, has a completely different artistic conception and, with its alternative way of staging, it is exceptional. Its attractiveness lies in experimenting with the decomposition of the classic biblical play. The directing and design concept is built on the staging and materialization of its creators' associations, while leaving room for spectators to make their own. Another specific feature is the creation of a Christmas atmosphere without the authors' direct illustration of the biblical story, yet the viewer perceives this story through his/her own associations. Russian theatre critics hailed the show as a *vertep* for the third millennium on the occasion of The Nativity Evenings Festival in Moscow in 2005. The imagery of the staging, if we compare it with the two previous *vertep* productions, is the most contemporary and reflexive, bringing all of the associative potentials of theatre to bear. Tradition here is less expressed, but it is still present, serving as a concrete starting point for new imagery. While the audience is not able to identify all the messages and allusions in their full richness, despite knowledge of the old tradition, this kind of show provides an opportunity for audiences to use their own imagination and find new meanings.

This third version of a "Nativity scene" is a contemporary *vertep* created through the free invention of the director and designer and based on the principles of collage. They used puppets and figures, which they found in a depository at the Puppet Theatre in Chmelnickij. In his essay "Letter to Author," Bryzhan describes how "associations appeared constantly as a mysterious mold on the walls" (Bryzhan 2012: 376). This expression corresponds to an image in one of the films of the famous Russian director Andrei Tarkovsky. The principle of collage is one of unexpected associations, which can appear autonomously. He says:

> It is not we who dictate to the puppets what they have to do, but vice-versa, it is the puppets who dictate to us. To use different puppets all would look differently. One needs only to feel where the puppets lead you. Only one thing I knew surely was that I would need a window. A window symbolizes expectation. When I was a child, I often used to be alone at home. At that time I would be sitting by the window watching the birds outside, the falling snowflakes, then I was not so sad.
>
> (Bryzhan 2012: 235)

Bryzhan and Nikolaev utilized a method of collage that made use of many different performing objects – objects that are not connected to the classical Christmas story but which could suggest a variety of meanings. For example, two cheesy old Santa Claus toys represented two of the kings, while an old Snow White toy stood in for the third. Use of these commercial figures evoked Christmas-shopping fever. In addition, there were portrait photos of different famous and lesser known personalities, mainly writers and artists, who "look out of the window, full of expectation." They are hanging on threads like puppets, and in Bryzhan's interpretation, their role of bearing spiritual messages is the same as a Nativity story.

This analysis of three Ukrainian Nativity stagings shows different possibilities for the treatment of the classical biblical theme through various directorial and artistic concepts. They confirm the use of a great variety of forms and puppetry techniques in this revived tradition. It is only up to the creators' invention as to how they tackle the theme. As one can see, the possibilities are endless.

As for respect for tradition in the sense of content and ideology, I conclude that puppet theatre-makers in Central and Eastern Europe do not significantly shift interpretation of the biblical message. Rather, the staging of a work like *Resonances*, presented in the spirit of postdramatic theatre, treats the theme in a distinctive style, avoiding the classical story and provoking the viewer's imagination at the same time.

In terms of form, the stagings are not intended to replicate the old folk puppet theatre and Christmas customs involving caroling around the puppet crèche. Instead, this new model derives inspiration from the traditional forms – puppetry technique, arrangement of the stage area, and the use of various cultural traditions. While these crèche performances are new stagings, they show that traditional forms can be a rich source of inspiration for theatre artists.

Figure 20.3 Resonances, Chmelnickij County Puppet Theatre, Chmelnickij, Ukraine (premiered July 1, 2003): Director: Sergij Bryzhan; designer: Michail Nikolaev. Photo courtesy of Sergij Bryzhan

Works cited

Bryzhan, S. (2012) "Letter to Author," in I. Uvarova (ed.) *Vertep – A Christmas Mystery*. Moscow: Progess-Traditsiia.
Lehmann, H.-T. (1999) *Postdramatic Theatre*, trans. K. Juers-Munby (2006). London: Routledge.
Slivka, M. (1992) *Slovenské ľudové divadlo: Genéza a vývoj hier* [*Slovak Folk Theatre: Genesis and Game Development*], vol. 1. Bratislava, Slovakia: Central Library and SIS Performing Arts.

Part III
CONTEMPORARY INVESTIGATIONS AND HYBRIDIZATIONS

Edited and Introduced by Dassia N. Posner

Theatre generates a kind of double vision, a parallel experience on multiple planes as audiences are confronted simultaneously with the real and the fictional. As Bert States muses in *Great Reckonings in Little Rooms*, "If we think of semiotics and phenomenology as modes of seeing, we might say that they constitute a kind of binocular vision: one eye enables us to see the world phenomenally; the other eye enables us to see it significatively" (States 1985: 8). Thus, we have no difficulty in weeping at the plight of a character while turning to a neighboring audience member to complement the quality of the acting. As Joseph Roach has observed, "Theatrical performance is the simultaneous experience of mutually exclusive possibilities: truth and illusion, presence and absence, face and mask" (Roach 2004: 559).

One of the recurrent aims of representational theatre has been to merge the lenses of theatre's metaphorical binoculars, to conflate these ways of viewing into a single image, a convincing illusion that real life is unfolding before an audience. Puppet theatre, which separates the actor from the character by including both a live performer (the puppeteer) and a conventionalized one (the puppet), does precisely the opposite. In fact, the co-presence of puppet and puppeteer is a physicalization of States's binocular vision. Particularly in performance modes where the puppeteer is fully visible, such as *bunraku*, most of the pleasure in watching lies in the mind's oscillations between remembering and forgetting that the puppeteer is there, between believing in and marveling at the fiction being created.

Puppetry excels at provoking binocular experiences of other kinds, too. Indeed, it assumes a kind of imaginative flexibility – even mental acrobatics – on the part of its viewers. The puppet is concomitantly alive and dead, serious and ironic, adult and childlike, mechanical and spontaneous, enthralling and uncanny. It is uniquely adept at simultaneity and fragmentation. Its voice can be separated from its body without generating confusion. It can be rent into pieces without the audience fearing for its life or soul. The puppeteer can be equally chameleonic: an impartial observer, an aspect of the puppet's personality, or invisible altogether.

Analyses of performing-object theatre thus must consider not only dramatic structures or character development but also these multiple modes of experience that cross over, diverge, and harmonize in the mind of the viewer like the discrete but interweaving instrumental lines in a symphony. Puppet performance rarely develops from a written text, or at least from a text that is generated in advance or that claims to capture the majority of a production's meaning. Instead, it relies on these sophisticated systems of nonverbal, visceral communication that are generated by its design, its physical transformations, or its interactions with the human and material world.

How, then, do we articulate how such material performances function theatrically? On one hand, thinking of puppetry in terms of medium specificity encourages us to identify and articulate the unique aesthetic laws and modes of communication that distinguish it from the theatre of live actors. On the other, it cannot be limited to this; its shifting boundaries make it uniquely adept at transformation in new mediums. This section of the book is therefore divided into two interrelated parts. In the first, "Material Performances in Contemporary Theatre," authors explore how the performing object functions theatrically through close analyses of contemporary productions. In the second, "New Directions and Hybrid Forms," authors define the puppet anew by testing the elasticity of its boundaries and examining its hybridizations in physical and virtual venues.

The authors included in "Material Performances in Contemporary Theatre" use a variety of theoretical lenses to investigate puppetry's structures, aesthetics, and philosophical significance. Jane Taylor and Dawn Tracy Brandes both explore, in different ways, the puppet in relation to the bifurcated self. Taylor analyzes the creation and South African premiere of her play *After Cardenio*, her contribution to a cluster of international plays commissioned by Stephen Greenblatt that generate culturally specific responses to Shakespeare's "missing" play *Cardenio*. Through the interweaving co-presence of the play's main character, Anne Greene, played simultaneously by a puppet and a live actor, Taylor investigates larger philosophical questions about the body/soul, object/subject dialectic inherent to puppetry. Brandes analyzes "compiled character" in *Or You Could Kiss Me*, a coproduction by South Africa's Handspring Puppet Company and the National Theatre in London. She illuminates the dramaturgical significance of this production's consciously created character mosaics that alternate between puppets and live actors, as well as among puppets that depict different versions of the same self, generated by the passing of time. Robert Smythe views Theater am Wind's *Hermann* through the lens of narrative theory, applying familiar definitions of *fabula* and *sjužet* in a new context that prompts a nuanced reading of the production's innovative spatial and character dynamics. In Smythe's analysis, space itself becomes a form of embodied *sjužet* that the puppeteer-auteur actively wields to construct the audience's experience. Mark Sussman analyzes two model theatre productions, Rimini Protokoll's *Mnemopark: A Model Train World* and Hotel Modern's *The Great War*, in conjunction with Walter Benjamin's essays on toys and the "mimetic faculty" of the child, to redefine the parameters and significance of model theatre. Sussman focuses on oscillations between miniature and vast, live and mediated, child and adult, to demonstrate the necessary, revolutionary potential of child's play in the adult world.

The authors included in "New Directions and Hybrid Forms" probe expanding definitions of puppetry and the new realms into which the puppet is moving. As articulated here, these shifting boundaries range from new technologies that reimagine the human through robotics and motion capture, to a project that replaces not the puppet but the puppeteer with an intelligent machine, to performance events that view the environment itself from a puppet perspective. Cody Poulton focuses on collaborations between two specialists in theatre and robot engineering: playwright and director Hirata Oriza and roboticist Ishiguro Hiroshi, specifically their productions that juxtapose human actors with robots and androids. Investigating these machine-populated theatre productions in the context of Mori Masahiro's "uncanny valley" and Chikamatsu Monzaemon's "slender margin between the real and the unreal," Poulton asks what it means to be human, whether a machine can attain consciousness, and what can be learned from examining the often uncomfortable boundaries between the illusion of life and life itself. Colette Searls explores how computer animation and puppetry are entering new realms through fusions of the two, using examples from contemporary live and recorded media that include the animated Magic Mirror in *Shrek the Musical*, the Wild Things with puppet bodies and animated faces in Spike Jonze's *Where the Wild Things Are*, and the eerie humans who populate Robert Zemeckis's performance-capture films. Searls both defines the boundaries of puppet theatre and productively challenges her own definition, arguing that a thorough awareness of the fundamental aesthetic laws of puppetry and animation is a necessary prerequisite to successful hybridizations. Elizabeth Ann Jochum and Todd Murphey discuss the *Pygmalion* Project, a collaboration between Northwestern University and Disney that aims to develop an automated robotic marionette play using traditional marionettes and a robotic puppeteer, or "actuator." They analyze how the *Pygmalion* Project has led to new understandings of motion planning and control by testing the limitations of engineering technology and the centrality of the human puppeteer.

The complementary conversations of these two sections intersect productively in Eleanor Margolies's chapter, with which this book concludes. Margolies analyzes specific performances – *Ubu Roi* by Nada Théâtre, *Claytime* by Indefinite Articles, and a participatory food-cycle event in London, *Feast on the Bridge* – to rethink the parameters of material performance. While the other chapters in this section redefine the puppet in the context of new technologies, Margolies instead ponders how performers interact with the Earth's most basic materials – clay, food, and compost – to understand our ethical responsibility to future generations.

Works cited

Roach, J. (2004) "It," *Theatre Journal* 56: 555–568.
States, B. O. (1985) *Great Reckonings in Little Rooms: On the Phenomenology of Theater*. Berkeley, CA: University of California Press.

Section V
Material Performances in Contemporary Theatre

21
From Props to Prosopopeia
Making *After Cardenio*
Jane Taylor

Mainly theoretical: "From Props to Prosopopeia"

Let me begin with the pairing of terms in my chapter title: I start with "props." In theatrical terms, the prop is something that makes no claims to agency. We get some good sense of what props are from Philip Henslowe, the Elizabethan theatrical entrepreneur, who lists the following props amongst his company's assets on March 10, 1598:

> 1 rock, 1 cage, 1 tomb, 1 hell mouth, 1 bedstead, 8 lances, 1 pair of stairs for Phaeton, 1 globe and golden scepter, 3 clubs, 1 golden fleece, 2 racquets, 1 bay tree, 1 lion's skin, 1 bear's skin, Phaeton's chariot, the city of Rome, Neptune fork and garland, one pot for the Jew, one boar's head and Cerberus' three heads.[1]
>
> (Henslow 1845: 273)

A workable definition of the prop is that it is an object used on stage by actors to further the plot or storyline. Although for all the passivity implied by this definition, the prop can also be at times *that without which the plot cannot advance*. (Let us think of the letter that Hamlet discovers and then rewrites in order to contrive the deaths of Rosencrantz and Guildenstern.)[2]

"Motion is the prop's defining feature," is the observation made by Andrew Sofer in his thoughtful introduction to *The Stage Life of Props* (Sofer 2003: iv). It is useful to consider Arjun Appadurai's suggestion that, while from a theoretical point of view human agents encode things with meaning, methodologically it is the "things in motion" which provide insight into social structure (Appadurai 1988: 5). Thus, for all of the object's ostensible "agentlessness," the study of how, where, and when things move on stage provides a set of traces for otherwise invisible interactions. Objects become bearers of affect, and so social, erotic, and economic relations that might be masked or opaque to characters on stage can be made legible via the ways in which things are transacted.

So much for the prop.

Of prosopopeia, then.

Prosopopeia is generally conceived of as a rhetorical device through which the speaker projects him or herself into the being of a second person or thing in order to communicate obliquely to a third term. The puppet, which can be anything from a sock to a bundle of sticks and cloth, is in some ways akin to the prop but rather radically veers toward personhood, becoming a materialization of the rhetorical device, prosopopeia. It thus provides an object-based site for the projection from a speaking subject. The puppet is that "other being or thing" onto which a speaking/thinking being is projected. Yet the puppet is a particular kind of illusionist, wedded to maintaining the fiction of its autonomy. A puppet would rather die than admit that it is not alive. As Basil Jones of Handspring Puppet Company has asserted, every puppet show has an *Ur*-narrative that can be framed by the question, "Will the puppet manage to hold onto its illusory existence for the duration of the show?" (B. Jones, pers. comm., 2011).

In this it differs distinctly from the ventriloquist's dummy. Within the conventions of ventriloquism, the dummy constantly draws attention to its captive status, abusing the manipulator, berating the man (!) who has a hand up its ass.[3] The puppet claims its own personhood, while the ventriloquist's doll in some uncanny way acknowledges, often acrimoniously, its status as prop. Most often a scene of ventriloquism entails the doll furiously battling to wrestle its agency from the manipulator, who is co-present in the performance. That performer is somehow rather poignantly usually the real substance of the narrative arc of the show, often trying to free himself (!) from the tyranny of the prop, as if in an extraordinary inversion of power, the manipulator is the dummy's puppet. There are enormous psychic and political implications to such scenes, which may account for the powerful feelings of anxious excitement and nausea we experience. It is, in ways, the enactment of an Oedipal inversion, with the parent being trounced by an ungovernable infant.[4]

Largely historical

After: "Succeeding, following on, not prior, not the first;" or, (after) "in imitation of, mimicking, in the style of;" or (after) "in pursuit of [as a detective is 'after a criminal'], hunting down."

This section is about the problem of writing a play that has already been written.

Some three years ago I was approached by Renaissance scholar Stephen Greenblatt to write a version of a so-called "missing" Shakespeare play, a work titled *Cardenio* that has come down through tradition as a play by the Bard, though no copy of the original play's text has ever come to light. The strongest clue to the play's possible plot arises from the fact that the title refers to a character, Cardenio, the name given to a melancholy hero from Miguel de Cervantes's celebrated novel *Don Quixote*. In the novel, Cardenio has lost his mind because he believes that his beloved has been seduced by the local overlord, and lives disguised as a shepherd in the mountains.

I did not immediately conceive of making a puppet play, although I am interested in the puppet text as both a theoretical idea and as a practical project. (I have written both a play-text and an opera libretto for puppets, working with Handspring Puppet

Company and artist/director William Kentridge.) When I received the commission to write a "*Cardenio*," my instinct was that I couldn't engage in making a pastiche of a Shakespeare play nor could I avoid wanting to engage with the force of his imagination. I had to locate an intellectual question that would assert its distinct validity within my work. How or why might Shakespeare have written in response to Cervantes? What in the vast, various novel *Don Quixote*, full of chivalric idealism, wild buffoonery, and irony, could be reconciled with Shakespeare's psychological portraiture, his wordplay, his scrutiny of statecraft and power? Was there real common terrain explored by both writers despite the vast differences in procedure, sensibility, ideology, and form? What would the book and the stage tell us about one another? And how does seventeenth-century Spanish Catholicism inform us about emergent Protestantism? These were the historical and literary questions.

The two extraordinary writers seem linked by more than chance. Both, curiously, are recorded as having died on the same date, though not the same day. Spain and England were on different calendars in 1613; the dates of deaths are somewhat unstable in this early modern period, and so it is perhaps by convention (and invention) that Cervantes died on April 23, some ten days before Shakespeare died on the same date, ten days later.

I began to undertake research, looking for ways into the project. Greenblatt and playwright Charles Mee had written a lighthearted comedy based on the motif of the sexual wager: one man challenges his friend to test the virtue of his wife. My response on reading that play was that, writing from South Africa in the twenty-first century, it was very difficult to perceive sexual infidelity as quite the same reckless riot that they were imagining. The context of AIDS, sexual violence, and infant mortality cast a particular kind of pall over the sport as so imagined. I was interested in the tough questions around the *droit de seigneur*: power, sexual domination, and betrayal.

In Cervantes's novel, Cardenio's love Luscinda escapes the enforced marriage being urged upon her by fainting at the altar. The plot device produced a readerly skepticism in me. "Possibly that swoon arose from a feigned circumstance," I thought; but even as I formulated that query, it struck me that my resistance to the text was informed at least in part by the patriarchal inclination not to believe the testimony of a woman's bodily performance.

I shifted procedures, trying to understand this trope of "fainting at the altar" not for its ostensible truth content but for its dramatic potential. Was there possibly a pregnancy concealed inside the plot that I was devising? That would locate a biological cause of the "vapors" and yet could carry narrative intrigue. The Luscinda I was imagining was perhaps more complex than suggested by the narrative of her as a one-dimensional feminine piety. The puppet is in a strange relation to transparency. There is a tradition of reception that more or less affirms that the puppet is without guile. (The ventriloquist's doll, by contrast, is notoriously deceptive.) I began to undertake research into early modern sexuality and the law, considering how I might work my theatre piece toward a dramatic situation concordant with Shakespeare's perennial investigations in the late plays.

My first imaginative journey was to consider the social and literary history in order to establish a store of historical fact that could inform, one way or another,

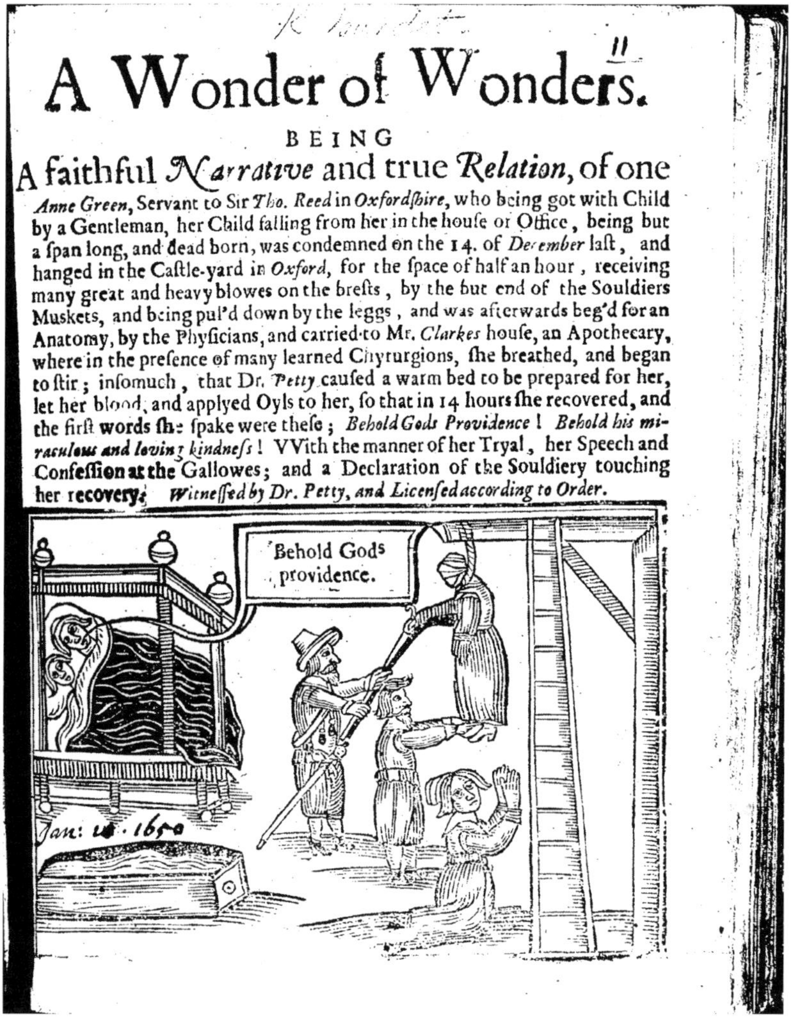

A Wonder of Wonders.

BEING

A faithful *Narrative* and true *Relation*, of one *Anne Green*, Servant to Sir *Tho. Reed* in *Oxfordshire*, who being got with Child by a Gentleman, her Child falling from her in the house or Office, being but a span long, and dead born, was condemned on the 14. of *December* last, and hanged in the Castle-yard in *Oxford*, for the space of half an hour, receiving many great and heavy blowes on the brests, by the but end of the Souldiers Muskets, and being pul'd down by the leggs, and was afterwards beg'd for an Anatomy, by the Physicians, and carried to Mr. *Clarkes* house, an Apothecary, where in the presence of many learned Chyrurgions, she breathed, and began to stir; insomuch, that Dr. *Petty* caused a warm bed to be prepared for her, let her blood, and applyed Oyls to her, so that in 14 hours she recovered, and the first **words** she spake were these; *Behold Gods Providence! Behold his miraculous and loving kindness!* VVith the manner of her Tryal, her Speech and Confession at the Gallowes; and a Declaration of the Souldiery touching her **recovery**. *Witnessed by Dr. Petty, and Licensed according to Order.*

Figure 21.1 "A Wonder of Wonders ... ," 1651 broadsheet recounting the story of Anne Green © The British Library Board General Reference Collection E.621(11). Image published with permission of ProQuest. Further reproduction is prohibited without permission. Image produced by ProQuest as part of *Early English Books Online*. www.proquest.com

the dramatic arc that I would establish. I was seeking a complex relation between history, literary precedent, and fresh invention.

So as a beginning, I turned to EEBO (Early English Books Online). Luck has something to do with it – and so does art history. I was drawn to an early modern text because it was illustrated. Any researcher will understand the hold that a vivid woodcut can have when one is sifting through endless textual accounts. The image is something of a rarity. That was how I settled upon the broadsheet recounting the story of Anne Green, who in 1650 was hanged for infanticide (Burdet 1651: 1).

Anne is not just a melancholy fact of history; rather, she becomes an unlikely *cause célèbre*. Because she lived and died in Oxford, England, her body was handed over to the university for an anatomy, a common practice with the corpses of the executed.[5] However, to the awe and shock of everyone attending, she regained consciousness on the anatomy table. When she was gathered enough to speak, her first words were allegedly "Behold God's Providence!" (Burdet 1651: 5). Her survival was, she claimed, testimony to her innocence.

What the broadsheet hints at is a bitter saga involving a young working girl, Anne Green, who was impregnated by the young Jeoffrey Read while she was in service in the great house of his grandfather, Sir Thomas Read. Her unhappy situation was disclosed when a fellow servant heard moans coming from an adjacent room and discovered Anne with a little corpse. The sometime friend immediately ran (one imagines the hollow shrieking of outraged piety) to the master and mistress of the house, disclosing Anne's misery and her alleged crime. Anne was found guilty of murdering her infant and sentenced to be hanged. This sad story is ordinary enough and would have had small interest. Her case becomes extraordinary to history when she revives on the anatomy table. Her notoriety is such that there are over 30 poems about her by young Oxford fellows (one of whom is Christopher Wren, who would later become the architect of London's own resurrection).[6]

The incredible Anne Green story was reminiscent for me of the late Shakespeare plays, with their haunting explorations of the possibility of renewal, resurrection, rebirth. The puzzle of a return from death to life is there even in his early plays: Juliet's feigned death is followed by her regaining consciousness, though tragically too late for Romeo, who kills himself in grief.

However, there is a quality of self-delusional hope in the face of despair that characterizes several of the mature plays. Here I have in mind the enigmatic structure of *The Winter's Tale*, in which Leontes accuses his wife, Hermione, of infidelity and banishes her, only to learn of Hermione's blamelessness after her death. Years pass, and the melancholy king has a statue made in commemoration of his wronged wife. The play concludes, implausibly, with Hermione's statue coming to life, and hope is restored. A comparable logic is implicit in the ending of *King Lear*. The old king, distraught and deluded at the end of the play, has his loving daughter Cordelia cut down from where she has been hanged. She is laid at the feet of Lear, who deceives himself that she still lives and breathes. At this point of wretchedness, he dies from shock and heartbreak, and so never has to come to terms with the fact that his daughter is irrecoverably dead and that he was the effective cause of her death.

Anne Green's story is substantially different in its detail, but it does allow for the apparently miraculous transformation from death to life of a hanged girl. Patriarchy is the cause of her death, much as it had been mortal for Cordelia. When I came across the broadsheet giving an account of the "miracle" of Anne's resurrection, I was attracted by what seemed to me an irresistible theatrical opening – the ostensible corpse of a woman "coming back to life" on an anatomy table. As I began to consider the theoretical and philosophical potential of this profoundly visual episode, it seemed to me that the incident could figure (in the sense of "embody") many of the major inquiries of the seventeenth century. Where did identity locate itself? In the body or some indefinable nonmaterial essence? The year of Anne Green's death,

1650, was coincidentally the year in which René Descartes died. The inquiry that had preoccupied the philosopher for much of his career was to set in place a dualistic model of the human being as partaking of both a metaphysical entity (the soul) and a physical one (the body). This model has defined subsequent Western metaphysics. Descartes went on to write extensively about the puzzle of how these realms interacted. How could an immaterial soul impel or interact with matter?

The philosophical quandary provided a set of metaphorics, as well as theatrical possibilities, for staging an event from the historical records of 1650. The tale also spoke of the seventeenth-century intersection of story and science.

After months of writing and thinking and deleting, I managed to compel the Anne Green story and the Cervantes plot to find common cause with social history. Shakespeare's *The Winter's Tale*, as outlined earlier, provides a strong study of patriarchal absolutism and its consequences, and in some ways this Shakespearean plot began to inform my thinking about Anne Green and her "Wonder of Wonders."

This led my research into early modern attitudes to the fetus, the infant, and conception. It has been asserted that during the seventeenth century between one quarter and one third of children died in their first year. I have no way of assessing the extent to which this is the result of urbanization and social transformation. Anne Green's story is a rather traditional one: a working girl who falls pregnant while in service in the house of the local gentry, Sir Thomas Read, whose grandson has impregnated her. The old man was a vociferous advocate that Anne be hanged again after her failed reckoning with the rope. It is the recorded irony that Read died three days after Anne was acquitted.

The status and meaning of "the infant" is obviously shifting in the seventeenth century, and new constraints and controls are instituted. In 1624 Parliament passed an act to "prevent the murthering of bastard children" (Williams 2004: 37). William Walsh by the end of the century asserts in *A Dialogue Concerning Women*, "Go but one Circuit with the Judges here in England; observe how many women are condemned for killing their Bastard children … " (Walsh 1691: 45)

The law intervened awkwardly and unevenly in such matters, and so it signaled its purposes through a decree that any birth kept secret could be inferred to signal danger and that the failure to disclose was itself criminal. The stories are grim and the circumstances hard to imagine.

Jane Lockwood confessed that she bore a stillborn child alone and that she left it on her bed, intending to bury it, but that her father's dogs pulled it off: "She was much to blame," she admitted, "she did not acquaint her mother and neighbours therewith" (cited in Gowing 1997: 111).

These were just some of the ideas percolating in the back of my mind as I began to imagine a viable play. But what was foremost was a visual event: that opening scene with a girl on an anatomy table, about to be dissected, who comes back to life. Nonetheless, I also wanted the work to be philosophical, about the relationship between the stage and the book, and about the seventeenth century. And what of quixotic idealism as a plot possibility? I was tantalized by the Don's religious chivalric zealotry and what it means now that we are again in an unlikely moment of commitment to sublime self-immolation for politico-religious causes.

Shakespeare, by contrast, is chock-a-block full of political cynicism, with persons who are climbing diverse ladders in the pursuit of self-aggrandizement or for revenge or out of rage, and Quixote's outlandish idealism looks rather like folly from outside of the system of its own delusions. What would Shakespeare make of the inquiry? Would this have interested him?

Substantially practical

The show was staged in the old anatomy theatre of the University of Cape Town, a space that was transformed into a performance venue for this production. The seating is at a high angle to allow for observation from above, down into the body. This would have allowed medical students proximity to the corpse, but also, in our situation, it facilitated focused and detailed observation of the puppetry.

I have for some years been interested in exploring what the arts of puppetry tell us about our disquiet at the uneasy dialogue between body and soul, spirit and matter.[7] These arts raise fundamental questions about the performance of the passions through the body in relation to a feeling or a thought that arises elsewhere. I am always struck at our investment in self-deception, such as puppetry allows. The story of Anne Green provided me with an opportunity to activate the archive in an uncanny mode that implicitly engages questions about substance and being. Puppetry necessarily always provides a set of metaphors through which to consider the passage between life and death. The puppet is an instrument that keeps in mind our double consciousness of the quick and the dead. Pinocchio's aspiration to live thematizes that yearning toward the metaphysical. Curiously, though, while Pinocchio's translation into a human boy gives him subjecthood through entry into consciousness, it also precipitates him into the flesh. He becomes captive to our time, our mortality, no longer within that curiously extended and ambiguous temporality of the world of things, which though they are subject to decay, might exceed our three-score years and ten. Pinocchio's consciousness becomes, in Yeats's unambiguous formulation, "fastened to a dying animal" (Yeats 1928: 2).

The technology of voice is part of the illusionism of the puppet. We know that the voice is not "coming from" the doll, yet we delight in believing that it is. The experiment in *After Cardenio* was also to test the limits, and the possibilities, arising from working with different puppeteers speaking Anne Green's voice at distinct points in the production. Would the character still hold?

The theatre is simultaneously a three-dimensional signifying space (say, Drury Lane) and a three-dimensional signified site (say, first-century Rome). Because our theatre was also an old anatomy theatre, it had a surplus of meaning deriving from that particularity. At any point in the performance, audience members would be unevenly aware of the complexities of the site-specific situation of the production. We had painted the back wall of the theater with blackboard paint, and Penny Siopis, a visual artist who had worked with me making several short experimental films, raised the question of how we might handle the projections. I was not keen on a screen, which would break the illusion for which the play text was reaching – namely, that the visual events were, at some level, actually dreams or thoughts and ideas. After Siopis engaged in a few experiments, the decision ultimately was to fill in a large chalk square to create a soft and rather diffuse block of white on the black wall. The mica from the chalk added good luminosity to the wall for bright projection, without foregrounding the projections as technologically derived. The white chalk cube was a kind of empty canvas upon which film and images were projected. The uneven chalk texture gave the projections a mark of the maker, with drawn ground and digital image supplanting each other, straddling ancient and modern art practices. As a way of acknowledging the relationship between the medical anatomy and the visual arts traditions, Siopis began a cycle of drawings that she generated live each evening at the start of the performance, in front of the arriving audience. Her works drew from the iconographies of the mythologies of medical history, as well as archaic notorious women narratives.

At the start of the show, we are in darkness, with a voice meditating on Time. Eventually the light picks up a figure lying in the darkness; she continues to speak and gives a brief account of the body's duel with the soul:

> My story was written and then was printed. Anne Green.
> Three times written down. Being one, yet three stories.
> Three in one. There was me who died.
> (My self was hang'd, and given over as dead.) She was first.
> And there was also me, the resurrection, just like our Lord.
> That second was all eternity.
> Then also the babe, so small, and still. "Is it breathing?"
> The little mouth as blue as water.
> Who can tell my guilt or my innocence?
> If you care to find evidence
> Watch my play, "Behold God's Providence!"
>
> (Taylor 2011)

As she says these words, the lights come up to reveal a group of doctors, one of whom, Dr. Petty, looks uncannily like the young Rembrandt, whose painting "The Anatomy Lesson of Dr Nicolaes Tulp" informs all such scenes.

The puppet of Anne Green/Dorotea[8] is a life-sized sculpture by South African artist Gavin Younge, who has in recent years been making persons, animals, and objects from molded vellum. They are simple but profound beings because of the luminous glow of the skin from which they are made. Of course, because the figure is vellum, she is both object and book. Younge sourced prosthetic eyes for her, so her gaze has a particular kind of focused intensity.

As the figure revives, she establishes a complex relation with the actress, Jemma Kahn, who is as much a body-double as a puppeteer, and who is a projective field of empathetic meaning. Much of the affective intensity of the puppet actually arises in the curious dialectical reciprocity between the actress and the puppet. The third figure in the triangular relation is puppeteer Marty Kintu, who occupies the more traditional role of the puppeteer for much of the performance. His performance is generally unvoiced, as he allows the figure to be "possessed" by Kahn; Kintu has a high order of physical dexterity and is a subtle and skilled manipulator. The puppet thus has a double set of competencies through which to express herself, the vocal

Figure 21.2 After Cardenio, University of Cape Town, South Africa (2011): Dylan Esbach as Cardenio; vellum puppet made by Gavin Younge; Marty Kintu as primary puppeteer. Photo: © Ant Strack 2011, www.antstrack.com

Figure 21.3 Puppet by Gavin Younge; Marty Kintu as primary puppeteer. Photo: © Ant Strack 2011, www.antstrack.com

and facial expressive sophistication of Kahn and the physical nuance and gestural language of Kintu. It was remarkable to observe how easily audiences embrace this complex triangular relation as embodying a single "person." In itself the visual field was superseding the Cartesian model of a dual subject.

The actress and the puppet are at times bound to one another as they might be in a *bunraku* performance, but on occasion it is as if the puppet is manipulating the actress, while on other occasions they prowl around the stage, as if they are body and soul searching for one another.

The interchange between them is volatile, and the question we repeatedly ask, undermining traditional Cartesian dualism, is "Is the body the technology for the soul, or is the soul a technology for the body?" As the play progresses, it is at times the puppet that consoles and comforts the actress; at other times, the actress who is defending the puppet. What is most astonishing is that the puppet and the girl can be at opposite sides of the stage and we still read the two as a single being.

The interrogation of Anne by the Church during the play turns on the question of the death of the child. Here is a fragment of the dialogue as the two wrestle with the resuscitated girl:

DOCTOR PETTY (*as if studying a case, he observes*): Her eyes are open.
Is this a scene that knows it is watched?
I have heard it said that one life is not sufficient;
And we enact through our dreams those things
That we do not perform in life.
ASSISTANT: Some have written that our dreams are prophecies.
DOCTOR PETTY: Yet another thinking on these matters has suggested
That when we sleep, the outward senses, as hearing,
Seeing and smell, retreat from their ordinary activities,

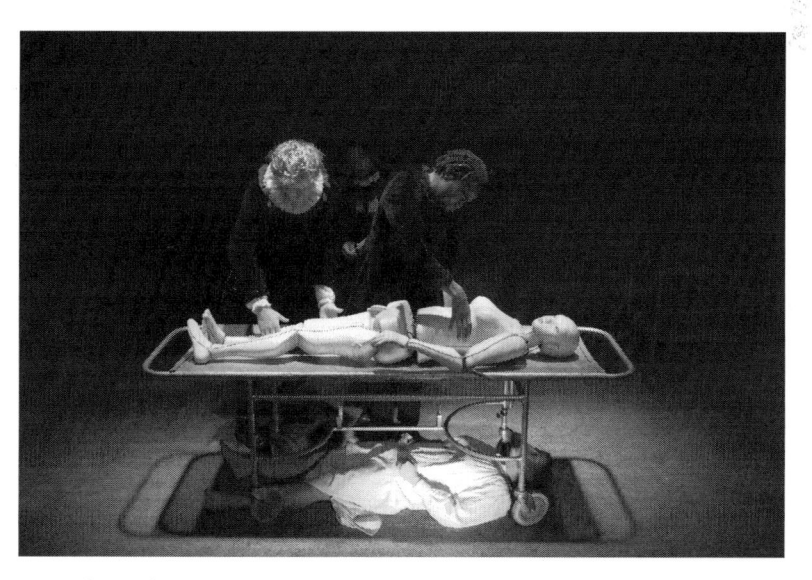

Figure 21.4 Dylan Esbach as Doctor Petty; Marty Kintu as primary puppeteer; puppet by Gavin Younge; and Jemma Kahn as Ann Green. Photo: © Ant Strack 2011, www.antstrack.com

And the inward powers, as memory and phantasy are enhanced.
Perhaps the Soul does at such times inspect its self?
ASSISTANT: I did dream once that I was the devil
And the devil I was, did dream of me.

(Taylor 2011)

The theological drama turns on whether Anne is guilty of infanticide, or whether, as she keeps asserting, there had been a spontaneous abortion:

ASSISTANT: A mother is advised to be not dark;
not to conceal the birth of a babe.
There's a taint of secrecy that is unlovely to the law's desire.
For this we know, a child undisclosed is a child in danger.
It is surely damned, having died without Church.
(*Anne looks distressed, her gaze darts across the ceiling.*)
ASSISTANT: See the child? Look you
It stands outside the door. Its hand too small to make a fist,
And cannot even knock at heaven to ask for entry.
See, it helpless pats the door. Pat, pat.
ANNE GREEN/DOROTEA: I never did dispatch the child. I'd have loved the boy,
For a memento of his father.

(Taylor 2011)

The tormented girl is left alone, and we enter a curious dream state that is structured to complicate the sketch of Anne as either victim or vicious because we do not entirely understand the status of what we watch or its claim as truth:

> The light changes to an unnatural dead white. Puppet and actress are seated side by side. The actress in a somnambulistic state gets up, wanders to the back of the room where there are instruments from the doctor's supplies, and takes a square of red cloth and two brass tankards. She wraps the mugs together in the rag, which becomes a kind of metaphoric swaddling cloth; she begins to rock the strange little bundle, making nurturing shushing noises. The puppet watches the make-believe event, amazed. The actress carefully and deliberately gives the bundle to the puppet, who, in turn, begins to rock and shush the swaddled package. At some point the puppet realizes that the puppet she holds will not quicken, and she flings it from her, violating the dream, as the mugs clatter onto the floor. The strange conceit of the puppet as mimic of the live is foregrounded here, and it is as if there is a tacit recognition that the offspring of the puppet cannot be anything but unnatural.
>
> The puppet figure rises and urinates on the castaway trinkets. In what is at one level an innocent moment, but which could also be a bit of collusive play, the two figures, actress and puppet, dress one another in Puritan-style

costumes and assemble themselves to challenge the church. We as audience members have been witness to an incomprehensible piece of playacting; as the actress and the puppet are caught in an activity that cannot be read as either guilt or innocence.[9]

(Taylor 2011)

For dramatic energy there is a wild disruption with the entry of the town crier (played by Jeroen Kranenberg), who has something of the freak show about him. (Anne was, after her release, allowed to exhibit herself for a small fee. The girl showed herself sitting beside her coffin. This is surely an early episode in the long history of entrepreneurial exhibitionism.)

This sequence is followed by a meta-critical scene in which the actress, the puppeteer, and the puppet all engage in a discussion about puppetry, the soul, and the body. One of the instructive revelations of this production was the extent to which the audience allowed for ambiguity about the site of intelligence in the figure, with the manufactured figure at times apparently following the actress, and the actress at times, it seems, following her. All the while we are subliminally aware of a kind of agency that facilitates the illusion through the silent figure of the master puppeteer. The illusion is broken in this, the so-called "philosophy scene," in which Marty Kintu performs alone on stage with the puppet. Here, there is an exploration of motives and desires, and Kintu speaks the voice of Anne Green, interrogating herself about her agency and her sexual drives. Ultimately, she asks whether she herself precipitated the liaison. Because Kintu has hitherto been the "unseen presence" behind the nuanced movement of Anne Green, the audience allows the shift in vocalizations without unease. So while for much of the production Jemma Kahn speaks for Anne, here in this segment, Kintu was able to be the puppet's ventriloquist, as it were.

This scene disrupts the action, but for many young adult audience members, this is what they engaged with most strongly.

The play ends with a dramatic shift in genre: the old Knight, a quixotic figure, arrives to save Anne, who has at this point in my drama been threatened with immolation. Here the performance aesthetic is very much within the idiom of Cervantes, whose character Cardenio somehow had prompted Shakespeare's play.

The Don dresses himself in battle regalia and equips himself to defend the threatened young woman. He wages a great battle to save her, but his sole warrior is a small Sardinian puppet made in traditional style and (rather ironically) wearing Moorish costume. The fight, as we know, is waged against windmills, and our piece makes marvelous use of very simple shadow puppetry with a wild piece of music, with marching bands and snorting horses. It is an ungovernable riot, and the Don (of course) succumbs in battle, slain in his defense of female virtue.

After Cardenio, then, is interested in the late Shakespeare; it is interested in Cervantes; and, oh, it is so interested in the languages of puppetry.

Afterword

When I first started working on the piece it occurred to me that John Locke, who was himself a student of philosophy and anatomy in the decade after Anne Green's death, must surely have known about this event – must have had her in his mind when he wrote in his famous chapter on identity and person that consciousness is what makes identity in persons. At the time of writing the play, I asserted as an act of faith that surely if 30 fellows had written doggerel about Anne Green, such as the following: "Strange metamorphosis this *dead-live* Woman, / Now differs from her self; and are such *Common?*" (Watkins 1651: 11), then her case was surely challenging assumptions about personhood and identity?

I began to investigate whether I could make a strong claim that Locke would have known about Anne Green, that she would have informed his thinking. The first document that began to confirm my speculation was a publication by Kenneth Dewhurst (1980) that provides an overview of the lectures by the seventeenth-century Oxford anatomist Thomas Willis. Such lecture notes are a fascinating rarity and show us the thinking and the theoretical practice of a man deemed now to be the originator of neuroscience in its earliest form. Willis was one of the anatomists involved in the resuscitation of Anne Green. The facts in the case survive because Willis's lectures have been recorded in summary form in the notes of two students of anatomy at Oxford: Richard Lower, a pioneer in cardiology, and Locke, philosopher.

This was to me a striking find. Here was evidence of an intellectual circuit of inquiry between the anatomist who resuscitated Anne Green and the foremost empirical philosopher of Europe. In my play, Anne herself suggests that Locke would have been interested in her, and she quotes him on resurrections:

> And thus we may be able, without any difficulty, to conceive the same Person at the Resurrection, though in a Body not exactly in make or parts the same which he had here, the same consciousness going along with the Soul that inhabits it.
>
> (Locke 1689: 229)

My interest in Locke, though, had preceded the production of *After Cardenio*. It is his wrestling with the question of identity and person that persistently provokes me. There is a rather remarkable series of thought experiments in Locke's *Essay Concerning Human Understanding*. Here's his question:

> Could we suppose two distinct incommunicable consciousnesses acting the same Body, the one constantly by Day, the other by Night; and on the other side the same consciousness acting by Intervals two distinct Bodies: I ask in the first case, Whether the *Day* and the *Night-man* would not be two as distinct Persons, as *Socrates* and *Plato*; and whether in the second case, there would not be one Person in two distinct Bodies; as much as one Man is the same in two distinct clothings.
>
> (Locke 1689: 233)

Locke's puzzle in the famous chapter on "Identity and Diversity" (Book II, Chapter XXVII) is this: in what does Personhood consist? The challenge he poses is to the commonsense presumption that body and consciousness are unified and co-extensive.

He writes in metaphor, and his remarkable trope of the body as "clothing for the Person" strikes us as a philosophical conundrum.

The discussion comes to us via the traditions of intellectual history. There is, though, another way of interpreting Locke's reverie, because his was no abstract conception of being, for he had a physician's understanding of the body. Recent research has revealed how extensive his medical library was, as well as the depth of his commitment to medical pursuits.[10] By 1667 Locke had become Lord Anthony Ashley Cooper's physician.[11]

Locke's philosophical inquiries are distinctly inflected by his familiarity with medical investigation at Oxford, and hence his challenge to an easy understanding of the relationship between the body and consciousness is provocative. Locke has us first imagine two consciousnesses inhabiting one body, alternately by day and by night; then he wants us to turn to the idea of one consciousness inhabiting two bodies. This is, at some level, a thinking-through of the continuum from the prop to prosopopeia and from the thing to the person. Psychoanalysis has gestured always to this as a dialectic and refers to anything which is not the subject (be it a thing or person) as the object. Through this modeling of the problem, he resolves (as he has clearly set out to do) that Personhood resides in consciousness.[12] Locke's influential thinking about being and number in all likelihood arises in some measure from the story of Anne Green. Philosophy and the natural sciences were co-emerging.

Notes

1. I have assembled this list from Henslow, selecting items for their interest.
2. A prop can certainly also function, as a costume or set might, to define context, conjure mood, or describe character. I would suggest that until recently it primarily was generally understood as *passively* facilitating *action*. Object theatre and puppetry challenge that presumed traditional quietism of the prop.
3. There are female ventriloquists, although they are so rare that the phenomenon is worth noting. Nina Conti is just such a noteworthy instance. Puppetry, by contrast, has many female professionals; the gender asymmetry between ventriloquists and puppeteers is suggestive of the signifying differences between the two art forms.
4. *Time* is obviously the manipulator here. As the riddle of the sphinx makes plain, positions of power are inverted as the human goes through the progress from infantile vulnerability on four legs, to adult autonomy on two, and to aged feebleness on three legs (the walking stick here as an early figure of the prosthetic limb).
5. In many European contexts, anyone hanged for a criminal offense might gain the right to be buried in hallowed ground if their corpse were handed over for an anatomy.
6. Wren, a student of Thomas Willis, one of Anne Green's anatomists, illustrated Willis's remarkable *Cerebri Anatomi* (1664), which would stand for 200 years as the definitive description of the brain.
7. I first worked with Handspring Puppet Company in 1996 when I wrote *Ubu and the Truth Commission*.
8. The protagonist is a composite of the historical figure of Anne Green and Dorotea, the literary love of Don Quixote. She thus had a double, or variable, appellation throughout the staging.
9. I was prompted in this by the protagonist in Daniel Defoe's *Roxana*. Roxana, a prostitute, dresses as a Quaker to escape her history. Quaker principles, of course, are antithetical to the idea of contrived performance.

10 See, for example, Meynell (1997).
11 This rather gives the lie to Meynell's comment that "for all his intelligence and interest in the subject, Locke appears to have remained an educated amateur in medicine" (Meynell 1997: 473). Or, at any rate, it provokes us to reconsider our contemporary understanding of "amateur" and "professional" as binaries.
12 He is also in dialogue with Descartes, who visited anatomies in the hope of finding some way of locating the site of intersection of material and nonmaterial being. For further discussion of Descartes's engagement with medical practice, see Carter (1983).

Works cited

Appadurai, A. (1988) *The Social Life of Things: Commodities in Cultural Perspective*. Cambridge, MA: Cambridge University Press.

Burdet, W. (1651) *A Wonder of Wonders. Being a Faithful Narrative and True Relation of One Anne Green …* . London: John Clowes.

Carter, R. B. (1983) *Descartes' Medical Philosophy: The Organic Solution to the Mind-Body Problem*. Baltimore, MD: Johns Hopkins University Press.

Dewhurst, K. (1980) *Willis's Oxford Lectures*. Oxford, England: Sandford Publications.

Gowing, L. (1997) "Secret Births and Infanticide in Seventeenth-Century England," *Past and Present* 156: 87–115.

Henslow, P. (1845) *The Diary of Philip Henslow, from 1591 to 1609*, J. P. Collier (ed.). London: The Shakespeare Society.

Locke, J. (1689; reprinted 1836) *An Essay Concerning Human Understanding*. London: Balne.

Meynell, G. G. (1997) "A Database for John Locke's Medical Notebooks and Medical Reading," *Medical History* 42: 472–486.

Sofer, A. (2003) *The Stage Life of Props*. Ann Arbor, MI: University of Michigan Press.

Taylor, J. (2011) "After *Cardenio*," unpublished play text.

Walsh, W. (1691) *A Dialogue Concerning Women*. London.

Watkins, R. (1651) *Newes from the Dead, Or a True and Exact Narration of the Miraculous Deliverance of Anne Greene, …* . Oxford, England: Leonard Lichfield (and H. Hall), for Tho. Robinson, D.

Williams, A. N. (2004) "Child Adoption in the Seventeenth Century," *Journal of the Royal Society of Medicine* 97: 37–38.

Willis, T. (1664) *Cerebri Anatomi*. London.

Yeats, W. B. (1928) "Sailing to Byzantium," *The Tower*. London: Macmillan.

22
"A Total Spectacle but a Divided One"
Redefining Character in Handspring Puppet Company's *Or You Could Kiss Me*

Dawn Tracey Brandes

In 2010, fresh from the sweeping success of *War Horse*, the National Theatre of London and Handspring Puppet Company from Cape Town, South Africa, teamed up again to produce a new work for actors and puppets entitled *Or You Could Kiss Me*. Unlike *War Horse*, an epic drama about a boy and his horse during World War I, *Or You Could Kiss Me* told an intimate story on a more human scale. As Handspring's artistic director Adrian Kohler wrote in the program for the play's premiere at the National Theatre, "The territory we now wished to further explore, was the puppet as human in a naturalistic piece devoid of fantasy. Could a puppet handle this task? Would the audience ask whether this could have been done more simply with actors?" (cited in Bartlett 2010: 11). In other words, what can puppetry bring to a human narrative? In this chapter, I will argue that the puppetry in *Or You Could Kiss Me* enables a distinctly postmodern approach to subjectivity that complements and complicates the quest for self-understanding explored in the narrative. By expanding the notion of character to encompass actors, puppeteers, and puppets, the play stages a simultaneous unity and fracture between various fragments of the same character, emphasizing the instability of the self without deconstructing it altogether.

At its core, *Or You Could Kiss Me* is a simple play about two men. Mr. A and Mr. B meet in 1971 on a beach in Cape Town at the ages of 19 and 20, respectively. Sixty-five years later, as Mr. B's health and memory simultaneously fail and Mr. A struggles to care for his ailing partner, the two attempt to come to terms with the knowledge that the next time Mr. B checks into the hospital, he will not be returning home. The text spirals through time, interweaving the past, present, and future of A and B's relationship as a series of overlapping vignettes culled from the memories and imaginations of the two characters.

The flexible chronology of the narrative is further complicated by the double- and triple-casting of puppets and human actors. Adrian Kohler and Basil Jones perform (sans puppets) the present-day, middle-aged A and B, respectively. They also provide the voices for the young and old puppet versions of their characters – Young A, Young B, Old A, and Old B – and often (but not always) participate in the manipulation of these puppets. Four other actors – Finn Caldwell, Craig Leo, Tommy Luther, and Mervyn Millar – act as a kind of chorus of assistants, manipulating the puppets when necessary, physically performing other characters in the story as needed, and conversing with the present-day A and B. The MC, played by Adjoa Andoh, serves a similar function but does not herself operate the puppets. Rather, the MC guides the narrative, instructing other characters on how they should interact with one another and encouraging the various incarnations of A and B to alternately reflect on the past and move through the present.

The puppets, designed and constructed by Kohler, are "five-sixths of life-size" (Kohler cited in Bartlett 2010: 13). While the detail of their carved wooden heads is astonishing, particularly in the older characters whose faces sag with age, the chisel marks remain visible, as do the joints of the puppets' fully articulated limbs. The puppets are not strictly naturalistic in their construction – there is no attempt to conceal their mechanics – nor are the puppeteers hidden. In the intimate black box of the National's Cottesloe Theatre, the audience surrounded the narrow alley stage on three sides, making it even more difficult for the two or three performers manipulating each puppet to recede into the background. Two stage managers and an accordionist were also visible to the audience, the former adding and subtracting minor set pieces and props from the relatively bare stage as needed, the latter providing musical accompaniment and, at times, the exaggerated inhalation and exhalation of the puppet characters' breathing through the use of the instrument's bellows.

By representing A and B in triplicate, *Or You Could Kiss Me* unsettles the notion of character as a unified entity that exists in a clear one-to-one relationship with the actor portraying it. This unsettling of character is a staple of postmodern theatre as understood by Elinor Fuchs in her seminal work *The Death of Character*. Fuchs writes that, just as postmodern philosophy declared its suspicion of metanarratives and stable subjectivity, so too did postmodern theatre reject character-driven representations of a seemingly autonomous subject, emphasizing instead fragmentation and exteriority. To quote Fuchs: "Nothing 'out there,' no one 'in here.' The interior space known as 'the subject' was no longer an essence, an in-dwelling human endowment, but flattened into a social construction or marker in language, the unoccupied occupant of the subject position" (Fuchs 1996: 3).

Thus, the postmodern character, if such a thing can be conceived, is one of division and construction, surface and masks. Rather than striving for a representation of coherent subjectivity, postmodern theatre argues that no such coherence exists and revels in the play of layer upon layer of fiction.

Fuchs's notion of postmodern theatre as one in which "the human figure is no longer the single, perspectival 'point' of stage performance" (Fuchs 1996: 12) is an important step towards defining this difficult model of theatre, but a caveat must be introduced. There is a danger in reading trends towards fracture, displacement, and exteriority too apocalyptically – that is, in sounding the death knell for character too hastily. As Patrice Pavis sagely suggests, "The character is not dead; it has merely become polymorphous and difficult to pin down" (Pavis 1999: 52). In his book *Postdramatic Theatre*, Hans-Thies Lehmann makes a related point when he cautions his readers against assuming that postmodern[1] theatre has lost interest in the human being. He asks:

> Is it not rather a matter of a changed perspective on human subjectivity? What finds articulation here is less intentionality – a characteristic of the subject – than its failure, less conscious will than desire, less the "I" than the "subject of the unconscious." So rather than bemoan the lack of an already defined image of *the* human being in postdramatically organized texts, it is necessary to explore the new possibilities of thinking and representing the individual human subject sketched in these texts.
>
> (Lehmann 1999 [2006]: 18)

Resisting past models does not eradicate character altogether, nor does it attest to a decreased interest in subjectivity. Rather, as Lehmann and Pavis imply, postmodern theatre offers a new approach to character, allowing the constructedness of identity and the slipperiness of subjectivity to be foregrounded rather than erased.

The written text of *Or You Could Kiss Me* gestures towards this slipperiness by dramatizing the desire to construct a stable sense of self, as well as depicting the impossibility of such a task. Old B's failing memory is emphasized throughout, and his attempts to recall his youth are often met with frustration. In one early scene, Old B desperately tries to reconstruct his past by searching through a box of photos while the other characters look on. The pictures prompt some memories but not without contradiction and uncertainty. As Old B rummages through his photographs, the MC lectures the audience about various kinds of memory loss, and Old B exhibits each in turn, appealing to Old A and the assistants to fill in the gaps left by the photos. When one of the assistants asks what Old B is trying to accomplish, B replies:

B: Trying to remember. To remember the first time.
ASSISTANT A: The first time what?
ASSISTANT [B]: The first time they – (*made love*)?
B: The first time he *knew*. The first time it felt like they were ...

(Bartlett 2010: 37)

As with much of the language throughout the play, the text of this exchange relies heavily on unspoken words and unanswered questions. The italicized "*made love*" is the most blatant example of this; the words appear in the printed text to clarify the subtext for the reader, but onstage the meaning of the sentence is only implied by the actor's delivery of the first half of the line. Old B is searching for one concrete moment that defines his life: a moment that no one is able to name. However, it is also a search for himself – one that comes up empty handed. When he asks those around him to identify a face in a photograph, Old A and the assistants assure him it's "You, when you still had your brown hair" (Bartlett 2010: 44), but Old B fails to recognize this image from his own past. Ostensibly, it is Old B's memory loss that prevents him from answering his own questions about who he is and who he was,

Figure 22.1 Or You Could Kiss Me, National Theatre, London (2010) presented in association with Handspring Puppet Company: written and directed by Neil Bartlett; Basil Jones (left) and Adrian Kohler (right) animate Old B and Old A. Photo: © Simon Annand/ Arena PAL

and at the climax of the play, the memory that Old B appears to be searching for – that is, the first time A and B made love – is reconstructed, with the assistants narrating the action and A and B wielding the Young A and Young B puppets. Read on its own, it is possible to see the reconstruction of this memory as the climactic restoration of the coherent subject.

There is an additional layer of fragmentation present in this production that needs to be addressed in order to fully grasp the extent of the postmodern character's instability. Thus, we turn now to the role of puppetry in the construction of postmodern character in *Or You Could Kiss Me*.

The connection between puppetry and postmodernism is an obvious one. Puppets are objects, after all, inherently devoid of interiority. In other words, if postmodern subjectivity can be likened to a series of masks under which no essential core can be found, then the puppet seems to be its perfect receptacle. Indeed, during recent years, puppetry in the West has tended to emphasize rather than conceal the fragmentary nature of its design. In an article tracing modern trends in European puppetry training, Cariad Astles suggests that over the past 20 to 30 years, puppetry training programs have transformed from a puppet-centric model to what she calls a "puppetesque aesthetic" (Astles 2010: 23). In the older model of the mid- to late twentieth century, "all focus and attention [was] on the puppet, which was the core of action, character, narrative, and plot" (Astles 2010: 23). More recently, the focus has dispersed, leaving the puppet as merely one element among many others contributing to the so-called "visual dramaturgy" (Astles 2010: 25) of the piece. Importantly, Astles does not explicitly align the puppetesque with the postmodern anti-character. However, by associating a visually undivided character with the puppet-centric model, the article implies a polarity: At one extreme, traditional puppet performances (particularly in the West) conceal the puppeteer and strive to create the impression of a unified character anchored in the puppet body. At the other, object theatre focuses instead on the transformative capabilities latent in the objects and matter, "suggesting that all things and all matter can be live, can have movement, and can interact with other elements" (Astles 2010: 31).

Astles's notion of the puppetesque supports my claim that contemporary puppetry, through its de-emphasizing of character and accentuation of fragmentation, has the potential to address uniquely postmodern themes. Like Fuchs, Astles defines a useful polarity (in this case, between traditional, puppet-centric puppet theatre and the contemporary, puppetesque aesthetic) without describing the space between the poles. While an extreme version of the puppetesque aesthetic might eradicate character altogether, an intermediary form might present an unstable but identifiable notion of character while retaining the same level of fracture and fragmentation espoused by the puppetesque aesthetic. One excellent example of this model of puppetry can be found in Roland Barthes's writings on Japanese *bunraku* puppet theatre, to which I now turn.

Barthes is interested in *bunraku* because of the tension resulting from the distance between the puppets, the puppeteers, and the chanter. An art dating back to the seventeenth century, contemporary *bunraku* utilizes puppets manipulated by three puppeteers. A chanter (*tayu*), accompanied by a samisen player, narrates the story and supplies all the character voices, from a small, separate side platform.[2] The division of character across so many elements has the potential to challenge the illusion of character as something that is unified and coherent, and yet the subject or character is not done away with entirely in this model. As Barthes (1970 [1982]: 55) suggests, *bunraku* is "a total spectacle but a divided one" in which the aesthetic is "not destroyed but somehow broken, striated" (1970 [1982]: 54). A kind of autonomy exists in the multiplicity; it is only a matter of understanding a character who is at once divided and complete, or striving towards completion.

This notion of a compiled character, made complete through pastiche, is crucial to the performance of *Or You Could Kiss Me*. In a promotional video for the show entitled "Choreographing Thought," Jones beautifully describes one way in which this style of puppetry affects the construction of character in the production. When the play's director/playwright Neil Bartlett asks the cast of *Or You Could Kiss Me* about their experience of manipulating a puppet in consultation with two other puppeteers, Jones answers:

> There's a sense in which ... the three people working together kind of mirror a real human being better than an "ordinary" actor onstage in that we always have several trains of thought working together in our heads. Some that are about our immediate physical environment, others ... we are so complex, really, in our minds, that we are able to have several [bodies at once]. And the fact that also our body is sort of "thinking" in a way. We've got an arm that's thinking and feet that are thinking. It's kind of a little bit more like a real human being than a real human being. Or certainly it highlights certain aspects of that multiplicity that is [in] us – the corporeal

nature of thought. So "what are you thinking?" is a huge question for a group of three puppeteers because there is an amazing congruence of thought and separation of thought.

(May 2010)

Jones's attention to the multiplicity of thought present in puppet performance echoes Barthes's notion of the striated-but-complete nature of *bunraku*. This connection is hardly surprising given Handspring's aesthetic, which is often inspired by *bunraku* techniques. Their puppets, designed and created by Kohler, almost always rely on more than one manipulator, who is often, to varying degrees, visible to the audience. And yet, as Jones's comments make clear, the presence of three manipulators (even visible ones) never demolishes the puppet-centric model that Astles associates with an early twentieth-century version of puppetry. On the contrary, skilled puppeteers can use their visibility to direct focus even more powerfully to the puppet. As American puppeteer Bruce Schwarz once wrote:

> I keep the mechanics out in the open because I don't want people to pay attention to them. … My theory is that watching me move the puppets with my hands will become dull after a little while. When it does, the puppets will be more interesting than I am.
>
> (cited in Tillis 1992: 132)

Jones's comments suggest a multiplicity *within* the character, not the breakdown of character as such. Watching the puppeteers in "Choreographing Thought" crawl awkwardly along the floor and contort their own bodies in order to invest their puppet with realistic movements, it is difficult to imagine a more puppet-centric model. All three puppeteers focus intently on the object they manipulate, and the audience is encouraged to do the same. What Jones is emphasizing here is not quite the split focus touted by Barthes but rather a rich character life that includes physicalized contradictions.

In *Or You Could Kiss Me*, these tensions and contradictions between the various iterations of each character form an essential part of the production. We see this in the opening moments of the show, when Old A and Old B enter for the first time. Encouraged by the assistants manipulating the puppets, A and B move hesitantly towards their older puppet selves, exchanging glances as they take up the controls of their respective selves. As Old B smokes his cigarette, Jones moves the arm holding the cigarette to the puppet's lips, inhaling a ragged breath. On the exhale, Jones blows the swirling smoke from the tip of the cigarette, a gesture that serves both to mimic breath (and therefore life) in Old B, but also to unite B and Old B as one character across time, while still maintaining the distinction between puppeteer and puppet, observer and observed, caretaker and patient. The *character* of B/Old B seems to exist somewhere between the two, in the smoke billowing from the cigarette.

This opening moment emphasizes the connection between the two versions of B. Elsewhere in the show, disjuncture is foregrounded. As Old B's failing memory takes center stage, it becomes more difficult to unite B's variously striated parts. In one flashback scene, for instance, Young A and Young B play squash, deftly wielded

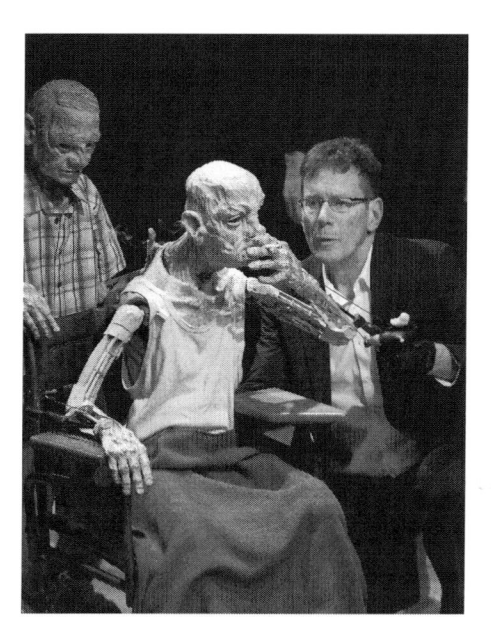

Figure 22.2 Basil Jones animates Old B. Photo: © Simon Annand/Arena PAL

by A and B with the help of the assistants. But when a janitor catches the two young men in the compromising position of what could have been their first kiss, A and B disagree on the order of events. A remembers B fighting back verbally, but B insists that he simply walked away. Old B and Old A, themselves puppets, mutely watch the debate from the sidelines, struggling to piece together these events that, for them, occurred over 60 years earlier. In the closing moments of the memory, Young B waves goodbye to his squash partner, who will become his life partner. The stage direction reads: "*B transfers the gesture of waving goodbye from Young B to Old B*" (Bartlett 2010: 64). The passing of the wave between three incarnations of the same character unites the past, present, and future of this single character, briefly collapsing time and space even as A and B struggle to get their stories straight. Did Young B confront the guard as A suggests? Or is B telling the truth when he says that he placidly walked away? Does the wave goodbye arise from a memory, or is it a performance on the part of B, retroactively attributed to his younger self and unknowingly adopted by his older one? A is similarly inscrutable in this scene; while reconstructing his side of the conversation, the stage directions tell us that "*A has had enough of this – he passes the line to an ASSISTANT to say*" (Bartlett 2010: 64). Character is not lost in this exchange; we continue to understand A and B as discrete individuals, but there is a degree of instability at the heart of these characters. Rather than bringing us closer to an essential core or a verifiable truth, these recollections and reminiscences raise more questions than they answer and remind the audience that such goals may be ultimately unattainable.

The simultaneous unity and fracture between these many pieces of the same character is even more apparent in another flashback sequence, in which Old B recalls his life before meeting A. At a party, Young B waits nervously to be approached by one of the other men at the end of the evening. The assistants, as the other partygoers, narrate an inner monologue – perhaps their own but perhaps Young B's: "come on come on come on somebody choose me" (Bartlett 2010: 54–55). Jones manipulates the Young B puppet alone, holding it aloft so that Jones's face is largely concealed behind its body. With its feet hovering off the floor and one arm dangling at its side, the puppet seems more like an object than ever before, especially when surrounded by the crush of non-puppet guests. Unlike the careful union of breath linking B and Young B in the opening scene, here the puppet seems more like a shield behind which B hides, protecting B from a memory that must be experienced by a surrogate rather than entered into. Thus when Jones utters the climactic line "Somebody please touch me" (Bartlett 2010: 55), it is unclear to whom the voice should be attributed. The voice seems to reach across all three iterations of the character (B, Old B, and Young B) as each one watches or participates in the unfolding action.

The elusiveness of subjectivity is not only apparent in the performance itself. Bartlett reveals in his program note that the script grew out of intensely personal stories shared between Kohler, Jones, and himself early in the collaboration, "encounters with the unspeakable" that he intertwined to create a story (Bartlett 2010: 10). The autobiographical nature of the creation process naturally leads to questions of veracity, as Bartlett acknowledges and cagily addresses:

> [S]everal people have asked me, as the project has developed, whether the characters A and B are "really" the performers whose initials they share in

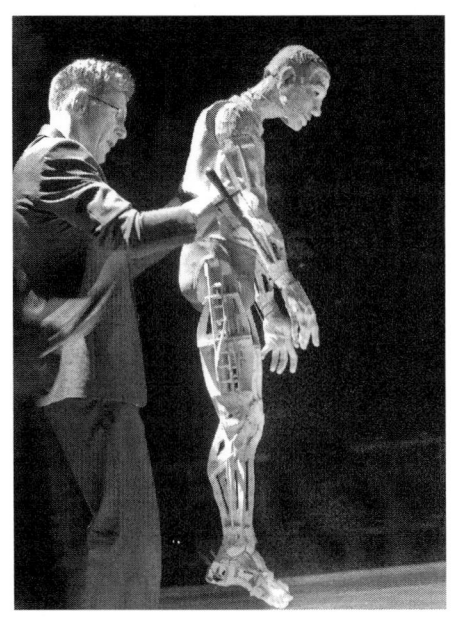

Figure 22.3 Basil Jones lifts Young B. Photo: © Simon Annand/Arena PAL

the cast list of the first production. I can only answer by saying that all the events of this play, both those which take place in the past and those which take place in the future, are true.

(Bartlett 2010: 10)

Bartlett swears authenticity while cleverly undercutting his own claim by insisting that the future events depicted are also "true." Bartlett's definition of truth is therefore called into question. Does he mean that all of these events happened, but not necessarily to Kohler and Jones? Or that the events depicted in the show, like losing a loved one or facing your own mortality, are predictable and inevitable?[3]

A photo included in the program further piques the audience's interest in the potentially autobiographical nature of the text: a full-page, black-and-white photograph reveals a young Kohler and Jones standing on a beach, with a caption that reads, "Adrian Kohler and Basil Jones in 1971. 'This did happen.'" The last three words echo the phrase "This is going to happen" (Bartlett 2010: 45), a line repeated by the MC character many times during the play. As the text weaves its way through the memories of Old A and Old B, often encountering contested recollections that destabilize the audience's understanding of what is true and what is false, this photo seems to imply that at least one component – the first meeting of Young A and Young B on a Cape Town beach – is true. But we shouldn't be so quick to accept its veracity; after all, when Old B rifles through his own box of photographs in search of a concrete memory, he comes up empty-handed. This reproduced photo is similarly elusive: it may provide a kernel of truth from within the layers of memory, fiction, fracture, and play, but it also draws attention to the gaps that remain. On another level, the photo is an object, not wholly unlike the puppets onstage. And like the puppets and bodies onstage, the photo re-extends the boundaries of character, incarnating not only a Young A and Young B, but also a Young Adrian and Young Basil. Put another way, the photograph slyly suggests that despite the contradictions, misdirections, and split focus plaguing the fictional characters in the play, a stable core exists in the real-life models of the story being told. "This did happen" – a statement of certainty. But this is all we get: a single photograph attesting to a connection back to something "real." There is a truth to these characters, the photograph seems to imply, but it is an essence that is not fully attainable.

Notes

1 Although Lehmann coins the term "postdramatic" to describe the avant-garde theatre to which he refers, his criteria align closely with Fuchs's description of postmodern theatre. For further discussion of the similarities between these two terms, see Karen Juerrs-Munby's "Introduction" to *Postdramatic Theatre* (Lehmann 1999 [2006]: 13–14).
2 It could be argued that the samisen player, who provides musical accompaniment to the performance in tandem with the chanter's narration, offers another potential site onto which the character may be grafted, but Barthes is less interested in this connection.
3 Bartlett is slightly more forthcoming about the inspirations for the piece in a platform event for the National Theatre. I am interested, however, in the questions that the play and its supplementary program notes raise, leaving aside information gathered by the audience after the performance has ended.

Works cited

Astles, C. (2010) "Puppetry Training for Contemporary Live Theatre," *Theatre, Dance and Performance Training* 1: 22–35.
Barthes, R. (1970) *Empire of Signs*, trans. R. Howard (1982). New York, NY: Hill and Wang.
Bartlett, N. (2010) *Or You Could Kiss Me*. London: Oberon Books.
Fuchs, E. (1996) *The Death of Character: Perspectives on Theater after Modernism*. Bloomington, IN: Indiana University Press.
Lehmann, H.-T. (1999) *Postdramatic Theatre*, trans. K. Juers-Munby (2006). London: Routledge.
May, D. (2010) "Choreographing Thought." London: The National Theatre, <http://www.nationaltheatre.org.uk/video/choreographing-thought> (accessed 6 July 2013).
Pavis, P. (1999) *Dictionary of the Theatre: Terms, Concepts, and Analysis*. Toronto, Ontario: University of Toronto Press.
Schwartz, B. (1983) "Working with Puppets: Bruce Schwartz, Theodora Skipitares, Julie Taymor," Interviews by C. Lee Janner, *Performing Arts Journal* 7(1): 103–116.
Tillis, S. (1992) *Toward an Aesthetic of the Puppet: Puppetry as a Theatrical Art*. Westport, CT: Greenwood Press.

23
Reading a Puppet Show
Understanding the Three-Dimensional Narrative
Robert Smythe

How do we read a puppet show? Are we looking at the same thing when we see Punch and Judy at a carnival or *War Horse* at Lincoln Center? What should we be thinking about? The design of the puppets? Whether the manipulation is lifelike? At present, while there is a growing body of knowledge about the history, techniques, and cultural uses and importance of the performing object, as exemplified by the excellent work of Blumenthal (2005), Bell (2008), and others, there are fewer guides to help in understanding, interpreting, or analyzing how performing objects and techniques communicate to audiences. Artists who tell stories and audiences who receive them need additional tools to interpret the content of performances created with puppets, a process of reading the relevant narrative features of nonverbal communication that the literary and film critic Seymour Chatman has called "reading out": "From the surface or manifestation level of reading, one works through to the deeper narrative level" (Chatman 1978: 41). In writing of film and literature, Chatman restricts reading out to the interpretation of a specific set of signs: words and film frames. Reading out from theatre performance is more complicated because of what Roland Barthes, the French literary theorist, philosopher, critic, and semiotician, has called its "real informational polyphony" and "density of signs" (Barthes 1964 [1972]: 262).

Sorting through material on stage, many modern-day theatre semioticians have been considerably influenced by the theories of the Prague School of the 1930s and 1940s, which analyzed the interrelationships of the communication systems at work in theatre, concluding that "theatre does not rely on a single system of signs, like the system of natural language for verbal narratives, but offers a polyphony of competing and overlapping signs that belong to many systems: verbal, paralinguistic, gestural, clothing, proxemic, color, and sound, and so forth" (Alter 1990: 93).[1] The Prague School's philosophy was perhaps best summed up by member Jiří Veltruský who wrote, "All that is on the stage is a sign" (Veltruský 1940 [1964]: 84).

The Prague School was heavily influenced by the Russian Formalists who preceded them[2] and for whom literary texts "resemble machines: they are the result of an intentional human activity in which a specific skill transforms raw material into a complex mechanism suitable for a particular purpose" (Steiner 1995: 18). Early film theorists used these ideas to recognize that movies could be seen as texts, in that cinema's mechanical arrangement of edited representations of reality (film clips) could result in the manipulation of time and space.

Performances with puppets are also edited representations of reality,[3] albeit in three dimensions. Given that puppetry and film have these similarities, existing modes of understanding the "reading out" of film, specifically narrative theory, may provide an additional methodology for analyzing puppet performance. Narrative theory provides a useful framework for analyzing puppetry because it posits that narratives are the creation of a single author – director, writer, or, perhaps, puppeteer – who alone controls the reader's access to the story.[4] Narrative theory's analysis of storytelling is related to semiotics, the study of how basic symbolic units combine to create language, whether verbal or visual, and therefore create meaning.[5] To understand how to read out puppetry, then, it is useful to understand how its language works.

Readers construct meaning by decoding the sequencing of basic units, each of which represents an idea or concept in the real world (McCloud 1994: 25–58). In written texts, the basic units are words, which are set into sequences of sentences. In cinema, the basic units are individual, visually composed frames of film set into sequences of clips. In comics, framed panels of hand-drawn art are sequenced in pages. In puppetry, the puppet itself is the basic semiotic unit of meaning (Jurkowski 1988: 55–61). Clearly, then, if a puppet is an abstracted, semiotic tool representing an idea in the real world, it is not the same as an actor interpreting a text or a design deriving from a text, because the puppet *is* the text. Moreover, like a word printed on a page, the puppet is infinitely reproducible and malleable: multiple copies of the same puppet are signifiers of the same meaning, one that can be continually shaped by context; yet, the puppet is unlike text – because puppets are also real objects, they can be destroyed and lost forever.

This idea of permanent loss can be seen as one of the central points in *Hermann*, a puppet show produced in 1982 by Theater im Wind of Braunschweig, Germany, written by Enno Podehl and performed by him and his wife Anne. *Hermann* gained notice for its exploration of the Holocaust using disturbing imagery of concentration camp victims, depicted by "a pile of false teeth and eyeglasses, perhaps the most haunting image of the death camps ... shovel[ed] into a box using a coal shovel" (Zucker 1987: 85). *Hermann* was performed throughout Europe, the United States, and Israel until the late 1990s and was described by Mitchell Zucker as being "among the best of the new, small, adult puppet theatre productions in Europe" (Zucker 1987: 79).[6] I would additionally suggest that examining *Hermann* through the lens of narrative theory allows us to view it as an exemplar of puppetry's potential for creating a unique narrative logic through its manipulation of space and time.

Enno Podehl's use of puppets as his basic units of meaning enable him to edit representations of reality, removing what is unnecessary for his story, in the way that literature does.[7] Podehl's puppets are spare evocations of the reality they represent: they are abstracted and painted in dull earth tones, with clothes to match. They consist of the barest minimum needed to suggest a human being: no real faces, no legs, no hands, only empty sleeves, through which the puppeteers sometimes slip their own hands. Podehl, like all puppeteers, creates three-dimensional edited representations of reality that cause the audience to fill in the blanks, creating meaning from any specifics they perceive, such as the bright red hair of a Roma woman, Johanna the Gypsy, the show's sole spot of bright color, startling and vividly memorable against the puppets' otherwise dull coloring. Details like this are the modifiers in the language of the puppet, and in the grammar of *Hermann*, Johanna's hair is a powerful adjective. Since Johanna is a performing object, Podehl can make her constantly twirl and play with her hair, alerting the reader that this information should be noticed, though its significance is not revealed until the end of the show. What appears to be a straightforward puppet show is, in fact, a precise arrangement of events designed to lead the audience on a journey of discovery and self-revelation.

Narrative theory posits that all storytelling embraces a duality: the plot of a story and how it is told are two separate things. Narrative theory carefully differentiates the "what" (events, characters, time and location, referred to as the *fabula*) from how the author reveals that information to the reader (the *sjužet*).[8,9] According to film theorist David Bordwell, authors create *sjužet* when they edit and arrange the events and facts of a story in a specific sequence of "cues prompting us to infer and assemble story information" (Bordwell 1985: 52). I suggest that, more than from the novelty and audacity of its images, the impact of *Hermann* comes from its organization, its *sjužet*.

When creators of narratives use words, film frames, puppets, or other edited representations of reality, they are not bound by the laws of physics, as film historian Rudolf Arnheim recognized in the early days of film theory:

> Time and space are continuous. Not so in film. The period of time that is being [represented] may be interrupted at any point. One scene may be immediately followed by another that takes place at a totally different time. And the continuity of space may be broken in the same manner.
>
> (Arnheim 1933 [1957]: 20–21)

When authors juxtapose scenes without either showing how a character got from one place to another or accounting for the passage of time, they force readers to use personal experience and creative thought to fill in that missing information.

Readers of a narrative are not idle spectators – they construct meaning through supposition and deduction, increasing their connection to the story because they have to fill in these missing bits. This happens at the beginning of *Hermann*, when Podehl manipulates a naked puppet of Hermann for seven minutes in a wordless, abstract ballet, causing the audience to question what is going on until Podehl looks directly at them and supplies the missing information with the play's first spoken line: "Hermann did his exercises every morning. Naked." The audience laughs: the joke contextualizes what they have been watching – it is their reward for trying to construct meaning out of abstraction. Podehl immediately switches the naked puppet for its fully clothed duplicate, a foreshortening of time that the audience can immediately understand: time has clearly passed in the narrative because Hermann is now dressed, though the events are simultaneous in the real world of the performance. The reader immediately accounts for the missing events: in order to get dressed in the morning, this character must have bought clothes and stored them in

Figure 23.1 Enno Podehl with Hermann performing his morning gymnastics.
Photo: © Sharon Baronofsky

his house. Bordwell notes that the reader's interpretation of the *sjužet* and subsequent creation of the accompanying *fabula* is automatic: "Presented with two narrative events, we look for causal, or spatial or temporal links. The imaginary construct we create, progressively and retroactively [is] the *fabula*" (Bordwell 1985: 49). A puppeteer's process of building a narrative, then, is one of shifting away from using such devices as sculpted puppets to simply reproduce the details of the real world and toward using them to make readers invest in constructing *fabula*. This process, because it draws on an audience's imagination and personal experience, is more powerful than presenting a straightforward, chronological telling of events.

Podehl appears to tell his story in just this manner. An old German man, Hermann, meets Johanna during the early days of World War II. She is taken away by the Nazis, who put her into a concentration camp, leaving Hermann to bring up her daughter, Rosa. Decades later, Podehl, a young college student, rents a room from Hermann. While he lives with him, the old man tells him about Johanna, and Podehl then decides to build a puppet show, with disastrous results, as we shall see. However, Podehl's *sjužet* intersperses these past events with his present-time telling of his story to an audience, compelling readers to make perceptive leaps of imagination and empathy to construct a *fabula* that includes those past events and Podehl's present-time storytelling.

Podehl's *sjužet* indicates that while the live aspect of the show makes it appear that all events are happening now, the story he is telling happened in the past, and no one, including him, can really know what happened then. To make this clear, Podehl establishes the relationship between the past and the present by mapping out a precise, three-dimensional *sjužet* where clearly defined stage spaces equal specific periods of time. Therefore, his location at any given moment in three-dimensional space indicates exactly where the narrative is in time.

Podehl carefully delineates three different kinds of time in his story by using these specific areas of his stage: an open space hung with black masking curtains and a waist-high table set in the center. The table is about 2 meters wide and less than 1 meter deep, covered in black fabric that hangs to the floor. On the floor in front of it sits a metal washbasin and a pitcher of water; stage left of it is a small table holding the lighting controls that the performers operate for themselves during the show. There is a meter or two of space on either side of the table and a few meters behind it, giving the performers, simply dressed in black, room to cross from one side to the other or to stand to directly address the audience. Each of Podehl's three main areas of the stage – downstage, the center table, and the space upstage of it – represent, respectively, a different period of time: the present, the past, and a place where time does not exist.

The downstage area represents *now*. It is the place where Podehl is not performing but rather shares the same space and breathes the same air as the audience. When he stands there, talking about the past from the perspective of the present, he and the audience are simply fellow humans and they, as a group, are included and implicated in his actions. He makes this clear from the beginning of the show as he stands and watches the audience enter the auditorium and sit, waiting for them so he can start his story.

The puppet table in the center of the stage represents the past, a fantasized period from the 1930s to 1944. Here Enno and Anne Podehl perform in full view of the audience as they operate the puppets in scenes from Hermann's life (as Podehl imagines it): Hermann performs morning exercises, talks to old woodstoves while hauling them in his cart, and meets Johanna. While the actions are sometimes fanciful (Hermann does a backflip to get into his cart; he floats into the air after suckling at Johanna's breast), the puppeteers are scrupulously precise in their manipulation; their focus never leaves the puppet stage, and there is never any indication that a world outside this invented one exists. The only exception is when Podehl himself leans or kneels on the stage table, sometimes sitting on it or even climbing up onto it.

When Podehl is physically on the puppet stage, he alerts readers that he is literally inserting himself into the story, supplying his point of view on details that he cannot know because he was not present. While describing how Hermann raised Johanna's daughter, Rosa, he uses the scarf that wrapped the baby Rosa to suggest Hermann's nurturing of her. Podehl wants us to understand exactly who is telling this part of the story; therefore, instead of clearing away the puppet of Hermann, he has it sit motionless and lifeless at his side, unneeded, while he uses the scarf as a swing, a folded fortune-telling cootie-catcher, and a blindfold to suggest how Hermann might have played with Rosa.[10] While telling this part of the story, Podehl supports himself with one foot on the stage and the other on the floor behind it, bridging the worlds of the author and his narrative. Podehl shows readers that they can literally gauge how much of the past he is inventing according to how much of the puppet stage he physically invades from his position just upstage of it.

This area behind the puppet table is a metaphorically infinite space where nothing exists until it is needed for the story. This area, similar to Harry Potter's Room of

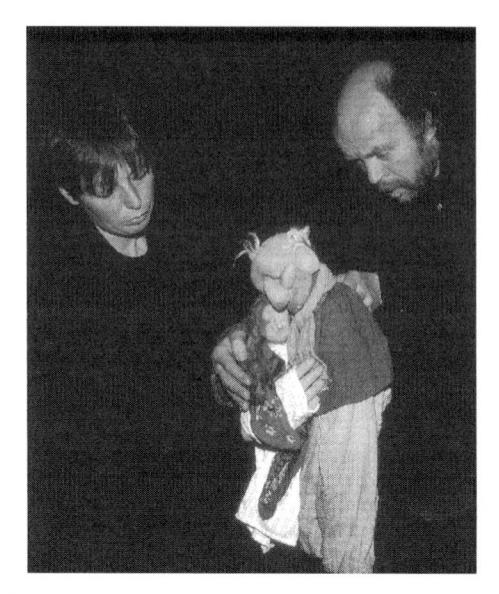

Figure 23.2 Anne Podehl, Rosa, Hermann, and Enno Podehl. Photo: © Sharon Baronofsky

Requirement or a blank page in a typewriter, is what I call "puppetland": a space that is found in most forms of puppetry but that the audience rarely sees. It is the place below the puppet booth's playboard and behind its curtains or behind the shadow screen just before or after the *wayang kulit* touches it. Everything necessary for the puppet show's narrative already exists in puppetland; it is the container for the puppeteer's prearranged *sjužet* in the form of the objects that will be used in the show. Puppetland's curtains and screens normally hide the puppeteer, but in *Hermann* he is indelibly visible behind the table, controlling the existence of the ideas represented by his objects.

The ability to literally tear characters from a story fully demonstrates the power of using editable representations of reality. After Hermann and Johanna meet and start to live together, the puppet of Johanna sleeps while Hermann strokes her cheek and exits, leaving Podehl to walk around to the front of the puppet table, his movement through three-dimensional space moving the narrative forward in time. Downstage, he tells the audience, "It was a time when people like Johanna – wayfarers, Gypsies, homeless people – were persecuted." He then pulls a black leather glove onto his hand, jumps onto the puppet table, and grabs the Johanna puppet by the throat, "now" bursting backward into the past. He carries the puppet upstage into the void of puppetland and lets it fall to the floor, her wooden head making a sickening thud as she disappears from view. In semiotic terms, Podehl's removal of a puppet from the narrative is akin to removing a word from a language, making Johanna's loss more than a symbolic death because, without the puppet, the ideas it represents can never be directly referenced again. This is made clear in the scenes that follow, while Hermann sits on the train platform through the progression of seasons, waiting for a sign of her. It is at this moment that the wagonloads of teeth and eyeglasses appear.

The power of these prosthetics comes from their indirect references to living people, a causal relation that has been set up by Podehl's *sjužet*. Shocking as these images are, Podehl's greatest achievement with *Hermann* is that his *sjužet* compels the reader to make a huge perceptive jump that vaults over the surface of these images and work to find personal meaning on a deeper narrative level. He does this with narrative logic.

Narrative logic is when the reader assumes that an event is "a consequence of another event, of a character trait, or of some general law" (Bordwell 1985: 51). The reader then constructs "causal networks that represent the relationships between the causes and consequences of events in a story" (Gerrig and Egidi 2003: 44). This form of logic enables readers to understand the chain of events that unfolds when Johanna, after having been taken by the black glove, eventually returns to Hermann's house, and he puts a real teakettle on the stove. While they wait for it to boil, there is a pounding on the door and the lights go out. In the pitch-dark auditorium, a flashlight isolates parts of the room: the closet, the teakettle boiling on the stove, Johanna sitting motionless at the table with no puppeteer to manipulate her. The flashlight stays on her face long enough to show a black-gloved hand grabbing her. The flashlight goes off. When the stage lights come back on, the Johanna puppet is gone and Hermann's kitchen table is turned over. In this sequence, specific signifiers (black gloves represent Nazis; Nazis searched houses) provide the necessary logical links between the events (the table was knocked over → they seized Johanna → they took her away).

While Podehl's choice of objects compels the reader to make connections between signifiers and their referents (black gloves = Nazis), his use of the stage space forces the audience to make causal connections between events within the show and to use them to evaluate the veracity of what they see – to realize they are watching fiction. For example, after the black glove grabs Johanna, Podehl stands upstage of the puppet table and says, "This much Hermann had always told me. But I could never get out of him where he actually was when it all happened." He then kneels on the puppet stage and picks up the fallen table to reveal the Hermann puppet lying inanimate behind it. Podehl quietly and deliberately looks the audience over, as if to ask, "Do you understand what I'm telling you?" Such causal connections between story events suggest that Hermann didn't try to save Johanna because he was a coward. However, the three-dimensional *sjužet* reveals that, by kneeling on the puppet stage, Podehl is again literally inserting himself into the story, clearly indicating that this indictment of Hermann's apparent cowardice is Podehl's version of what happened.

Podehl inveigles the audience to believe in Hermann's guilt because his ultimate goal is to have them join him in forgiving Hermann for his imagined trespasses. Through his arrangement of the story's events in space, Podehl indicates that he is an unreliable narrator and that the audience should not rush to judgment. His three-dimensional *sjužet* counteracts the "truthiness" of his story. Since Podehl plays himself in the show and is, therefore, simultaneously a sign and its own referent, he can be interpreted as reliable because he is what he appears to be; likewise, his puppet of Hermann is a sign for a real Hermann who once existed and who is also alive onstage, so his actions must refer to real events. However, as the *sjužet* makes clear,

Podehl's – and the audience's – indictments of Herman are actually self-criticisms, because Hermann only exists as a literal extension of Podehl, his creator.

When the fully dressed Hermann first appears, he is a small puppet with a blank face, a cheerful disposition, and Podehl's comically oversized human hand inserted through the puppet's sleeve. Hermann's first action after his morning exercises is to cook his breakfast. Podehl, manipulating Hermann, has him strike a real match to light a real gas stove, then crack open and fry a real egg, wiping his (Podehl's real) hand on his (Hermann's) scarf. Finally, when the puppet realizes that, without a mouth, he cannot eat what he has made, Podehl leans down to eat the egg from Hermann's fork, saying, "We had a special relationship." The audience responds with a laugh of recognition at this reference to the obvious point that, despite the disguise of the puppet, Podehl and Hermann are one and the same. Following this punch line, Podehl carefully removes the Hermann puppet and all the cooking paraphernalia from the stage, giving the audience time to read out from the surface level of the joke to its deeper narrative implications: Hermann exists in the "now" only because Podehl and the audience have constructed him.

Podehl's *sjužet* leads the audience to realize that *Hermann* is a carefully created narrative, designed to reveal something deeper than its brilliant tour de force of a puppet who lights matches. As Jorge Luis Borges said of *Citizen Kane*, which constructs its *sjužet* in a similar way:

> ... the theme (at once metaphysical and detective-fictional, at once psychological and allegorical) is the investigation of the secret soul of a man. ... Overwhelmingly, infinitely, [the author] ... shows fragments of the life of the man ... and invites us to combine them and to reconstruct them.
>
> (Borges 1941 [1980]: 12–13)

Figure 23.3 Enno Podehl and Hermann light a match. Photo: © Franz Kramer

As Podehl's *sjužet* continuously indicates, the man being examined here is not Hermann but Podehl, and the experience of what we learn, when we learn it, and how we learn it is what *Hermann* is ultimately about: a man who confronts his ignorance and learns to forgive.

Just after Podehl reveals the Hermann puppet hiding under the table, he stretches a clothesline across the stage, saying, "Then came the time that I was living with [Hermann] twenty years later. I was building a puppet and used a piece of hemp rope for its hair. I put it over the stove to let it dry and went upstairs to my room." As he relates this information he casually pulls a bit of frayed rope from his pocket and pins it to the clothesline. Though he does not describe it, the rope is bright red.

Until now, the only bright red in the muted palette of the entire narrative has been a signifier for Johanna; filling in details from this fragment, the reader understands that the puppet the young Podehl is building must be of her.[11] Similarly, the reader can make other causal relations from all the information presented to this point, leading to the understanding that, as a college student living with Hermann in post-war Germany, Podehl intended to make a show that would expose the cowardice of an old man who didn't stand up to the Nazis when they took away his Gypsy lover.

However, this plan is thwarted, as shown in horrifying detail when Podehl manipulates Hermann to again light a real match and accidently set Johanna's drying hair ablaze. As real fire consumes the dyed rope and leaps across the puppet stage, Podehl confirms what the audience infers from the real fire they see: "Everything was in flames. The table. The chairs. The ceiling. The walls." He strikes the Hermann puppet below the stage, saying: "We had to leave the house." Podehl, now alone on stage, surveys the puppet table: the fire has left nothing behind. He speaks what must be seen as truth because there are no edited representations of reality in sight: "'My God!' I thought, 'he's ninety years old! He'll never survive this.'" Clearing the stage of debris, he brings up the puppet of Hermann, letting it dangle from his hand as he continues: "In that moment Hermann stood very quiet, looked at me and said, 'All right now, [my house is] gone, the firemen will come, there is nothing more to do.'" Since Podehl is not manipulating his edited version of Hermann, Podehl is quoting the real person here, reminding us that Hermann is not Podehl's invention but a man who truly lived, loved and, apparently, forgave Podehl for the loss of his house. This moment of truth suggests the reason behind Podehl's narrative: his guilt as he replays and relives his actions in every performance.

The last few minutes of *Hermann* are as quietly intense as the black-gloved Nazi scenes are loud and powerful. The Hermann puppet surveys the ashes of his house and then asks Podehl to help him. Podehl lifts him off the stage table, ostensibly so Hermann can whisper in his ear, "Now I'd like a bath. My boy, will you wash me?" but actually to show the true relationship between them. The moment is shocking because it reminds us that the Hermann we thought we knew has always been just a small and insignificant puppet, a product of Podehl's imagination. Importantly, this is the last time Podehl speaks for him; Podehl removes him from sight to below the stage table and, like Johanna before him, Hermann disappears.

The scene that follows is so different in style that it can be read as a coda to what has come before. Podehl moves from his upstage narrator position in puppetland to the downstage position that indicates he is in the same physical and temporal space as the audience. Here he picks up the galvanized tub and pitcher of water from the floor in front of the table where they have been – and where we have forgotten about them – for the entire performance. He carries them upstage, his three-dimensional map of time indicating that these present-time articles play a role in the past and that, once again, he is acting as the audience's proxy. Reaching below the stage, he lifts the puppet of the naked Hermann out of puppetland and places the tiny, naked, vulnerable puppet into the tub. He pours water over him while a recording of Hermann's (Podehl's) voice is heard: a two-minute nonsensical monologue relating how he confounded the insurance company that investigated the fire. While this plays, Podehl ritualistically dips a sponge into the water and squeezes it over the inanimate Hermann, all the while watching the audience as he did before, again inviting them to join him in his treatment of Hermann. As the story ends, Podehl squeezes the sponge one last time and simply says, "Hermann." The lights fade to black.

This coda separates the events of the past from the present. Everything Podehl has presented to that point could have been part of the puppet show he had been planning as the college student who blamed Hermann (and his generation) for being weak. Had the house not burned down (and who is at fault is not entirely clear), Podehl would have had his puppets finished and could have produced a show in 1964. But, instead, he waited 18 years, until 1982, to create *Hermann*.

Throughout his show, Podehl has taught his audience that the narrative derives from his relationship to it as the author of the material. The coda's shift in style and tone, then, signal to the reader that Podehl's attitude toward his subject has changed: for the first time Podehl lets Hermann speak for himself. This is a crucial moment, and there is a causal link between it and Hermann's act of forgiving Podehl for burning down the house. It is possible to deduce that this absolution changed Podehl's mind in regards to creating a show about Hermann's failure to save Johanna because, 18 years later, Podehl bathes Hermann in a ritual of forgiveness. We, like Podehl, realize that we were not present during the events in Hermann's life and, therefore, cannot judge him. Ultimately, then, *Hermann* is the story of Podehl's journey toward forgiveness, a journey he has crafted as a narrative assembled to compel the reader to not only judge him, but also to judge themselves, to ask what they would do when a knock on the door comes in the middle of the night. It is an invitation to join him as he washes away his own lack of understanding.

The genius of *Hermann* is that Podehl's use of signs and narrative structure makes the audience supply information from their lives and experiences to fill in the gaps in the "fabula": they become complicit in the telling of the story, in the blaming of its characters, and in its celebration of the human capacity for forgiveness. Podehl's artistic aims are to create a specific relationship with his audience, to start a dialogue with them after they see the work. He says in an interview,

> I don't know how I would have reacted at that moment in history if I were as socially unaware of what was taking place as Hermann. So, this is a question for me, and I hope for you too. I know there are many people who reacted like Hermann during the war. I ask you why and you ask me why.

And I hope if we talk about it together, something will happen and we will both become more responsible

(Zucker 1987: 83).

Narrative theory, with its emphasis on structure, is a useful tool for the analysis of puppetry performance because it recognizes that puppets, edited representations of reality, enable authors to manipulate space and time. Additionally, because puppets limit the quantity of sign systems in a performance, they give authors great control over the referents available to an audience, and, therefore, to its meaning. Most importantly, using narrative theory to delineate a three-dimensional *sjužet* in a puppet show creates the possibility of using time as a referent system on stage. Analyzing puppet shows with this conceptual framework can help us to explore the essence of puppetry, providing an understanding of its relationship to other systems of performance analysis.

Notes

1. Analysis of theatrical signs began in the 1930s, when a former member of the Russian Formalists, Petr Bogatyrev, charted the basics of theatrical semiotics (Elam 2002: 7).
2. "The close genealogical link between Russian Formalism and the Prague School is undeniable. The two not only had common members (Bogatyrev and Jakobson), but the Prague group consciously named themselves after the Moscow branch of the Formal school – the Moscow Linguistic Circle. Also, several leading Formalists (Tomashevsky, Tynyanov, and Vinokur) delivered in the 1920s lectures at the Prague Circle, and thus familiarized Czech scholars with the results of their research" (Steiner 1995: 14–15).
3. While human actors and puppets are both signs that refer to outside characters and events, the puppet is a product of specific choices as to what to include and exclude, therefore controlling an audience's access to referents by reducing the number of signs in use. According to Veltruský (1940 [1964]: 84–85), "The actor's body, on the other hand, enters into the dramatic situation with all of its properties. A living human being can understandably not take off some of them and keep on only those he needs for the given situation." For instance, even as he imitates a wild animal, the actor playing the tiger in Rajiv Joseph's *Bengal Tiger at the Baghdad Zoo* necessarily references his existence as a human, including the fact that he is alive and, therefore, subject to the laws of time and space.
4. Chatman (1978: 41) uses the term "reader" to include "not only readers in their armchairs, but also audiences at movie houses, ballets, puppet shows, and so on." Use of the term throughout supposes such inclusion.
5. Most importantly, for narrative theory, through the work of Barthes.
6. *Hermann* was performed in German and simultaneously orally interpreted into the language of the country where it was performed. Quotations from the production used here are from the English translation used in the September 18, 1992, performance at the Joseph Papp Public Theater in New York for the Henson International Festival of Puppet Theater.
7. Chatman (1978: 30) assesses verbal narratives as being "imprecise" in their representations of the real world because they "may elect not to present some visual aspect, say, [of] a character's clothes. It remains totally *unbestimmt* [(unstated, undetermined)] about them, or describes them in a general way: 'He was dressed in street clothes.'" At the same time, cinema "cannot 'say,' simply, 'A man came into the room.' He must be dressed in a certain way. In other words, clothing, *unbestimmt* in verbal narrative, must be *bestimmt* in a film." Puppetry straddles both modes of representation: certain things can simply be witnessed, as in cinema or theatre; they can also be *unbestimmt* (gender, features, etc.) because they can be edited from a puppet; a puppet can even have non-clothing, indistinguishable from its being.

8 Chatman delineates "resolved plots" that unravel events and "revealed plots" that tend to be "strongly character-oriented": where the:

> ... function of the [sjužet] is not to answer [the question of what happened] nor even to pose it. Early on we gather that things will stay pretty much the same. It is not that events are resolved (happily or tragically), but rather that a state of affairs is revealed.
> (Chatman 1978: 48)

9 The terms *fabula* and *sjužet* were first used in the 1920s: "Various technical terms were introduced and used by [early Russian Formalists Viktor] Šklovskij, [Boris] Ejchenbaum, [Jurij] Tynjanov, and others in order to distinguish the main constructive factors in a literary work" (Fokkema and Ibsch 1978: 18–19).

> Disjunction was the key logical principle by which mechanistic Formalism organized its basic notions. This principle split art decisively from non-art and expressed their mutual exclusivity in terms of polar opposition. The now famous pair, story and plot (fabula and sjuzhet [sic]) is an application of this binarism to artistic prose. Story is a sequence of events unfolding as it would in reality, according to temporal succession and causality. This series serves the writer as a pretext for the plot construction, the liberation of events from their quotidian context and their teleological distribution within the text. The devices of repetition, parallelism, gradation and retardation scramble the natural order of happenings in literature and render its form artistic. The events depicted are relegated to an ancillary position and deprived of any emotional, cognitive, or social significance. Their only value rests in how they contribute to the technique of the work itself.
> (Steiner 1995: 18).

10 Veltruský states that it is possible for the human actor to have action that falls to the "zero" level (1940 [1964]: 86). Keir Elam describes an actor's role in this state as "analogous to that of the prop" (2002: 14). This is, of course, completely different for a puppet, where the inaction or stillness that results from the loss of the manipulator does not change its role in the play but, instead, can suggest that time has stood still for that character. Inactivity for the puppet, then, becomes a sign referring to time rather than a transformation from one state to another.

11 Studies of psychological cognition support the idea that authors can rely on readers' memory structures to fill in details. "To understand narrative, readers retrieve information from memory. The author can provide the fragments that are critical to her story, with the strong expectation that readers will fill in the rest" (Gerrig and Egidi 2003: 40).

Works cited

Alter, J. (1990) *A Sociosemiotic Theory of Theatre*. Philadelphia, PA: University of Pennsylvania Press.

Arnheim, R. (1933; 2nd edn 1957) *Film as Art*, trans. L. M. Sieveking, I. F. D. Morrow, and R. Arnheim (1933; 1957). Berkeley, CA: University of California Press.

Barthes, R. (1964) "Literature and Signification: Answers to a Questionnaire in *Tel Quel*," in *Critical Essays*, trans. R. Howard (1972). Evanston, IL: Northwestern University Press.

Bell, J. (2008) *American Puppet Modernism: Essays on the Material World in Performance*. New York, NY: Palgrave Macmillan.

Blumenthal, E. (2005) *Puppetry: A World History*. New York, NY: Harry N. Abrams.

Bordwell, D. (1971) "Citizen Kane," *Film Comment* 7: 38–47.

——(1985) *Narration in the Fiction Film*. Madison, WI: University of Wisconsin Press.

Borges, J. L. (1941) "An Overwhelming Film," trans. G. Waldman and R. Christ (1980), *October* 15: 12–14.

Chatman, S. B. (1978) *Story and Discourse: Narrative Structure in Fiction and Film*. Ithaca, NY: Cornell University Press.

Elam, K. (2002) *The Semiotics of Theatre and Drama*, 2nd edn. London: Routledge.

Fokkema, D. W. and Ibsch, E. (1978) *Theories of Literature in the Twentieth Century: Structuralism, Marxism, Aesthetics of Reception, Semiotics*. New York, NY: St. Martin's Press.

Gerrig, R. J. and Egidi, G. (2003) "Cognitive Psychological Foundations of Narrative Experiences," in D. Herman (ed.) *Narrative Theory and the Cognitive Sciences*. Stanford, CA: CSLI Publications.

Jurkowski, H. (1988) "The Sign Systems of Puppetry," in P. Francis (ed.), *Aspects of Puppet Theatre: A Collection of Essays*. London: Puppet Centre Trust.

McCloud, S. (1994) *Understanding Comics: The Invisible Art*. New York, NY: Kitchen Sink Press/Harper Perennial.

Podehl, E. (1992) *Hermann*, performed by Enno and Anne Podehl at the Joseph Papp Public Theater, New York, September (New York: The Jim Henson Foundation, 2010), DVD.

Steiner, P. (1995) "Russian Formalism," in R. Seldan (ed.) *The Cambridge History of Literary Criticism, Vol. 8: From Formalism to Poststructuralism*. Cambridge, MA: Cambridge University Press.

Veltruský, J. (1940) "Man and Object in the Theater," reprinted in P. L. Garvin (ed. and trans.) (1964). *A Prague School Reader on Esthetics, Literary Structure and Style*. Washington, DC: Georgetown University Press.

Zucker, M. (1987) "Hermann: The Puppet Anti-Hero," *The Drama Review: TDR* 31(2): 79–87.

24
Notes on New Model Theatres
Mark J. Sussman

La Petite Geante, the giant girl marionette of the Royal de Luxe troupe from Nantes, France, strides into a park or a street in Guadalajara, Liverpool, or Berlin. Suspended from a motorized crane and manipulated by a crowd of red-liveried engineers with ropes, guy-lines, and pulleys – attendants who seem Lilliputian next to her – she takes a nap, receives a shower from the equally gigantic Sultan's Elephant, takes a boat ride, and meets a mysterious undersea diver who emerges from a local river or canal. The pageant of giant puppets and tiny human operators is surrounded by an audience that forms in the street and follows the troupe, their daily routine interrupted. Huge, calm, and silent despite all the human activity of tending to the puppets, these urban theatrical interventions take four or five days to perform.[1]

The work of Royal de Luxe is manifestly gigantic, dwarfing the surrounding buildings, streetlamps, and bridges. It is also miniature. The human performers in antiquated uniforms, who operate the machinery, animating the giant marionettes on their stroll through the city, appear to be on the scale of toys. They work as a team of pilots, builders, circus roustabouts, and parade marshals. The girl, the elephant, and the diver move slowly, silently, and expressively, the focus of the audience's attention. The puppets' actions are mundane, and yet they completely transform the surrounding street, rendering it as a kind of model, the made-up landscape of an oversized child's imagination. Toys and players have switched positions, an effect, I think, of what we might come to think of as a contemporary form of model theatre, incorporating, among other things, a collision of material and imaginary scales and a liberatory reversal of the ways in which adults and children play.

The term "model theatre" appears within the context of some puppetry literature as roughly synonymous with toy theatre, "model" signaling a relation of the miniature or toy proscenium stage to adult-scale theatre architecture and scenography that is analogous to the relation between a child's model airplane, train, or dollhouse and the real thing in the adult world.[2] Here, however, I propose to broaden our understanding of "model" beyond the largely two-dimensional paper landscape of the toy theatre stage and to emphasize the performer's attitude of total absorption while demonstrating, inhabiting, or animating models in a three-dimensional field, borrowing elements from puppetry, dance, performance, and installation art. Furthermore, the proliferation of cheap, readily available image capture-and-control technologies affords new means of projecting, magnifying, and animating models, manipulating their scale in real time.

Writing of the artist Sarah Sze's large-scale installations incorporating thousands of banal mass-produced products arranged in precise abstract compositions that evoke fantastic landscapes, the critic Jeffrey Kastner asks, "Does Sze's work evoke the grandeur of the immense or the hidden life of the miniature? Does her practice conjure the daydream of the infinite or the infinitesimal?" (cited in Norden 2007: 9). Gazing at her works arrayed across the floors, walls, and ceiling of a Chelsea gallery, one is immediately absorbed by the repetitions and patterns formed by everyday objects. Scale collapses and becomes deeply alien. Are these landscapes monumental sculptures, microscopic performance landscapes, or somehow both?[3] These questions come to mind in response to certain contemporary object-based performances that work, like Sze's installations and Royal de Luxe's performance interventions, with multiple scales and, in particular, with startling appearances of the miniature or the gigantic.

A further set of questions emerges concerning models, adults, and children: how might the image of the adult performer playing with puppets, models, or toys – situations in which multiple scales collide – suggest a new way of thinking about children and their habits of play?

Performers working with objects and puppets regularly appear across a range of public spaces, from political demonstrations to museums, from off-festival cabarets to Olympics opening ceremonies, from urban interventions to rural pageantry. Puppetry is being taken increasingly seriously, embodying adult-oriented stories, themes, and images, and moving across the fields of the performing, visual, and projected arts.[4] And yet, the question of whether puppetry is inherently an art form for children – and whether it is perceived as such by the critical and popular press, as well as by festival curators and season presenters – persists. The eternally recurring discovery of serious puppetry for adults proclaims that performances using puppets are, amazingly, not exclusively for children.[5] Why, we might ask, does this discovery recur? And is it somehow engaged in the reinscription of a normative sense of puppetry as a children's art form, not to mention the reinforcement of a Western bourgeois separation of the world of the child from that of the adult, a separation that Walter Benjamin pondered in his essays on children's toys and play?

I propose three admittedly sketchy scenarios: one, in which a hypothetical critic has genuinely never considered puppets as serious business beyond the realm of entertainment aimed exclusively at children or family audiences; two, an instrumental scenario in which said critic has been assigned an adult-oriented show or festival and is faced with commenting on, in the examples discussed below, either a performance staged on and around Rimini Protokoll's miniature Swiss landscape and model-train layout or Hotel Modern's cinematic staging of letters written by soldiers from a World War I battlefield, animated for live cameras on model landscapes. This critic imagines a public that simply connects puppets, models, and toys to children and then proceeds to enlighten that imagined naïve public with the discovery that, in fact, puppets have a long history of social commentary, taboo speech, and subversive gesture. This rhetoric of discovering serious puppetry for adults seems somehow by negation to strengthen and reinforce the notion of puppetry as inherently for children in the first place. And maybe it is, in a third possible scenario, which affirms that, despite their serious subject matter or nonlinear narrative construction, performances grounded in radical collisions of scale may well belong to the realm of children. Perhaps contemporary model theatre, instead of reinforcing the commodified or disempowered subject position of childhood in a liberal economic marketplace, can, in fact, reimagine how we conceive of children (and, by extension, adults) in the first place – as experts in play with scale.

Children, according to Walter Benjamin, "form their world of things by themselves, a small world in the large one ... full of the most incomparable objects that capture the attention of children who use them," especially "garbage and junk left over from building, gardening, housework, sewing, or carpentry" (cited in Zipes 2003: 9). Roland Barthes calls the child who engages in this world-forming play a "demiurge," a creator using objects that can instantly change what they are, rather than merely a "user" of an overly determined plastic toy (Barthes 1957 [1984]: 54). Model theatre combines this juvenile tendency towards improvisatory bricolage with the realm of stories that range from the mythic to the banal and from the ridiculous to the documentary, given its powerful ability to show big ideas within the limits of the tiny proscenium frame or the tabletop landscape.

Benjamin considered the value of early Soviet revolutionary children's theatre: "Everything is turned upside down, and just as master served slave during the Roman Saturnalia, so during the performance, children stand on stage and teach and educate their attentive educators" (Benjamin 1999d: 205). Why "revolutionary"? Children here are conceived as always potential revolutionary subjects not yet formed by bourgeois civilization, in love with movement, action, and mimetic play – which again raises for us the question of what might be at stake when adults build models, play with toy theatres, and animate miniature landscapes.

New model theatres

Architects, urban planners, military officers, stage designers, and film special-effects artists all play, in some form, with models, animating them with and for serious, even deadly, intentions and effects. In bridging the crafts associated with puppetry, architecture, and cinema, the following examples of model theatre bring together the handmade and the technological, the miniature built environment, and the absorbed, methodical performance of the manipulator of objects.

In a time when the miniature is increasingly associated with technology and when theatre magic is becoming ever more invisible, portable, and cheap, the handmade model is technologically enlarged and reframed in two recent stage productions juxtaposing tabletop landscapes, live manipulation of miniature figures and objects, and video projection. The German-Swiss company Rimini Protokoll and Rotterdam-based Hotel Modern illustrate closely related approaches that carefully choreograph a collision of gigantic and miniature architectural scales onstage and, implicitly, an inversion of typically adult and children's forms of play. These performances merge documentary and imaginary elements to reanimate events of the historical past, staged and manipulated with a child's method of play before the eyes of an audience.

Rimini Protokoll, a three-member company founded in 2000, has pioneered a "theatre of experts." Not exactly site-specific, their work is more personnel-specific, which is to say that it uses nonprofessional performers who are experts in some field. Director Stefan Kaegi shapes the community's message into theatrical material using the talents of what he calls "specialists" of daily life or "experts of the everyday" (Mumford and Garde 2012: 26). In the case of Mnemopark, shown at Montréal's Festival TransAmériques in 2007, the performers were model-train enthusiasts – Swiss "retirees who love model trains," according to the program. A professional actress functioned as MC, introducing and framing each performer's story.

An extraordinary portrait of modern-day Switzerland emerges in this show, staged on and around a large working model-train layout complete with miniature mountains, lakes, rural depots, and farmland, organized on rows of waist-high tables around the stage. Mounted on the toy locomotive is a wireless video camera, so the train's-eye view appears on a large screen at the back of the stage. As the miniature landscape rushes past, simultaneously tiny and huge, the performers narrate stories of growing up in Switzerland, building a portrait of the nation out of memories and fragments, including personal "flashbacks" in which each performer in turn jumps in front of a green screen backdrop at the side of the stage, allowing a second camera's signal to mix their live image into the miniature memory landscapes. Thanks to the magic of the green screen, which affords the possibility of the miniature landscape becoming background for human-scale performers in the foreground, one man jumps into an airplane and flies into the sky. Another rides atop a train car.

In these moments of narrative layering, simultaneous stages exist side by side: the blank space of the green screen is total cinematic artifice, and the miniature-train landscape is tabletop toy theatre in three dimensions. They mix in real time, thanks to the trick of crude, onstage video compositing, merging the performer's rough,

Figure 24.1 Mnemopark: A Model Train World, Rimini Protokoll (2005): Director: Stefan Kaegi. Photo: © Lex Vögtli

task-based choreography with the complex background landscapes rushing past. Other places and times are evoked, as well. As in the classical puppet theatre of *bunraku*, the presence of the character has been exploded in the division of functions. Music, language, movement, and the expression of emotion have been divided, only to be put back together again before our eyes in the merging of object-based tasks. Here, the technology of the proscenium is enriched by the addition of cameras, screens, and projectors, not to mention the live score provided by the Foley artist with his sound effects table. These older adults each take their turns, animating and being animated inside the model, in a visual dramaturgy of constantly shifting scale.

An imaginary Switzerland emerges here, a model in both senses of the term, constructed with the clean, lifeless beauty of the static landscapes complete with snowy mountains, happy cows, green rolling hills, and picturesque villages. The performers, both detached storytellers and giddy time travelers, imply that the Swiss are living in something like a model nation, preserved in its pre-war state. Meanwhile, the pleasure the audience takes in their serious play continues when, after the curtain call, we are invited onto the stage to observe the switches, tracks, bells, and whistles at close range with the artists: railway engineers, tour guides, and new friends. We share the performers' experience of absorption into and by the model, a mechanical landscape both vast and tiny, which surrounds us.

Hotel Modern is a company of two trained actresses and an architectural model-maker, accompanied by a sound designer mixing live and prerecorded sound effects. Since their founding they have evolved a performing style grounded in the animation of models, sometimes accompanied by language, sometimes not.

In *The Great War*, three silent performers construct scenes from the trenches of World War I, accompanied by recordings of soldiers' letters from the battlefield. The stage consists of a series of tabletop film sets, with small cameras transmitting live to an upstage screen. Cameras are mounted in and around miniature landscapes, at times positioned on model trains, at times handheld. We hear the words of one soldier's diaries and letters home, as the camera tracks his unsteady footsteps across the ground, first under shelling, later emerging into a destroyed landscape of flame, smoke, and corpses. In a series of shaky, subjective tracking shots, the intimacy is heightened by synchronized live sound effects: shells exploding in the distance and the soft impact of footsteps on soil in the auditory foreground. As audience members, we split our focus from the narrative on the screen above to the elaborate situation of the live filmmakers, working on tables of earth with torches and air compressors to make fire and shell bursts, not to mention the small, fragile human figures. The object manipulators – graceful, calm, and totally absorbed – focus on the tasks at hand, achieving the complex choreography of objects, cameras, and special effects, simulating warfare in miniature and blowing it up to the gigantic proportions of cinema.

The Great War and *Mnemopark* each illustrate how precise, deliberate play with models and the resulting fusions of scale resonate with the techniques of children's play. Although neither group describes their work as puppetry, there is a deep connection to the methods, techniques, and attitudes of puppeteers – namely, a deliberate combination of small-scale elements, tabletop dramaturgy, and conscious

Figure 24.2 The Great War, Hotel Modern (2001): created and performed by Herman Helle and Pauline Kalker (pictured) and Arlène Hoornweg. Photo: © Joost van den Broek

manipulation of a simultaneous multiplicity of scales. The matrix of camera, live projection, model landscape, and tiny objects renders the miniature world instantly gigantic and positions the performer both as a manipulator of toys and as a manipulated object within an animated stage environment. This visual rhetoric of live cinema, in which the projected image shifts quickly from close-up to long shot and back, combined with the live choreography of puppet theatre, creates a productive tension, neatly suited to demonstrating the burdens of history and the careful making and unmaking of the world.

Model theatre, then, may be considered a genre at the intersection of puppetry and cinema, child and adult play, and the miniature and the larger-than-life.[6] Questions regarding the experience of scale remain to be investigated: what compressed or expanded dynamics of presence are created when performance takes place on multiple scales at once? And how might the notion of model theatre allow for a more careful consideration of the implication of adults playing with toys? The model affords a child's palpable sense of agency and demonstrates the wielding of power, if temporary or imagined, over concrete dramatic events. The ability to invert the loss of control we experience in contemporary life may be part of what's at stake in the rediscovery of model theatre. Given the acceptance of the seriousness of the puppetry arts, it seems worthwhile to reconsider the trope of the child's privileged affinity for playing with toys.

On grown-ups and toys

The history of toys, at least in their early modern incarnation in the West, is mirrored in the experience of the individual child's growing up. "A history of the evolution of children's toys can therefore hardly be written," writes Karl Gröber in the wistfully titled *Children's Toys of Bygone Days*, "since with each child there begins afresh the same cycle of the play instinct, if we may so call that instinct to imitate which forces its way to expression in the heart of every human being" (Gröber 1928: 1). A curious way to begin a lavishly illustrated history of toys from antiquity to the nineteenth century (reviewed by Benjamin in 1928), this passage signals Gröber's insistence that, although toys belong to a history of material culture created by adults for children, the activity of play, particularly the mimetic impulse to copy the world of adults, belongs to the world of children, no matter how detailed or naturalistic, hand- or machine-made toys become. "The fantasy of a grown-up, be it ever so winged," he writes, "can never recover the wealth of visions which course past the heart of every child when it is absorbed in its playthings, undisturbed, oblivious of its surroundings" (Gröber 1928: 1). This quality of absorption in play belongs, of course, to the puppeteer as well as to the performer visibly animating a model on a tabletop.

Model theatre also stages the comparatively ancient, some say primitive, impulse that Benjamin called "the mimetic faculty," that ability, particularly strong in children, not only to copy the actions, emotions, and characteristics of adults but also to recognize "non-sensuous" correspondences between nature and culture. "The child plays at being not only a shopkeeper or teacher," he writes, "but also a windmill and a train. Of what use to him is this schooling of his mimetic faculty?" (Benjamin 1999c: 720). Benjamin refers to this faculty as a "gift" for producing similarities and recognizing them. Furthermore, this gift has become increasingly fragile in proportion to modernity's elimination of "magical correspondences and analogies that were familiar to ancient peoples" (Benjamin 1999c: 721). The mimetic faculty resides in our language – perhaps the clearest example of those non-sensuous kinds of correspondences that children take for granted when playing with objects or those specially designed objects that adults call toys.

In the vocabulary of model theatre, the performers are visible, absorbed in their tasks. Their presence is both masked and heightened by the focus required to make the inanimate objects expressive and to conjure a suspension of disbelief, which – in puppet theatre of all kinds – combines the audience's willingness to grant liveness to the inanimate object despite, or thanks to, the visible evidence of the concrete gestures of the puppeteer. If all goes well, the audience believes in the truth of the act and endows the proceedings with a sense of magic and the illusion of illusion. Belief and artifice, truth and faking, reality and magic nervously coexist. The spectator, as Barthes said famously of the art of professional wrestling, "does not wish for the actual suffering of the contestant; he only enjoys the perfection of an iconography" (Barthes 1957 [1984]: 20).

The "perfection of an iconography" brings to mind the freeze-frame of the tableau, in the sense meant by Hans-Thies Lehmann when he uses this painterly term to refer to narrative progression in the postdramatic theatre. "As is well known," he writes, "it is generally painters who speak of states, the states of images in the process of creation, states in which the dynamics of image creation are crystallizing and in which the process of the painting that has become invisible to the viewer is being stored. Effectively, the category appropriate to the new theatre is not action but states" (Lehmann 1999 [2006]: 68). "Scenically dynamic formations" here suggest a model theatre that proceeds by a sequence of tableaux rather than primarily through unbroken narrative flow borne by language and features the live performer as supporter, manipulator, narrator, and animator of the stage picture. In the cases of *The Great War* and *Mnemopark*, the video image is supplemented by the performers' intensely absorbing tasks of animating the model and playing with miniatures, processes that are, in most cinema experiences, kept offscreen.

Benjamin viewed the relationship between toys as a particular category of commodity objects and play as a formative practice for children. For it is not in the toy that play exists, but in the playing – improvisation and imitation; not in mimicry of the world of adults, but in the completion of tasks where the toy becomes a necessary accessory. Toys are not only commodities, but also the artifacts that we use to construct the world on a small scale (Benjamin 1999a: 115–116). *Mnemopark* and *The Great War* demonstrate a method of calm, intentional, and focused remembering and remaking of the world from ordinary objects and materials in which dramatic action is produced by the nervous tension between the big screen and the miniature landscape. In both of these pieces, the performers are located midway between the scale of the film and the scale of the toy, simultaneously dwarfed and gigantic.

Benjamin wrote a series of meditations on toys and an essay on the politics of children's theatre in the years 1928–1929, a period during which he published newspaper and magazine articles, short, aphoristic "thought figures" (the German word is *Denkbild*), and gave radio lectures on diverse topics. This was at the height of his short-lived career as a public intellectual in Germany. Writing reviews of toy histories and exhibitions in Berlin, as well as specifically on the topic of proletarian children's theatre, Benjamin is careful to strategically emphasize the radical otherness of the world of the child.

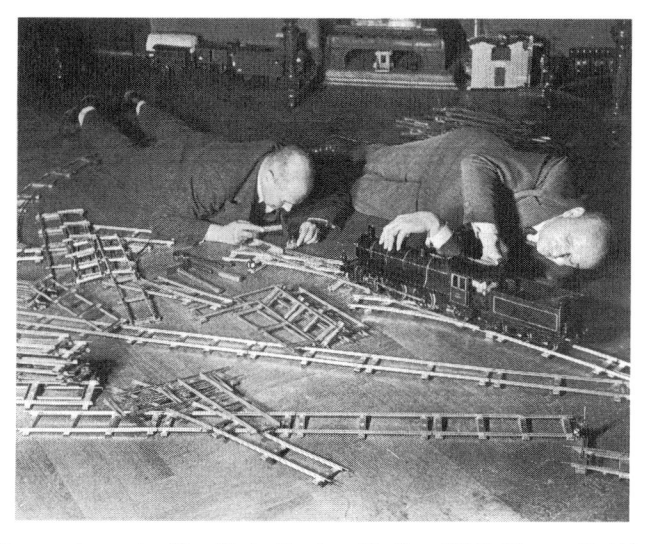

Figure 24.3 Fixing tracks at the Toy Train Society (Berlin, 1931). Photo: © Alfred Eisenstaedt/ Time & Life Pictures/Getty Images

"Surrounded by a world of giants," he writes, "children use play to create a world appropriate to their size." Fair enough. But then comes the more cunning dialectical insight: "But the adult, who finds himself threatened by the real world and can find no escape, removes its sting by playing with its image in reduced form." Here, Benjamin accounts for the adult's "growing interest in children's games and children's books since the end of the war" (1999b: 100–101). The adult is not simply regressing to childhood but rather making light of a life grown unbearable. And this is only 1928 – the Great War ten years in the past, the war of the *Mnemopark* performers' generation not quite yet on the horizon.

Puppet masters, puppet slaves

But what is a child, anyway? Writing on the figure of the child in the works of Jean-François Lyotard, Avital Ronell reminds us that the child "constitutes a security risk for the house of philosophy" (Ronell 2007: 140), by which I understand that the child stands in for a defenseless subject, one that has not yet learned to play by the rules of philosophy, law, or reason. She quotes Lyotard, asking: "What shall we call human in humans, the initial misery of their childhood, or their capacity to acquire a 'second' nature, which, thanks to language, makes them fit to share in communal life, adult consciousness and reason?" (cited in Ronell 2007: 141–142). The child's performance of mimetic dances, playing with and becoming objects, belongs then to a "first" nature, before language. The adult, absorbed in and by objects and collapsing an everyday sense of worldly scale, recovers some aspect of the child's play, mobilizing the muscle memories of childhood, telling stories of war and cultural history, or turning entire city streets into accumulations of building blocks.

"By childhood," Ronell continues in her reading of Lyotard's analysis, "Lyotard means that we are born before being born to ourselves. 'We are born from others but also to others, given over defenseless to them'" (Ronell 2007: 142). A counterintuitive notion of the child emerges – one who is not yet his or her own self:

> … an age that is not marked by age – or rather, it does not age but recurs episodically, even historically. Childhood can last a whole lifetime if you find yourself throttled and unable to root out some representation of what is affecting you; this can happen every day.
>
> (Ronell 2007: 142)

No wonder, then, that adults, particularly since the industrialization of modern toy-making from the mid-nineteenth century onwards, have taken an interest in the toys of children, particularly in those toys that give children the language and habits of a modern productive life. The bourgeois domestic scene required that children be separated from the chaos of the street, from "uncontrollable socialization," and from anything that might "undermine the construction of their children's bourgeois identity" (Hamlin 2003: 859). The toy, then, presumes a home, a set of relations, and a regime for the formation of children as future subjects of their nation and class. And the model proposes a means of returning to the past, to retell stories and simultaneously embody them in the present.

Model theatre, then, occupies an animated landscape created by adults, for adults, in the manner of child's play. Think of the testimonies by Great Men attesting to the importance of the English toy theatre in their boyhoods: Laurence Olivier, Robert Louis Stevenson, G. K. Chesterton, Winston Churchill, Charles Dickens, and J. B. Priestley all played melodramas of the amateur toy theatre genre as children and as citizens-in-training. Toys and play can be read as occupying a staging ground poised between the worlds of children and the projections of adults. "After all," Benjamin writes, "a child is no Robinson Crusoe; children do not constitute a community cut off from everything else. ... their toys cannot bear witness to any autonomous separate existence, but rather are a silent signifying dialogue between them and their nation" (Benjamin 1999a: 116). The habits of adulthood are tried on for size in child's play and the mimetic habits of childhood are embodied by the contemporary puppeteer animating models. The model-train lovers of *Mnemopark* jump, via video magic, into the remembered landscapes of their youth. The actors and model-makers of Hotel Modern demonstrate the physical facts of terrible global events, re-enacting the footfalls and inner life of an anonymous soldier in the trenches of the Great War. Model theatre, with its cunning collapses and reversals of scale, reawakens the mimetic faculty, reminding us to be educated by child's play, to play again with models and toys at moments of crisis in the world of adults.

Notes

The author wishes to thank MJ Thompson, Dassia Posner, John Bell, and John Pemberton for their generous comments on drafts of this chapter, as well as Josette Feral for the invitation to present an early version as a talk for the 2009 colloquium "Effets de Présence et Effets de Réel: Formes Indisciplinées" at l'École supérieure de théâtre, Université de Québec à Montréal.

1 Footage of a Royal de Luxe video is online at <https://www.youtube.com/watch?v=Bc0PoWfPzmI> (accessed 22 April 2014).
2 See Arthur B. Allen, *The Model Theatre* (1950), and Allen J. Allport, *Model Theatres, and How to Make Them* (1978), as cited in Peter Baldwin, *Toy Theatres of the World* (1992).
3 I'm thinking in particular of the mixed-media works "Proportioned to the Groove" (2005) and "Still Life With Fish" (2005) in her self-titled solo exhibition at the Marianne Boesky Gallery in New York, 12 May to 1 July 2005.
4 For a recent compendium of both literal and metaphorical treatments of the figure of the puppet in recent works of art, see *The Puppet Show*, the catalog from a 2008 exhibition organized by the Institute of Contemporary Art at the University of Pennsylvania. Included in the show were works by an array of artists from William Kentridge and Mike Kelly to Louise Bourgeois and Laurie Simmons, attesting to the art world's ongoing fascination with puppets, dolls, and masks as ambiguous, powerful, or uncanny figures, fetishes, human doubles, automata, and philosophical toys. See also the recent reviews of puppet theatre performances by *New Yorker* dance critic Joan Acocella in that magazine, including "Puppet Love: The Artistry of Basil Twist," April 15, 2013: 34–40; "Lifelike: Puppets in New York," March 23, 2009: 80; and "Doll Houses: Basil Twist's 'Petrushka' and the Kirov at City Center," April 21, 2008: 140–141.
5 For example, Carolyn Battista, "Puppets Are Not Just for Children Anymore," *The New York Times*, March 17, 1985: CN31; Leslie Talmadge, "The Puppets Take Manhattan; Think Puppets Are Strictly for Kids? Think Again. On Broadway and at Other Venues, Puppet Shows Are Breaking the Mold by Tackling Rossini Operas and Mature Subjects," *Christian*

Science Monitor, August 1, 2003: 13; and Amy S. Rosenberg, "A Show Where Puppets Are Not Child's Play," *Philadelphia Inquirer*, February 13, 2008: D01.

6 Another example combining dance, model architecture, and cinema is the recent tabletop ballet *Kiss and Cry* by Belgian choreographer Michèle Anne de Mey and cinematographer Jaco Van Dormael, in which a full film-making crew constructed live, projected images of a series of dances performed primarily by the two dancers' hands on a shifting series of elaborate tabletop sets.

Works cited

Allen, A. B. (1950) *The Model Theatre*. Redhill, England: W. Gardner, Darton.
Allport, A. J. (1978) *Model Theatres, and How to Make Them*. New York, NY: Scribner.
Baldwin, P. (1992) *Toy Theatres of the World*. London: A. Zwemmer.
Barthes, R. (1957) "Toys," in *Mythologies*; trans. A. Lavers (1984). New York, NY: Hill & Lang.
Benjamin, W. (1999a) "The Cultural History of Toys," in M. W. Jennings, H. Eiland, and G. Smith (eds) *Selected Writings, Vol. 2: 1927–1934*. Cambridge, MA: Belknap Press, Harvard University Press.
——(1999b) "Old Toys," in M. W. Jennings, H. Eiland, and G. Smith (eds) *Selected Writings, Vol. 2: 1927–1934*. Cambridge, MA: Belknap Press, Harvard University Press.
——(1999c) "On the Mimetic Faculty," in M. W. Jennings, H. Eiland, and G. Smith (eds) *Selected Writings, Vol. 2: 1927–1934*. Cambridge, MA: Belknap Press, Harvard University Press.
——(1999d) "Program for a Proletarian Children's Theater," in M. W. Jennings, H. Eiland, and G. Smith (eds) *Selected Writings, Vol. 2: 1927–1934*. Cambridge, MA: Belknap Press, Harvard University Press.
Gröber, K. (1928) *Children's Toys of Bygone Days: A History of Playthings of All Peoples from Prehistoric Times to the XIXth Century*. trans. P. Hereford. London: B. T. Batsford.
Hamlin, D. (2003) "The Structures of Toy Consumption: Bourgeois Domesticity and Demand for Toys in Nineteenth-Century Germany," *Journal of Social History* 36: 857–870.
Kuoni, C. and Schaffner, I. (eds) (2008) *The Puppet Show*. Philadelphia, PA: University of Pennsylvania Press.
Lehmann, H. (1999) *Postdramatic Theatre*, trans. K. Jürs-Mundy (2006). London: Routledge.
Mumford, M. and Garde, U. (2012) "Experts of the Everyday," *RealTime Arts* 108: 26, <http://www.realtimearts.net/article/issue108/10617> (accessed 18 November 2013).
Norden, L. (2007) "Show and Hide: Reading Sarah Sze," in *Sarah Sze*. New York, NY: Abrams.
Ronell, A. (2007) "On the Unrelenting Creepiness of Childhood: Lyotard, Kid-Tested," in C. Nouvet, Z. Stahuljak, and K. Still (eds) *Minima Memoria: In the Wake of Jean François Lyotard*. Stanford, CA: Stanford University Press.
Zipes, J. (2003) "Political Children's Theater in the Age of Globalization," *Theater* 33(2): 3–25.

Section VI
New Directions and Hybrid Forms

25
From Puppet to Robot
Technology and the Human in Japanese Theatre

Cody Poulton

String Puppet Sanbasō, a *kabuki* dance performed to the accompaniment of a *nagauta* ballad,[1] is one of a long series of felicitous *sanbasō* plays, a performance type that can be found in every major genre of traditional theatre. Indeed, the *sanbasō* (a kind of divine clown who is the sidekick of another god, the Old Man *okina*) is a character whose performance predates Japan's oldest full-fledged dramatic genre, the *nō*, and points to the sacred and ritual origin of all traditional Japanese performance. In the *kabuki* dance, two actors play a marionette of the little god and its puppeteer. When the puppeteer pulls an invisible string, for example, the puppet's hand rises, and it seems as if his entire body is at the beck of his manipulator: limp, inert matter until animated by his controller. It is a brilliant dance, the actor mimicking the jerky, awkward – yet gravity-defying – movements of the little god made of wood and strings.

Watching a performance of this play at the Kabukiza in Tokyo in December 2009, I was struck afresh by the traditional Japanese theatre's delight in metatheatrical techniques that reference not only a plethora of other forms, narrative motifs, and performance patterns (*String Puppet Sanbasō* also references *ningyōburi*, the technique in which *kabuki* actors imitate *bunraku* puppets), but also call to attention the meaning of mimesis itself, its chief purpose arguably being an effort to cheat death. Art's pedigree can be traced back to the Orphic quest to resurrect the dead, to retrieve through recollection what has been lost.[2]

In her book *Phantasmagoria*, Marina Warner notes that "Thomas Aquinas singled out animation as the defining quality of soul, calling the soul 'the starting point of all motion in things which live'" (Warner 2006: 47). The uncanny exists when immaterial ("spiritual") forces are able to reach through and affect physical objects. Thus, there is something uncanny about puppets, where human energy animates lifeless objects. In this sense, puppets serve as a synecdoche of mimesis. In a recent study of automata, Kara Reilly discusses what she calls an "onto-epistemic mimesis" – in short, a "mimesis that changes a person's way of knowing, and by extension their way of being" – which she claims has been at work in the production and reception of automata and other lifelike effigies in European culture since classical times, a process analogous to the introduction of perspective (Reilly 2011: 7).

Recent experiments in robotics, artificial intelligence, and graphic fiction reflect a fascination with the techniques of animation and simulation in Japan that go at least as far back as the puppets of the seventeenth-century theatres of Osaka. The puppet plays for which Chikamatsu Monzaemon wrote in the late seventeenth and early eighteenth centuries were large dolls held, like a ventriloquist's dummy, by a single manipulator. Alongside the theatres on Dōtombori Canal in Osaka, where Chikamatsu premiered his plays, were shows of mechanical automata (*karakuri ningyō*) by artists such as Takeda Ōmi. Yūda Yoshio has suggested that the levers and moving parts that were a feature of the *karakuri ningyō* found their way into the bodies of the puppets used in *ningyō jōruri* (*bunraku*).[3] Movable eyes, eyelids, mouths, and finger joints necessitated larger bodies that had to be manipulated by three men visible to the audience. These puppets, ancestors of the *bunraku* dolls of today, made their stage debut in 1734. Linking the evolution of puppetry to Japan's robotics industry, Christopher Bolton remarks that, "the gradual internalization of technology is the central trope of the cyborg and the key step in blurring the lines between bodies and tools, or humans and machines" (Bolton 2003: 741).

It is well known that the term "robot" (derived from the Czech word *rab*, meaning "slave," and its cognate *robota*, meaning "indentured servitude") was coined by Karel Čapek in his stage play *R.U.R* (*Rossum's Universal Robots*), which premiered in Prague in 1921. The play was staged in Japan as early as 1924 under the title *Jinzō ningen* (*Artificial Humans*) at the state-of-the-art Tsukiji Little Theatre and was directed by Hijikata Yoshi, who had seen it performed in Europe. Miri Nakamura has pointed out that *Artificial Humans* sparked a booming interest in robots in Japan, but we have seen that the existence of clockwork automata and sophisticated puppets since as early as the seventeenth century in Japan had already created a fertile environment for technological innovation in this field (Nakamura 2007: 169–190). The country today is at the vanguard of robotics research and development. It was here that industrial robots were first employed on a massive scale during the 1980s as a measure to reduce labor costs, and today Japan produces more robots for domestic and consumer use than any other country in the world (Robertson 2010: 7–8).

Recent collaborations between two leading specialists in the areas of theatre and robot engineering illustrate how these two seemingly disparate fields can stimulate mutual innovation. Ishiguro Hiroshi, born in 1963, is the director of the Intelligent Robotics Laboratory at Osaka National University and has an international reputation for creating doppelganger androids of himself, his daughter, and other people. Hirata Oriza, born in 1962, won the Kishida Kunio Award, Japan's top drama prize, in 1995 for his play *Tokyo Notes*. He is internationally known for his self-styled "contemporary colloquial theatre" – what critics have dubbed "quiet drama" – hyper-realistic plays that present ordinary people in realistic and singularly undramatic situations (Poulton 2002: 1–8). Hirata has toured extensively abroad, both with his company Seinendan and alone, and frequently collaborates with artists in Korea, France, and Belgium. Hitherto a special advisor on international and cultural affairs to the Japanese prime minister's cabinet, Hirata has been a member of the faculty of the School of Communication Design at Osaka University since 2006. Ishiguro and Hirata's earliest collaboration was a 20-minute play called *I, Worker* (2008), arguably the first play ever presented in which a robot performed the role of a robot.[4] *I,*

Figure 25.1 The Wakamaru robot, Takeo, converses with his employer, Yūji, in *I, Worker* (2008): written and directed by Hirata Oriza. Photo: © Osaka University & Eager Co. Ltd

Worker is set in the near future. A couple, Yūji and Ikue, live with two robot servants, Takeo and Momoko. As if mirroring the unemployed Yūji, Takeo the "male" robot has also lost his desire to work.

A robot that no longer wants to work can be said to be almost human – he is certainly experiencing an identity crisis as a robot! Hirata and Ishiguro's aim for this work is to explore the potential for machines to communicate with human beings, and, by extension, the possibility that machines can acquire, at the very least, a semblance of will or consciousness or even feelings – the very stuff that makes us human, a quality which in Japanese is summed up in a single word, *kokoro* (the "heart-mind"). The Wakamaru robots used in this play, created by Mitsubishi Heavy Industries, may look primitive, but they are capable of recognizing individual differences in people and acting accordingly. Their sensors allow them to move through space and manipulate objects. They appear to have free agency and communicate with their human counterparts in this play, but their dialogue has been programmed down to the split second.

Sensors, programming, and remote control: these are the three technical devices that afford a semblance of agency to the modern automata that Hirata and Ishiguro employ in their robot plays. Ishiguro and Hirata followed *I, Worker* with *In the Heart of the Forest*, which premiered at the Nagoya Triennale in August 2010. Hirata had originally written this play for Le Théâtre Royale Flamande in Brussels. Inspired by Joseph Conrad's *Heart of Darkness*, Hirata conceived of a team of Japanese scientists conducting research in the Congo to precipitate the evolution of bonobos. The work is a meditation on not only race but species as well; in this version, two of the scientists are robots, presenting an opportunity for a further inquiry into whether consciousness can exist in inorganic matter. Having created intelligent machines, humans in this play are poised to create primates that rival humans in their development, anticipating the premise of the Hollywood film *Rise of the Planet of the Apes* (Rupert Wyatt, director, 2011). Longer-lasting batteries allowed the technicians of *In the Heart of the Forest* to extend the performance life of the Wakamaru robot from 20 minutes to close to an hour and a half; but in the performance I saw, the two robot scientists had run out of "juice," and "Plan B," an alternate human scenario, was hastily substituted for that of the robots, who were originally supposed to end the show.[5]

What is human? How do primates, or even robots, differ from humanity? If emotion and fellow feeling – compassion – is the link between humans and primates, what of intelligent machines, who can reason and communicate, but do not feel? Ishiguro has said repeatedly that he is only interested in making robots for what they can teach us about human beings. "Robots and androids," he says, "are mirrors reflecting what it is to be human" (Ishiguro 2009: 66). And so, to understand what makes humans "tick," he has decided that the best method is to build one! For his part, Hirata has likened actors to chess pieces, to be controlled by the playwright and director. His unique directorial method is not based on any notion of interiority or quest for a character's motivation. Instead, his hyper-realistic style is created out of a multitude of formal elements of closely observed human behavior: gestures and speeches modulated by precise calibrations of movement and timbre, volume, and pause of speech. Hirata has said that by carefully calibrating the pacing of dialogue he could create the eerie sensation of consciousness and agency in his automata. By making his audiences weep at a robot's predicament, he boasts that he has beaten Stanislavsky at his own game:

> Most human communication is not empathic but rather based on learned patterns of response to stimuli. My actors were shocked to learn this, but what makes it so congenial to work with Ishiguro is that in fact I used precisely the same vocabulary with Ishiguro's robots as I do to direct my actors.
>
> (Hirata and Ishiguro 2010: 18)

For his part, Ishiguro Hiroshi claims that "androids can express themselves just as well as human actors. I believe that in theatre there is fundamentally no difference between a human and a robot" (Ishiguro 2009: 19). He is interested in learning more about what he calls "emotional affordances in human-robot interaction."[6] This interest mirrors the influence of James J. Gibson's theory of affordances on Hirata's own dramaturgical theory. In Gibson's ecological psychology, the social environment is the key determinant, not individual agency, in human behavior (Gibson 1979).

The Wakamaru robot clearly does not look human, but movement and speech can create the illusion of life. Ishiguro and Hirata even resorted to the traditional puppet theatre to learn how to manipulate their robots, hiring the *bunraku* puppeteer Kiritake Kanjūrō III to give their engineers a primer in the humanizing and gendering of movement.

In his desire to understand what it is that makes us human, Ishiguro is driven by a desire to create even more lifelike androids. For Ishiguro, *ningen rashisa* – human likeness – is almost as good as being human, such that the quest for semblance has

Figure 25.2 Ishiguro Hiroshi and his Geminoid HI-1 (2006): Geminoid HI-1 was developed by Hiroshi Laboratory, Advanced Telecommunications Research Institute International (ATR). Geminoid is a registered trademark of ATR. Photo courtesy of ATR Hiroshi Ishiguro Laboratory

arguably come to trump an understanding of the real: *paraitre* stands in for *être*. There is a sense that for Ishiguro a human is a highly sophisticated somatic machine, and all one has to do in order to understand it is to replicate one. Writing for *Wired* magazine's online Malcontents blog, John Brownlee expresses an almost atavistic aversion to Ishiguro's android double of himself, Geminoid HI-1: "It is part cyborg, part real doll, part Shigeru Miyamoto, part Dracula. It is horrible. It hates you. Professor Ishiguro seems oblivious to the bladder-evacuating creep factor of his Geminoid robot" (Brownlee 2007: 1). I find it interesting that in this comment, Brownlee personifies the Geminoid: "*it* hates you," not "*I* hate *it*." The source of his aversion seems to be reflective of a fear that, though it is not human, it is *alive*.

Brownlee's "creep factor" was analyzed 40 years earlier in an article by roboticist Mori Masahiro in the Japanese journal *Energy* (Mori 1970) as "the uncanny valley," whereby excessively realistic simulations of living creatures elicit an instinctive sense of revulsion:

> The vertical axis marks the degree to which we feel familiarity with an object. The horizontal axis measures the extent to which that object looks human, with the most mechanical-looking objects at the left end and the most humanlike on the right. [The Wakamaru robot would be located on the graph roughly midway between the industrial and the humanoid robot.]
> (Mori 1970 [2012]: 100)

Mori comments that:

> As healthy persons, we are represented at the second peak in Figure [25.3] (moving). Then when we die, we are unable to move; the body goes cold,

and the face becomes pale. Therefore, our death can be regarded as a movement from the second peak (moving) to the bottom of the uncanny valley (still), as indicated by the arrow's path in Figure [25.3]. We might be glad that this arrow leads down into the still valley of the corpse and not the valley animated by the living dead.

I think this descent explains the secret lying deep beneath the uncanny valley. Why were we equipped with this eerie sensation? Is it essential for human beings? I have not yet considered these questions deeply, but I have no doubt it is an integral part of our instinct for self-preservation. ...

We should begin to build an accurate map of the uncanny valley so that through robotics research we can begin to understand what makes us human.

(Mori 1970 [2012]: 100)

Intriguingly, in Mori's scheme, *bunraku* puppets have crossed the uncanny valley to the other side where verisimilitude is balanced with familiarity. In the same essay, he writes:

I don't think that, on close inspection, a *bunraku* puppet appears similar to a human being. Its realism in terms of size, skin texture, and so on, does not even reach that of a realistic prosthetic hand. But when we enjoy a puppet show in the theater, we are seated at a certain distance from the stage. The puppet's absolute size is ignored, and its total appearance, including eye and hand movements, is close to that of a human being. So, given our tendency as an audience to become absorbed in this form of art, we might feel a high level of affinity for the puppet.

(Mori 1970 [2012]: 99)

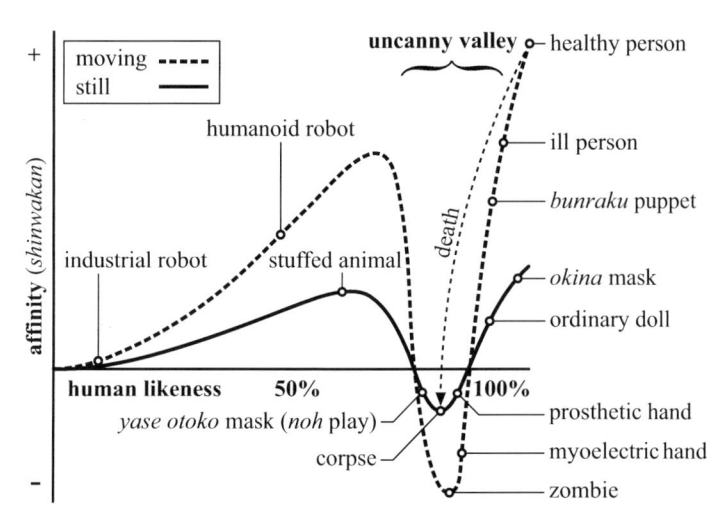

Figure 25.3 Diagram of Masahiro Mori's "Uncanny Valley." Image courtesy of Karl MacDorman. Originally published in *IEEE Robotics and Automation*, 2012, 19(2): 99

It seems significant that puppets and automata have been at the center of many discussions of the uncanny. The classic work on the subject is, of course, Freud's "The Uncanny" ("Das Unheimliche"), (1919) which analyzes E. T. A. Hoffmann's "Der Sandmann" (1816), a story featuring an automaton by the name of Olimpia. But even prior to Freud's groundbreaking work, Ernst Anton Jentsch's "On the Psychology of the Uncanny" (1906) discussed the fear engendered by inorganic matter, like wax figurines and automata, that seemed to be alive.

Perhaps if there comes a time when the appearance, movement, and speech of Ishiguro's androids are refined so much that it becomes impossible to distinguish them from human, they will have succeeded in crawling out of the uncanny valley they still inhabit, and humans will learn to befriend them. Hirata and Ishiguro's theatrical experiments nevertheless serve to refine the communicative (one might even say social) qualities of intelligent machines, a project in which contemporary Japan, with its rapidly aging and decreasing population, is heavily invested. In the near future, Japan's elderly will need companions and caregivers. There is arguably a xenophobic angle to this project: many have commented that robots would be more acceptable to many Japanese than the presence of foreign labor. "When men were no longer found, their place was supplied by machines," Edward Gibbon (1776 [1897]: 15) wrote, referring to the increasing reliance by Roman legions on machines of war to replace old-fashioned military valor, but his remark has a ring of truth when applied to the contemporary scene in Japan.[7]

Humanity's replacement by machines may be said to be the covert message of another Hirata-Ishiguro collaboration, *Sayōnara*, which also premiered in August 2010 at the Nagoya Biennale.[8] Ishiguro's Geminoid F, modeled after a real woman in her mid-20s, is paired with an American actress of about the same age, Bryerly Long, who plays a woman who has been given an android to keep her company in her last hours of life. While the two quote lines of poetry, "dead" matter comes alive as a living organism dies. Depending upon the lighting and the spectator's proximity to the stage, it is difficult for audiences to determine initially which actor is human – both are chair-bound – and having one played by a non-Japanese is an alienation effect that adds to the uncanny nature of the performance. (This uncertainty is confirmed by surveys taken of audiences who have seen the play. According to Yoshikawa Yūichirō, 90 percent of audience members polled found the android "beautiful." This may indicate that, given the appropriate setting, Ishiguro's androids may have crawled out of the uncanny valley.) We understand in the play that the android has been designed to develop increasingly sophisticated algorithms of behavior so as to respond to the "emotional affordances" of the sick Caucasian woman. The poetry the Geminoid recites is intended to express the essence of the woman's state of mind as she faces her own extinction. "Now, who is the girl talking to, her android or herself? Can we call their 'conversation' a dramatic dialogue? Or is it more of a monologue of the invalid girl, since the android chooses the poems she recites to suit her owner's inner state?" asks theatre critic Noda Manabu. "Their dialogue is not strictly between two independent subjectivities," he adds. "Rather, the subjectivity of the invalid girl is defined in terms of inter-subjectivity between her consciousness and the other within her through the play's beguilingly neoclassical dialogic structure" (Noda 2011: 6). This is assuming that the android has no

Figure 25.4 Geminoid F and Bryerly Long in *Sayōnara* (2010): written and directed by Hirata Oriza. Photo: © Tatsuo Nambu/Aichi Triennale 2010

consciousness, no subjectivity. Given the present state of the technology, this is no doubt true; but the play is suggesting that there may well come a time in the near future when androids will be aware of themselves and others. Noda himself acknowledges this possibility when he remarks, "We are no longer sure who she is reciting his poem for. Is [the android] addressing her mistress, or has she started to malfunction and begun to talk to herself?" (Noda 2011: 7).

The android, as it were, emerges into self-consciousness through its mirroring of the memories and feelings of others – namely, the terminally ill woman and her dead father, thus perhaps suggesting an immortality of the "soul" through technological means. Ishiguro (2009: 25) has written that he is interested in what would remain of a human when everything had been downloaded into a machine. Could a machine then acquire consciousness? The fundamental difference between a machine and a human being, he suggests, is the presence in the human of "noise" (*yuragi*), the term used in electronics to contrast with "signal" – that is, order. Perhaps the element of chaos – what cannot be predicted or programmed – is what makes us human after all. One should add that this uncertainty regarding the existence of agency in the android is compounded by the fact that Geminoid F's speech is performed by an act of ventriloquism: an operator behind the scenes speaks for and electronically directs the movement of the android as one would a puppet. Ishiguro has said that operating an android often gives one an eerie sense of extending one's perceptual field, such that one becomes, as it were, embodied by the android and can feel when the android is touched, for example (H. Ishiguro, pers. comm., 4 August 2011).

One of Ishiguro's latest androids, Geminoid DK, modeled after Associate Professor Henrik Scharfe of Aalborg University in Denmark, is a significant advance on earlier models, both in appearance and realistic movement.[9] Scharfe's wife jokes that she prefers Body #1 – Scharfe himself – and that Body #2 – the android – should be sent on the road to lectures and conferences. Maybe we should all get one, but at US$1 million for a Geminoid, the cost is still prohibitive. Such a scenario is nevertheless the premise for the Bruce Willis vehicle, *Surrogates* (Jonathan Mostow, director, 2009). Featuring a cameo by Geminoid HI-1, this film imagines a future in which most of us will have android doubles to do our work and even live our lives.[10] (The film's conclusion, ironically for Ishiguro but predictably for Hollywood, is the destruction of the androids and a return to embodied humanity, warts and all.) Nevertheless, Ishiguro's emphasis on appearance over movement – his androids are paraplegic and their upper bodies still move rather awkwardly – limits their practical use and, perhaps even more significantly, suggests, to this writer at least, a failure on the part of Ishiguro to understand such matters as emotional affordance and familiarity. I suspect that Ishiguro's quest to create ever-more-realistic human simulacra will literally lead to a dead end because humans appear to be hard-wired to recognize movement, even more than physical resemblance, as the prime indicator of life – hence, animation's etymological link to *anima* (spirit). Current theory posits a neurological basis for our privileging movement over appearance in detecting sentience in others (see, for example, Rizzolatti et. al. 2001). Yet, Ishiguro's research is exciting because of its interdisciplinary nature: he draws upon the work of not only cognitive scientists and neurologists, but artists as well, and by the same token his research will have important applications to all of these fields. Ishiguro's collaboration with a playwright and stage director is an especially good sign that artists should have an increasingly significant role to play in technological innovation. Aesthetic considerations have profound existential and social repercussions. As the electronic artist Zaven Paré (who has worked with Ishiguro) has put it, what is required today in robotics research and development is "more dramaturgy, less programming." In other words, theatre is being used as a platform here for robotics research in order to explore the social dynamics of human discourse, something for which programming alone cannot account (Paré 2011).

In the meantime, Mori's uncanny valley has now entered the lexicon of popular culture. Roger Ebert (2004: 3) referred to it in a review of the film *Lord of the Rings* and, from Godzilla to Gollum, the idea almost inevitably enters discussions of how far to push realism in animation, animatronics, and computer-generated special effects. Animated features like the film versions of *Final Fantasy: The Spirits Within* (2001) and *Polar Express* (2004) flopped, it is argued, because they were *too* realistic. Lawrence Weschler quotes Andy Jones, director of *Final Fantasy*, in commenting that the replication of a real human being "can get eerie. As you push further and further, it begins to get grotesque. You start to feel like you're puppeteering a corpse" (Weschler 2002: 4).

From *The Golem* to *Frankenstein* to *Ghost in the Shell*, writers have explored the philosophical and ethical issues surrounding the creation of artificial life. For his part, Ishiguro's inquiries into the nature of humanity and the impact of technology upon the human are fact, not science fiction. These issues are too big to do justice to here, but I would like to suggest a few ideas as to what these technologies may bode for the direction that our art, puppetry, may take in the coming years. And here Chikamatsu ought to get the last word.

Mori's idea of the uncanny valley, which has become so central not only to robotics design, but also to the use of animatronics and computer graphics in the film and gaming industries, was surely inspired by remarks by Chikamatsu recorded some 300 years before. As related in Hozumi Ikan's *Naniwa miyage* (Souvenir of Naniwa), Chikamatsu saw the task of the playwright as one in which "the author must impart to lifeless wooden puppets a variety of emotions, and attempt in this way to capture the interest of the audience" (Hozumi 1738, cited in Keene 1955: 386). The text must be animated, "all living and full of action" (Hozumi 1738, cited in Keene 1955: 386). Nevertheless, realism is not the ultimate goal: "In writing *jōruri*, one attempts first to describe facts as they really are, but in so doing one writes things which are not true, in the interest of art" (Hozumi 1738: 388):

> Someone said, "People nowadays will not accept plays unless they are realistic and well reasoned out." ... I answered, "Your view seems plausible, but it is a theory which does not take into account the real methods of art. Art is something which lies in the slender margin between the real and the unreal."
> (Hozumi 1738, cited in Keene 1955: 389)

Chikamatsu goes on to relate the story of a noblewoman who had a doll made in the likeness of her lover that was so realistic that:

> ... the only difference between the man and this doll was the presence in one, and the absence in the other, of a soul. However, when the lady drew the doll close to her and looked at it, the exactness of the reproduction chilled her, and she felt unpleasant and rather frightened. Court lady that she was, her love was also chilled, and as she found it distressing to have the doll by her side, she soon threw it away.
> (Hozumi 1738, cited in Keene 1955: 390)

In his famous analysis on *bunraku* in *L'Empire des Signes*, Roland Barthes (echoing Kleist's famous characterization of the marionette as an embodiment of prelapsarian grace) argues that *bunraku* problematizes dualistic Western notions of flesh and spirit:

> It is not the simulation of the body that [*bunraku*] seeks, but, so to speak, its sensuous abstraction. Everything which we attribute to the total body and which is denied to our actors under cover of an organic, "living" unity, the little man of Bunraku recuperates and expresses without any deception: ... in short, the very qualities which the dreams of ancient theology granted to the redeemed body. ... This is how it rejects the antinomy of *animate/inanimate* and dismisses the concept which is hidden behind all animation of matter and which is, simply, "the soul."
> (Barthes 1970 [1982]: 60)

That is not to say, however, that Chikamatsu ignored the metaphor of spirit animating matter in the puppet theatre. It is likely more a problem of translation that the word "soul" is applied here for the Japanese *tamashii*, a concept of spiritual force which many have noted is not quite equivalent to the traditional Western idea of a "soul." The Japanese have since ancient times accorded a sense of spirit or consciousness (*kokoro*) to all natural phenomena, from insensible stones to plants and animals. As Ki no Tsurayuki said in his preface to the *Kokinshū*, Japan's first court anthology of poetry: "when we hear the warbling of the mountain thrush in the blossoms or the voice of the frog in the water, we know that every living being has its song" (Ki no Tsurayuki 1920 [1984]: 35). This animistic instinct at the heart of all puppetry is something which Basil Jones, one of the founders of Handspring Puppet Company of South Africa, the creators of *War Horse*, has also eloquently identified as:

> A belief in the life of objects and the life of things around us. We suspect that objects may have life and that dead people might have an afterlife. So when we go into the theatre and the lights go down and we once again are shown objects – i.e., puppets – that are brought to life, I think it ignites a smoldering coal of ancient belief in us that there is life in stones, in rivers, in objects, in wood. I feel it's almost part of our DNA that we all left Africa believing in the life of things, as animists.
> (*Lincoln Center Theater Review* 2011: 12)

Jones has stressed that the *Ur*-narrative of all puppet plays is an existential one: puppets want to live, for puppets can do what no human actor can, and that is play death convincingly.[11]

What have been called animistic tendencies in Japanese culture find their counterpart in contemporary attitudes toward technology. Jennifer Robertson (2007, 2010) and Robert Geraci (2006), among others, have suggested that Shinto belief has enabled the Japanese people to be more accepting of the presence of robots in their daily life. The issue is more complex, however: for one thing, Japan's commercial and domestic development of robotics, in contrast to the US focus on military applications, is surely an important factor determining the "friendliness" of Japanese robots. At the same time, modern cognitive science, neurology, and philosophy point toward a more nuanced understanding of consciousness. As Masamune Shirow puts it in his *Ghost in the Shell manga* series, "Generally speaking, what we refer to as 'spirit' or 'soul' is a very vague concept, including things programmed into, or closely related to, the physical body, such as memory, the results of chemical reactions, etc" (Masamune 1989–1990 [2009]: 100n).

The aim of many traditional Japanese performing arts, like that of contemporary robotics or much computer-generated media, is to create virtual realities. A certain aura of the uncanny is necessary, perhaps, for any work of art – it calls our attention to its own intrinsic energy as a kind of "second life." But when realism is exploited to the limits of what is technologically possible at any given time, an instinctive human reaction kicks in: realism becomes its opposite, accentuating the falseness of the likeness, and in this falseness lies a kind of weird spiritual charge. Marina Warner notes that "the virtual reality of the internet has forged a new narrative of spirits and specters" (Warner 2006: 376). If monsters are, as Goya said, born of the dreams of reason, if the uncanny is the disconcerting byproduct of the mimetic instinct in Western art especially, then perhaps the Japanese have discovered a way to domesticate the otherworldly by accommodating it into the common practices of their art and technology, familiarizing it while still acknowledging and even celebrating its essential strangeness. New art and science thus serve to redefine what is "human" by probing the limits of life, where it begins and ends, and who (or what) possesses it. New media and technology, in particular, seem poised to undermine traditional Judeo-Christian concepts of human uniqueness and individual agency, opening us perhaps to something closer to the traditional Japanese worldview – one that is basically pagan – a world of gods and not God. And, as Warner (2006: 378) points out, "a non-Christian, classical, mythical idea about individual potential and polyvalence has set aside a traditional concept of the soul."

Notes

1. A *nagauta* (literally, "long song"), a ballad typically found in *kabuki* dance plays, is sung by a chorus to the accompaniment of a *shamisen*, a three-stringed instrument.
2. Margaret Atwood, for example, has suggested that "perhaps all writing, is motivated, deep down, by a fear of and fascination with mortality – by a desire to make the risky trip to the Underworld, and to bring something or someone back from the dead" (Atwood 2002: 156).
3. Takeda Ōmi (d. 1704) was the father of Takeda Izumo I (d. 1747), who became manager of Chikamatsu's theatre, the Takemoto-za, after the retirement of Takeda Gidayū. Takeda Izumo I's supervision of Chikamatsu's *Kokusen'ya kassen* (*The Battles of Coxinga*, 1715), with its emphasis on spectacular effects, had a profound impact upon the development of the puppet theatre. See Yūda (1975: 21–40).
4. The Portuguese artist Leonel Moura, who in 2010 staged the first-ever version of R.U.R. to use robots, claims wrongly that his was the first theatrical production ever to feature real robots and humans together. See http://www.leonelmoura.com/rur_en.html (accessed January 9, 2013).
5. Hirata typically factors in the possibility for machine malfunction, scripting alternate scenes for human actors, into his robot plays. This happened in the case of a delayed entrance by the android Geminoid F in a performance in Tokyo in October 2012 of his recent work *Three Sisters: Android Version*.
6. See Noda (2011).
7. Jennifer Robertson (2007, 2010) has written extensively on Japan's production of consumer robots as an answer to the declining birthrate.
8. Hirata has written a sequel to *Sayōnara*, which premiered in New York at an event commemorating the first anniversary of the March 11, 2011, Eastern Japan earthquake and tsunami. *Sayōnara* and its sequel toured North America in February 2013.
9. Videos of the Geminoid DK can be viewed at <http://www.youtube.com/user/GeminoidDK> (accessed November 21, 2013).
10. A trailer for *Surrogates* can be viewed at <http://www.youtube.com/watch?v=Qyg4GEjKkM4> (accessed July 28, 2013).
11. Personal communication with Basil Jones at the Puppetry and Postdramatic Performance Conference, University of Connecticut, 2 April 2011. The death of the horse Topthorn in *War Horse* was eerily reminiscent of Enya Hangan's ritual suicide in the classic puppet play *Kanadehon Chūshingura* (*Treasury of the Loyal Retainers*, 1748). Upon the deaths of both Topthorn and Enya Hangan, the manipulators in these plays abandon their puppets and leave the stage, turning a once-animate character into inert matter.

Works cited

Atwood, M. (2002) *Negotiating with the Dead: A Writer on Writing*. Cambridge, England: Cambridge University Press.

Barthes, R. (1970) *L'Empire des Signes*; trans. Richard Howard (1982) *The Empire of Signs*. New York, NY: Hill and Wang.

Bolton, C. (2003) "From Wooden Cyborgs to Celluloid Souls: Mechanical Bodies in Anime and Japanese Puppet Theatre," *Positions: Asia Critique* 10: 729–771.

Brownlee, J. (2007) "Professor Ishiguro's Creepy Robot Doppelganger," *Wired* April 26, <http://www.wired.com/table_of_malcontents/2007/04/ professor_ishig/ > (accessed July 28, 2013).

Ebert, R. (2004) "Gollum Stuck in 'Uncanny Valley' of the 'Rings,'" *Chicago Sun Times*, January 11: 3.

Freud, S. (1919) "The Uncanny," in J. Strachey (ed. and trans.) (1959) *The Standard Edition of the Complete Psychological Works of Sigmund Freud*, vol. 17, *An Infantile Neurosis and Other Works*. London: Hogarth Press.

Geraci, R. (2006) "Spiritual Robots: Religion and Our Scientific View of the Natural World," *Theology and Science* 4: 229–246.

Gibbon, E. (1776 [1897]) *The History of the Decline and Fall of the Roman Empire*, vol. 1. London: Methuen.

Gibson, J. J. (1979) *The Ecological Approach to Visual Perception*. Boston, MA: Houghton Mifflin.

Hirata, O. and Ishiguro, H. (2010) *Robotto engeki* (Robot Theatre). Osaka, Japan: Osaka University Center for the Study of Communication-Design.

Hozumi, I. (1738) "Chikamatsu on the Art of the Puppet Stage," in D. Keene (ed. and trans.) (1955) *Anthology of Japanese Literature*. New York, NY: Grove Press.

Hozumi, I. (1738) "Naniwa miyage," Excerpted in *Nihon koten bungaku taikei* [Collected Works of Classical Japanese Literature], vol. 50, *Chikamatsu jōrurishū (ge)* [Chikamatsu's *jōruri* (part 2)]. Tokyo: Iwanami Shoten.

Ishiguro, H. (2009) *Robotto to wa nani ka? Hito no kokoro wo utsusu kagami* [What Is a Robot? A Mirror Reflecting the Human Mind]. Tokyo: Kōdansha Gendai Shinsho.

Jentsch, E. A. (1906) "Zur Psychologie des Unheimlichen"; trans. R. Sellars (1995) "On the Psychology of the Uncanny," *Angelaki: Journal of the Theoretical Humanities* 2: 7–16.

Ki no Tsurayuki, (1920) "Kanajo," in L. R. Rodd (trans. and ann.) (1984) *Kokinshū: A Collection of Poems Ancient and Modern*. Princeton, NJ: Princeton University Press.

Lincoln Center Theater Review (2011) "The Magical Life of Objects: An Interview with Adrian Kohler and Basil Jones," *Lincoln Center Theater Review* 55 (Spring): 10–14.

Masamune, S. (1989–1990) *Kōkaku Kidōtai* [Mobile Armored Riot Police], vol. 1; trans. Frederick L. Schott and Toren Smith (2009) *Ghost in the Shell*. New York, NY: Kōdansha Comics.

Mori, M. (1970) "Bukimi no tani," *Energy* 7: 33–35; K. F. MacDorman and N. Kageki (trans.) (2012) "The Uncanny Valley," *IEEE Robotics and Automation* 19(2): 98–100.

Moura, L. (2010) "Robot Theatre," <http://www.leonelmoura.com/rur_en.html > (accessed July 28, 2013).

Nakamura, M. (2007) "Marking Bodily Differences: Mechanized Bodies in Hirabayashi Hatsunosuke's 'Robot' and Early Shōwa Robot Literature," *Japan Forum* 19: 169–190.

Noda, M. (2011) "Dramatic Intersubjectivity Called into Question: Oriza Hirata's Robot/Android-Human Plays," Paper presented at the annual conference of the International Federation for Theatre Research, Osaka, Japan, 11 August 2011.

Paré, Z. (2011) "More Dramaturgy, Less Programming," Paper presented at the Puppetry and Postdramatic Performance Conference, Storrs, Connecticut, 3 April 2011.

Poulton, C. (2002) "Introduction to *Tokyo Notes*, a Play by Hirata Oriza," *Asian Theatre Journal* 19: 1–8.

Reilly, K. (2011) *Automata and Mimesis on the Stage of Theatre History*. Basingstoke, England: Palgrave MacMillan.

Rizzolatti, G., Fogassi, L., and Gallese, V. (2001) "Neurophysiological Mechanisms Underlying the Understanding and Imitation of Action," *Nature Reviews Neuroscience* 2: 661–670.

Robertson, J. (2007) "*Robo sapiens japanicus*: Humanoid Robots and the Posthuman Family," *Critical Asian Studies* 39: 369–398.

——(2010) "Gendering Humanoid Robots: Robo-Sexism in Japan," *Body and Society* 16(2): 1–36.

Warner, M. (2006) *Phantasmagoria: Spirit Visions, Metaphors and Media into the Twenty-First Century*. Oxford, England: Oxford University Press.

Weschler, L. (2002) "Why Is This Man Smiling?" *Wired* 10(6), June, <http://www.wired.com/wired/archive/10.06/face.html> (accessed July 29, 2013).

Yūda, Y. (1975) "The Formation of Early Modern *jōruri*," *Acta Asiatica* 28: 21–40.

26
Unholy Alliances and Harmonious Hybrids
New Fusions in Puppetry and Animation

Colette Searls

Animation and special-effects studios today are making increasing use of motion capture, computer-generated imagery (CGI), and digital puppetry in television, theatre, commercial films, and videogames. As CGI grows ever-more capable and pliant, it is not only changing the way in which actors and puppets appear in various media, it is enabling animated characters to perform like puppets and vice versa. Actors are controlling cartoon characters, while visual-effects teams are seamlessly mingling objects with images, blurring the lines between acting, animation, puppetry, and special effects.

Hybrids are appearing in a range of environments, including live theatre, theme parks, and – most commonly – fantasy films. In the latter, animation and puppetry are sometimes combined to achieve human likeness through motion-capture technology. In this chapter, I will argue that successful hybrids are radically transforming what puppetry and animation can do. In some cases, however, where these fusions are used to achieve naturalistic human likeness, their creators are setting aside what is most advantageous about puppetry and animation, thus diminishing their creative impact.

I will begin by looking at definitions of puppetry and animation and at how digital puppetry has already expanded these classifications and the creative reach of both forms, using examples from live performances. I will then investigate principles of unity and distance, which puppetry and animation share, and demonstrate what happens when artists fail to apply these principles in their use of animation/puppetry hybrids, using both the Spike Jonze-directed film *Where the Wild Things Are* (2009) and several "performance-capture" animated films as examples. I will conclude by analyzing actor Andy Serkis's most well-known digital film roles to demonstrate how animation and puppetry are harmoniously intersecting in creature effects[1] through advanced motion-capture technology.

Definitions

Emerging digital technology has challenged animation and puppetry artists to redraw the boundaries of their crafts. Interestingly, scholars have long struggled to settle upon a clear universal definition of animation. According to Maureen Furniss, author of *Art in Motion: Animation Aesthetics*:

> One of the most famous definitions of animation has come from Norman McLaren, the influential founder of the animation department at the National Film Board of Canada. He once stated:
> Animation is not the art of drawings that move but the art of movements that are drawn; What happens between each frame is much more important than what exists on each frame; Animation is therefore the art of manipulating the invisible interstices that lie between the frames.
>
> (Furniss 1998: 5)

McLaren's statement is significant not only for its lasting influence as a widely referenced definition, but for the way he places the performance of movement (rather than the creation of pictures) at the heart of animation.

When I use the term "animated character," I am broadly referring to the common perception of what this means: imagined characters drawn or sculpted by visual artists (via paintbrush, pencil, software tools, clay, or other means) and given the illusion of life through movement. I follow the common American understanding that animation refers to drawn or CGI-rendered images in motion, including those created through claymation and other types of stop-motion puppetry (a long-established hybrid).

Penny Francis, who analyzes historical classifications of puppetry in *Puppetry: A Reader in Theatre Practice*, concludes that a puppet is:

> [A] representation and distillation of a character, the repository of a persona perceived by both creator and spectator within its outward form. It can be any thing, any object, if brought to imagined life through the agency of a human player who inspires and controls it directly. The control may be through corporeal contact (hands-on, hands-in), or via strings, wires, wooden or metal rods. The figure animated electronically or even remotely is still a puppet if the performer is present at the other end of the cable or machinery, controlling the movements … .
>
> (Francis 2012: 13)

Here, Francis points to how the creator and spectator jointly participate in perceiving character in a puppeteered object. John Bell makes a similar suggestion in *American Puppet Modernism*, referring to a "performance triad" in object performance in which "performer and spectator are both focused on the object, not on each other" (Bell 2008: 5). In offering remote animation as a valid form of puppeteering, Francis still holds puppetry to the bounds of human agency and presence. In light of digital puppetry's emergence, I would add that a puppet can be any inanimate object or *image* manipulated by a performer to create the illusion of a life, so long as it falls within these same parameters. To be a puppeteer, the person controlling the image/object must be present during the performance, even if it is recorded and otherwise retouched before intended audiences perceive it (like Frank Oz puppeteering Miss Piggy before a film camera). Puppeteering is also a type of acting, and I categorize it as physical theatre because its chief communication tool is movement, making it particularly close to mask performance and mime.

The digital age has generated a new breed of character, often called a "digital puppet" or "virtual character," that is confusingly part image, puppet, and human performer. The most common instance of this hybrid arises from reading an actor's movements and expressions through motion-capture technology to create animated images. With motion capture, actors wear sensors on their faces and/or bodies (often on form-fitting suits designed for this purpose) and, as they perform, a computer uses the information to map the movements onto an image of a character. The captured information in this way drives the character's movements. This technique distinguishes motion capture (commonly called "mocap") from traditional animation[2]: with mocap, animators are no longer wholly responsible for creating the illusion of movement; character action is now coming in large measure from an actor's choices.

In today's advanced mocap studios, actors can interact with one another as they would in a live-action film[3] or theatre rehearsal and can even respond to instantaneous commands from a director, who is often watching the resulting animations on a monitor in real time. These are the animated characters featured in films such as *The Polar Express* (2004), *Avatar* (2009), and *The Avengers* (2012), as well as television shows produced by the Jim Henson Company's Digital Puppetry Studio (the most well-known being *Sid the Science Kid*). This particular type of hybrid brings performers into the animation picture by enabling them to choose the movements of the character image using gadgetry and/or their bodies as controllers (hence the term "digital puppet"). Author Stephen Kaplin has pointed to the profound effect this has on the way images can be animated from a puppetry standpoint: "With the motion capture suit, the performer can again achieve a kind of direct contact with the object, performing as though from inside the object" (Kaplin 1999: 35).

The very existence of these performed animations forces two radical ideas within the fields of animation and puppetry. It means that an animated character can perform live and that an image can be a puppet. A number of puppetry scholars have addressed the question of how to categorize these new species and how they might destabilize traditional understandings of what constitutes puppetry. Steve Tillis's article "The Art of Puppetry in the Age of Media Production" draws a clear distinction between what he calls "tangible puppets" and intangible images that are operated *as* puppets "i.e., intangible objects that are tangibly moved." He then suggests that these manipulated images make up a new category called "virtual puppets," a term coined by Stephen Kaplin (Tillis 1999: 192). I have adopted some of this language here. I ultimately conclude, however, that virtual puppets have transcended their intangibility in some of the most advanced uses of motion capture for film.

Digital puppets in real life

Though most of what I discuss in this chapter relates to recorded performances for film, I will first examine how digital puppetry in live settings exploits puppetry's interactive, spontaneous abilities, thereby expanding the powers of animated characters. For illustrative examples, I will look at two cartoon characters that have been transformed into interactive digital puppets for live audiences: Magic Mirror from DreamWorks Animation's *Shrek* (2001) and Crush from Pixar's *Finding Nemo* (2003).

When *Shrek the Musical* (a stage adaptation of the film) was brought from Seattle to Broadway in 2008, digital puppetry proved an artistic problem solver for the Magic Mirror character, a talking mask that floats inside a mirror frame. Joe Strike of *Animation World Network* describes how the *Shrek* team used digital puppetry to make an animated character perform live onstage:

> In the old days the producers might have settled for an actor on the other side of a pretend mirror, or perhaps a pre-produced piece of animation. Today however, the same technology that brings these moments to life onscreen can perform the identical magic onstage – and thanks to modern motion capture technology, go one better by doing it live, every night in real time ... The Mirror face the audience sees is identical to the one in the original animated Shrek ... .
>
> (Strike 2009)

Puppeteer John Tartaglia (*Sesame Street*, *Avenue Q*) had sensors placed on various parts of his face for each performance in order to manipulate Magic Mirror with his own expressions. He could see his virtual puppet move in real time, and he could react to other characters with the kind of organic spontaneity a recorded animation could never offer.

Going a step further, Disney has built theme park attractions with digital puppets that interact with their audiences. Digital puppets in live environments are actually not that rare – they can often be spotted at trade shows and conference attractions in the form of computer game-style characters. But Disney/Pixar offers something more transcendent in its conversion of animated characters into digital puppets. A mainstay Disney World attraction, "Turtle Talk with Crush" invites visitors into a dark room facing a large screen, lit up with what looks like a scene from the film *Finding Nemo* – a slice of colorfully animated ocean. Crush, the surfer-dude turtle from the movie, swims in to playfully joke around with individual children. The setup is totally cinematic: Crush and the other sea creatures who float by on the screen look exactly like their *Nemo* originals and their environment mirrors the movie. Only now, Crush can see through the screen. With this kind of live digital puppetry (the puppeteer hidden but able to view the audience), the animated character makes eye contact with people, calls them by name, and engages in actual conversations.

These examples from live theatre and interactive attractions demonstrate how alliances between puppetry and animation yield more territory to each field. Because of digital puppetry, animated characters can, like puppets, *be present*. By turning the screen from a projected recording into an interactive puppet stage, cartoon creatures can act on spontaneous impulse and experience the vulnerability to accident that actors and puppets have always exploited. And puppetry has updated its identity: puppets can now be instantly transformable images. I do not suggest digital puppetry is a useful solution in all forms of animation or an attractive new alternative to tangible puppets. Naturally, traditional animation and puppets that exist outside of a computer will always carry unrivaled charms and particular aesthetic powers. But hybrid creations do give artists substantial new tools and help keep puppetry and animation at the forefront of inventive make-believe.

Unity and distance in puppetry and animation

Animation and puppetry have always shared common links and practices, though the training and skills required for each, as well as their final outcomes and relationships to audiences, are naturally quite different. I am interested in where the two forms overlap and have identified unity and distance as two principles they both rely on to create convincing illusions.

First, artists in both fields must strenuously apply their craft to make fictional characters convincingly unified within themselves and their environments. With animation, bodies must be drawn from one frame to the next in a way that makes them appear to physically react, consistently and reliably, as a living being would. As animator Chris Webster explains in *Animation: The Mechanics of Motion*:

> In order for animation to be believable the action must demonstrate those qualities that we are familiar with in our day-to-day experience. Even the fantastic will become credible if it appears to respect those same laws of nature that we ourselves are subject to.
>
> (Webster 2008: 3)

He then details, like many animation technique authors, how to convey physical laws in renderings of human, animal, or object movement. For example, particular emphasis is placed on how characters cope with gravity (also a key component of puppetry training). Puppeteer/director Eric Bass similarly emphasizes the importance of consistency and unity in his "Notes on Puppetry as Theatrical Art," stating that "each production sets its own rules; I only insist that the production be consistent within its rules, and that the rules be organic to the complete aesthetic of the production" (Bass 1999: 39). Whether a story takes place in a magical wonderland or a dense rain forest, this principle of wholeness is critical to building credible illusion.

The second principle is distance. Interestingly, this rule points to one way in which puppetry and animation work differently from human-character acting. When actors portray other human beings, there is no physical detachment between themselves and the characters they portray: performer and performed are one entity and cannot exist in separate spaces. Conversely, puppeteers and animators are separate and distinct from the characters they bring to life. In *Acting for Animators*, Ed Hooks illustrates the difference this way:

An actor does not "become" a character. He doesn't stop being himself and become somebody else. He experiences the process of acting as if the emotions of the character are his own and of course they really are. The animator doesn't work like that because there is a physical distance between him and the character he is creating.

(Hooks 2011: 49)

Basil Jones of Handspring Puppet Company makes this curiously aligned point about the difference between actors and puppets:

The actor is a living person and therefore automatically possesses life ... His or her *livingness* is obvious and certainly doesn't need to be "performed" ... the primary work of the puppet is the *performance* of life, whilst for the actor this fundamental battle is already won ... .

(Jones 2009: 254)

Indeed, both puppets and animations pretend to be alive. They are removed from their creators by this simple fact of nature as well as basic physics. But the gap between performer and performed has actually been obscured in a number of attempts by fantasy film directors to mix human-character acting with animation through motion capture. In these cases, which I will discuss in detail further along, the failure to understand this essential rule of distance has resulted in rather flat, uncompelling characters.

The centrality of these two principles, unity and distance, comes from my investigations into how animation is taught, compared with my research and experience as a puppetry artist. The following case studies of several films show how distance and unity become particularly critical when animation and puppetry are hybridized.

What the Wild Things are

In 2009, filmmaker Spike Jonze (*Being John Malkovich*, *Adaptation*) conceived a script with writer John Eggers based on Maurice Sendak's illustrated book, *Where the Wild Things Are*. To capture the iconic titular beasts in his live-action film, Jonze and his team worked with tangible puppets that would eventually become partially animated with CGI. While this is not an uncommon technique (it is often used in stop-motion animation), the hybrids in this film illustrate particularly well the importance of unity.

Jonze commissioned Jim Henson's Creature Shop to create large suit puppets for the Wild Things,[4] and the resulting figures look remarkably similar to their two-dimensional originals, with their design seeming to capture the beasts in spirit as well. Jonze and Eggers devised a screenplay that would lend these creatures nuanced emotions and an extensive amount of human dialogue. Jonze recognized early that these enormous, heavy puppets would require flexible, articulate faces in order to perform this dialogue, so he planned to employ animatronics (remote-controlled machines) to manipulate the facial expressions. However, the inherent challenges of working with the large puppet suits in rough outdoor locations, reinforced by advice from director David Fincher (*The Curious Case of Benjamin Button*), convinced Jonze and his team to remove the heavy motors from the costumes and pursue "[their] own hybrid visual effect process" with London's premier special-effects studio, Framestore (Billington 2009). Applying some of the same tools used to make live animals appear to speak on film, the Framestore artists rendered faces with CGI to match the images of each puppet and applied them to the film. The CGI mouths and other facial features were designed to respond to the vocalizations of the voice actors' pre-recorded dialogue so that the creatures onscreen would appear to speak naturally (Bennett 2009).

The creatures' faces on film do, indeed, lend a range of expression to these puppets: the effect is remarkably seamless in that the CGI blends in with the puppets' heads quite believably. But the movement itself does not match: the puppets' faces (particularly their mouths) are highly detailed and articulate, while their limbs and torsos appear clumsy and heavy. The irony of this problem – the dual masters Jonze was serving by creating this hybrid – comes through in his motivation: "we were just trying to get real, subtle, complex, nuanced performances out of these giant, wild, furry, huge-headed beasts" (quoted in Billington 2009). Such performances are certainly possible with either puppetry or animation, but this particular division of face and body resulted in a mismatched effect, as if a body composed of wide brushstrokes was supporting a head painted in extreme detail.

The issue here is lack of unity. Jonze's Wild Things read visually as terrestrial beings, inhabiting the Earth and confronting the same obstacles as any other large animals would. They run in the water; sling mud at their human friend, Max; and traverse the Earth like elephants, lumbering along with heavy footsteps. On several occasions, however, one leaps several times its own height into the air as if lifted from above. Since there is no apparent physical force (or exertion of magic) to create this impossibility, it discredits the Wild Things by making them look like marionettes on invisible strings, rather than the earthbound, living beasts they were until that moment.

The Wild Things' speech and dialogue also hamper unity. The script makes them sound not only like people but specifically American people from young Max's suburban world. While their physical appearances signal a crudeness we associate with animals, they engage in sophisticated small talk, petty gossip, and passive-aggressive group politics. As critic Kenneth Turan observes:

> The problem with this cast of characters is not so much their personalities but the way screenwriters Jonze and Eggers have turned them into neurotic adults with dysfunctional relationships. To hear them talk among themselves is to feel like you've stumbled onto a group therapy session involving unfunny refugees from an alternate universe Woody Allen movie.
>
> (Turan 2009)

The idea of presenting the Wild Things as humans in beast form is both imaginative and doable. But Jonze's puppeteers could not (or were directed not to) express with a full range of physical movement what they were communicating verbally or experiencing emotionally. During scenes of energetic group conversation, for example, their bodies are often incongruously limp. When he made the choice to use a hybrid puppetry/animation technique, Jonze did not fully consider the principle of unity to deliver consistently credible creatures.

Performance capture: How to escape the zombies

Today's most successful fantasy film directors are beginning to work with motion capture on a frequent basis. They tend to use an alternative term, "performance capture," to underscore the actors' contributions to the animated work. This type of puppetry/animation hybrid is particularly powerful when used in creature effects. But several film directors have used performance capture to try to make animations look like real people, often with unsettling results. The eeriness of these human cartoons is routinely attributed to the "uncanny valley," a term coined by Japanese roboticist Masahiro Mori. Mori posits that as artificial figures grow increasingly human-looking by design, they begin to dip into a "valley" of repulsiveness (Mori 1970). While the uncanny valley is an important consideration, I believe that it is the second principle shared by animation and puppetry that animated humans more perilously violate: the necessity of distance between performer and performed object/image.

Film directors Robert Zemeckis, Steven Spielberg, Peter Jackson, and James Cameron have all used extensive performance capture in their own twenty-first-century high-budget fantasy films. The three latter directors worked with Weta Digital, the New Zealand-based special-effects studio noted for its pioneering motion-capture work in *The Lord of the Rings: The Two Towers* (2002), *King Kong* (2005), *Avatar* (2009), *Rise of the Planet of the Apes* (2011), and *The Adventures of Tintin* (2011). While Weta was working with motion capture for the earliest of these films in the early 2000s, American film director Robert Zemeckis (*Back to the Future*, *Death Becomes Her*) was using mocap to make realistic-looking animated humans in his ImageMovers film studio. Zemeckis has a history of successfully mixing film from diverse sources, directing the famous interactions between people and cartoons in *Who Framed Roger Rabbit* (1988) and between new and historical film footage in *Forrest Gump* (1994). But in his particular brand of performance capture, he moved away from juxtaposing animation with live action (as seen in *Roger Rabbit*) and towards a *blending* of human with cartoon by turning a human actor into her animated likeness. The child characters in his first fully animated film, an adaptation of Chris Van Allsburg's *The Polar Express* (2004), were famously criticized for their eeriness – for impersonating humans too well. One critic called them "likeable zombies" (Burr 2004), another "as blank-eyed and rubbery-looking as moving mannequins" (McDonagh 2004). But as a producer and director, Zemeckis remained committed to advancing this style of naturalistic animation for several films that followed: *Beowulf* (2007), *A Christmas Carol* (2009), and *Mars Needs Moms* (2011). Effects technology improved considerably between each film, and the characters grew ever more detailed and convincingly human-looking. But the criticism of his animation style remained steadfast, and critics began to note that his experiments actually diminished the power of animation in his studio's work. *New York Times* critic Manohla Dargis offered a particularly interesting analysis of the performance capture in *Beowulf*:

> I don't yet see the point of performance capture, particularly given how ugly it renders realistic-looking human forms. Although the human faces and especially the eyes in "Beowulf" look somewhat less creepy than they did in "The Polar Express," ... they still have neither the spark of true life nor that of an artist's unfettered imagination. The face of [Anthony] Hopkins's king resembles the actor's [face] in broad outline, in the shape and curve of his physiognomy. But it has none of the minute trembling and shuddering that define and enliven – actually animate – the discrete spaces separating the nose, eyes and mouth. You see the cladding but not the soul.
>
> (Dargis 2007)

According to this critique, these hybrids are less believable and compelling than either human actors or pure animations (using the "artist's unfettered imagination") might have been. The creators borrowed from the crafts of acting and animation to build these realistic humans but lost the advantages of both.

The digital characters in Steven Spielberg's more recent performance-capture film *The Adventures of Tintin* (2011) have proven that animating humans without falling into the uncanny valley is now feasible. Critic John Beifuss conceded that the film "more or less climbs out of this [uncanny] valley," but then continues:

> The animation is extraordinarily impressive, yet the final impression remains: So what? ... If you're going to have Tintin more closely resemble a boy actor than Hergé's drawings, why animation? The stylishly flat cartooning of the opening credits is more attractive than the 3D animation that follows.
>
> (Beifuss 2011: 3)

This "what's the point?" response echoes the *Beowulf* review above, as well as a number of other reviews of *Tintin* and earlier performance-capture films. So if we accept the idea that near-photographic human animation is tolerable but boring, why are directors pushing so hard to do it? There may be anthropological, artistic, budgetary, and logistical answers to this question, but what interests me is the implicit assumption that human likeness itself expresses humanity. Embedded in this perspective is a mistrust of animated images and performing objects. This excerpt from an interview with *Beowulf* visual-effects artists Ken Ralston and Jerome Chen reveals this curious ambivalence:

> ... there was no razor stubble on the Tom Hanks character in "Polar (Express)." But here (in Beowulf), on Anthony Hopkins's Hrothgar and even on Ray Winstone's Beowulf, we wanted to see scars on their faces, as if they'd had to shave with knives. We wanted to see the pores. We kept on adding things until we really felt engaged by this character. ... "Beowulf" is a

movie for adults about deep, dark emotional journeys, and you can't get any sense of that in a cartoon character ... .

(quoted in Kehr 2007)

It is illuminating that artists working on a major *animated* feature believe that animation cannot convey serious feelings and that naturalistic detail creates engaging characters. In fact, puppetry and animation excel at portraying the deepest human emotions by their own means. Animation and puppetry reflect particular, selected characteristics of what they represent; they distill, filter, and exaggerate. As Penny Francis asserts, a puppet is a "representation and distillation of a character" (Francis 2012: 13), which could also be said of a fictional creature in an animated film. Pursuing perfect human mimesis in animation (as in puppetry) is to misunderstand its nature. Indeed, it is a symptom of a common bias towards naturalistic human acting and a tendency to view all performance forms through its lens.

Additionally, actors performing animated images of realistic human beings lack the requisite distance between creator/performer and character that good animation requires. Actor Jamie Bell's actual in-studio performance of Tintin was diminished in translation in the same way the work of *Beowulf* actors Robin Wright and Anthony Hopkins was visually muted by their animated semi-likenesses. In Wright's case, for example, the movie audience misses the full force of her character work and sees instead an overlay of her face with less authentic qualities: those of an artificial woman.

It helps to contrast Wright's example with a performance-capture character from the same film (significantly, not a human one) that does apply the distance principle and puts performance capture to good use. Actor Crispin Glover performed Grendel, an intensely contorted humanoid monster, in Zemeckis's performance-capture studio with a full grasp of the character's strange physical dimensions (*A Hero's Journey* 2008). He was necessarily conscious of the vast difference between his own body and that of his monster. This is what links effective performance capture to puppetry. Glover was portraying a creature quite physically distant and different from himself, as if he were inside a highly sophisticated, virtual costume puppet. Actors who climb into costume puppets know that their own performances will be obscured; only their manipulation of the puppet will read to the audience. In this way, the mocap suit works like a suit puppet of the imagination.

Based on these examples, I posit that simple human mimesis is a misplaced goal for hybrids. Creature effects, however, present powerful opportunities for mixed-breed technologies because they automatically offer the requisite distance between performer and performed. And, when done well, performance-capture effects for animals and other fantastical beings also achieve the unity necessary for plausibility. A more specific look at actor Andy Serkis's work will illustrate how performance capture for creatures is analogous to puppetry and how it enhances both the way film actors work with, and audiences interpret, nonhuman characters.

John Bell writes about the significance of Serkis's first experience with performance capture for the role of Gollum in Peter Jackson's *The Lord of the Rings: The Two Towers* (2002). Serkis describes how he first witnessed the animated creature's image through special goggles and was astonished by the way it reacted to his own movements. That experience of puppeteering was his introduction to the art of digital acting:

> Ramon ... [a "Mexican puppeteer"] explained it was more like controlling or driving a puppet than acting the character, and that I had to project life into the Gollum on the screen. Thinking I understood what he meant, I donned the goggles. What a buzz! Instantly it made sense. I got into the character as Gollum, hunching my back and crouching on my haunches, splaying my fingers, and in the goggles Gollum responded, simultaneously mirroring my every action, only in a more extreme way.
>
> (quoted in Bell 2008: 161)

Many considered this intense actor/animator collaboration a critical breakthrough in creature effects. It lent the not-quite-human, tortured Gollum a complex psychology and allowed him to fit in with the fantastical, live-action world he was to inhabit.

Serkis has since created a niche for himself as a digital actor, most notably performing the iconic ape in Peter Jackson's *King Kong* (2005) and Cesar, the lead chimpanzee in Rupert Wyatt's *Rise of the Planet of the Apes* (2011) [henceforth *Rise*]. In both films, Serkis performs photorealistic animals that possess some depth of character and interact extensively with humans in live-action settings.

Author Dan North bookends his study of virtual acting and special effects in *Performing Illusions* with references to the evolution of the *King Kong* films. He concludes that Kong's character benefits from the "vestiges of that human-ness" lent by Serkis in 2005, posing that "*King Kong* marks a point of convergence between physical performance, visual effects and animation" (North 2008: 180).

The artistry of rendering the creatures before and after Serkis performed them belonged to a team of animators and effects artists. How much of Serkis's performance plays out in the final images has varied from project to project (North 2008: 180). But in all of these examples, principles of unity were observed. Even with multiple artists at the helm, each of the resulting illusions presents whole creatures that honor physical laws and the particular confines of their well-researched anatomies.

Some of the effectiveness of naturalistic animal hybrids may also lie in audience relationships to the familiar-but-nonhuman. I suggest that we see the animal as *other* (as we do puppets and animated characters), and though an animal may exhibit aspects of what we call humanity, it is still of a different species. I draw this idea in part from an observation Basil Jones has shared from his *War Horse* experience:

> The audience quickly develop an affinity and fascination with the horses. They clearly want to understand what the horse is feeling and thinking and as a result, they become avaricious readers of horse semiotics. Whatever the horse puppeteers do (from ear twitching, flank shivering and eye-line alteration, to whinnying, nickering and blowing), the audience hungers to interpret.
>
> (Jones 2009: 261)

A human-performed animal like Cesar generates a range of expressions, gestures, and sounds that invite this type of audience interpretation. And this engagement does not require the kind of photorealism we see in *King Kong* and *Rise*, as the semi-transparent wooden puppets in *War Horse* prove. But Jackson's team built a Kong that would give the audience additional information to interpret: the more finely nuanced feelings and experiences of this complex primate. Indeed, performance capture seems ideally suited to the portrayal of *hybrid* human characters: an ape who falls in love with a woman (*Kong*), a chimp cursed with human intelligence (*Rise*), and emotionally tormented humanoid beasts like Grendel and Gollum.

Weta Digital's ability to create a whole club of diverse, realistic, tangible, and spontaneously performed animals in *Rise* has even further implications for puppetry and animation.[5] Prior to such successful hybrids, directors more or less had to choose between animation and puppetry for creature effects, weighing the complementary pros and cons of each. There was a time when George Lucas essentially had the options of either building conventional puppets for his *Star Wars* creatures, with all of the attending physical limitations and challenges (e.g., Yoda in *The Empire Strikes Back*), or creating post-production animated characters that no one could ever touch (e.g., Yoda in *Attack of the Clones*). As advanced hybrids, the CGI apes and chimpanzees in *Rise* capitalize on the advantages of both animation and live-action puppetry as spontaneous, tangible, artificial images (the film abounds with primate-human touching). And part of the reason these hybrid characters can embrace people is because they are present in the studio with them: they are actors performing together.

Performance-capture creatures can honor both unity and distance, and consequently expand the boundaries of both animation and puppetry. They also bring other logistical and creative advantages (as well as added complexities), but their contributions to animation and puppetry are clear. They make animation more spontaneous and lend the possibility of naturalism if that is desired for a particular kind of communication with audiences. To puppetry, they bring the possibility of operating photorealistic images and participating in the creation of a new species of make-believe.

Conclusion

The types of hybrids I have discussed here all follow a tradition of energetic invention. Artists generate new tools, combine forms, and devise technologies to make imaginative creatures, effects, worlds, and relationships. With digital puppetry, animation and puppetry are gaining new ground and changing the way in which audiences interact with fictional characters. And performance capture is enabling film directors to more precisely communicate what is inside their heads. Animation and puppetry are asserting their lasting relevance via this intermixing, even as (and perhaps because) it destabilizes definitions of both. As more hybrids come into regular use, artists newly experimenting with animation and puppetry will have to shake off inherited notions that they are limited, simplistic crafts and trust the considerable aesthetic powers of images and objects that perform.

Notes

1 "Creature effects" is a common term for special effects applied to fantastical creatures or animals, such as the dinosaurs in *Jurassic Park* (Steven Spielberg, director, 1993).
2 By "traditional" I am referring to the type of animation (drawn or CGI) that relies on the animator's art without use of motion capture or other digital puppetry tools.
3 "Live-action" generally refers to the filming of actual actors, animals, and/or puppets, as opposed to animated characters.
4 A suit puppet (sometimes called a costume puppet) is a large figure worn like a costume by its manipulator, who is fully concealed within. Big Bird, Chewbacca, and C3PO are all suit puppets.
5 To view a short documentary on the making of *Rise of Planet of the Apes*, see <http://www.youtube.com/watch?v=XM9Pvfq1KhE> (accessed August 14, 2013).

Works cited

A Hero's Journey: The Making of Beowulf (2008) DVD, Herzog-Cowen Entertainment, North Hollywood, California.

Bass, E. (1999) "Notes on Puppetry as a Theatrical Art: Response to an Interview," *Contemporary Theatre Review* 10: 35–39.

Beifuss, J. (2011) "'The Adventures of Tintin' – a Review: Steven Spielberg and the Uncanny Valley of Doom," *The Bloodshot Eye*, December 20, <http://blogs.commercialappeal.com/the_bloodshot_eye/2011/12/the-adventures-of-tintin—a-review.html> (accessed August 14, 2013).

Bell, J. (2008) *American Puppet Modernism: Essays on the Material World in Performance*. New York, NY: Palgrave Macmillan.

Bennett, N. (2009) "Framestore Goes to *Where the Wild Things Are*," December 23, <http://digitalartsonline.co.uk/features/creative-lifestyle/framestore-goes-where-wild-things-are/#ixzz2FBxwtn7o> (accessed August 14, 2013).

Billington, A. (2009) "Interview: *Where the Wild Things Are* Director Spike Jonze!," *FirstShowing.net*, October 15, <http://www.firstshowing.net/2009/interview-where-the-wild-things-are-director-spike-jonze/> (accessed 13 August 2013).

Burr, T. (2004) "Santa's Mixed Bag: 'Polar Express' Has Cool Visuals but Characters Lack Warmth," *Boston Globe*, November 10, <http://articles.boston.com/2004-11-10/news/29198606_1_polar-express-hero-boy-cool-visuals> (accessed August 14, 2013).

Dargis, M. (2007) "Confronting the Fabled Monster, Not to Mention His Naked Mom," *New York Times*, November 16, <http://movies.nytimes.com/2007/11/16/movies/16beow.html?scp=84&sq=movie&st=Search&pagewanted=print> (accessed August 14, 2013).

Francis, P. (2012) *Puppetry: A Reader in Theatre Practice*. Hampshire, England: Palgrave Macmillan.

Furniss, M. (1998) *Art in Motion: Animation Aesthetics*. Sydney: John Libbey Publishing.

Hooks, E. (2011) *Acting for Animators*, 3rd edn. London: Routledge.

Jones, B. (2009) "Puppetry and Authorship," in J. Taylor (ed) *Handspring Puppet Company*. Johannesburg, South Africa: David Krut Publishing.

Kaplin, S. (1999) "A Puppet Tree: A Model for the Field of Puppet Theatre," *TDR/The Drama Review* 43(3): 28–35.

Kehr, D. (2007) "Duplicate Motion, then Capture Emotion," *The New York Times* November 18, <http://www.nytimes.com/2007/11/18/movies/18kehr.html?pagewanted=all> (accessed August 14, 2013).

McDonagh, M. (2004) "*The Polar Express*: Review," *TV Guide*, <http://movies.tvguide.com/the-polar-express/review/137271> (accessed August 14, 2013).

Mori, M. (1970) "Bukimi no tani," *Energy* 7: 33–35; K. F. MacDorman and N. Kageki (trans.) (2012) "The Uncanny Valley," *IEEE Robotics and Automation* 19(2): 98–100.

North, D. (2008) *Performing Illusions: Cinema, Special Effects and the Virtual Actor*. New York, NY: Wallflower Press.

Strike, J. (2009) "Autodesk Reveals the Secrets of the Shrek Magic Mirror," *Animation World Network (AWN)* May 13, <http://www.awn.com/news/technology/autodesk-reveals-secrets-shrek-magic-mirror> (accessed August 13, 2013).

Tillis, S. (1999) "The Art of Puppetry in the Age of Media Production," *TDR/The Drama Review* 43: 182–195.

Turan, K. (2009) "Review of 'Where The Wild Things Are'," *Los Angeles Times* October 16, <http://articles.latimes.com/2009/oct/16/entertainment/et-wild-things16> (accessed August 14, 2013).

Webster, C. (2008) *Animation: The Mechanics of Motion*. Burlington, MA: Focal Press.

27
Programming Play
Puppets, Robots, and Engineering

Elizabeth Ann Jochum and Todd Murphey

> Art lies halfway between scientific knowledge and mythical or magical thought.
> Claude Lévi-Strauss (1962: 22)

In this chapter we introduce the *Pygmalion* Project, our collaboration between Northwestern University, the Georgia Institute for Technology, the University of Colorado, and Disney Research to develop a robotic platform for controlling marionettes. While engineers at Carnegie Mellon University, Nanyang Technological University in Singapore, and National Chiao Tung University in Taiwan have experimented separately with automating marionette and glove puppets, many efforts to combine robots and puppets have focused on using mechanical limbs to reproduce human and animal motions exactly.[1] These automated puppets often appear rigid and perfunctory and fail to stimulate the imagination in the same way that puppets operated directly by live puppeteers can. In the *Pygmalion* Project the robots are not the puppets, but rather the agents that operate the puppets. Our goal is to emulate the control technique of human puppeteers to develop automated puppets that are capable of dynamic movement typically beyond the range of traditional animatronics – such as walking and flying. Using the natural dynamics of marionettes, where puppets create the illusion of life through the art of indication rather than precise mechanical reproduction, we anticipate that our robotic marionette platform will allow for a wider, more artistic range of automated motions for entertainment robots.

Since antiquity, both artists and engineers have been interested in the creation and animation of material objects that create the illusion of life. Through the artful imitation of human and animal motions – using either the techniques of traditional puppetry (objects operated through direct human manipulation) or automated motion (objects that move autonomously) – inanimate objects succeed in creating compelling illusions because of what Bert States calls "binocular vision" (1985: 8). In the theatre, States argues, the spectator has the ability to "hold in mind two categories – that of the real and that of the imaginary – that are fused into a single phenomenon" (States 1985: 169). Binocular vision is what allows theatre audiences to grant fictive life to characters or objects based on their behaviors and the performance setting, encouraging spectators to project psychology and emotions onto human actors or inanimate objects. Binocular vision is especially pronounced in puppetry and productions that feature robot actors; but the nature of the theatrical illusion is problematized because, unlike human actors, puppets and robots are inanimate objects that simultaneously occlude and expose their artificiality, purposefully challenging distinctions between the real and imaginary (Bergamasco and Ghedini 2010: 731).[2] While a human actor never has to prove their "liveness" to a spectator, puppets and robots hover in a liminal space between the animate and the inanimate and must therefore work differently than human actors to provoke binocular vision. In marionette performance, puppeteers create the illusion of life by directing the dynamic swing motions of the marionette to generate movements that indicate human and animal behaviors but do not copy them precisely. Conversely, robots and other animatronics have typically eschewed dynamic motions in favor of ultrarealistic design, which results in objects that may look lifelike but have a limited range of motion. This approach raises expectations about how believably and convincingly the object should be able to perform, challenging the spectator's binocular vision by presenting an illusion of life that can sometimes appear frightful or uncanny.

Following Ernst Jentsch's 1906 essay "On the Psychology of the Uncanny," Freud defines the uncanny as the emotional response of fear or dread that arises from an encounter with a person or object that provokes doubt about its liveness (Freud 1919 [2003]: 135). Freud argues that specific situations provoke a strong sense of the uncanny – for example, "when the boundary between fantasy and reality is blurred, when we are faced with the reality of something that we have until now considered imaginary, when a symbol takes on the full function and significance of what it symbolizes" (Freud 1919 [2003]: 150). If States's binocular vision arouses delight in the simultaneous perception of "that of the real and that of the imaginary," then the uncanny can be understood as the inverse of that experience, where the spectator becomes frightened or anxious because of the uncertainty surrounding whether the object is living or dead, real or imagined. Recognizing the implications for robotics, Masahiro Mori coined the term "uncanny valley" to define this problem for robot engineers: human beings delight in the illusion of inanimate objects that appear to be alive, such as dolls and puppets, but if an object reaches a remarkable likeness without actually achieving liveness, the illusion is no longer pleasurable but disturbing (Mori 1970 [2012]: 99). Unlike robots, many traditional puppets manage to avoid the uncanny valley through design choices and the implied presence of the human puppeteer.[3] Because a puppet never has to convince a spectator of its autonomy, spectators can enjoy the illusion without experiencing uncertainty about the puppet's liveness. For example, Mori cites *bunraku* as an art form where the audience becomes "absorbed" in the performance and is able to "feel a high level of affinity for the puppet" despite the puppets' physical resemblance to humans (Mori 1970 [2012]: 99). We might say that for puppets, binocular vision supersedes the experience of the uncanny. Unlike puppets, robotic actors always risk appearing uncanny because they are designed to perform autonomously and independently from a human operator. The tendency towards the uncanny is furthered when robots are designed to physically resemble humans, such as the Geminoid F (discussed by Cody Poulton in Chapter 25). To create compelling theatrical illusions that provoke binocular vision, engineers would do well to design robots that avoid appearing uncanny.

In both puppetry and robotics, expressive movement is an integral aspect of mimesis, influencing how deftly the illusion of life is created and sustained. Joseph Roach observes that "expressive movement is becoming a lingua franca, the basis of a newly experienced affective cognition and corporal empathy. Mimesis, rooted in drama, imitates action; kinesis embodies it" (Roach 2010: 2). Recognizing the importance of expressive movement to puppetry and robotics, we might extend the metaphor of movement as a *lingua franca* for communication and interaction between humans and robots, and in particular for robots tasked with imitating human motions. Mori argues that movement is fundamental to how humans perceive animate and inanimate objects, proposing that the presence of movement "changes the shape of the uncanny valley graph by amplifying the peaks and valleys" (Mori 1970 [2012]: 99). The ability to generate expressive movement is directly related to how readily humans develop an affinity for inanimate objects. Mori's consideration of movement articulates for engineers a truth long understood by puppeteers: how an object moves, rather than its physical appearance, provokes binocular vision and creates the illusion of life.

The field of puppetry has a rich history of generating expressive movement that suggests the illusion of life without precisely copying human or animal motions. While puppetry is rooted in mimesis (puppets are imitative of human behavior in appearance), puppets operate according to a different set of physical laws than the creatures they imitate. From the perspective of movement, puppets are interesting because they partly resist a puppeteer's attempts to direct them: puppeteers are forced to reach a compromise with the physical dynamics of the puppet to create believable and expressive characters. This tension was explored in Heinrich von Kleist's 1810 essay "Über das Marionettentheater" ("On the Marionette Theatre"), here summarized by Kenneth Gross:

> The puppeteer knows he cannot control each limb separately, and thereby imitate in perfect detail the natural movements of human bodies. Rather, the manipulator learns to yield himself to the specific weight, the pendular motion and momentum of that thing suspended from strings. That's where the puppet's soul is found, in its merely physical center of gravity, which is the line of its spirit.
>
> (Gross 2011: 63)

The puppet's power of artistic expression is therefore not determined by how well it mimics human behavior, but rather by its ability to abstract the human experience and throw it into a type of relief, offering an artistic projection of a recognizable world from which we are partly or wholly free. That puppetry privileges artful imitation over precise replication confirms States's notion of binocular vision, grounding puppetry's underlying aesthetics more firmly in the Aristotelian notion of theatre as the imitation of an action. For marionettes, puppeteers have developed approaches that enable them to balance the dynamics of the puppet against the need to execute expressive choreography that convincingly imitates – but does not replicate – human and animal motion. Because puppets resist mimicry, they are capable of creating the illusion of life (or a different kind of life) in a way that pure mechanical replication does not. For this reason, we anticipate that entertainment robots might benefit from incorporating puppet-inspired design choices: not limited by the need to realistically replicate motions, engineers can learn from puppetry how to generate motions that provoke binocular vision and avoid appearing uncanny.

Traditionally, engineers have approached the task of imitating movement through mechanization, powering the motions of robotic limbs through individual motors or hydraulics located inside the puppet. Because of the tremendous difficulty of reproducing complex movements such as walking or dancing, entertainment robots are often heavily stabilized and equipped with a limited set of pre-programmed gestures. This reduced set of behaviors ensures that the robotic actors are reliable and stable, but the mechanisms involved with replicating the motions make the robots heavy and difficult to work with. Because these robots attempt to realistically mimic facial expressions and refined gestures, their jerky, mechanical motions are jarring and appear uncanny; the contrast with their lifelike appearance provokes uncertainty over whether the object is alive or not. Engineers who wish to develop mechanical performers that are better able to imitate the human experience must learn how to create the illusion of life through other means. Our research suggests that one way to achieve this is through dynamic motion that does not aim at precise mimicry. We use puppetry as a model for creating expressive automated robots that avoid the limitations of conventionally automated figures. For entertainment robots, kinesis is the new mimesis.

The *Pygmalion* Project is a collaboration begun in 2007 between artists and engineers to develop an automated platform for operating and controlling marionettes. After preliminary conversations with puppeteer Jon Ludwig at the Center for Puppetry Arts in Atlanta, we devised an experiment that uses string marionettes as a model for developing a new approach to automated motion. Our approach is fundamentally different than that of traditional animatronics, androids, and automata: we automate the physical motions of the human puppeteer and the forces outside of the puppet body rather than powering the motions from within the puppet. The robots in the *Pygmalion* Project are not the actors and do not appear onstage, but like human puppeteers, they act as the external agents of puppet motion. Removing the machinery from the puppet body may result in automated motion that is less rigid and more graceful because the sources of automation are indirect and hidden from view. Furthermore, the use of traditional marionettes invites the phenomenological gaze – or binocular vision – normally reserved for puppets (rather than robots), thereby helping our system to avoid the uncanny. Marionette puppetry has proven to be a useful method for investigating the dynamic, interactive processes between automated machines and passive agents, and represents a novel approach to automated motion that avoids the trappings of pure mechanization.

The Pygmalion myth – the story of the Greek sculptor who carves an ivory statue of a woman, which is then magically brought to life – provides the plot for our play and the title of our project. We were interested in a narrative that prompted reflection about the nature of our research: the relationship between humans and their attempts at creation. The metamorphosis in Pygmalion is a movement from the inanimate towards the animate, a theme that resonates in both puppetry and robotics. We determined that the story could be told though movement alone, using only two characters, and that the choreography for each puppet could be isolated. The last feature would prove important once the design for the system was finalized.

At the time of writing this essay, we have completed a prototype and programmed the robots to perform sections of the play. Our system was featured at the Museum of Science and Industry in Chicago during National Robotics Week in 2012 and 2013, where we performed short choreographic segments and demonstrated the user interface. Visitors were invited to interact with the system and design marionette choreography in real time by using software that translates their movements into choreographic sequences for marionettes. While we have not yet realized a full production, our ongoing research has led to useful findings about the complex task of automating human motion and the profound difficulties involved with computing mathematically what a puppeteer does intuitively. Our results suggest how the developers of entertainment robots might use puppetry as a model for designing and programming robotic performers that are more dynamic than the current generation of entertainment robots.

Kinesis in the age of mechanical reproduction

Automated mechanical figures have delighted audiences from antiquity to the present, but because of the technical and conceptual difficulties involved with replicating human and animal locomotion, these figures have traditionally focused on reproducing small, precise gestures, such as speaking, drawing, or playing musical instruments, rather than ambulatory movement, such as dance or acrobatics.[4] The automata of Heron of Alexandria (first century BCE), Leonardo Da Vinci (fifteenth century), Jacques de Vaucanson (eighteenth century), and Henri-Louis and Pierre Jaquet-Droz (eighteenth century) are forerunners to contemporary entertainment robots found in stage productions and theme parks. Because we are interested in kinesis, we can divide entertainment robots into two categories according to how they move: automated and tele-operated figures.

Automated figures – or automata – imitate human and animal behaviors and gestures, and although they appear to operate independently and without human agency, they require a human operator to set them in motion – for example, by turning a crank or pressing a button. Automated figures can be operated by pneumatics (pressurized gases) or hydraulics, through a system of springs and pulleys, or by clockwork mechanisms. Animatronic figures, such as those found in Disney's "The Hall of the Presidents," are automata that are powered electronically and rely on hydraulics and individual motorized joints to move. They operate according to a predetermined program run on a computer that determines the time, sequence, and duration of their movements. While automated figures might feature a variety of programmed movements – Vaucanson's life-size flute player (1739) could play 12 different melodies and Jaquet-Droz's "The Draftsman" (1771) could sketch four different drawings – their range of expression is limited to a predetermined set of behaviors. The benefit of these types of machines is that the performances are reliable over time; however, their rote performances do not always provoke binocular vision.

Tele-operated figures are mechanical figures in the shapes of humans, animals, or other fanciful creatures operated in real time by a human operator who controls the movements remotely. Like automata, these figures have a narrow range of expression that is limited by a set of preprogrammed expressions and gestures. However, because the figures are operated by human agents, they can often appear to be more interactive and expressive than their automated counterparts. Tele-operated figures have more in common with puppets because they are operated by external agents.[5] Examples of tele-operated robots are the Geminoid F and the Disney/Pixar animatronic *Wall-E* robot, each of whose expressive limbs and facial gestures simulate human motions and behaviors through the agency of human "puppeteers" who tele-operate the puppets remotely.

Because of the exigencies of live performance, including the presence of human actors and a live audience, the developers of entertainment robots must decide how to design and program robots that create pleasurable theatrical illusions without compromising the stability of the system or the safety of the audience. In some ways, theatre is an ideal venue for tele-operated robots because a stage production is a narrowly defined domain in which automated figures can excel. In a scripted production, the dialogue, technical cues, and choreography of the other actors are predetermined and guided by a human agent (the stage manager), who oversees the event from offstage. This approach makes it relatively easy to insert tele-operated robots into a live performance alongside human or other robotic actors. However, introducing fully automated robots into this setting is a more difficult task and often involves a trade-off between more dynamic behaviors – such as responsive facial gestures and speech which require a human operator – and those that favor more stable and repeatable motions not requiring an operator. The latter performances are unvarying, which often leads to motions that appear dull or predictable. In both cases, tele-operated and fully automated figures are heavily stabilized, and because of the machinery involved, are cumbersome to work with. The combination of weight and safety concerns and motion-control challenges makes it difficult to create compelling theatrical illusions that provoke binocular vision.

In terms of movement, both automated and tele-operated robots are similar to rod puppets, where movement is defined in kinematic, geometric terms – that is, by precisely mapping the motions of joints to the motions of the puppet. In rod puppetry, the puppeteer provides stability for the puppet, and the movements are directly controlled by the geometry of the human-powered rod. Programming a stabilized robot to reproduce these gestures mechanically is a rather straightforward engineering task (as demonstrated by Disney's Audio-Animatronics), but because there is no human intention or artistry powering the motions, the resulting movements look mechanical or rigid. We might call this a kinematic version of Mori's uncanny valley, where the absence of human feeling and impulse make it nearly impossible for mechanical figures to communicate any truths other than mechanical ones.

How is it possible, then, that Kleist can locate a marionette's soul in its "merely physical center of gravity," while animatronics and other entertainment robots are habitually perceived as soulless? Part of this can be explained by the presence of the human puppeteer, who enters into the gravity of the marionette, allowing "his own human feeling and impulse to be drawn toward and translated through the inanimate body, finding a home for them there, making the puppet itself into an actor" (Gross 2011: 64). But we might also suggest that puppets avoid appearing mechanical precisely because they resist perfect imitation. This is especially true for marionettes, where the distance between the puppeteer and the puppet and the indirectness of the control system make it difficult to replicate precisely human or animal motions. Because marionettes are controlled indirectly by strings (rather than by rods or human limbs), they present a different problem for automating motion than a stabilized automaton seated at a desk or playing a piano.

To automate the motion of a marionette, we cannot program a motor to move the individual joints directly. Rather, we must approach the problem indirectly by considering how the human puppeteer interacts with the puppet to control its movements – balancing the need for descriptive motions against the reality of the physical motions – and automate that process. Focusing on the indirect control of the human puppeteer, we account for the marionette's unique properties by using an approach called "optimal control." In this approach, the puppet's geometric movements are used to specify how and when a robotic puppeteer should be programmed to exert forces on the puppet in order to create the desired motion. To represent a person walking, we start with the marionette body and calculate how to operate the strings and controller in a way that best creates the illusion of walking, given that a marionette cannot precisely reproduce human locomotion. For engineers, optimal control is an essential step for programming robots that are able to navigate their environment independently. Because engineers want to design robotic systems that can move and operate in the real world, and human puppeteers have demonstrated a reliable ability for controlling dynamic objects in the physical world, puppetry makes a good test bed for exploring these issues.

Marionettes have significantly more degrees of freedom than other types of puppets, albeit far less than a human body: depending upon the number of strings, a typical marionette has between 45 and 60 degrees of freedom, while a healthy human possesses a number far greater than that. And yet, in the hands of a skilled puppeteer, marionettes are capable of a wide range of expressive and nimble choreography that emulates human movement. Rather than replicate the mechanical processes of a person walking, a marionette indicates walking, using the ground only as reference point and not as a physical constraint. As Kleist observed, marionettes appear immune from gravity's forces: "Puppets need only to touch upon the ground, and the soaring of their limbs is newly animated through this momentary hesitation" (Kleist 1810 [1972]: 24). Within this abstracted framework – where puppets operate according to a different set of dynamic and aesthetic laws than humans and humanoid robots – puppeteers have developed a system to control figures that is artful, stable, and reliable. This is the process that we emulate.

The *Pygmalion* Project

To understand how marionettes are operated, we met with puppeteers at the Center for Puppetry Arts in Atlanta. From puppeteer Jon Ludwig, we learned of an approach to designing puppet motion known as the "Imitate, Simplify, Exaggerate" method: imitate an observed behavior, simplify the motion to its basic components, and exaggerate the behavior to an appropriate level of animation that creates the illusion of that motion. To translate this approach into engineering terms, our first task was to describe this three-step process in computational terms. To do this, we had to model mathematically what a puppeteer does intuitively.

Ludwig describes how marionette choreography is divided into small units of motion, each lasting a specific amount of time (Egerstedt et al. 2007: 192). Puppeteers coordinate the timing of a motion so they can interact with other puppeteers, sometimes collaborating to control a single marionette or groups of puppets, ensuring that the marionettes remain animated throughout the performance. Scripts of puppet plays describe the action using four parameters: temporal duration, agent, space, and motion (i.e., when, who, where, and what). These motions are grouped and executed according to counts that specify when each motion begins and ends. During rehearsals and performance, the puppeteer makes decisions about the use of force, dynamics, and movement qualities that determine the expressive characteristics and the overall visual effect, handling complex choreographic sequences and solving problems of uncertainty. Using puppetry as our model, we developed robotic controllers and corresponding software that would replicate this process as closely as possible.

Unlike the puppeteer who can rely on a combination of heuristics and improvisation, engineers must work with comparatively simple building blocks to design marionette choreography. For the *Pygmalion* Project, we used two interdependent approaches: we created a software program called "Trep" that mathematically translates human motions into feasible puppet choreography, and we designed a robotic platform for controlling the marionettes (Johnson and Murphey 2007; Martin et al. 2011). Trep programs the robots to "perform" a marionette play, essentially enabling the robotic controllers to assume the role of a human puppeteer. Unlike traditional puppetry, however, we cannot rely on a human agent to interpret the kinetic "script." In a fully automated system, the marionette and its robotic controllers remain passive and mechanical; therefore, we must consider other factors, such as how many robots should operate one puppet and how to coordinate the movements of several robots controlling a single puppet. Unlike robots, puppeteers rely a great deal on intuition, and they are continually aware of where the audience is seated and of the positions of their left and right hand at any given moment. One of the most challenging parts of the experiment was coordinating and controlling the movement and efforts of the robotic controllers to approximate this level of intuition and awareness.

We devised the choreography with professional dancers – an approach not dissimilar from digital or puppetry – to generate a set of data points that would provide a mathematical "script" to start with. First, we encouraged the dancers to move with their natural gait and full range of motion; we then simplified the choreography to a level that would sufficiently communicate the story and recorded the choreography using a motion-capture system (see Figure 27.1). This system uses infrared sensors to track individual points attached to the dancer's body that record each motion.[6] From the data, we calculated the speed, duration, and forces for each movement and choreographic sequence and used this information to develop software that would

Figure 27.1 Dancers Stephen Loch and Stephanie Johnson (Brooks & Company Dance) performing choreography that was recorded using motion-capture technology; Georgia Institute for Technology, Atlanta (January 2009). Photo courtesy of the authors

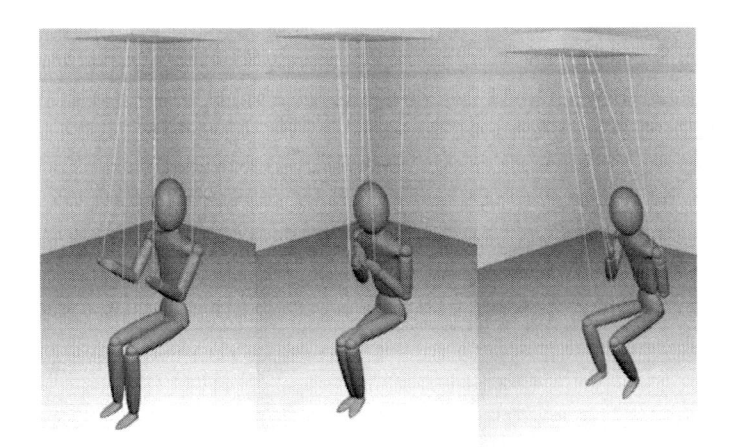

Figure 27.2 A computer rendering of marionette choreography based on motion-capture data and simulated using the original Trep software program. Image courtesy of the authors

translate human motion into abstracted marionette motion. Trep software uses algorithms to determine how to program each individual string attached to the marionette and simulates what this motion will look like using computer animations (see Figure 27.2). The "inputs" are then used to program robotic controllers that, like a human puppeteer, control the marionette by pulling on passive strings from above.

By indirectly operating the puppet, we are able to create expressive, automated puppet motion without mechanically reproducing human motions.

One might ask why we did not use marionettes to choreograph the play from the outset. Wouldn't it be simpler to use the motion-capture system to record the motions of marionettes directly operated by a professional puppeteer? The answer is that this approach would have sidestepped the more difficult – and more interesting – question of abstraction. As marionettes have fewer degrees of freedom than humans, their movements are already abstracted. Because we are interested in exploring kinesics – that is, understanding what motions are recognizably "human" and can be reliably reproduced using a minimum amount of effort and control – it was necessary to begin with the fullest range of dynamic and expressive motion possible.

Originally, we intended to control the puppets using two pivoting mechanical arms equipped with motor-powered winches for operating the marionette strings.[7] While this design partially imitated the process of a human puppeteer, it was limited because the marionettes could not traverse the stage as human-operated marionettes can. In some respects, this early design was as limited as the heavily stabilized systems we were trying to avoid because fixed robotic arms cannot approximate the fluid, dexterous, and extensive range of motion of a human puppeteer. In 2008, we began collaborating with engineers at Disney Research to develop a more flexible system for controlling the *Pygmalion* Project marionettes. We first experimented with the design of a single, freely moving robotic controller operating a single-stringed butterfly marionette. This design enabled a range of motion that more closely approximated the motions of a human puppeteer: the robotic controller (and, by extension, the marionette) could move around the entire stage fluidly and quickly, although not very reliably. To operate larger, heavier, and more articulated marionettes would require a redesign of the robotic controllers.

Following the butterfly experiment, we replaced the robotic arms of the original design with a custom-designed metal chassis equipped with individual winches for operating the strings and separate motors to drive around the stage (see Figure 27.3). A unique feature of the design is that the robotic controller is suspended from above using magnetic wheels that attach to a plastic "roof" covering the stage. This allows for a significantly wider range of motion than the original design, increasing opportunities for locomotion for the robot and the suspended marionette. The robot has three main functions: to move around the stage synchronously; to bear the weight and force of the puppet; and to reliably animate the limbs of the puppet using winch-operated strings. After early experiments with lightweight objects, such as a ball and a plastic skeleton, we determined that each puppet would require more than one robotic controller to operate it. Currently, a single human-shaped marionette is controlled by three robots attached with six strings at fixed points: two head strings, left forearm, right forearm, left knee, and right knee.

We approach the task of imitating human movement from two directions: automated motion and tele-operated motion. For automated motion, we use Trep to replicate as closely as possible the original choreography recorded from the human dancers.[8] Working with short choreographic phrases, we can learn which motions are the most aesthetically interesting and stable; however, controlling the natural swing of the marionette in between movement phrases is challenging. The second

Figure 27.3 Three robotic controllers operate a wooden marionette suspended from a plastic ceiling that covers a stage at the McCormick School for Engineering at Northwestern University: the robots each control two puppet strings and collaborate with each other to generate marionette motion; Evanston, Illinois (January 2011). Photo courtesy of the authors

approach involves tele-operating the robots in real time using remote controls. This allows us to experiment with the system more directly, as a puppeteer would operate a marionette controller, only without the tactile feedback that a puppeteer senses when controlling a marionette. The lack of feedback makes it difficult to develop an intuition for operating the puppets. In light of this limitation, we have experimented with Microsoft's Kinect®, a motion-tracking system, to record movement and reproduce the motions using Trep.[9] This method of tele-operation provides a more intuitive interface that allows users to design choreography in real time and observe the effects of their movements on the marionette. Kinect has proven to be a useful tool for designing animations in 2-D and virtual environments (Moore 2012), and our system demonstrates how it can be used to animate motion for inanimate objects in the physical world.

Currently, we are experimenting with variations of the automated marionette system. At Disney, engineers are working with lightweight marionettes equipped with individual motors on the puppet joints to create more controlled and defined movements; the forces created by the individual motorized joints help to stabilize some of the swing dynamics of the marionette. In our lab at Northwestern, we continue to develop the *Pygmalion* choreography using only the robotic controllers and are focusing on grouping together longer choreographic phrases. In addition, we are using the marionette platform to conduct other research experiments concerning optimal control and human-robot interaction.

Puppetry and future entertainment robots

From an engineering perspective, the most significant aspects of a puppeteer's process are coordination, improvisation, and intuition. Learning to coordinate the movements of robots so that they perform synchronously and collaboratively is a challenge for our experiment, in particular, and for robotics research, in general. For puppeteers, this process happens intuitively: in the direct-contact horse puppets Handspring Puppet Company designed for *War Horse* (2007, National Theatre), spectators witness how skillfully three puppeteers can instinctively and silently interact with one another while controlling a single puppet, collaboratively creating the illusion of life through the artful manipulation of an inanimate object. Designing automated systems that operate with a comparable level of collaboration and intuition remains a difficult task. Our research demonstrates that puppetry can be a powerful tool for exploring these complex processes. Puppetry is not only a metaphor for mechanical motion but also a useful method through which we can investigate the dynamics of expressive movement and its influence on binocular vision and the uncanny.

The *Pygmalion* Project is an example of how emerging technologies might be combined with well-established art forms to create new types of performing objects. Invariably these new technologies will prompt discussion concerning the relationship between the human artist and the performing object. Just as automata and animatronics challenged traditional notions of human agency by distancing the live human puppeteer from the act of animation, our automated marionette platform further distances the human artist from the live performance. The absence of a human puppeteer is potentially problematic for marionette puppetry, where the visual aesthetics are so profoundly intertwined with the physical relationship between the human puppeteer and the performing object. However, automated marionettes will not eliminate the need for human artists any more than robots have eliminated the need for human labor or puppets have eliminated the need for human actors. Rather, just as industrial robots changed the type of work that humans could do and empowered them to do other things, and just as puppets continue to artfully imitate the human condition without replacing human performers, entertainment robots will enable new types of performances and theatrical illusions. Automated marionettes invite us to consider how human puppeteers might negotiate new technological interfaces to enter the gravity of the marionette and how such technologies might shape the future of live performance.

Acknowledgments

This material is based upon work partially supported by the National Science Foundation under Award IIS-0917837. Any opinions, findings, and conclusions or recommendations expressed in this material are those of the author(s) and do not necessarily reflect the views of the National Science Foundation. The robotic system was developed in collaboration with Lanny Smoot at Disney Research (patent pending). Choreography was developed with dancers from the University of Colorado and Brooks & Co in Atlanta, Georgia. The authors wish to thank Oliver Gerland III and Jon Ludwig for their insight and contributions. Photo credits: Elliot Johnson, Todd Murphey, and Elizabeth Ann Jochum.

Notes

1 See Chen et al. (2005); Hu et al. (2009); and Yamane et al. (2003).
2 For further discussion of "binocular vision" in puppetry, see Tillis (1992).
3 Jurkowski (1988: 55) defines puppetry as:

> a theatre art distinguished from the theatre of live performers by its most fundamental feature, namely that the speaking, acting subject makes temporal use of vocal and motor sources of power which are outside it, which are not its own attributes. The relationships between the subject and its power sources are constantly changing, and this variation has essential semiological and aesthetic significance.

4 Kang (2011) describes the Western fascination with automata and humanoid robotics, tracing the intellectual, cultural, and artistic representations of the automaton from antiquity to the present.
5 Following Jurkowski's definition, tele-operated figures would be considered puppets because they require an outside force to animate them but automated figures would not.
6 Motion capture is used to generate computer graphic images in animation and film and has been adapted for video gaming and home animation with the Microsoft Kinect®.
7 The initial design was not unlike those used in Chen et al. (2005) and Yamane et al. (2003).
8 Videos of the *Pygmalion* Project are available at <http://vimeo.com/channels/numarionette>.
9 Kinect® is a gaming console that functions as a motion-capture system. The portable device has been used in many virtual simulations and animations. See Moore (2012).

Works cited

Bergamasco, M. and Ghedini, F. (2010) "Robotic Creatures: Anthropomorphism and Interaction Contemporary Art," Paper presented at IEEE International Symposium in Robot and Human Interactive Communication (RO-MAN), Viareggio, Italy, September 2010.

Chen, I., Xing, S. and Yeo, S. (2005) "Robotic Marionette System: From Mechatronic Design to Manipulation," Paper presented at IEEE International Conference on Robotics and Biomimetics (ROBIO), Hong Kong, July 2005.

Egerstedt, M., Murphey, T. and Ludwig, J. (2007) "Motion Programs for Puppet Choreography and Control," *Hybrid Systems: Computation and Control*, 4416: 190–202.

Friedman, T. (2012) "I Made the Robot Do It," *The New York Times*, August 25, 2012: SR11.

Freud, S. (1919) "The Uncanny," trans. D. McLintock (2003). New York, NY: The Penguin Group.

Gross, K. (2011) *Puppet: An Essay on Uncanny Life*. Chicago, IL: University of Chicago Press.

Hu, J., Wang, J. and Sun, G. (2009) "Self-Balancing Control and Manipulation of a Glove Puppet Robot on a Two-Wheel Mobile Platform," Paper presented at IEEE/RSJ International Conference on Intelligent Robots and Systems (IROS), St Louis, October 2009.

Johnson, E. and Murphey, T. (2007) "Dynamic Modeling and Motion-Planning for Marionettes: Rigid Bodies Articulated by Massless Strings," Paper presented at IEEE International Conference on Robotics and Automation (ICRA), Rome, April 2007.

Jurkowski, H. (1988) *Aspects of Puppet Theatre*, ed. P. Francis. London: Puppet Centre Trust.

Kang, M. (2011) *Sublime Dreams of Living Machines*. Cambridge, MA: Harvard University Press.

Kleist, H. (1810) "Über das Marionettentheater," trans. T. Neumiller (1972) "On the Marionette Theatre," *TDR/The Drama Review* 16(3): 22–26.

Lévi-Strauss, C. (1962) *La penseé sauvage*, trans. G. Weidenfeld (1966) *The Savage Mind*. Chicago, IL: University of Chicago Press.

Martin, P., Johnson, E., Murphey, T. and Egerstedt, M. (2011) "Constructing and Implementing Motion Programs for Robotic Marionettes," *IEEE Transactions on Automatic Control* 56: 902–907.

Moore, S. (2012) "Microsoft's KinEtre Animates Household Objects," *IEEE Spectrum*, August 8, <http://spectrum.ieee.org/video/consumer-electronics/audiovideo/microsofts-kinetre-lets-you-possess-people-inanimate-objects> (accessed August 8, 2013).

Mori, M. (1970) "Bukimi no tani," *Energy* 7: 33–35; trans. K. F. MacDorman and N. Kageki (2012) "The Uncanny Valley," *IEEE Robotics & Automation Magazine* 19(2): 98–100.

Murphey, T. and Egerstedt, M. (2007) "Choreography for Marionettes: Imitation, Planning, and Control," Paper presented at IEEE IROS, San Diego, California, October 2007.

Murphey, T., Egerstedt, M. and Johnson, E. (2011) "Control Aesthetics in Software Architecture for Robotic Marionettes," Paper presented in proceedings at American Control Conference, San Francisco, California, June 2011.

Roach, J. (2010) "Up Front: Kinesis Is the New Mimesis," *Theater* 40(1): 1–3.

States, B. (1985) *Great Reckonings in Little Rooms*. Los Angeles and Berkeley, CA: University of California Press.

Tillis, S. (1992) *Toward an Aesthetics of the Puppet*. Westport, CT: Greenwood Press.

Yamane, K., Hodgins, J. and Brown, H. B. (2003) "Controlling a Marionette with Human Motion Capture Data," Paper presented at IEEE ICRA, Taipei, Taiwan, September 2003.

28
Return to the Mound

Animating Infinite Potential in Clay, Food, and Compost

Eleanor Margolies

This chapter explores the live animation of food and clay in theatrical contexts, suggesting that "object animation" or "material animation" can help to dissolve the conceptual division between living and inert matter. Although this division appears to be one of the most fundamental concepts in everyday use, when we seek to understand processes such as the food cycle or the effect of radioactivity on genes, a more complex picture emerges. For example, a loaf of bread may appear to be an inert block of matter when sliding along a supermarket conveyor belt, but when it is eaten, its proteins, vitamins, and minerals interact with acids, enzymes, and bacteria in the body; the bread becomes integrated in the living body as well as fueling it. The science of the twentieth century opened up many new fields of study in which living and (apparently) inert matter interact. We are still digesting these concepts in the wider culture. Jane Bennett argues in *Vibrant Matter* (2010) that a rigid division between "matter" and "life" is partly to blame for our difficulties in conceiving of active interactions between substances, people, and animals. I will suggest that some contemporary puppetry succeeds in dramatizing the potential of matter to play an active part in life.

In a classical view of puppetry, the puppeteer creates the illusion of independent life in matter by manipulating it. "The term 'puppetry' denotes the act of bringing to imagined life inert figures and forms (representational or abstract) for a ritual or theatrical purpose" (Francis 2012: 5). The sense of "life in things" is thus no more than a pleasant illusion. However, some contemporary manipulation of objects, particularly the animation of formless materials in full view of the audience, evokes the unseen liveliness of matter by making visible material qualities such as weight, acoustic potential, and elasticity. Rather than attempting to create an illusion of life in the lifeless, such performances highlight the process of humans noticing and responding to fundamental material properties, as well as the variety of possible interactions between humans and the material world.

This chapter focuses on three performances, each modeling a different kind of relationship to the material world. In their version of *Ubu Roi* (1990), Nada Théâtre remain within a traditional performance context: they present a puppet version of a classic play, with a clear distinction between audience and performers. Yet, by using vegetables as their puppets, they disturb the boundary between living and dead matter. The parallels they make between vegetable and human substance revive our sense of the fragility of human life, embodied as it is in organic matter.

In the second performance discussed, *Claytime* by Indefinite Articles (2006 to present), the puppeteers sculpt figures from clay, improvising in response to audience requests. The use of clay adds another level of meaning to the dramas, conveying a sense of the infinite potential of formless materials. With its improvised musical accompaniment and interplay with the audience, *Claytime* springs from a tradition of improvisation. It establishes a relationship between the different kinds of "listening" that the puppeteers employ: they listen not only to fellow performers and audience members but also to the raw materials of performance, attentive to all suggestions and implicit invitations.

The third performance, "Feast on the Bridge" (2007–2012), further dissolves the boundary between performer and audience. Artist-curator Clare Patey has created a day-long, agglutinative performance along the length of a city bridge; a series of everyday interactions with materials, such as kneading bread dough, are framed as heightened performances, drawing in hands-on participants from the public. As a series of linked yet independent performances, the form of Feast on the Bridge is analogous to the macroscopic structure of the British food chain or the microscopic activity within a lump of live bread dough – it is a complex structure of interactions between living and inert matter. In an important essay, Bruno Latour proposes that such complex structures encompassing both material facts and social beliefs might be described as *"matters of concern*, not *matters of fact"* (Latour 2004: 231). He mentions global warming, the hormonal treatment of menopause, and the Space Shuttle Columbia as further examples of "matters of concern." I suggest that Patey's Feast on the Bridge might usefully be considered as an attempt to dramatize an important matter of concern and that this performance (extended in time and space) falls within the remit of puppetry studies because it focuses audience attention on the diversity of possible interactions (both everyday and extraordinary) between human and nonhuman matter.

In the case of the performances discussed here, the notion of puppetry as a form of "mastery" of inanimate things must be set aside. Far from aiming to "master" the inanimate, these animators "listen" to their particular materials, sensing their physical properties and potential for movement or metaphorical deployment. This approach has wider ethical implications. Phelim McDermott and Julian Crouch who, as Improbable Theatre, play extensively with puppetry and animation, often improvising with materials such as newspaper, sellotape, and foam, note that in "watching a puppeteer animating materials, we see her attitude to the world she inhabits" (Crouch and McDermott 2000: 13). Another example of this approach in actor training is given by director Enrique Pardo, who often asks actors to work with:

> ... a large and abstract object, too large to control cleverly, like a large piece of material, or cardboard, or a metal coil reel, or a set of bamboo sticks, etc. Respectful handling of such an object (and not "manipulating" it) will bring out its autonomous movements and sensual qualities, its "will" and caprice.
>
> (Pardo 1988: 170)

Pardo holds that respectful handling and receptivity help "to establish a dialogue with the object-world, beyond personal psychology and its expressivity" (Pardo 1988: 170). His approach to objects that are "too large to control cleverly" is particularly suggestive when considering human relations to substances, forces, and phenomena that seem beyond human control. Though a receptive, listening approach to matter does not constitute an ecological philosophy, it is perhaps a precondition for ecological thinking. Mark Down and Nick Barnes of the puppet company Blind Summit work mainly with table-top puppets operated in full view by three puppeteers each.[1] They make a suggestive analogy:

> In Japanese Bunraku puppetry three puppeteers work closely together to make lifelike human movement. In order to master the art, puppeteers listen to the puppet and enable it to move the way it suggests. They allow it to live. By submitting to the puppet in this way the puppeteers fall naturally into collaboration. This reverses the way puppets are popularly thought of today. Maybe from this perspective the Earth should be thought of as humanity's biggest puppet?
>
> (Down and Barnes 2012: 146)

As Down and Barnes suggest, the metaphor of planet-as-puppet depends upon redefining the popular understanding of puppetry, removing the implied relation of dominance and the implication that the human "gives life" to the inanimate.

Though well-worn phrases such as "puppet master" and "puppet state" emphasize a relation of dominance and manipulation, the notion of puppeteers "listening" to the kinetic inclinations of their puppets also has a long history. Many teachers of puppetry describe the practice of animation as starting from "following" or "listening to" a puppet or object. For example, Henryk Jurkowski writes of puppet manipulation: "Tin, cloth, wood, plastic, willow-cane – every one of these materials has its own peculiarities, and that is why [Edward Gordon] Craig, in *Puppets and Poets*, has rightly remarked: ... 'you don't move it; you let it move itself; that's the art'" (Jurkowski 1967: 26). Craig's recommendation to puppeteers finds an echo in sculptor Stephen De Staebler's approach to clay: "What I have tried to do for a long time is find out what the clay wants to do" (quoted in Adamson 2007: 50).

What might it mean to listen to the Earth, as Down and Barnes suggest? And why has it proved so challenging to do so? Any ecology is constituted by interactions on scales that escape direct human perception: transformations occurring in milliseconds or across millions of years, at the microscopic level or right across the globe. Climate change represents a particularly salient cluster of interactions that have proved hard to absorb intellectually or emotionally. It is difficult to grasp how burning fossil fuels in the nineteenth century could be implicated in alterations in twenty-first-century weather patterns or how the gas that heats my London flat could have anything to do with the inundation of coastal Bangladesh or the melting of polar ice-caps.

Puppetry, celebrated for its capacity to play with scale, offers one way to help audiences visualize interactions at scales beyond ordinary human perception. The performances described below take their audiences imaginatively into the heart of events they could not otherwise perceive: death and destruction on a nineteenth-century battlefield in a nonexistent country, collisions between particles at the subatomic level, and the "gargantuan" activity involved in feeding a modern city. Further, the "hands on" work of object animation and improvisation with formless materials transmits to puppeteers and audiences alike a heightened awareness of material properties such as weight and texture, a sense of dialogue between the human and the material, and a vision of matter as having independent agency – insights which might help to alter patterns of overconsumption without denying the pleasures of consumption.[2] Giving a new name to people interested in the mutual interactions between human and nonhuman matter, Bennett suggests that "vital materialists" will "linger in those moments during which they find themselves fascinated by objects, taking them as clues to the material vitality they share with them" (Bennett 2010: 17). The following discussion lingers over moments that have been deliberately constructed to draw attention to the materials of performance.

Playing with food

French puppet company Nada Théâtre adapted Alfred Jarry's play *Ubu Roi* for "two actors, some fruit and a lot of vegetables" in 1990.[3] Two performers, Guilhem Pellegrin and Babette Masson, play the central characters, Père and Mère Ubu. They animate a barrowload of fruits and vegetables serving as puppets that represent the other characters, such as noblemen and soldiers. When the tall, skinny, pale noblemen played by leeks are hacked to death on a Polish battlefield, shreds fly across the performance space, a sharp, sulfurous smell fills the air, and fluids drip from the table. There is a visceral sense of the destruction of living substance that takes place in war. Nada's decision to use food as characters reflects a trope that runs through Jarry's play: in the original text, as translated by Barbara Wright, the king is said to have been "cut in two like a sausage" (*"en deux comme une saucisse"*) (Jarry 1966: 43; 1922: 60). In the vegetable version, the metaphor is made literal as the actors playing Père and Mère crush a bunch of grapes representing the king. The Ubus appear as amoral demigods who casually animate and destroy. In numerous speeches in the play, they blur the distinction between people and food: Mère Ubu dismisses the troops as *"une cinquantaine d'estafiers armés de coupe-choux"* ("fifty flunkeys armed with nothing but cabbage-cutters") (Jarry 1966: 28; 1922: 10); while Père Ubu threatens her: *"Vous me faites injure et vous allez passer tout a l'heure par le casserole"* ("Insult me, and you'll find yourself in the stewpan in a minute") (Jarry 1966: 29; 1922: 11). Many of Ubu's orders are carried out by puppet or robot-like subalterns known as *palotins*; for Ubu, other human beings are nothing more than cannon fodder. Food puppets thus become a metaphor for the instrumentalization of people.[4]

Figure 28.1 Leek nobleman from Nada Théâtre's *Ubu Roi* (1990; photo from 2013 remounting). Photo © Nada Théâtre

Nada Théâtre is working here in the tradition of object animation. A puppet is an object designed to move in particular ways, the distribution of weight and points of suspension facilitating particular kinds of characterful movement. Any "found" object – like the leek in *Ubu Roi* – can also be considered in terms of its center of gravity and potential for movement.[5] Object animation draws the spectator's attention to the relationship between performer and everyday objects by overturning expectations: the performer picks up a teapot in an unexpected manner, gazes at it, turns it upside down, explores its potential for movement as a vehicle, a creature, a character. Through this process, object animation can reveal normally hidden material properties, such as the sound potential of an eggbeater or the springiness of a hose.

The animation of food in this production draws our attention to all the resemblances between humans and fruit and vegetables: the bodies – bulbous or elongated, firm or tender – as well as skin, flesh, and pulpy interiors. The live animation is rather different from the use of fruits and vegetables to generate characters in cartoons aimed at children.[6] Food items in such cartoons are usually little more than logos: stylized shapes (an elongated orange triangle is a carrot; a red circle is a tomato), with no roots, shoots, or seeds; no specific properties of taste, texture, or nutrients; and no connection to the process of growing food. Those cartoon characters are never peeled, let alone sliced open. The anthropomorphism is cozy: with the addition of cute voices and googly eyes, anything can become a character. The aesthetic of Nada Théâtre is, however, closer to Rabelais than to Mr. Potato Head, exploring the unhappy resemblances between human and nonhuman matter – both subject to violence, death, and decay.

The puppeteers in *Ubu Roi* add voices and movement to their cast of vegetables, just as the food-based cartoons do, but a more complex sensory identification takes place in live performance: audience members not only recognize forms visually but also activate a corporeal memory of weight, smell, taste, and texture. The same process applies to watching other forms of object animation such as, for example, the family of teaspoons of different sizes in Peter Ketturkat's *Keine Angst vor großen Tieren (The Crazy Kitchen Crew)*, touring since 2006.[7] As neurological research suggests, audience members bring their own bodily experience to performance; when I observe a performer peeling potatoes, it activates my own corporeal memory of performing the same action, a memory held in the muscles as well as the mind.[8]

Though the same principles of object animation apply, the impact upon an audience of using edible objects is different from work with objects such as cutlery. Food engages performers and audience in the sense of the provisional because it is so fragile, easily damaged, and quick to decay. By animating and then literally destroying food as the performance material, Nada Théâtre intensifies Jarry's themes of waste and wanton destruction. The familiarity of the vegetable and its closeness to the human body – peach skin to lip, potato peel to calloused thumb – can provoke a visceral reaction to the play's violence.

The hands dream

When animating formless materials, such as clay or paper, a performer responds to material qualities such as weight, elasticity, and resonance without any recourse to the social meaning of pre-existing forms. The dialogue between the performer and the material therefore becomes central to the meaning of the performance.

An improvisatory response to matter might be characterized as an alternation between "listening" to assess material properties, such as weight, grain, and surface tension (as discussed above), and "responding" with empathy, breath, and intention, shaping and adding movement in the search for human meaning. Gaston Bachelard captures this duality when he writes, "Matter, to which one speaks according to the rules when he is working it, swells under the hands of the workman. This *anima* accepts the flatteries of the *animus* which makes it emerge from its torpor. The hands dream" (Bachelard 1971: 72). Work with matter involves both a respectful address ("according to the rules") and creative shaping (matter "swells" and "emerges"). His image of dreaming hands evokes the experience of improvisation with materials: the performer's impulse is sculptural, but as it takes place before an audience that interprets and responds to the evolving forms, it is also aligned to storytelling. This delicate balance is exemplified in British theatre company Indefinite Articles, a collaboration between sculptor Sally Brown and actor Steve Tiplady.

Improvisation with formless materials has long played a significant role in the work of this company. Many of their performances have explored the expressive possibilities of a single material, most notably in *Dust* (2002), a retelling of Homer's *Odyssey*. In it, the performers drew a series of rapid sketches in a layer of fine sand spread on the plates of overhead projectors, projecting the images produced onto sheets, the walls of the space, or even a stream of falling sand. The material evoked the ancient world and the impermanence of life, "dust to dust."[9] The improvised performance *Claytime* (2006 to present) similarly brings characters to life for a brief moment of existence before they return to the earth.

Claytime grew out of storytelling and modeling workshops in a Cambridge nursery.[10] Originally developed for children from three to six years of age, it has also been performed for adults.[11] In both versions, the stage is set with a mound of soft terracotta clay. The performers initially work with the clay in a nonfigurative way, exploring its properties and establishing a relationship with each other and the audience, before inviting suggestions for an improvisation: "What would you like to see?" According to what is suggested, they sculpt landscapes, dinosaurs, dragons, or people, working the figures and themes into an improvised story that is accompanied by a musician. At the end of the performance, audience members are invited onto the stage to play for themselves. The resulting sculptures are photographed but not physically preserved – the clay is returned to the mound. This decision emphasizes the provisional nature of the performance: figures come into existence just for the time of storytelling and are preserved only in the memory. At the same time, it promises boundlessness: these marvelous creations of skill and imagination need not be saved since the clay contains infinite potential.

In a performance of *Claytime* that was part of the Suspense festival of puppetry for adults, an audience member requested a story about "the universe." This was November 2009, the month in which the Large Hadron Collider, the high-energy particle accelerator, was due to start operating. The underlying scientific principles were widely discussed in the news media, accompanied by speculation about apocalyptic disasters (e.g., it was suggested that microscopic black holes might drill right through the Earth).[12] The *Claytime* improvisation at Suspense developed into a sci-fi adventure: a man walks into a pub at the moment when an accident at the Large Hadron Collider sends the universe racing backwards towards the Big Bang; he falls through a jukebox portal into a parallel universe and eventually manages to put the world back on the right course. Although the plot is conventional in outline, the performance provided room for a more spacious response to the materials of the story. The performers unhurriedly molded clay into planets and showed them

Figure 28.2 The Sugar-Eating Sea Monster. Photo © Sally Todd/Indefinite Articles

moving through empty air, morphing and transforming: we seemed to look at Earth from the perspective of deep time or to follow a high-energy particle in slow motion.

Here, the use of clay added an important metaphorical dimension to the performance. Its emotional effect depended upon the evocation of a web of associations – some conscious, some unconscious – that might be called the "poetics" of the material. Clay is familiar childhood play stuff, dug out of the earth, but here it represents the vast strangeness of planet Earth; it forms geological strata but is malleable by the smallest hands; it is inanimate but is also the *Ur*-material out of which humanity was formed in many creation myths. The combination of this generative material and the actors' improvisation allowed the audience to daydream around big questions or the feelings provoked by them: the sense of wonder and of being small in the universe, the fear of being subject to processes that are out of our control.

The theme chosen for this performance of *Claytime* arose from the interests of a particular audience and the news stories of the day, but the cosmological scale is not unusual when working with formless materials, such as newspaper, cloth, or clay. Workshop improvisations with materials often take the shape of life cycles: bringing inanimate matter "to life" through the first touch of the puppeteer's hands, proceeding through growth and transformation, then to death or decay, finally ending with a return to inanimate formlessness as performers lift their hands away.[13] Audiences looking at the improvised manipulation of formless masses often imagine them to represent processes geological (volcanoes, continental shifts, lava flows) or biological (cells dividing, animals migrating, evolving) that might in reality take place over thousands of years.

At the end of *Claytime*, audience members are given a small lump of clay and invited to model a person or object that figured in the story. This private absorption in a creative response seems to follow naturally from the improvisatory approach – in every sense, the performance needs to be completed by the audience.

A giant playboard

As a substance, food acts on and alters the eater; it is the material most apt to call into question the fixed division between living and lifeless matter. Bennett describes the activity of eating as a series of "mutual transformations between human and nonhuman materials" (Bennett 2010: 40). In Feast on the Bridge, the materials of performance – in this case, foodstuffs – are not only animated by designated artists or performers, audience members also directly interact with the food. The performance is a structured assembly of everyday and fanciful interactions that cumulatively represent the life story of food:

> Feeding cities takes a gargantuan effort; one that arguably has a greater social and physical impact on our lives and planet than anything else we do. Yet few of us in the West are conscious of the process. Food arrives on our plates as if by magic, and we rarely stop to wonder how it got there.
> (Steel 2008: ix)

To understand the process by which food arrives on our plates, as Carolyn Steel invites us to do in her book *Hungry City* (2008), is very complex work, bringing together science, culture, agriculture, architecture, health, and economics, and ranging from the microscopic to the global. It requires a large canvas: if Feast on the Bridge can be interpreted as object animation on a giant scale, its playboard is a road bridge over the Thames, and the performance runs for ten hours, with a cast of thousands.

Over the last 20 years, artist Clare Patey has investigated food through a variety of means and with different constituencies.[14] In 2007, she created Feast on the Bridge, an annual festival that stages the whole life cycle of food, inviting "the participation of an urban public to explore the cyclical narrative of food production" (Patey 2012: 154). For one day a year, a bridge over the Thames in London is closed to road traffic. Trestle tables covered with hand-printed tablecloths run down the center of the bridge, forming two long banqueting tables. Around 40,000 strangers sit down and eat together over the course of the day, buying snacks from the stalls run by local producers or bringing food to share. But more than just a festival, with food as the means of encouraging sociability, Feast on the Bridge offers a coherent presentation of the story of food, focusing on a different staple produce each year.

Along the sides of the bridge there are dozens of stalls teaching specialist or forgotten food techniques, such as filleting fish, beekeeping, and bread-making. Participants grind wheat into flour, knead dough, bake bread, and eat it. They might also take part in playful activities that twist these artisanal interactions with food into art: they might decorate a hat with herbs, cut pumpkin lanterns, or toss a giant fruit salad in a tarpaulin held taut by dozens of people. Along the way, the story behind the raw materials is told conversationally by the artists and performers: the luscious peaches and berries in the giant fruit salad, for example, were destined for landfill because they did not meet the standards of uniformity, physical perfection, and longevity imposed by the supermarkets.

The handling of food in playful ways that might be regarded as wasteful from a purely utilitarian standpoint is part of the artistic program, alongside the very visible collection and reuse of waste. There are terracotta flowerpots on every table for leftovers, emptied by volunteers garlanded with flowers who push wheelbarrows down the bridge to onsite compost heaps. Nothing disappears or arrives "as if by magic": here are the cows that provide milk; there are the static bikes where cyclists generate power for a cinema. Feast on the Bridge is both a carnival, temporarily permitting new relationships and conversations to take place through the medium of food, and a participatory performance spread out along the bridge, describing the whole journey of food from growing, cooking and eating to decomposition.

If in *Ubu Roi*, the specific form, color, and texture of the leeks were intrinsic to their potential for animation as Polish noblemen (even if they had to be replaced for each performance), in Feast on the Bridge, the performance draws our attention both to the specific qualities of the material (i.e., there are particular fruits,

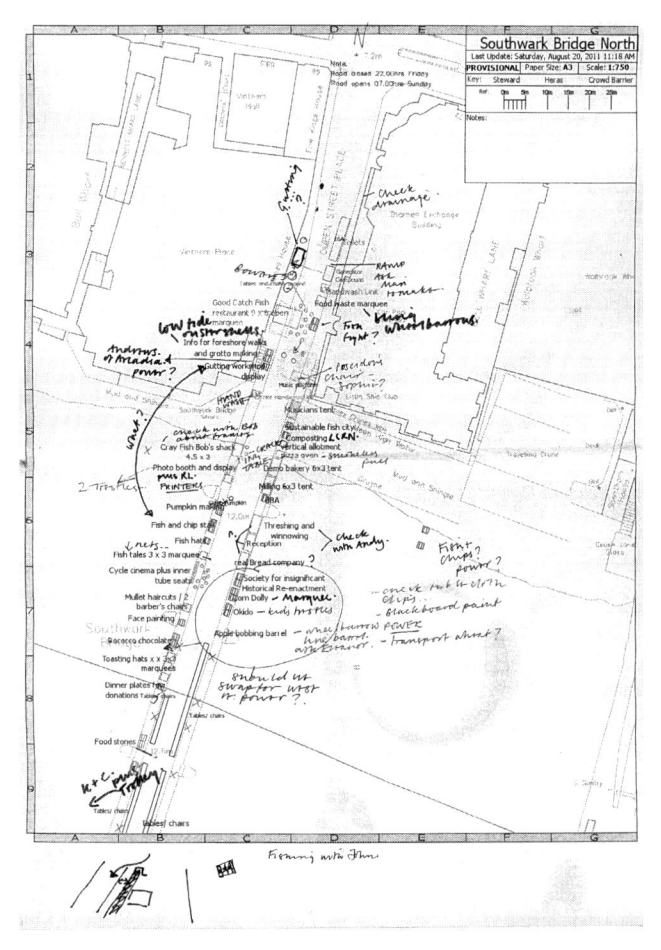

Figure 28.3 Map dated 20 August 2011 showing the location of individual stalls in that year's Feast on the Bridge in London. Image courtesy of Clare Patey

vegetables, grains of wheat, and loaves of bread, each with their own properties and available for manipulation by individual members of the audience) and to the nature of food as a commodity, substance, and "matter of concern" (i.e., "food" as it is manipulated by the collective forces that constitute the food chain). In this second sense, the foodstuffs used in Feast on the Bridge are more like the clay in *Claytime* than the vegetables in *Ubu Roi* – together, they constitute a formless mass with infinite potential. Taking this viewpoint on the material requires us to consider Feast on the Bridge as a new kind of animation in which Patey curates hundreds of independent interactions between humans and nonhuman matter, unified by her larger theme. One might recall Edward Gordon Craig's advice to the puppeteer, "You don't move it; you let it move itself."

Patey's work as artist-curator of this event is perhaps best described through Nicolas Bourriaud's notion of "relational aesthetics." Bourriaud identifies relational works as "formations" rather than "forms," providing opportunities for conviviality and ways of "learning to inhabit the world in a better way." No longer is the role of artworks "to form imaginary and utopian realities"; relational works are instead "ways of living and models of action within the existing real, whatever the scale chosen by the artist" (Bourriaud 2002: 13). In terms of the manipulation of objects, Feast on the Bridge operates on a very large scale, but one that is not unknown to puppetry.[15]

Treated as a material, food is "too large to control cleverly" in Enrique Pardo's resonant phrase (Pardo 1988: 170), both in terms of the geographically distributed physical space it occupies in production, distribution, and consumption, and in terms of the difficulties that we have in imagining the processes that lie behind its magical appearance on our plates. Food is one of many "matters of concern" (to use Latour's term) that have proved too large to represent when handled in an everyday, naturalistic way by an actor. As a result, important matters of concern, such as climate change, the future of radioactive waste, or the scarcity of resources, have generally been left outside the naturalistic theatre.[16]

What makes it so difficult to dramatize subjects such as climate change? According to playwright Caryl Churchill, as paraphrased by critic Robert Butler, the essential problem is distance: "What happens in one place affects people in another place. What happens in one generation affects people in another. Plays tend to frame individuals within a world of cause and effect that is immediate and visible" (Butler 2009: 110).

At a dramaturgical level, working with formless materials such as food and clay opens up the possibility of telling stories that extend beyond the human in time and space, working on cosmological, geological, or evolutionary timescales. More importantly, performances that involve animating such materials offer implicit alternatives to two equally destructive ideologies: the ceaseless exploitation of resources and the indiscriminate restriction of all consumption. Instead, performances such as *Claytime* and Feast on the Bridge transmit a receptive attitude to matter that emphasizes its intrinsic value and a joyful sense of material abundance.

A sense of abundance in performance may appear an unlikely goal when looking for ways of understanding climate change. But as Simon Bayly points out in a recent article, a genealogy of performance that traces its origins back to ritual is inevitably invested in "energy, excess and expenditure" (Bayly 2012: 38). In contrast, the trend in environmental politics that takes its cue from the title of the 1972 report to the Club of Rome – *The Limits to Growth* – stresses the need for limitations and constraints on consumption. But research has shown that well-intentioned exhortations encouraging sacrifice, restraint, and limitation for the sake of the planet not only fail to motivate change but can be counterproductive, arousing anxiety and suspicion or even a perverse determination to use resources right up to the permitted limit.[17] Thus, restrictions may prove ineffective from the environmental point of view, while destroying the efficacy of performance as ritual. Meanwhile, it could be argued that the creativity, playfulness, and invention embodied in performance are exactly what is needed in an ecological crisis – so long as the materials used are renewable.[18]

In festive mode, performers destroy barrowloads of vegetables and audiences make garlands that will quickly wilt and sculpt models that will be squashed back into a mound of soft clay. Performing with abundant, renewable materials spotlights interactions between human and nonhuman matter in the context of larger social and ecological formations. The barrowload of vegetables nightly destroyed in *Ubu Roi* could be made into soup or deposited on the compost heap. Either way, it constitutes a renewable resource for performance; the living matter so horrifyingly wasted in the performance need not be literally wasted in the real world, precisely because it is organic and biodegradable. This relationship with materials is made more explicit in *Claytime* and Feast on the Bridge: although apparently limitless quantities of clay and food are available for play and improvisation, the materials are not thrown away but are visibly "returned to the mound" or wheeled off to the compost heap. This action in itself generates a sense of renewal, potential, and abundance: children in the audience for *Claytime* refer to the "stories in the clay," while the creation of a compost heap represents an investment in the soil and the promise of future years of food-growing.

Notes

1 See <http://www.blindsummit.com>.
2 See, for example, Simms and Potts (2012).
3 The full title of the piece was *Ubu, adaptation pour deux comédiens, quelques fruits et beaucoup de légumes*. Directed by Jean-Louis Heckel, the production was first presented at the Avignon Festival in 1990 and toured extensively in the following years.
4 There have been numerous versions of *Ubu* exploring tyranny through the use of puppetry, including *Ubu and the Truth Commission* (Handspring Puppet Company, 1997; written by Jane Taylor) and *Mori el Merma* (1978, revived in 2006; a collaboration between Joan Miró and La Claca, directed by Joan Baixas). According to Jill Fell, Ubu's earliest appearances were in plays put on by the schoolboy Jarry and his friend Morin, "first with live actors, then as a shadow play and finally with actual puppets"; a version for puppets was shown to the public at the Théâtre des Pantins in 1898 (Fell 2010: 23).
5 Henryk Jurkowski distinguishes actors from objects, props, and puppets as follows: "Actors are human beings fulfilling theatrical functions; objects are things made by human beings not for theatrical use; props are things made for theatrical use; puppets are objects made to be theatre characters" (Jurkowski 1988: 80). I use the term "object animation" here to refer to the live animation of objects not made for theatrical use.
6 See, for example, the BBC children's series *OOglies* <www.bbc.co.uk/cbbc/shows/ooglies>. Cartoon characters based on vegetables are often used to promote a "healthy living" message, confident that viewers' pleasure in the characters will extend to the unanimated vegetables on the plate.
7 See <http://ketturkat.com/>.

8 Research into mirror neurons has shown that the same areas of the brain engage when performing an action and when watching someone else perform the same action. This is particularly marked among spectators who have direct physical experience of the action. See Calvo-Merino et al. (2005) for an account of an experiment measuring the neurological responses of a capoeira dancer and a ballet dancer to video clips of ballet and capoeira sequences.
9 Reviewer Lyn Gardner wrote of *Dust*: "When Penelope's suitors are dispatched by the returning hero, a constant stream of falling sand stands in for the screen itself: ghostly faces suddenly emerge from amid the falling grains and disappear. The sense of dust to dust, of walking in the footsteps of those who came before us, is palpable" (Gardner 2004: 1).
10 The resulting show that toured to theatrical venues in the UK (2006 to present) was co-devised and directed by Carey English of Quicksilver Theatre.
11 The workshops in the Cambridge nursery engaged with the investigative approach to art in education pioneered in the Reggio Emilia region of Italy. The Reggio schools employ artists in residence who reflect on the children's activities and help to deepen the quality of their explorations, using an artistic process of purposeful investigation, building on children's interest in natural phenomena such as shadows, the behavior of water, etc. As Sally Brown (Indefinite Articles 2006) puts it in the *Claytime* marketing materials, "When working with clay, children become scientists, alchemists, sculptors and architects in their investigations of what the material can do and what its properties are." She reports that children involved in the workshops would re-enact stories weeks or months later, referring to the "story in the clay."
12 See, for example, the detailed online rebuttal by CERN (the European Organization for Nuclear Research) of a number of such suggestions at <http://press.web.cern.ch/backgrounders/safety-lhc> (accessed 10 August 2013).
13 Observations of object-animation workshops run by Steve Tiplady and Rachel Riggs (1998) and Julian Crouch (1988) are documented in Margolies (1999, 2002).
14 Feast on the Bridge grew out of an earlier yearlong primary school project based on a local allotment, culminating in a meal for 400, cooked by the children using food they had grown.
15 For example, on Steve Kaplin's "puppet tree" diagram (1999 [2001]), which distributes puppets on a grid with axes representing the distance between performer and object and the ratio of performer to object, Feast on the Bridge would fall into the same region as Bread and Puppet's *Domestic Resurrection Circus* (1999 [2001]: 20–21). *Commute of the Species* operated on a comparable scale to Feast on the Bridge to dramatize a story that took place across hundreds of years: in the 2010 performance, animal puppets boarded a commuter train running up the Hudson Valley in New York State in order of their historical colonization of the area, creating "an allegory of migration, habitat expansion, and unforeseen consequences – in effect, condensing 400 years of eco-history into a single one-hour train ride" (Processional Arts Workshop 2010).
16 Though these themes are largely absent from naturalistic theatre, they have been explored in other forms of performance, such as street theatre and performance art. The timeline in *Culture and Climate Change: Recordings* (Butler et al. 2011) notes significant landmarks in drama, literature, and art addressing climate change.
17 For discussions of the psychology of climate change see Weintrobe (2012), Hulme (2009), and Butler et al. (2011).
18 See, for example, the essays edited by Goodbun et al. (2012) that form a special issue of *Architectural Design*.

Works cited

Adamson, G. (2007) *Thinking Through Craft*. Oxford and New York: Berg.
Bachelard, G. (1971) *The Poetics of Reverie*. Boston, MA: Beacon Press.
Bayly, S. (2012) "The Persistence of Waste," *Performance Research* 17(4): 33–41.
Bennett, J. (2010) *Vibrant Matter: A Political Ecology of Things*. Durham, NC, and London: Duke University Press.

Bourriaud, N. (2002) *Relational Aesthetics*, trans. S. Pleasance and F. Woods. Dijon, France: Les presses du réel.
Butler, R. (2009) "Closing the Distance" in E. Margolies (ed.) *Theatre Materials*. London: Central School of Speech and Drama.
Butler, R., Margolies, E., Smith, J. and Tyszczuk, R. (eds.) (2011) *Culture and Climate Change: Recordings*. Cambridge: Shed.
Calvo-Merino, B., Glaser, D. E., Grèzes, J., Passingham, R. E. and Haggard, P. (2005) "Action Observation and Acquired Motor Skills: An fMRI Study with Expert Dancers," *Cerebral Cortex* 15: 1243–1248.
Crouch, J. and McDermott, P. (2000) "The Gap," in A. Dean (ed.) *Puppetry into Performance: A User's Guide*. London: Central School of Speech and Drama, 21–23.
Down, M. and Barnes, N. (2012) "What Is a Puppet?" in R. Tyszczuk et al. (eds) *Atlas: Geography, Architecture and Change in an Interdependent World*. London: Black Dog Publishing.
Fell, J. (2010) *Alfred Jarry*. London: Reaktion Books.
Francis, P. (2012) *Puppetry: A Reader in Theatre Practice*. Houndmills, Basingstoke: Palgrave Macmillan.
Gardner, L. (2004) "Dust," *The Guardian* Online, January 16, 2004, <www.guardian.co.uk/stage/2004/jan/16/theatre> (accessed February 2, 2012).
Goodbun, J., Till, J. and Iossifova, D. (eds) (2012) *Scarcity: Architecture in an Age of Depleting Resources*, Special issue of *Architectural Design* 82(4).
Hulme, M. (2009) *Why We Disagree About Climate Change*. Cambridge: Cambridge University Press.
Indefinite Articles (2006) *Claytime* Marketing Pack, Developed with Colleges Nursery Cambridge, Junction Theatre Cambridge, Lyric Hammersmith, Colchester Mercury Theatre and the New Wolsey Theatre Ipswich.
Jarry, A. (1922) *Ubu Roi ou Les Polonais*. Paris: Librarie Charpentier et Fasquelle.
——(1966) *Ubu Roi*, trans. Barbara Wright. London: Gaberbocchus Press.
Jurkowski, H. (1967) "The Eternal Conflict," in M. Niculescu and UNIMA (eds) *The Puppet Theatre of the Modern World*. London: Harrap.
——(1988) *Aspects of Puppet Theatre*, ed. P. Francis. London: Puppet Centre Trust.
Kaplin, S. (1999) "A Puppet Tree: A Model for the Field of Puppet Theatre," *TDR/The Drama Review* 43(3): 28–35; reprinted in J. Bell (ed.) (2001) *Puppets, Masks and Performing Objects*. Cambridge, MA: MIT Press.
Latour, B. (2004) "Why Has Critique Run Out of Steam? From Matters of Fact to Matters of Concern," *Critical Inquiry* 30: 225–248.
Margolies, E. (1999) "Actors and Artisans: The Use of Objects in the Training of Actors," Unpublished thesis, University of Glasgow.
——(2002) "Dancing with Forks: A Study of Objects in Contemporary Performance," Unpublished thesis, London College of Printing.
Pardo, E. (1988) "The Theatres of Boredom and Depression," *Spring: A Journal of Archetype and Culture* 166–176.
Patey, C. (2012) "Feast on the Bridge," in R. Tyszczuk et al. (eds) *Atlas: Geography, Architecture and Change in an Interdependent World*. London: Black Dog Publishing.
Processional Arts Workshop (2010) "Commute of the Species," <www.superiorconcept.org/SCMpages/KMA.htm> (accessed February 2, 2012).
Simms, A. and Potts, R. (2012) *The New Materialism: How Our Relationship with the Material World Can Change for the Better*. London: The Real Press.
Steel, C. (2008) *Hungry City: How Food Shapes Our Lives*. London: Chatto and Windus.
Weintrobe, S. (2012) *Engaging with Climate Change: Psychoanalytic and Interdisciplinary Perspectives*. London: Routledge.

INDEX

A Christmas Carol 301
A Christmas Mystery (Bryzhan) 220–22, 222
A Wrapped Heart Inside the Refrigerator (Bungkusan Hati di Dalam Kulkas) 187
Aalborg University, Denmark 287
Abbott and Costello Meet Frankenstein 100
Abyor 183
Academy of Performing Arts, Prague 76
Acapella Mataraman 187
actant 6
action-images 88
actor-object relationship 3
actuator 227
Adoration Crucis 166, 169
Adorno, Theodor 186
The Adventures of Tintin 301, 302, 303
aerophones 69, 70, 74 n3
affect 15, 40, 86, 87, 88, 171, 230, 237, 310,
affection images 86, 87, 88
After Cardenio (Taylor) 226, 230–43, 233, 238, 239, 333 n4; historical approach 231–35; practical approach 236–41; theoretical approach 230–31
agency 3, 4, 5–6, 9, 45–46, 48–49, 131, 140–41, 173, 230, 231, 241, 273, 282–83, 287, 291, 295, 312, 313, 319, 325
Agus Nur Amal 7
AIDS 323
Akbari, Suzanne Conklin, Idols in the East: European Representation of Islam and the Orient 1100–1450 146
All Hallows' Eve Ritual Celebration (Redmoon Theater) 99
amagatsu 156–57, 156, 163 n2
Andoh, Adjoa 246
androids 3, 227, 281–84, 282, 284, 286–88, 287; see also automata; robots/robotics
animal hide, as material 6, 14, 94, 207, 211
animate 3, 21–25, 27, 46–47, 47, 49, 289, 291 n11, 309–10, 312
animation 294–305

Animation World Network 297
animatronics 288–89, 299, 308, 309, 311, 312, 313–14, 319
animism/animist 44, 46, 48, 49, 51, 290
Anoman Immolated (Anoman Obong) 182
Anselm of Canterbury 171–72
anthropomorphism 2, 5, 6, 22–23, 26, 46, 86, 112, 170, 326
Apollinaire, Guillaume 50
Arabic: culture 112, 144–52; language 149, 183
Argento, Vincenzo (e Figli) 147, 149, 149
Ariendra, Yenu 187, 188, 189
Arnott, Peter 125, 126
Arnstein, Sherri 102
artist-entrepreneur 206, 215
Ashley, Leonard 117–19
Association House of Chicago 100
Association of Southeast Asian Nations 185
Atwood, Margaret 291 n2
audience reception 65–66, 171
Audio-Animatronics (Disney) 313
automata 7, 9, 46, 49, 139, 277 n4, 280–81, 282, 283, 286, 311, 313; Disney 227; Gothic era 166; Greek temple 136–37; see also androids; robots/robotics
avant-garde 8, 15, 49–50, 51, 67, 78, 185, 201
Avatar 296, 301
The Avengers 296
Avenue Q 2, 297
Avvakum (Russian Archpriest) 48
Awaji (island) 154
Awaji (puppetry) 154, 162
Awaji Puppet Theatre 162

Babelfish 28 n11
Bachelard, Gaston 93, 327
Bak Byeong-o see Park Chun-hee (Bak Byeong-o)
Bak Cheomji (Old Man Park, namsadang character) 195, 199–200, 203 n1

INDEX

Baixas, Joan 24, 26, 28 n9, 333 n4
Barnes, Nick 324
Baroque theatre 218
Barrow, William, of Walden 166
Barthes, Roland 126–27, 249, 250, 253 n2, 255, 270, 274; *L'Empire des Signes* 289
Bartlett, Neil 245, 246, 247, 248, 249–50, 251–53, 253 n3; *see also Or You Could Kiss Me* (Handspring Puppet Company/ National Theatre, London)
Baruth, Philip 117, 128 n3, 128 n6
Bass, Eric 11, 14, 54–59, 141, 298; *see also* Sandglass Theater
The Bat (*Chauve-Souris*) (cabaret) 130
batlejka 218; *see also* crèche performances; Nativity; vertep
Bauhaus 15, 25, 78
Bayly, Simon 332
behavior, modes of 88
Beifuss, John 302
Béjart, Maurice 31
Bell, Jamie 303
Bell, John 2, 6, 10, 11, 13–15, 43–52, 108, 255, 277, 295, 303–4; *American Puppet Modernism: Essays on the Material World in Performance* 9, 295; *Puppets, Masks, and Performing Objects* 9
Benjamin, Walter 226–27, 269, 270, 274–77
Bennett, Jane 325, 329; *Vibrant Matter* 6, 9, 322
Benois, Alexandre 130
Beowulf 302–3, 305
Berlian Ajaib (*Magical/Wonder Diamond*) 187, 188
Bernstein, Robin 173
Between Sand and Stars (Sandglass Theater) 56, 57
Bhagavati/Bhadrakali 207
Bhat, Puran 72
biblical stories 120, 221–22; Creation 91; Nativity 218–24, 224
"big bang" 193–94, 195–96, 202
Big Bang theory 91, 329
Big Petrushka 140, 140
binocular vision 225, 308–11, 313, 319
Bishop, Claire 100, 102
Blackburn, Stuart 9, 208, 210, 211; *Inside the Drama-House: Rama Stories and Shadow Puppets in South India* 216 n4
blenchong lamp 93
Blind Summit 30, 324
Blumenthal, Eileen 122, 124, 255; *Puppetry: A World History* 10
bodhisattva 158, 159
body: and gaze 36–38; Sartre on 36–37

body-movements, and co-presence 33–35
Boerwinkel, Henk, *Metamorphosis* 56
Bogart, Anne 54, 56
Bogatyrev, Petr 265 n1, 265 n2
boli 72
Bolton, Christopher 281
Bonté, Patrick 31; *see also* Compagnie Mossoux-Bonté; *Twin Houses*
Borrowed Fire (Stone) 207, 209
Bourriaud, Nicolas 180, 186, 189, 311
Boxley, Kent 166
Brandes, Dawn Tracey 245–53
Brandon, James 10
Bread and Puppet Theater 15, 45, 51, 108, 334 n15
breath 57, 66, 246, 250, 252, 327
Brecht, Bertolt 43, 44
Brecht, Stefan 9
Brehm, Kate 11, 15, 84–90
"The Brementown Musicians" (Showcase Beat Le Mot) 82
Bride of Frankenstein 100
British Museum 117, 179
Brodiachyi Vertep see Vagrant Booth Theatre
Brooks and Co. Dance 316, 319
Brown, Sally 327, 334 n11
Brownlee, John 284
Bryzhan, Natasha 221
Bryzhan, Olga 221
Bryzhan, Sergij 219–20, 221, 222–23, 222, 224
Buddhism 92, 154, 158, 159, 163 n5, 194–95, 201
Bufano, Ariel 24
bunraku 2, 3, 112, 161–62, 193, 225, 239, 249–50, 272, 280–89, 309, 324
Bunraku company 178
Burke, Peter 48, 49
Butler, Robert 323
Butterworth, P. 166

Caldwell, Finn 246
camera, eye of 84, 89
camera obscura 8
camera-consciousness 84
Cameron, James 301
Camille, Michael 165, 166, 172
Cañellas, Carles 28 n7
Čapek, Karel 49; *R.U.R. (Rossum's Universal Robots)* 49, 281, 290 n4
capitalism 2, 15, 101, 106–7, 108, 118
Carnegie Mellon University 308
Carrignon, Christian 27 n2
Cartesian dualism 238

337

INDEX

Catholicism/Catholic Church 49, 112, 122, 150, 166, 212, 232
causal networks 261
Cebolang Minggat 190
Center for Puppetry Arts 311, 314
Cervantes, Miguel de 232; *Don Quixote* 231–32, 234, 241
CGI 4, 93, 230 n6, 288, 290, 294, 295, 299–301, 305, 306 n2, 316
Chagall, Marc 56
Charke, Charlotte 116–27
Chandradasan 213
character 86–87, 88–89; compiled 226, 249; fragmentation of 2, 11, 55, 225–26, 245, 246, 248–49; refining 245–53
Charlemagne 144
Chatman, Seymour 255, 265 n4, 265 n7, 265 n8
Chazelle, Celia 170–71
Chekhov, Anton: *The Seagull* 50
Chen, Fan Pen Li 10
Chen, Jerome 302–3
Chernubles (Saracen character) 146, 148
Chesterton, G. K. 277
Chikamatsu Monzaemon 13, 227, 281, 289, 291
children/child's play 226–27, 268, 269–70, 272, 274–77
children's theatre *see* postdramatic children's theatre; theatre for young audiences
China, shadow theatre 92, 96
Chinese Theatre Works 15, 96
Chmelnickj County Puppet Theatre 219–20, 222, 224
Cho Yong-su (Jo Yong-su) 196
Cho Yong-suk (Jo Yong-seok) 196
Christianto, Wisma Nugraha 181, 182
Churchill, Caryl 322
Churchill, Winston 277
Cibber, Colley 116, 117, 122, 128 n7; *Dawn and Phillida* 128 n4
Cirebon 181, 183
clay, as material 5, 50, 227, 295, 322, 323, 324, 327–29, 331, 333, 334 n11
Claytime (Indefinite Articles) 227, 323, 328–29, 331, 333, 334 n11
"Cloisters Cross" 168–69, 169
close-up 87, 89
Cloud, Christine 127
cognition 266 n11
Cohen, Matthew Isaac 11, 112, 178–90
Cole, Jeffrey 151–52; *The New Racism in Europe: A Sicilian Ethnography* 145
collage 201, 223

Collins, P. H. 127 n2
colonialism 45
comics 85, 89
commedia dell'arte 122, 135, 199, 201
Communism/Communist regime 218–19, 221
communitas 15, 102
Commute of the Species (Processional Arts Workshop) 334 n15
Compagnie Mossoux-Bonté 30–31; *see also Twin Houses*
Compagnie Skappa! 76
compiled character 226, 249
computer-generated imagery/graphics *see* CGI; computers
computers 4, 93, 206, 215, 227, 288–89, 296, 297, 298, 312, 316; *see also* CGI
Confucian ideology 194–95
Conrad, Joseph, *Heart of Darkness* 282
consciousness 290
Conti, Nina 243 n3
Contractor, Meher 210
co-presence 3, 30–31, 225, 226, 231; defining 31; and the Other 35–38; perception and imagination 38–41; through body movements 33–35; through speech 32–33
Corneille, Pierre, *Le Cid* 59 n1
cosmogenesis 91
costume 25, 141, 185, 189, 197, 198, 199, 201, 221, 240, 243 n2, 300, 303, 306 n4
"courtly consort" 193–94, 196, 202
Covent Garden 120
Craig, Edward Gordon 8, 10, 14, 28 n6, 120, 131, 137, 142, 313, 324; "The Actor and the Über-marionette" 3, 133, 136
Creative Group NONI 193, 194, 195, 198–202, 203 n3
creature effects 294, 301, 303–4, 305, 306 n1
crèche performances 9, 218, 219–20, 223; *see also batlejka*; Nativity; *vertep*
Critchley, Simon 38
Cross, the: in context 168–69; as performing object 165, 166–68; as puppet 165, 166–68; puppet perspective 173–74; in ritual performance 170–74, 174 n1; speaks 169–70; and the "temporal contract" 171–73
cross-dressing 116, 117, 118, 122, 123, 126, 127, 127 n1, 128 n3, 128 n8, 194
Crossley-Howard, Kevin 171
Crouch, Julian 323
Crusades 150
cubism 94, 141
Cungkring 183
Cungkring Runs for Office (*Cungkring Nyaleg*) 183

Cuniculus (Stuffed Puppet Theatre) 30, 31–33, *32*, 34, 36, 39
cuts *see* montage

da Vinci, Leonardo 312
Dada 78
dalang 92, 93, 95
Damasio, Antonio, *The Feeling of What Happens* 40
dan Droste, Gabi 77; *Theater von Anfang an!: Bildung, Kunst und frühe Kindheit* 82
dance/dancers 4, 11, 13, 26 n6, 31, 34, 44, 181, 185; children's theatre 77, 79, 82; *kabuki* 280, 291 n1; Korea 6, 196–200; new model theatres 268, 276, 278 n6; Petrushka 67, 71, 72; robots/robotics 312, 315–18, *316*, 333; Russian modernist 130, 135–36, 140; shadow 95–96, 205
Daniel, Norman, *Heroes and Saracens: An Interpretation of the Chansons de Geste* 145
Dargis, Manohla 302
Darika 207
Dastur, Françoise 38
De Leon, Moses, *Zohar* (*The Book of Splendor*) 91
De Staebler, Stephen 324
de Vaucanson, Jacques 312
de Weever, Jacqueline, *Sheba's Daughters: Whitening and Demonizing the Saracen Woman in Medieval French Epic* 146
Death (character) 219–20
death: and marionettes 137; of the puppet 18–27, 56; and puppets 3, 11, 14, 62, 73, 156–57, 160, 199–200, 202, 219–20, 236, 238–39, 246–47, 260, 280, 284–85, 290, 291 n11, 325, 326, 329
Deleuze, Gilles 15, 84, 85, 87, 88, 89, 90 n3; *Cinema 1: The Movement Image* 84
Deong deong kung ta kung (Hyundai Puppet Theatre) 196–97, 203 n2
Depositio Crucis 164, 166, 170, 171
Derrida, Jacques 9
Descartes, René 235, 243 n12
Desfosses, Angès 76
Deutsch-Sorbisches Volkstheater Bautzen (German-Sorbian People's Theatre Bautzen) 78, 79
Devil (character) 50, 219–20, 239
Dickens, Charles 277
digital media 4, 44, 179
digital puppet(ry) 51, 294, 296, 297–98, 305, 306 n2
director 219, 220
Disney 227, 297, 308, 312–13, 318
Disney Research 308, 317, 319

disobedient obedience 130–42
Dis/RePlacement (Redmoon Theater) 103–4, *104*
Dobuzhinsky, Mstislav *135*
doll(s) 24, 26, 84, 88, 155–56, 158, 159–61, 162 n2, 196, 198, 202, 231, 232, 236, 277 n4, 281, 284, *285*, 289, 309
Don Cossack (character) 220
Dondoro Theatre 30
Dono, Damiet van Dalsum Heri 186
double consciousness 5, 236
doubling 237, 243 n8, 245–46, 277 n4, 284
Down, Mark 324
"The Draftsman" (Jaquet-Droz) 312–13
dramaturgy 31, 219, 226; physical 54, 56; tabletop 272; visual 54–59, *57*, *58*, 141, 248–49, 272–73
"The Dream of the Rood" 171
DreamWorks Animation 297
Drury Lane *see* Theatre Royal, Drury Lane
duality 140–42
Dupont, Lauren 76
Dürrenmatt, Friedrich 56
Dust (Indefinite Articles) 326, 334 n9

Ebert, Roger 288
Efimov, Ivan 139, 140
eidophusikon 8
Eisenstein, Sergei 90 n3, 135
Ejchenbaum, Boris 266 n9
Elam, Harry J. 189
Elevatio Crucis 164, 166, 169, 172
Elizabeth of Spalbeek 173
Energy (journal) 284
English, Carey 334 n10
Enlightenment 49
Eruli, Brunella 9
"The Extraordinary Ordinary" 106, 107–9
eye of the camera 84, 89
The Eye Which We Do Not Have 87, 88, 90 n4

fabula 226, 257–58, 266 n9
family-theatre 220; *see also* children's theatre
Faust tradition 135
Feast on the Bridge (Patey) 227, 323, 330–33, 334 n14, 334 n15
Fell, Jill 334 n4
feminist theory 112, 118, 122, 123–27, 128 n3, 128 n8
Festival Mondial des Théâtres de Marionnettes 77
Festival Morgana 144–45
FIDENA (Puppet Theatre of the Nations) 77

Fielding, Henry 116, 122–26; *The Covent Garden Tragedy* 122, 123–25, 128 n4; *The Mock Doctor* 128 n4; *The Old Debauchees* 128 n4
figurative puppet(s) 4, 11, 18, 23–24, 26–27, 219, 291 n11
Figurentheater Triangle 56
film xxiii, 4, 84, 88, 93, 100, 111, 207, 255–56, 257, 265 n7, 272, 287 n6, 289, 294, 296, 297, 301, 305, 306 n3, 320 n6
film animation xxiii
film theory 84, 257
Final Fantasy: The Spirits Within 288
Fincher, David 300
Finding Nemo 297
Fluxus 8
Fokine, Mikhail 130
Foley, Kathy 6, 112–13, 192–202
folk plays 9, 73, 74 n9, 126, 199, 218–19, 223
food: as material 5, 227, 322, 323, 329–33, 334 n14; as performing object 5, 21, 27, 325–27, *326*; as offering to puppets 21
forces, and action-image 88
The Forces of Love and Magic (Slonimskaia) 130, 131, 134–35, *135*
form, theatrical 219
formalism 255, 265 n1, 265 n2, 266 n9
formlessness 19, 27, 322–23, 325, 327, 331, 332
Forrest Gump 301
Foucault, Michel 9
Frabetti, Roberto 76, 77
Frabetti, Valeria 76
Framestore 300
framing 85, 85–86
Francis, Penny 9, 122, 124, 131, 132, 141; *Puppetry: A Reader in Theatre Practice* 10, 295–96, 303, 322
Frankenstein 100–102, 288
Frankenstein Unbound 100
Freud, Sigmund: on "discarded beliefs" 50, 51; dreamwork 67; on performing objects 47–49, 50–51, 52 n2, 62, 92, 93, 112, 165; on the uncanny 43, 44, 45, 47–49, 50–51, 67, 131, 286, 309; "The Uncanny" 46, 286, 309
frivolity business 105, 107
Furniss, Maureen, *Art in Motion: Animation Aesthetics* 295

Gallini, Clara 147–48
Gandhi, Mahatama 205, 211–12
Gardner, Lyn 334 n9
gaze 36–38
Geertz, Clifford 179, 180
Geminoid DK 287–88, 291 n9
Geminoid F 286–87, *287*, 291 n5, 309, 313
Geminoid HI-1 284, *284*, 288
gender 116, 118, 123–24, 126, 127, 127 n1, 128 n3, 142 n9, 158
Genesis 1:3 91
Genet, Christian 34
Genty, Philippe 18, *19*, 20, 23, 24, 25, 26, 27 n1, 28 n7, 30, 56, 141; and Pierrot marionette 18, *19*, 23, 24, 25, 27 n1, 28 n7, 56; *Round Like a Cube* 56; and stage magic 24–25, 26, 28 n12
Georgia Institute for Technology 308
Geraci, Robert 290
Gerland, Oliver 319
Ghost in the Shell 288, 290
ghosting (Carlson) 6
Gibbon, Edward 286
Gibson, James J. 283
Giddens, Anthony 178
Gilles, Annie 31
glove puppets 4, 69, 76, 142 n10, 308; *see also* Petrushka; Punch, Mr; Punch and Judy
Glover, Crispin 303
Godzilla 288
Goethe, Johann Wolfgang von 8
Gollum 288, 303–4, 305
The Golem 288
Googe, Barnaby 166
Gorbachev, Mikhail 219
govorok *see* swazzle
Goya, Francisco 290
The Great War (Hotel Modern) 226–27, 272, *273*, 275, 276, 277
Green, Anne 226, *233*, 234–35, 236–42, *239*, 243, 243 n6, 243 n8
Greenblatt, Stephen 231–33
Gref, Alexander 11, 14, 69–73
Grips Theater Berlin 77
Gröber, Karl, *Children's Toys of Bygone Days* 274
Gross, Kenneth xxiii, 131, 310
Grotowski, Jerzy 31
Guercio, Francis M. 148, 150, 151
Guidicelli, Carole, *Über-Marionettes and Mannequins: Craig, Kantor and Their Contemporary Legacies* 10
Guignol (character) 4
Gundono, Slamet 180, 190
Gunning, Tom 49
Gyeonggi (Korean traditional music center) 196

INDEX

Hahoe (Korean village) 197
halogen projector bulbs 93, 94
hand puppets *see* glove puppets
Handspring Puppet Company 5, 14, 61–67, 141, 178, 226, 231, 243 n7, 245–253, 290, 299, 319; *see also* Jones, Basil; *Ubu and the Truth Commission*; *War Horse*; *Or You Could Kiss Me*
Hanks, Tom 302
Hardacre, Helen 163 n3
Harman, Graham 8
Harris, Michael, *Colored Pictures: Race and Visual Representations* 147
Haymarket (theatre) 119, 122
Haymarket Company 128 n7
Heidegger, Martin 8
Helsdingen Trio 190
Henslowe, Philip 230
Henson, Jim *see* Henson International Festival of Puppet Theater; Jim Henson Company's Digital Puppetry Studio; Jim Henson's Creature Shop
Henson International Festival of Puppet Theater 265 n6
Hermann (Theater am Wind) 226, 256–65, *258, 260, 262,* 265 n6
Hernes, L. 77
Hero (Heron) of Alexandria 8, 312
Herod, King 219–20
Hetherington, Norman 25
Heungbu and Nolbu 196
Hijikata Yoshi 281
Hilborn, Debra 9, 11, 112, 164–74
Hill, Thomas 166
Hirata Oriza 227, 281–84, *284,* 286, 287–88, 291 n5, 291 n8
Hitchcock, Alfred 85, 89
hitogata 155, 162 n1
Hledíková, Ida 11, 113, 218–24
Hoffmann, E. T. A. 8, 52 n2; "The Sandman" 46, 49, 286
Hohnsteiner Puppentheater 76
Holocaust 256
Holy Week 112, 164–74
Homer, *Odyssey* 327
homosexuality 194–95
Hong Dongji (*namsadang* character) 195
Hooks, Ed, *Acting for Animators* 298–99
Hopkins, Anthony 302, 303
Hotel Modern 226–27, 269, 270, 272, *273,* 277; *see also The Great War* (Hotel Modern)
Howdy Doody 4
Hrabanus Maurus 170
Hugh of St. Victor 165

human agency 4, 295, 312, 313, 319
Human Scripture (*Kitab Sucieng Manusa*) 183, *184*
Husserl, Edmund 39
hwakwan (Korean dance) 196
hwarang (Korean Buddhist youth organization) 194, 195
hypocrisy-artist 107
Hyundai Puppet Theatre 192, 194, 195–98, 202, 203 n2

I, Worker (Hirata) 281–82, *282*
iconostasis 221
icons 48, 49, 221
Il Teatro e il nido (Theatre and the Nursery) 76
illusion, visual 19, 295
imagination, and co-presence 38–41
imon ningyō 159–61, 163 n2
Improbable Theatre 323
improvisation 64, 66–67, 78–79, 179, 197, 270, 275, 315, 318, 323–24, 325, 327–29, 332–33
In the Heart of the Forest 282, *283*
inanimate 2, 3, 5–6, 14, 20, 21–25, 46–47, 84, 131, 155, 165–66, 274, 289, 296, 308–10, 311, 314, 318, 319, 323–24, 329
Indefinite Articles 227, 323, 327, *328*; *see also Claytime*
Indian shadow puppetry 92, 205–16, *214*
Indonesian shadow puppetry 92, 93, 94, 95, 147, 193, 260; *see also wayang kulit*
Indramayu 181
Institut Seni Indonesia Surakarta 190 n1
intersectionality 118, 119, 127 n1
Iran, string puppets 193
Ishiguro Hiroshi 227, 281–84, *284,* 286, 287–88
Islam 144, 145–46, 150, 180, 182–83; fundamentalism 181
Italy 218

Jackson, Peter 301, 303–4, 305
Jakarta 179
The Jakarta Post 181
Jamieson, Nigel 190
Japan: hybridity 280–91; ritual performance 154–62, *162,* 163 n3, 280
Jaquet-Droz, Henri-Louis and Pierre 312–13
Jarry, Alfred 8, 14, 50, 178, 327, 333 n4; *Ubu Roi* 50, 325–27
Java 178–90; Department of Education and Culture 181; post-tradition 178–90; ritual performance 178, 179, 180, 181–83; shadow theatre 37, 93, 94–95, 179–80, 181–82, 285, 189–90
al-Jazari, Ibn 8

Jentsch, Ernst: "On the Psychology of the Uncanny" 286, 309; on the uncanny 43, 44, 45, 46–47, 48, 131, 286, 309
Jesuits 218
Jesus Christ 168, 212, 219–20, 221; *see also* Cross, the; Nativity
Jew (character) 220
Jim Henson Company's Digital Puppetry Studio 296
Jim Henson's Creature Shop 299
Jizō 158–59, 163 n2
Jo Yong-seok *see* Cho Yong-suk (Jo Yong-seok)
Jo Yong-su *see* Cho Yong-su (Jo Yong-su)
Jochum, Elizabeth Ann 11, 227, 308–19
Joffrey Ballet 55
Joly, Yves, *Tragédie de Papier* (*Tragedy in Paper*) 19, 20, 20, 21, 23, 24, 26, 28 n7
Jones, Andy 288
Jones, Basil 5, 10, 11, 14, 45, 61–67, 231, 245, 248; on actors and puppets 299, 304; on puppetry style and character construction 249–50, 251, 252–53, 252, 290, 291 n11; *see also* Handspring Puppet Company
Jonze, Spike 227, 294, 299–301
jōruri puppet plays 13, 124, 281
Joseon dynasty (Korea, 1392–1910) 194–95, 200, 202
Joseph, Rajiv, *Bengal Tiger at the Baghdad Zoo* 265 n3
Joseph Papp Public Theater, New York 265 n6
Judson Church 8
Jurassic Park 306 n1
Jurkowski, Henryk 9, 18, 19–20, 26, 120–21, 122, 124, 131, 132, 141, 167, 320 n3, 320 n5, 324, 333 n5
juru bicara (spokespeople) 182

Kabbala 91
kabuki 280, 291 n1
Kabukiza 280
Kahn, Jemma 237–38, 239, 241
kalam-ezhuthu 208
Kalmakov, Nikolai 135, *135*
Kamba Ramayana 206, 216 n3
Kambar (Kamban) 206
Kamerny Theatre, Moscow 141, 142 n11
Kanadehon Chushingura (*Treasury of the Loyal Retainers*) 291 n11
Kang, Minsoo, *Sublime Dreams of Living Machines* 320 n4
Kant, Immanuel 8
Kantor, Tadeusz 7, 31

Kaplin, Stephen 11, 15, 91–97, 167, 296; "puppet tree" model 165, 334 n15; *see also* Chinese Theatre Works
Karagöz theatre 70
karakuri ningyō 281
Karloff, Boris 100
Kathputli (Rajasthani marionette theatre) 193
Kaufman, Moisés 7
kavalapura 209
kayon (Tree of Life) 92, 184, 185, 190 n3
kazoo 70, 73 n2
KBS-TV (Korean Broadcasting System) 196
kebathinan 184
Keene, Donald 10, 289
keimeh shab bazi (Iranian string puppets) 193
Kentridge, William 10, 62, 67 n3, 232, 277 n4
Kerala, India 113, 205–16
Kermit 4
Ketturkat, Peter, *Keine Angst vor großen Tieren* 327
Kino Tsurayuki 290
Kimbrough, R. Keller 163 n5
Kinder-und Jugendtheaterzentrum der BRD (German National Center for Children's Theatre) 77
Kinect (Microsoft) 318, 320 n9
kinesis 310, 311, 312–14
King Kong (Jackson) 301, 304, 305
Kintu, Marty 237–38, 238, 239, 241
Kirchmayer, Thomas 166
Kkok Du (Creative Group NONI) 198–202
kkokdu gaksi (male homosexual performers) 194
Kkokdu Gaksi (*namsadang* character) 196
kkokdu gaksi (*namsadang* puppet play) 192–93, 195
kkokdu noreum 192, 193, 194, 196–97, 198–200, 200
Klangfugl – kulturformidling med de minste (Glitterbird – cultural education for the smallest) 77
Kleist, Heinrich von 8, 10, 52 n2, 289, 313–14; "Über das Marionettentheater" ("On the Marionette Theatre") 13–14, 308
Kneehigh Theatre 141
Kohler, Adrian 45, 62, 245–46, 248, 250, 252, 253; *see also* Handspring Puppet Company
kokeshi 157–58
Kokinshū 290
kokoro 3, 282, 290
Kokusen'ya kassen (Chikamatsu) 291 n3, 291 n4
komunitas 180, 181–83
koothoo-madam 207

Korea: dance/dancers 196–200; ritual performance 199; traditional rod puppetry 112–13, 192–202; shadow theatre 202
Kranenberg, Jeroen 240
kraton 179
Krymov, Dmitry 7
Kua Etnika 187
Kukla (character) 4
Kuncoro, Catur "Benyek" 187
kuroko 161, *162*
Kusumadilaga 186

La Baracca 76
La Claca 333 n4
La Conica Laconica 27 n2
Lacy, James 122
Lafleur, William R. 163 n3
lakon 179
Lamb Chop 4
Lancashire, Ian 165
Landau, Tina 54
Langer, Monika 37
Lanka Lakshmi 213
Large Hadron Collider 328–29
Lasko, Jim 6, 11, 15, 98–104; *see also* Redmoon Theater
Latour, Bruno 6, 9, 44–46, 51, 323, 332
Law, Jane Marie 3, 10, 11, 112, 154–62
Le Petit Chaperon Rouge 27 n3
leather shadow puppetry 205–16, *214*; *see also wayang kulit*
LED lights 93
Lee Mi-yong 196
Léger, Fernand 8
Lehmann, Hans-Thies: and postdramatic children's theatre 76–83, *79, 80*; and postdramatic theatre 23, 25, 28 n8, 31, 220, 246–47, 253 n1; *Postdramatic Theatre* 274–75
lenses 93, 225, 226
Leo, Craig 246
Lepage, Robert 45
Levinas, Emmanuel 30, 41; on the Other 38, 41; *Totality and Infinity* 36, 38
Lévi-Strauss, Claude 308
Lewis, Peter 124
Liber ordinaries 165
Licensing Act (1737) 119, 121, 122, 128 n6, 166
life-death 130–42
light *see* Primal Light; shadow performance, light/shadow architecture
The Limits to Growth 323
Lion King 2, 95
literature 4, 7–10, 52 n3, 77, 96, 124, 132, 134, 145, 159, 255, 256, 266, 268

live actors xxiii; method acting 31; and puppetry 61–62, 63, 65, 66, 221–22
live-actor theatre 4, 112, 131
liveness 89
Locke, John 241, 242; *Essay Concerning Human Understanding* 242–43, 243 n11
LoDico, Giusto 144, 150
Lokadharmi 213
Long, Bryerly 286, *287*
Lord of the Rings (Jackson) 288
Lord of the Rings: The Two Towers (Jackson) 301, 303–4
Lotus Sutra 154
Love, Kermit 55
Lucas, George 305
Ludwig, John 311, 314–15, 319
Luluk Purwanto 190
Luther, Tommy 246

Macbeth (Simonovich) 140, *141*
MacDorman, Karl 285
machines 6, 8, 22–23, 24, 25, 26, 28 n6, 28 n7, 28 n13, 43, 44, 46, 49, 50, 62, 134, 225, 227, 268, 274, 281, 282–83, 284, 287, 291 n5, 311, 313; *see also* androids; robots/robotics
Mackie, Erin 123, 128 n3
Maeterlinck, Maurice 8, 50, 130; *The Blue Bird* 130
magic lantern 8
magic puppet 26
The Magic Tinder Box 25
Magnin, Charles, *Histoire des Marionnettes en Europe* 9
Mahábali, Demon King 212
Mahabharata 179, 183
Mahabharata Jazz and Wayang 190
The MahabharANTa 190
Mahayana Buddhism 154, 158
Malayalam 206–7, 215
Malaysia 185, 190
Mamane, Moussa 71
Margolies, Eleanor 227, 322–33, 334 n13
Margueritte, Paul 137
marionettes: xxiii, 5, 11, 18, 20, 25, 56, 57, 104, 120–22, 138, 139, 141, 144, 178, 193, 227, 268, 280, 289, 300, 308–320 and death 137; and fate 136; freedom of movement 314, 317; Russian modernist 130, 132–33; souls of 134–37; as tireless 137; and the uncanny 131
Mars Needs Moms 301
Marxism 101
Masamune Shirow 290

Masao Yamaguchi 156
masks 98–99, 101, *101*, 225, 230, 246, 248, 274, 277 n3, 285, 296, 297
Masson, Babette 325
material xxiii; animal hide 94; clay 5, 50, 227, 295, 322, 323, 324, 327–29, 331, 332–33, 334 n11; dramaturgies of 5; food 5, 227, 322, 323, 325–27, *326*, 329–33, 334 n14; leather 5, 205–16, *214*; poetics of 329
material animation *see* object animation
material performance 1, 2, 4, 10, 27, 44, 98, 140, 173, 226, 227, 229, 322, 323, 325, 327, 329, 330; defining 5–7
materiality xxiii, 14, 19, 21, 22, 24, 27, 37, 39, 40, 41, 173
McCloud, Scott 15, 256; *Understanding Comics: The Invisible Art* 85
McCormick, John 9
McDermott, Phelim 323
McLaren, Norman 295
McPharlin, Paul 9, 118, 119
meaning, unit of (semiotics) 256
Mee, Charles 323
metamorphosis xxiii, 312
metaphysics 3, 8, 14, 91, 235, 236, 262
Method acting 31
Metropolitan Museum of Art, New York 169
Meurant, René 9
Meyerhold, Vsevolod 44, 130, 133, 135
micromovement 63
Microsoft 318, 320 n9
Middle Ages 164, 165, 166, 169, 172, 173, 174 n1
migawari 156
migawari ningyō 159–61
Miklashevsky, Konstantin *135*
milieu 88
Millar, Mervyn 246
mimesis 280, 303, 310, 311
mirlitones 69–70
Miró, Joan 333 n4
mirror neurons 334 n8
mizuko Jizō 158–59, *159*, 163 n3
Mnemopark: A Model Train World (Rimi Protokoll) 226–27, *271*, *272*, *275*, *276*, 277
mocap *see* motion capture (mocap)
model theatre 226–27, 268–77; *see also* toy theatre
modernism 112, 162 n2, 182, 202; and Russian marionettes 130, 131, 132–33; and the uncanny 49–51
modernity 3, 8, 14, 43, 44–46, 49–51, 198, 274; and the uncanny 44–46

Molina, Victor 19, 27
Molnár, Gyula 22, 23, 24, 26, 27, 27 n3; and *Piccoli Suicidi (Small Suicides)* 19–21, *21*, 28 n7
monad 186
monastic community 164, 165, 167, 168, 172–73, 185
montage 88–89, 92
Morgan, Fidelis 118, 121, 123, 127 n1, 128 n7
Mori Masahiro 227, 284–86, *285*, 288–89, 301, 309–10, 313
Mori et Merma 333 n4
Morpurgo, Michael 63
Morse, Lisa 11, 112, 144–52
Moscow Art Theatre 130, 133
Mossoux, Nicole 34–35, *35*, 36, 37; theory of the Other 35–36, 37; *see also* Compagnie Mossoux-Bonté; *Twin Houses*
motion capture (mocap) 4, 11, 51, 227, 294, 296–97, 299, 306 n2, 315–17, *316*, 320 n6, 320 n9
movement 63, 66–67
Mrázek, Jan, *Phenomenology of a Puppet Theatre* 37, 180
Mrs. Sun and Mr. Moon Make Weather 78–82, *79*, *80*
Mudra School 31
Muhammadiya (modernist Islamic movement) 182
Murphey, Todd 11, 227, 308–19
Museo Internazionale delle Marionette 144
Museum of Science and Industry, Chicago 312
music, the swazzle as 70–72
Myanmar 193

Nada Théâtre 227, 323, 325–27, *326*
Nagata Kōkichi 162 n1
nagauta 280, 291 n1
Nagoya Biennale 286
Nagoya Triennale 282
Nair, C. N. Sreekantan 213
Nair, Sreedharan 210
namsadang nori 192, 194–200, 201, 202, 203 n1
Nanang HP 190
nang sbek thom 193
nang yai 92, 193
Naniwa Miyage (Souvenir of Naniwa) 13, 289
Nanyang Technological University, Singapore 308
narration 207, 253 n2
narrative; three-dimensional 245–53; Ur-narrative 61–67, 231, 290

narrative theory 226, 256–57, 264–65
narrator 63, 71, 74 n7, 261, 263, 275
National Chiao Tung University, Taiwan 308
National Film Board of Canada 295
National Shadow Puppetry Festival, Dharmasthala 205
National Theatre, London 63, 226, 245, 248, 253 n3, 319
Nativity 218–24, *224*
Nativity puppets *see batleija*; crèche performances; Nativity; *vertep*
Neale, John Mason 170
Needham, Elizabeth 123, 125
Nelson, Victoria 165–66; *The Secret Life of Puppets* 9
networks (Latour) 45, 51
New Order dictatorship 179, 182
New York City Ballet 55
Nikolaev, Michail 219–20, *221*, 222–23, *222*, 224
ningen rashisa 283
ningyō jōruri 281
ningyō 112, 155–56, 157, 159–61, 280, 281
ningyōburi 280
nō 193, 280, 285
Noda Manabu 286, 287
North, Dan 304
Northwestern University 308, *318*
Norway: Ministry of Culture 77
Nugroho, Eko 187, 189, 190 n4

object(s) 85, 87–88; food as 5, 21, 27; *see also* performing object
object animation 322, 325–27, 330, 333 n5
objectified bodies 28 n11
object-oriented ontology 8, 174
Obraztsov, Sergei 137, 141
Obraztsov State Central Puppet Theatre, Moscow 134, *140*, *141*
October Revolution (Russia, 1917) 132, 218
O'Hagan, John 146, 148
okina 280, 285
Olivier, Laurence 277
ontology 44, 45, 46; object-oriented 8, 174; of the puppet 14, 30–41, 62–63
OOglies 333 n6
opera dei pupi 144–52
Or You Could Kiss Me (Handspring Puppet Company/National Theatre, London) 226, 245–53, *248*, *251*, *252*
Orenstein, Claudia 111–13, 205–16
Orlando 148–50
Orlando e Rinaldo per amore di Angelica (Argento) 149

Os, E. 77
Osaka National University 281
oscillation 3, 92, 225, 227
Osman, Jena 44
Other: body and gaze 36–38; and co-presence 35–38; Levinas on 38, 41; Mossoux on 35–36, *37*; Petrushka as 72–73, 74 n7; puppets as 38, 40–41, 72–73; Sartre on 30–31, 36, 37, 38, 41; Tranter 35–36, *37*
other world 72–73
Our Domestic Resurrection Circus (Bread and Puppet) 334n15

Padepokan Seni Bagong Kussudiardjo (Indonesian arts company) 187
Paiva, Duda 30
Paladins 144, 145, 147–50, 152
Palermo 144, 145
Panchatantra 211–12, 216 n11
panorama 8
pansori 196
papier-mâché/Paper Maché 6, 14, 104, 106, 109
Pardo, Enrique 323–24, 331
Paré, Zaven 288
Park Byung-oh (Bak Byeong-o) 197
Park Chung-hee 192
Parker, Elizabeth 168–69
Parr, Philip 28 n7
Pasqualino, Antonio 9, 144, 145, 149, 150, 152
pastorales sacrae 218
pastorals 218
Patey, Clare 323, 330–31, *331*; *see also Feast on the Bridge* (Patey)
patriarchy 118, 125, 126–27, 128 n3, 234
Pellegrin, Guilhem 325
Pemberton, John 179
Pepadi (*wayang* organization) 179, 189–90
perception, and co-presence 38–41
perestroika 219
performance capture 227, 294, 301–5
performing objects xxiii–xxiv, 1, 2, 3, 5, 6, 7, 11 n2, 13, 23, 44–45, 46–47, 257, 319; the Cross as 165, 166–68; Freud on 47–49, 50–51, 52 n2, 62, 93, 112, 165; medieval attitudes to 165–66, 174, 174 n3
perspective (painting) 221
Petersen, Nils Holger 171–72
Petrushka (ballet) 130
Petrushka (Russian glove puppet) xxiii, 14, 69–73, *70*, 130, 137–38, *139*, *140*, 142 n9, 219; as Other 72–73, 74 n7; and swazzle 69–70, 74 n10

Phénomène Tsé-Tsé 76
phenomenology 5, 6, 9, 14, 15, 30, 38–39, 66–67, 103, 164, 225, 311
physical dramaturgy 54, 56
physics, laws of 66, 257
Picasso, Pablo 68 n3; *Parade* 50
Pierrot (marionette) 18, *19*, 23, 24, 25, 26, 27 n1, 28 n7, 56
Piris, Paul 11, 14, 30–41
Piscator, Erwin 44
pishchik see swazzle
Pixar 297, 313
Plassard, Didier 9, 30
Plato, "Allegory of the Cave" (*The Republic*) 8
playboard 260, 329–33
Players' Halt (cabaret) 130, 142 n5
Podehl, Anne 260
Podehl, Enno 256–64, *258, 260, 262*; *see also* Hermann
The Polar Express 288, 296, 301, 302
portrait puppets 121–22
Posner, Dassia 1–11, 15, 44, 52 n3, 112, 130, 142, 225–27
post-colonialism 194–96
postdramatic children's theatre 76–83, *79, 80*
postdramatic theatre 23, 25, 28 n8, 31, 220, 246–47, 253 n1
postmodernism 45, 51, 245, 246–47, 248–49, 253 n1
post-tradition 11, 112, 219; Java 178–90; *wayang kulit* 184–86, 189–90
Poulton, Cody 280–91
Prague Linguistic Circle (Prague School) 9, 225–56, 265 n1
Prague School *see* Prague Linguistic Circle (Prague School)
Priestley, J. B. 277
Primal Light 91
Processional Arts Workshop 334 n15
props, definition of 230
Proschan, Frank 5, 6, 72, 74 n9, 126, 127, 165–66; "Puppets, Masks, and Performing Objects from Semiotic Perspectives" 9
prosopopeia: 230–31, 242–43
proto-instruments 69, 73
pulavar 207, 209, 210
Pulavar, Krishnankutty 205, 206, 209–10, 211, 213, 215–16
Pulavar, Rahul 210
Pulavar, Rajeev 210, 212–13, 215–16
Pulavar, Rajitha 210, 214–16
Pulavar, Ramachandra 205, 206, 207, 209–16, *212*, 216 n2, 216 n6

Pulavar family 206, 209, 211–13, 215–16
Punch 4, 27 n1, 72, 73, 74, 111, 120–22, 130; proto-feminist 123–26; *see also* Punch and Judy
Punch and Judy 51, 70, 108, 125, 135, 202, 255
Punchdrunk 7
Punch's Theatre 119–20, 121
puppet(s): and agency 3, 4, 5–6, 9, 45–46, 48–49, 131, 140–41, 173, 230, 231, 241, 273, 282–83, 287, 291, 295, 312, 313, 319, 325; and anthropomorphism 2, 5, 6, 22–23, 26, 46, 86, 112, 170, 326; as collaborator 6, 7, 28 n9, 131, 132–33; and community 8, 98–99, 102, 145; and control xxiii; the Cross as 165, 166–68; cubism/cubist forms 94, 141; and death 3, 11, 14, 62, 73, 156–57, 160, 199–200, 202, 219–20, 236, 238–39, 246–47, 260, 280, 284–85, 290, 291 n11, 325, 326, 329; death of 18–27, 56; and disobedient obedience 130–42; dramaturgy of 54–59, 141; food offered to 21; hybrid forms/hybridization 11, 31, 45, 51, 226–27, 294–305; as idea xxiii–xxiv; intangibility 11, 141, 296; and life 137–40; and life-death 130–42; in media xxiii, 328; as mediator 104; ontology of 14, 30–31, 62–63; as Other 38, 40–41, 72–73; poetics of 1, 10; powers and qualities 87, 88; as text 7–10, 256; work of 61–62
puppet control, and metamorphosis xxiii, 312
puppet death 18–27, 56
puppet doubles xxiii, 34, 36, 237–38, 277 n4, 284, 288
puppet perspective, and the Cross 173–74
The Puppet Show (exhibition) 67 n3, 277 n4
puppet slam 2
puppet think 154–63
"puppet tree" model (Kaplin) 165, 334 n15
puppeteer(s) 118–20, 127; as magicians 24–25, 26, 28 n12
puppetland 260, 263–64
puppetry: and audience reception 65–66; and authorship 61–67; and the avant-garde 67; and breath 57, 66, 246, 250, 252, 327; and life 61–62, 63, 66; and live actors 61–62, 63, 65, 66, 221–22; and movement 63, 66–67; new technologies 3–4, 39, 49; and ontology 14, 30–31, 62–63; practice xxiii; and stillness 66, 174, 266 n10; theory xxiii–xxiv
Puri, Rajika 44
Purjadi 182–83, 184, *184*

pusaka 179
Pygmalion Project (Northwestern University and Disney) 227, 308, 311–12, 314–18, 316, 318, 319, 320 n8

"qualisign" 87–88
queer theory 118, 127 n1, 128 n3, 128 n8
Quicksilver Theatre 334 n10

radical listening 100, 103
Raffles, T. S. 179
Rahardjo, Sri Djoko 190
Ralston, Ken 302–3
Rama 207–8, 216 n5
Ramayana 179, 206–7, 209–10, 211, 212, 213, 216 n5
Ravana 207, 216 n5
Raw, Barbara 168
reading out (Chatman) 255, 256, 265 n4
reality: edited representations of 256, 257, 263, 264–65; virtual 290
Redmoon Theater 15, 98–104, 99, 101, 104
Reed, Larry 94
referents and signifiers 145, 146, 147, 256, 261, 265, 265 n3
Reformasi 182
Reggio Emilia 334 n11
Regularis Concordia 164–74
Reilly, Kara 280
Reiniger, Rike 11, 14–15, 76–83
Reiyūkai 154
religious performance: ban on 218; *see also* ritual performance
Rembrandt, "The Anatomy Lesson of Dr Nicolaes Tulp" 237
Resonances 219–20, 222, 223, 224
rhythm 70–72
Rice, Emma 7; *see also* Kneehigh Theatre
Rimini Protokoll 226–27, 269, 270–71; *see also* Mnemopark
Rinaldo 149
Rise of the Planet of the Apes 283, 301, 304, 305
ritual performance 4, 8, 9, 14, 51, 92, 112, 113, 136, 223, 264, 291n11, 322, 332; the Cross 170–74, 174 n1; Indian shadow puppetry 206, 207, 210, 212, 213, 214; Japanese 154–62, 162, 163 n3, 280; Javanese 178, 179, 180, 181–83; Korean 199
Roach, Joseph 225, 310
"Robber Hotzenplotz" (Showcase Beat Le Mot) 82
Robertson, Jennifer 290, 291 n7

robots/robotics 3, 4, 7, 11, 49, 198, 227, 280–91, 282, 284, 285, 287, 291 n4, 291 n5, 301, 308–19, 316, 318, 325; *see also* androids; automata
rod puppetry 112–13, 192–202
Romani (Gypsy, as character) 71, 220, 257, 263
Romanticism 8
Ronell, Avital 276
"Rood of Grace" 166
Rovenski Puppet Theatre 220–22, 222
Royal de Luxe 268, 269, 277 n1
R.U.R. (*Rossum's Universal Robots*) 49, 281, 290 n4
Russell, John 120
Ruwatan (ritual drama ceremony) 183

Saint-Exupéry, Antoine de, *Wind, Sand and Stars* 56
sampakan theatre 189
samul nori 196, 197
Sanata Dharma University 190 n1
sanbasō 280
Sand, George 139; *The Snow Man* (*L'homme de neige*) 142 n10
Sandglass Theater 14, 56, 57
Sangeet Natak Akademi 206, 214
Sanskrit 206, 216 n11
Saracens 146; identity 146; image 112, 144, 146–48, 147, 149, 150–52; in literature 145; use of term 145
Sartre, Jean-Paul 38, 39–40, 41; *Being and Nothingness* 30–31, 37; and the body 36–37; *The Imaginary* 31, 41; theory of the Other 30–31, 36, 37, 38, 41
Sayōnara (Hirata) 286, 287, 291 n8
Sazonov, Pavel 134–35, 142 n5
scale, use of 269–70, 271–73, 275, 277, 325
scenic design 221
Scharfe, Henrik 287–88
Schattschneider, Ellen 159–60, 163 n4
Schechner, Richard, *Performance Studies: An Introduction* 102
Schiller, Friedrich 8
Schlemmer, Oskar 8
Scholem, Gershom 91
Schönbein, Ilka 30
Schonewolf, Herte, *Play with Light and Shadow* 94
School of the Art Institute of Chicago 101
Schumann, Peter 3, 5, 8, 11, 15, 45, 105–9, 161; *Domestic Resurrection Circus* 334 n15; drawings 106, 107; *see also* Bread and Puppet Theater
Searls, Colette 11, 227, 294–305

Segel, Harold 9
Seinendan 281
Sekolah Mengenah Karawitan Indonesia 187
Seltman, F. 213
Semar Builds the Heavens (*Semar Mbangun Kahyangan*) 182
Semar Goes on the Hajj (*Semar Munggah Haji*) 183
Semar's Journey 190
semiotics 9, 14, 44, 64, 65, 165, 223, 225–56, 260, 265, 304
Senawangi (*wayang* organization) 179, 189–90
Sendak, Maurice 299
Seno, Mas 182
Seno Aji, Andy 187, 188
separation (Latour) 44–46
sequence/sequencing 89, 256, 257, 266 n9, 312
Serkis, Andy 294, 303–4
Shadowlight Productions 94
shadow performance: and focal plane 95; leather 205–16, *214*; and light source 93–94; light/shadow architecture 95–97; and shadow figure 94–95
shadow theatre 8, 15, 91–97, *94*, *96*, 140; China 92, 96; India 92, 205–16, *214*; Indonesia 92, 93, 94, 95, 147, 193, 260; Javanese 37, 93, 94–95, 179–80, 181–82, 185, 189–90; Korea 202; Tamil 70; Thailand 92, 193; *see also* leather shadow puppetry; *wayang kulit*
ShadowBang 190
Shakespeare, William 54, 122, 126, 127, 211–12, 234, 235; *Cardenio* 226, 231–32, 241; *Hamlet* 58, 230; *Henry IV* 128 n4; *Henry VIII* 128 n4; *King Lear* 234; *Richard III* 128 n4; *Romeo and Juliet* 234; *A Winter's Tale* 234
shamanism 92, 96, 194, 195, 197–202
Shelley, Mary 101
Shershow, Scott Cutler 121, 123, 124, 126
Shevelow, Kathryn 116, 119–20, 121, 122, 123, 126, 128 n7
Shils, Edward 178–79, 180, 189
shoe/shoeness 104
shots *see* montage
Showcase Beat Le Mot 82
Shrek the Musical 227, 297
Sicily 112, 144, 148; immigration 151; invasion and occupation 145; racism 148, 151; *see also* Opera dei Pupi
Sid the Science Kid 296
Sidia, I Made 190
sign systems *see* semiotics

signifiers 145, 146, 147, 256, 261, 265, 265 n3
Silk, Dennis xxiii; and "thing theatre" 22; "The Thing Theatre and Thing Language" 28 n4
Silla Dynasty (57 B.C.E.–935 C.E.) 194, 195
Silver Age (Russia) 132
Simonovich-Efimova, Nina 11, 72, 112, 130, 131–32, 134, 137–41, *140*, *141*, 142 n7, 142 n8, 142 n9; *Notes of a Petrushka Player* (*Adventures of a Russian Puppet Theatre*) 138
Singh, Salil 178, 205, 206, 209, 212
Siopis, Penny 236
SITI Company (Bogart) 54
sjužet 226, 257–59, 260–63, 265 n8, 266 n9; three-dimensional 258–59, 261, 265
Šklovskij, Viktor 266 n9
Slonimskaia, Iulia 112, 130, 131, 132, 134–37, *135*, 139, 140–42, *140*, *141*, 142 n5
Slonimskaya, Elena 11, 14, 69–73
Small Size Network for the Diffusion of Performing Arts for early Childhood 77
Smythe, Robert 7, 11, 226, 255–65
Soedharsono, Ki Manteb 179
Soeharto, President 179, 181, 182
Sofer, Andrew 5, 171; *The Stage Life of Props* 164, 230
Sogolon Puppet Troupe 178
Sokolov, Vladimir 141, 142 n11
Sologub, Fedor 132, 133–34, 142
Somu mask 197
Son of Frankenstein 100
The Song of Roland 146, 148
Southeast Asia 70, 147, 183, 185, 216 n5; *see also individual traditions*
Soviet Union 218
Sowell, Thomas, *Race and Culture: A World View* 151
space, meaning of 102–4; stage 120–22, 164, 258–59, 261
space and time 25, 178, 251, 256, 257, 265 n3, 323, 332
Speaight, George 9, 117, 118–19, 120, 123
spectatorship 3, 23, 27
speech 70–72; and co-presence 32–33; the Cross 169–70
Spielberg, Steven 301, 302
spirit xxiii, 3, 91–93, 96, 126, 181, 190, 201, 236, 288, 289–90; in the flame 91–93
stage magic 24–25, 26, 28 n12
stage space 120–22, 164, 258–59, 261
Stanislavsky, Konstantin 50, 130, 283

Star Wars 305
Stasiuk, Andrej, *Dukla* 59
State Institute of Islamic Studies 182
States, Bert O. 225, 308, 309, 310
Steel, C. 330
Stevenson, Robert Louis 277
Stewart, Susan, *On Longing* 9
stillness, and puppetry 66, 174, 266 n10
Stone, Marc 209
story 88, 219–20
storytelling 55, 56, 62, 84, 206, 213, 219, 220, 256, 257, 258, 272, 327–28
Straub, Kristina 123
Stravinsky, Igor 130
Strike, Joe 297
String Puppet Sanbasō 280
Stuffed Puppet Theatre 30, *32*; see also *Cuniculus* (Stuffed Puppet Theatre)
Styles, John 24
subjectivity 3, 37, 174 n3, 245, 246, 247, 248, 252, 272, 286–87
Sugiarto, Ignatius "Clink" 189
suit puppets 299, 303, 306 n4
Sukasman, Sigit (dalang) 185–86, *186*, 189
Surakarta 179, 186, 190 n1
Surrogates 288, 291 n10
Surwedi, Ki 181–82
Suryatm, Joned 187
Susmono, Enthus 187
Suspense festival 328–29
Sussman, Mark J. 11, 226–27, 268–77
Swastika, Alia 187, 189
swazzle 69–70, 74 n10, 126–27, 195
The Sydney Front 25, 28 n12
Symons, T. 170, 172
Sze, Sarah 269

table-top puppetry 27 n2, 272, 324
Takeda Gidayū 291 n3
Takeda Izumo I 291 n3
Takeda Ōmi 281, 291 n3
Takemoto-za 291 n3
talchum, mask dance of the Bongsan (Pongsan) 197
Tall Horse 178
tamashii 290
Tamil: language 206, 207; shadow theatre 70
Tarkovsky, Andrei 223
Tartaglia, John 297
Tarte Ramey, Lynn, *Christian, Saracen, and Genre in French Literature* 146
Taylor, Jane 5, 11, 226, 230–43, 333 n4; *Handspring Puppet Company* 10; *Ubu and the Truth Commission* 243 n7, 333 n4; see also *After Cardenio* (Taylor)
Taymor, Julie 45, 141; *Lion King* 95
Teater Garasi 189
Teater Gardanella 187
Teater Salihara 187
Teatre de la Claca 28 n9, 333 n4
Teatro Giocca Vita 94
television 4, 28 n7, 44, 111, 179, 196, 197, 207, 294, 296
Templeraud, Jacques 27 n2
"temporal contract" 171–73
text: puppets as 7–10, 256; visual 66
Thai shadow puppetry 92, 193
Theater am Wind 226, 256–65, *258*, *260*, *262*, 265 n6
Theater as der Parkaue 82
Theater junge Generation 82
Theater von Anfang! (Theater from the Beginning!) 77
Theatre de Cuisine 27 n2
théâtre d'objets 5
theatre for young audiences: common practices 77–78; current trends 82–83; development 76–77; *Mrs. Sun and Mr. Moon Make Weather* 78–82, *80*; and performance 81–82
Theatre of Objects 5, 14, 19, 21, 23, 27, 27 n2, 219
Theatre Royal, Drury Lane 116, 120
theatrical form 219
theatrical signs 171, 265 n1; see also semiotics
The Theft of Sita 187
Theo Tinkerer Invents the Hare 82
"thing theatre" 22
Things Done in a Seeing Place (Bread and Puppet Theater) 51, *108*
Thomas Aquinas, Saint 172, 280
Three Sisters: Android Version (Hirata) 291 n5
Tillis, Steve 31, 166, 250, 296
time 89; map of 258–59; and space 25, 178, 251, 256, 257, 265 n3, 323, 332
Tiplady, Steve 327
tōgalugōmbeaṭṭa 178
Tōhoku region (Japan) 156, 157, 158
Tokugawa period (Japan) 158
Tokyo Notes 281
tholu bommalata see Indian shadow puppetry
topeng 181
toys 273–76, *275*
tradition: practice 206–7, 208, 210, 211, 213, 214, 215; preserving 205–6, 210, 216 n7;

transformation of 205–6, 213, 215; translating 194–96
translation: tradition 194–96; and the uncanny 44–46
Tranter, Neville: *Cuniculus* 32–33, *32*, 39, 40; theory of the Other 35–36, 37
Triangel 27 n1
"Tribute in Light" (World Trade Center) 95, 96
trick puppets 25, *149*
Tsukiji Little Theatre 281
Turan, Kenneth 300
Turkle, Sherry, *Evocative Objects* 9
Turner, Victor 102
Twin Houses (Compagnie Mossoux-Bonté) 30, 31, 33–35, *35*, 36, 40
Twist, Basil 7, 45, 141, 161; *Seafoam Sleepwalk* 44
Tydeman, W. 166
Tynjanov, Jurij 266 n9

Über-marionette (Craig) 3, 133, 136
Ubu and the Truth Commission (Taylor/Handspring Puppet Company) 243 n7, 333 n4
Ubu Roi (Nada Théâtre) 227, 323, 325–27, *326*, 331, 332
uncanny, the 11, 14, 43, 44–46, 225, 227 n4, 280, 291, 309, 311, 131; Freud on 43, 44, 45, 46, 47–49, 50–51, 67, 131, 286, 309; Jentsch on 43, 44, 45, 46–47, 48, 131, 309, 386; and modernism 49–51
uncanny valley (Mori) 227, 284–86, *285*, 288–89, 301, 302, 309–10, 311, 313, 319
Un Cid (Compagnie Émilie Valantin) 58, *58*, 59 n1
UNESCO 144, 193, 203 n1
UNIMA (Union Nationale de la Marionnette) 210, 216 n8
University of Cape Town 235, *237*
University of Colorado 308
University of Giessen 76, 82
Ur-narrative 61–67, 231, 290

Vagrant Booth Theatre 69, *70*, 73 n1, 74 n4
Valantin, Émilie 58, 59 n1; *Un Cid* 58
Van Allsburg, Chris 301
Velo Théâtre 27 n2
Venantius Fortunatus 170
ventriloquism 32, 231, 241, 243 n3, 287, 323
Verfremdungseffekt (Brecht) 43, 44
vertep (genre) 113, 135, 218–24, *222*, *224*; see also crèche performances; *batlejka*; Nativity
Vertep (performance) 220, *221*
vibrant matter (Bennett) 6, 9, 322

Viewpoints (Bogart) 54
virtual 24, 29 n9, 226, 290–91, 296–97, 303, 304, 318, 320 n9
virtual reality 290
Visitatio Sepulchri 172
visual, reading the *see* visuality
visual, the *see* visuality
visual agency 33, 37
visual art/artist 4, 28 n9, 112, 130, 200, 236, 295
visual design 198–99, 200
visual dramaturgy 54–59, *57*, *58*, 141, 248–49, 272–73
visual gaze 37
visual illusion 19, 295
visual metaphor 220
visual storytelling 84, 85
visual text 66
visual-effects 294, 295, 300, 302, 304
visuality 4, 5, 24, 28 n9, 74 n5, 74 n10, 78, 141, 147, *186*, 192, 201–2, 219, 234, 235, 238, 256, 265 n7, 269, 300, 303, 315, 319, 327
visualizing 169, 220, 325
Vivisector 28 n11
voice modifiers 69–70, 72, 74 n9, 126; *see also* swazzle

Wadehra, Anurag 209
Wagner, Otmar 78–79, 82
Wakamaru robot 282–84, *282*
Walker, Cheryl 127
Wall-E 313
Walsh, William, *A Dialogue Concerning Women* 235
War Horse (Handspring Puppet Company) xxiii, 63–65, 219, 245, 255, 290, 291 n11, 304, 305, 319
Warhol, Andy 100
Warner, Marina 291; *Phantasmagoria* 280
Wart (*Daging Tumbuh*) 187
wayang beber 180
wayang bocor 187, 188
wayang gedhog 179
wayang Hiphop 187
wayang Indonesia 190
Wayang Kartun 187
wayang kontemporer 180, 185
Wayang Kontemporer Dual Core 187
Wayang Kreasul 187–88
wayang krucil 179
wayang kulit 37, 92, 112, 147, 178–90, 193; porous 187–89; post-tradition 184–86, 189–90; tradition in context 180–82; tradition in performance 182–84
Wayang Legenda 186

INDEX

Wayang Pixel 187
wayang ukur 185
wayang wong 185
Webster, Chris, *Animation: The Mechanics of Motion* 298
Weschler, Lawrence 288
West, Amber 112, 116–28
Weta Digital 301, 305
"The What Ordinary" 105–6, 107–9
Where the Wild Things Are (Jonze) 227, 294, 299–301
Where the Wild Things Are (Sendak) 299
Who Framed Roger Rabbit 301
"The Why Ordinary" 106, 107–9
Wider, Kathleen 36
Wija, I Wayan 190
Williams, Margaret 3, 5, 11, 14, 18–27, 56
Willis, Bruce 288
Willis, Thomas 241–42, 243 n6
Wilson, Peter 190
Wilson, Robert 23
Winstone, Ray 302
Wired magazine 284
women 11, 112, 116, 124–25, 136, 211, 213–15, 216 n13

"Wonder of Wonders" 233, 235
Wood, Ian 172
World of Art 135
World Trade Center *see* "Tribute in Light" (World Trade Center)
World War I 245, 269, 272
World War II 154, 159, 218, 258
Wren, Christopher 234, 243 n6
Wright, Barbara 325
Wright, Robin 303
Wu (Emperor, Han dynasty) 96

Yeates, Richard 120
Yi Mi-yong 196
Yoda 305
yokthe pwe 193
Yoshikawa, Yūichirō 286
Yoshio, Yūda 281
Young Frankenstein 100
Younge, Gavin 238, 239

Zemeckis, Robert 227, 301, 303
Ziporyn, Evan 190
zobo 70, 73 n2
zoetrope 8

eBooks
from Taylor & Francis

Helping you to choose the right eBooks for your Library

Add to your library's digital collection today with Taylor & Francis eBooks. We have over 45,000 eBooks in the Humanities, Social Sciences, Behavioural Sciences, Built Environment and Law, from leading imprints, including Routledge, Focal Press and Psychology Press.

Choose from a range of subject packages or create your own!

Benefits for you
- Free MARC records
- COUNTER-compliant usage statistics
- Flexible purchase and pricing options
- 70% approx of our eBooks are now DRM-free.

Benefits for your user
- Off-site, anytime access via Athens or referring URL
- Print or copy pages or chapters
- Full content search
- Bookmark, highlight and annotate text
- Access to thousands of pages of quality research at the click of a button.

ORDER YOUR FREE INSTITUTIONAL TRIAL TODAY

Free Trials Available

We offer free trials to qualifying academic, corporate and government customers.

eCollections
Choose from 20 different subject eCollections, including:
- Asian Studies
- Economics
- Health Studies
- Law
- Middle East Studies

eFocus
We have 16 cutting-edge interdisciplinary collections, including:
- Development Studies
- The Environment
- Islam
- Korea
- Urban Studies

For more information, pricing enquiries or to order a free trial, please contact your local sales team:

UK/Rest of World: **online.sales@tandf.co.uk**
USA/Canada/Latin America: **e-reference@taylorandfrancis.com**
East/Southeast Asia: **martin.jack@tandf.com.sg**
India: **journalsales@tandfindia.com**

www.tandfebooks.com